Taking SIDES

Clashing Views on Controversial Issues in
Science, Technology, and Society

Edited, Selected, and with Introductions by

Thomas A. Easton
Thomas College

The Dushkin Publishing Group, Inc.

Photo Acknowledgments

Part 1   The Dushkin Publishing Group, Inc.
Part 2   Sunshine and Wilson Peaks/Colorado Tourism Board
Part 3   National Aeronautics and Space Administration
Part 4   Frank Tarsitano/The Dushkin Publishing Group, Inc.
Part 5   Courtesy of the Yerkes Primate Research Center/Emory University

Cover Art Acknowledgment

Charles Vitelli

Library of Congress Cataloging-in-Publication Data

Main entry under title:
   Taking sides: clashing views on controversial Issues in Science, Technology, and Society/edited, selected, and with introductions by Thomas A. Easton.—1st ed.
   Includes bibliographical references and index.
   1. Science—Social aspects. 2. Technology—Social aspects. I. Easton, Thomas A., *comp.*
      Q175.5.E23   303.48′3—dc20
      1-56134-386-2   94-26749

 Printed on Recycled Paper

DPG

The Dushkin Publishing Group, Inc.

Taking
SIDES

**Clashing Views on
Controversial Issues in
Science,
Technology, and
Society**

PREFACE

Those who must deal with scientific and technological issues—scientists, politicians, sociologists, business managers, and anyone who is concerned about a neighborhood dump or power plant, government intrusiveness, expensive space programs, or the morality of medical research, among many other issues—must be able to consider, evaluate, and choose among alternatives. Making choices is an essential aspect of the scientific method. It is also an inescapable feature of every public debate over a scientific or technological issue, for there can be no debate if there are no alternatives.

The ability to evaluate and to select among alternatives—as well as to know when the data do not permit selection—is called critical thinking. It is essential not only in science and technology but in every other aspect of life as well. *Taking Sides: Clashing Views on Controversial Issues in Science, Technology, and Society* is designed to stimulate and cultivate this ability by holding up for consideration 19 issues that have provoked substantial debate. Each of these issues has at least two sides, usually more. However, each issue is expressed in terms of a single question in order to draw the lines of debate more clearly. The ideas and answers that emerge from the clash of opposing points of view should be more complex than those offered by the students before the reading assignment.

The issues in this book were chosen because they are currently of particular concern to both science and society. They touch on the nature of science and research, the relationship between science and society, the uses of technology, and the potential threats that technological advances can pose to human survival. And they come from a variety of fields, including computer and space science, biology, environmentalism, law enforcement, and public health.

Organization of the book   For each issue, I have provided an *issue introduction*, which provides some historical background and discusses why the issue is important. I then present two selections, one pro and one con, in which the authors make their cases. Each issue concludes with a *postscript* that brings the issue up to date and adds other voices and viewpoints.

Which answer to the issue question—yes or no—is the correct answer? Perhaps neither. Perhaps both. Students should read, think about, and discuss the readings and then come to their own conclusions without letting my or their instructor's opinions (which perhaps show at least some of the time!) dictate theirs. The additional readings mentioned in both the introductions and the postscripts should prove helpful. It is worth stressing that the issues covered in this book are all *live* issues; that is, the debates they represent are active and ongoing.

i

The list of contributors at the back of this volume provides information about the authors of the 38 selections reprinted in this book.

A word to the instructor   An *Instructor's Manual With Test Questions* (multiple-choice and essay) is available through the publisher for the instructor using *Taking Sides* in the classroom. It includes suggestions for stimulating in-class discussion for each issue. A general guidebook, *Using Taking Sides in the Classroom*, which discusses methods and techniques for integrating the pro-con approach into any classroom setting, is also available.

Acknowledgments   Of immense assistance in the preparation of this book were Mimi Egan, publisher for the Taking Sides series, and the libraries of the University of Maine at Orono and at Augusta, Colby College, and Thomas College. I am also grateful for the existence of computers, modems, information services, and photocopiers.

Special thanks are due to John Quigg of Thomas College.

Thomas A. Easton
Thomas College

CONTENTS IN BRIEF

CONTENTS

Purnell Choppin, the president of the Howard Hughes Medical Institute, argues that society must provide funding for basic research in order to promote scientific progress. Senator Barbara A. Mikulski (D-Maryland) argues that it is the place of science to lead to new ideas, new technologies, and new jobs, and that funding must therefore go for applied research.

Robert Costanza, a professor of environmental studies, and policy analyst Laura Cornwell argue that when uncertainty about potential future damage to health or the environment is high, compensation based on a worst-case scenario should be set aside by those who are potentially responsible. Wendy Cleland-Hamnett, the acting deputy assistant administrator for policy, planning, and evaluation at the U.S. Environmental Protection Agency, insists that worst-case scenarios are far too unlikely to be used as the basis for policy.

Howard K. Schachman, a research biochemist, argues that the phrase "other serious deviations from accepted research practices" should not be included in the definition of scientific misconduct because it is ambiguous and unfair to scientists. Scientist Donald E. Buzzelli argues that the "other serious deviation" clause is necessary to cover cases that do not involve fabrication, falsification, or plagiarism.

Michael J. Mandel, an economics writer, argues that the computer and the telecommunications and information-processing industries will benefit the entire nation. The Center for Media Education et al. argue that current plans for the construction of the information superhighway discriminate against minorities and the poor.

Researcher David Norse argues that new agricultural policies can ensure adequate food for a much greater human population than that which exists today. Marine geologist K. O. Emery asserts that continued population growth will inevitably exceed what the Earth's resources can accommodate, and the human species may become extinct as a result.

Christopher Flavin and Nicholas Lenssen, researchers at the Worldwatch Institute, argue that the technology currently exists to meet most energy needs from renewable sources. Chauncey Starr, Milton F. Searl, and Sy Alpert, researchers at the Electric Power Research Institute, argue that renewable energy is limited particularly by its intermittency and lack of portability.

Mary H. Cooper, a staff writer for *CQ Researcher*, asserts that scientific findings in recent years indicate that the ozone layer is being depleted, exposing Earth's living organisms to increasing levels of harmful ultraviolet radiation from the sun. James P. Hogan, a science fiction writer, maintains that reports of the ozone being destroyed by chlorofluorocarbons are unsupported by any valid scientific evidence.

Professor of geology Wallace S. Broecker argues that human-caused increases in the level of greenhouse gases in the atmosphere will warm the world, with potentially serious consequences for human life. Economists Wilfred Beckerman and Jesse Malkin argue that global warming, if it even occurs, will not be catastrophic and warrants no immediate action.

Associate professor of physics Doug Beason argues that a U.S. government program oriented to the manned space exploration of Mars would provide many benefits for the nation. David Callahan, a foreign-policy analyst, argues that fiscal realities will force greater reliance on automated (unmanned) missions in space.

Professor of astronomy Frank Drake and science writer Dava Sobel argue that scientists must continue to search for extraterrestrial civilizations because contact will eventually occur. Professor of astronomy Richard G. Teske doubts that there are any beings outside of Earth with the technological capability to send signals that scientists can receive.

Professor of computer science Dorothy E. Denning holds that law enforcement agencies have a legitimate interest in ensuring access to private communications, including those done via computer. Mike Godwin, staff counsel for the Electronic Frontier Foundation, argues that the individual's right to privacy must take precedence over the government's power to intrude, even at the risk of diminished national security.

Research scientist Hans Moravec asserts that computers that match and even exceed human intelligence will eventually be developed. Professor of philosophy John R. Searle argues that artificial (machine) intelligence and human intelligence are so different that it is impossible to create a computer that can think.

Mark A. Findeis, a group leader at OsteoArthritis Sciences in Cambridge, Massachusetts, argues that genetic therapy holds great promise for battling diseases. Andrew Kimbrell, the policy director of the Foundation on Economic Trends in Washington, D.C., argues that the development of genetic engineering is so marked by scandal and moral blindness that society should be deeply suspicious of its purported benefits.

Writer Paul Brodeur argues that there is an increased risk of developing cancer from being exposed to electromagnetic fields given off by electric power lines. Scientist Thomas S. Tenforde argues that the evidence indicating adverse health effects from electromagnetic fields is very weak.

Andrzej E. Olszyna-Marzys, who works in a food and drug control laboratory, argues that no hazards have been demonstrated with respect to the sterilization of food by means of ionizing radiation. Donald B. Louria, a consultant in infectious diseases, argues that the studies used to judge the safety of food irradiation are flawed and that irradiated food may prove to increase the consumer's risk of developing cancer.

Virus researcher Brian W. J. Mahy and his colleagues argue that there is no reason to keep potentially dangerous samples of the deadly smallpox disease alive in the laboratory. Professor of microbiology Wolfgang K. Joklik and his colleagues argue that the smallpox virus must be preserved so that scientists may study it further.

Physiologist Jerod M. Loeb and his colleagues at the American Medical Association argue that the use of animals for testing medical drugs and procedures is essential to human welfare. Research attorney Steven Zak argues that for society to be virtuous, it must recognize the rights of animals not to be sacrificed for human needs.

Science writer Charles C. Mann makes the point that, under certain conditions, experiments done on human beings can be ethically sound. Arjun Makhijani, president of the Institute for Energy and Environmental Research in Takoma Park, Maryland, argues that experiments performed on humans in which the subjects are exposed to great risks without their knowledge are grossly unethical.

The American Medical Association's Council on Scientific Affairs and Council on Ethical and Judicial Affairs argue that using fetal tissue to treat adult illnesses is ethical, provided appropriate precautions are taken. Theologian James Tunstead Burtchaell asserts that research with aborted fetal tissue is unethical because informed consent cannot be obtained from a fetus.

INTRODUCTION

Analyzing Issues in Science and Technology

Thomas A. Easton

INTRODUCTION

As civilization approaches the dawn of the twenty-first century, it cannot escape science and technology. Their fruits—the clothes we wear, the foods we eat, the tools we use—surround us. Science and technology evoke in people both hope and dread for the future, for although new discoveries can lead to cures for diseases and other problems, new insights into the wonders of nature, and new toys (among other things), the past has shown that technological developments can also have unforeseen and terrible consequences.

Those consequences do *not* belong to science, for science is nothing more than a systematic approach to gaining knowledge about the world. Technology is the application of knowledge to accomplish things that otherwise could not be accomplished. Technological developments do not just lead to devices such as hammers, computers, and jet aircraft, but also to management systems, institutions, and even political philosophies. And it is, of course, such *uses* of knowledge that affect people's lives for good and ill.

It cannot be said that the use of technology affects people "for good *or* ill." As Emmanuel Mesthene said in 1969, technology is neither an unalloyed blessing nor an unmitigated curse.[1] Every new technology offers both new benefits and new problems, and the two sorts of consequences cannot be separated from each other. Automobiles, for example, provide rapid, convenient personal transportation, but precisely because of that benefit, they also cause suburban development, urban sprawl, crowded highways, and air pollution.

OPTIMISTS VS. PESSIMISTS

The inescapable pairing of good and bad consequences helps to account for why so many issues of science and technology stir debate in our society. Optimists tend to focus on the benefits of technology and to be confident that society will be able to cope with any problems that arise. Pessimists tend to fear the problems and to believe that the costs of technology will outweigh any possible benefits.

Sometimes the costs of new technologies are immediate and tangible. When new devices fail or new drugs prove to have unforeseen side effects, people can die. Sometimes the costs are less obvious. John McDermott, one of Mesthene's opponents, expressed confidence that technology led to the centralization of power in the hands of an educated elite; to his mind, technology was therefore antidemocratic.[2]

The proponents of technology answer that a machine's failure is a sign that it needs to be fixed, not banned. If a drug has side effects, it may need to be refined, or its list of permitted recipients may have to be better defined (the banned tranquilizer thalidomide, for example, is notorious for causing birth defects when taken early in pregnancy; it is apparently quite safe for men and nonpregnant women). And although several technologies that were developed in the 1960s seemed quite undemocratic at the time, one of them —computers—developed in a very different direction. Early on, computers were huge, expensive machines operated by an elite, but it was not long before they became so small, relatively inexpensive, and "user-friendly" that the general public gained access to them. Proponents lauded this as a true case of technological "power to the people."

CERTAINTY VS. UNCERTAINTY

Another source of debate over science and technology is uncertainty. Science is, by its very nature, uncertain. Its truths are provisional, open to revision.

Unfortunately, people are often told by politicians, religious leaders, and newspaper columnists that truth is certain. By this view, if someone admits uncertainty, then their position can be considered weak and they need not be heeded. This is, of course, an open invitation for demagogues to prey upon people's fears of disaster or side effects (which are always a possibility with new technology) or upon the wish to be told that greenhouse warming and ozone depletion are mere figments of the scientific imagination (they have yet to be proven beyond a doubt).

NATURAL VS. UNNATURAL

Still another source of controversy is rooted in the tendency of new ideas —in science and technology as well as in politics, history, literary criticism, and so on—to clash with preexisting beliefs or values. These clashes become most public when they pit science against religion and "family values." The battle between evolution and creationism, for example, still stirs passions a century and a half after naturalist Charles Darwin first said that human beings had nonhuman predecessors. It is nearly as provocative to some to suggest that homosexuality is a natural variant of human behavior (rather than a conscious choice), or that there might be a genetic component to intelligence or aggressiveness, or that the traditional mode of human reproduction might be supplemented with in vitro fertilization, embryo cloning, surrogate mother arrangements, and even genetic engineering.

Many new developments are rejected as "unnatural." For many people, "natural" means any device or procedure to which they have become accustomed. Very few realize how "unnatural" such seemingly ordinary things as circumcision, horseshoes, and baseball are.

However, humans do embrace change and are forever creating variations on religions, languages, politics, and tools. Innovation is as natural to a person as building dams is to a beaver.

PUBLIC VS. PRIVATE: WHO PAYS, AND WHY?

Finally, conflict frequently arises over the function of science in society. Traditionally, scientists have seen themselves as engaged solely in the pursuit of knowledge, solving the puzzles set before them by nature with little concern for whether or not the solutions to those puzzles might prove helpful to human enterprises such as war, health care, and commerce. Yet, again and again, the solutions discovered by scientists have proved useful—they have even founded entire industries.

Not surprisingly, society has come to expect science to be useful. When asked to fund research, society feels that it has the right to target research on issues of social concern, to demand results of immediate value, and to forbid research it deems dangerous or disruptive. And society's control of the purse strings gives its demands a certain undeniable persuasiveness.

PUBLIC POLICY

The question of how to target research is only one way in which science and technology intersect the realm of public policy. Here the question becomes, How should society allocate its resources in general? Toward education or prisons? Health care or welfare? Research or trade? Encouraging new technologies or cleaning up after old ones? The problem is that money is limited—there is not enough to finance every researcher who proposes to solve some social problem. Faced with competing worthy goals, society must make choices. Society must also run the risk that the choices made will turn out to be foolish.

THE PURPOSE OF THIS BOOK

Is there any prospect that the debates over the proper function of science, the acceptability of new technologies, or the truth of forecasts of disaster will soon fall quiet? Surely not, for some issues will likely never die, and there will always be new issues to debate afresh. (For example, think of the population debate, which has been argued ever since Thomas Malthus's 1789 "Essay on the Principle of Population," and then consider the debate over the manned exploration of space and whether or not it is worthwhile for society to spend resources in this way.)

Since almost all technological controversies will affect the conditions of our daily lives, learning about some of the current controversies and beginning to think critically about them is of great importance if we are to be informed and involved citizens.

Individuals may be able to affect the terms of the inevitable debates by first examining the nature of science and a few of the current controversies over issues of science and technology. After all, if one does not know what science, the scientific mode of thought, and their strengths and limitations are, one cannot think critically and constructively about any issue with a scientific or technological component. Nor can one hope to make informed choices among competing scientific or technological priorities.

WOMEN AND MINORITIES IN SCIENCE

There are some issues in the area of science, technology, and society that, even though they are of vital importance, you will not find directly debated in this volume. An example of such an issue might be, "Should there be more women and minorities in science?" However, this is not a debate because no one seriously responds to this question in the negative. Nonetheless, you should keep such considerations in mind as you read the issues in this book. And you should consider how the problems of discrimination and prejudice (based on race or class or gender) are played out in some of these debates— the debate on the information revolution and the debate on the use of humans as "experimental animals" would be two examples.

Every spring the American Association for the Advancement of Science publishes a special issue of its journal *Science* that deals with women in science. The March 13, 1992, issue dealt with obstacles in women's way. The April 16, 1993, issue dealt with the culture of science; its lead article was "Is There a 'Female Style' in Science?" And the March 11, 1994, issue focused on international comparisons of men and women working in science.

Also, every fall *Science* has a special issue on minorities in science. The November 13, 1992, issue dealt with the "pipeline problem," or the diversion of minority science students into other lines of study and work. And the November 12, 1993, issue focused on expanding minority representation in science careers.

These special issues contain a wealth of statistical information, interviews, and analyses invaluable to anyone considering whether or not to pursue a career in science. There are also, of course, vast amounts of other material available. See, for example, *Women's Work: Choice, Chance or Socialization? Insights from Psychologists and Other Researchers*, by Nancy Johnson Smith and Sylva K. Leduc (Detselig Enterprises, 1992).

THE SOUL OF SCIENCE

The standard picture of science—a world of observations, hypotheses, experiments, theories, sterile white coats, laboratories, and cold, unfeeling logic— is a myth. This image has more to do with the way science is presented by both scientists and the media than with the way scientists actually perform their work. In practice, scientists are often less orderly, less logical, and more prone to very human conflicts of personality than most people suspect.

The myth remains because it helps to organize science. It provides labels and a framework for what a scientist does; it may thus be especially valuable to student scientists who are still learning the ropes. In addition, the image embodies certain important ideals of scientific thought. These ideals make the scientific approach the most powerful and reliable guide to truth about the world that human beings have yet devised.

THE IDEALS OF SCIENCE: SKEPTICISM, COMMUNICATION, AND REPRODUCIBILITY

The soul of science is a very simple idea: *Check it out.* Years ago, scholars believed that speaking the truth simply required prefacing a statement with "According to" and some ancient authority, such as Aristotle, or a holy text, such as the Bible. If someone with a suitably illustrious reputation had once said something was so, it was so.

This attitude is the opposite of everything that modern science stands for. Scientific knowledge is based not on authority but on reality. Scientists take nothing on faith; they are *skeptical.* When a scientist wants to know something, he or she does not look it up in the library or take another's word for it. Scientists go into the laboratory, or the forest, or the desert—wherever they can find the phenomena they wish to know about—and they "ask" those phenomena directly. They look for answers in nature. And if they think they know the answer already, it is not of books that they ask, "Are we right?" but of nature. This is the point of scientific experiments—they are how scientists ask nature whether or not their ideas check out.

The concept of "check it out" is, however, an ideal. No one can possibly check everything out for himself or herself. Even scientists, in practice, look up information in books and rely on authorities. But the authorities they rely on are other scientists who have studied nature and reported what they learned. And, in principle, everything those authorities report can be checked. Experiments performed in the lab or in the field can be repeated. New theoretical or computer models can be designed. Information that is in the books can be confirmed.

In fact, a good part of the "scientific method" is designed to make it possible for any scientist's findings or conclusions to be confirmed. For example, scientists do not say, "Vitamin D is essential for strong bones. Believe me. I know." They say, "I know that vitamin D is essential for proper bone formation because I raised rats without vitamin D in their diet, and their bones became soft and crooked. When I gave them vitamin D, their bones hardened and straightened. Here is the kind of rat I used, the kind of food I fed them, the amount of vitamin D I gave them. Go and do likewise, and you will see what I saw."

Communication is therefore an essential part of modern science. That is, in order to function as a scientist, you must not keep secrets. You must tell others not just what you have learned but how you learned it. You must spell out your methods in enough detail to let others repeat your work.

Scientific knowledge is thus *reproducible* knowledge. Strictly speaking, if a person says, "I can see it, but you cannot," that person is not a scientist. Scientific knowledge exists for everyone. Anyone who takes the time to learn the proper techniques can confirm any scientific finding.

THE STANDARD MODEL OF THE SCIENTIFIC METHOD

As it is usually presented, the scientific method has five major components: *observation, generalization* (identifying a pattern), stating a *hypothesis* (a tentative extension of the pattern or explanation for why the pattern exists), *experimentation* (testing that explanation), and *communication* of the test results to other members of the scientific community, usually by publishing the findings. How each of these components contributes to the scientific method is discussed below.

Observation
The basic units of science—and the only real facts that the scientist knows —are the individual *observations.* Using them, scientists look for patterns, suggest explanations, and devise tests for their ideas. Observations can be casual or they may be more deliberate.

Generalization
After making observations, a scientist tries to discern a pattern among them. A statement of such a pattern is a *generalization.* Cautious experimenters do not jump to conclusions. When they think they see a pattern, they often make a few more observations just to be sure the pattern holds up. This practice of strengthening or confirming findings by replicating them is a very important part of the scientific process.

The Hypothesis
A tentative explanation suggesting why a particular pattern exists is called a *hypothesis.* The mark of a good hypothesis is that it is *testable.* But there is no way to test a guess about past events and patterns and to be sure of absolute truth in the results, so a simple, direct hypothesis is needed. The scientist says, in effect, "I have an idea that X is true. I cannot test X easily or reliably. But if X *is* true, then so is Y. And I can test Y." Unfortunately, tests can fail even when the hypothesis is perfectly correct.

Many philosophers of science insist on *falsification* as a crucial aspect of the scientific method. That is, when a test of a hypothesis shows the hypothesis to be false, the hypothesis must be rejected and replaced with another. This is not to be confused with the falsification, or misrepresentation, of research data and results, which is a form of scientific misconduct.

In terms of the X and Y hypotheses mentioned above, if it has been found that Y is not true, can we say that X is false too? Perhaps, but bear in mind that X was not tested. Y was tested, and Y is the hypothesis that the idea of falsification says must be replaced, perhaps with hypothesis Z.

The Experiment

The *experiment* is the most formal part of the scientific process. The concept, however, is very simple: an experiment is a test of a hypothesis. It is what a scientist does to check an idea out. It may involve giving a new drug to a sick patient or testing a new process to preserve apples, tomatoes, and lettuce.

If the experiment does not falsify the hypothesis, that does not mean that the hypothesis is true. It simply means that the scientist has not yet come up with a test that falsifies the hypothesis. As the number of times and the number of different tests that fail to falsify a hypothesis increase, the likelihood that the hypothesis is true also increases. However, because it is impossible to conceive of and perform all the possible tests of a hypothesis, the scientist can never *prove* that it is true.

Consider the hypothesis that all cats are black. If you see a black cat, you do not really know anything at all about the color of all cats. But if you see a white cat, you certainly know that not all cats are black. You would have to look at every cat on Earth to prove the hypothesis, but only one (of a color other than black) to disprove it. This is why philosophers of science often say that *science is the art of disproving,* not proving. If a hypothesis withstands many attempts to disprove it, then it may be a good explanation of the phenomenon in question. If it fails just one test, though, it is clearly wrong and must be replaced with a new hypothesis.

Researchers who study what scientists actually do point out that most scientists do not act in accord with this reasoning. Almost all scientists, when they come up with what strikes them as a good explanation of a phenomenon or pattern, do *not* try to disprove the hypothesis. Instead, they design experiments to *confirm* it. If an experiment fails to confirm the hypothesis, then the researchers try another experiment, not another hypothesis.

The logical weakness in this approach is obvious, but it does not keep researchers from holding onto their ideas as long as possible. Sometimes they hold on so long, even without confirming the hypothesis, that they wind up looking ridiculous. Other times the confirmations add up over the years, and any attempts to disprove the hypothesis fail to do so. The hypothesis may then be elevated to the rank of a theory, principle, or law. *Theories* are explanations of how things work (the theory of evolution *by means of* natural selection, for example). *Principles* and *laws* tend to be statements of things that invariably happen, such as the law of gravity (masses attract each other, or what goes up must come down) or the gas law (if you increase the pressure on an enclosed gas, the volume will decrease and the temperature will increase).

Communication

Each scientist is obligated to share her or his hypotheses, methods, and findings with the rest of the scientific community. This sharing serves two purposes. First, it supports the basic ideal of skepticism by making it possible for others to say, "Oh, yeah? Let me check that." It tells the skeptics where to look to see what the scientist saw and what techniques and tools to use.

Second, communication allows others to use in their work what has already been discovered. This is essential because science is a cooperative endeavor. People who work thousands of miles apart build with and upon each other's discoveries—some of the most exciting discoveries have involved bringing together information from very different fields.

Scientific cooperation stretches across time as well. Every generation of scientists both uses and adds to what previous generations have discovered. As Sir Isaac Newton said in 1675, in a letter to fellow scientist Robert Hooke, "If I have seen further than [other men], it is by standing upon the shoulders of Giants."

The communication of science begins with a process called "peer review," which typically has three stages. The first stage occurs when a scientist seeks funding—from government agencies, foundations, or other sources—to carry out a research program. He or she must prepare a report describing the intended work, laying out the background, hypotheses, planned experiments, expected results, and even the broader impacts on other fields. Committees of other scientists then go over the report to determine whether or not the applicant knows his or her area, has the necessary abilities, and is realistic in his or her plans.

Once the scientist has acquired funding, has done the work, and has written a report of the results, that report will be submitted to a scientific journal, which begins the second stage. Before publishing the report, the journal's editors will show it to other workers in the same or related fields and ask them whether or not the work was done adequately, the conclusions are justified, and the report should be published.

The third stage of peer review happens after publication, when the broader scientific community can judge the work.

It is certainly possible for these standard peer review mechanisms to fail. By their nature, these mechanisms are more likely to approve ideas that do not contradict what the reviewers think they already know. Yet, unconventional ideas are not necessarily wrong, as German geophysicist Alfred Wegener proved when he tried to gain acceptance for his idea of continental drift in the early twentieth century. At the time, geologists believed that the crust of the Earth—which is solid rock, after all—did not behave like liquid. Yet, Wegener was proposing that the continents floated about like icebergs in the sea, bumping into each other, tearing apart (to produce matching profiles like those of South America and Africa), and bumping again. It was not until the 1960s that most geologists accepted his ideas as genuine insights instead of harebrained delusions.

THE NEED FOR CONTROLS

Many years ago, I read a description of a "wish machine." It consisted of an ordinary stereo amplifier with two unusual attachments. The wires that would normally be connected to a microphone were connected instead to a pair of copper plates. The wires that would normally be connected to a speaker were connected instead to a whip antenna of the sort usually seen on cars.

To use this device, one put a picture of some desired item between the copper plates. It could be, for instance, a photo of a person with whom one wanted a date, a lottery ticket, or a college that one wished to attend. One test case used a photo of a pest-infested cornfield. The user then wished fervently for the date, the winning lottery ticket, a college acceptance, or whatever else one craved. In the test case, the testers wished that all the pests in the cornfield would drop dead.

Supposedly, the wish would be picked up by the copper plates, amplified by the stereo amplifier, and then sent via the whip antenna to wherever wish orders go. Whoever or whatever fills those orders would get the message and grant the wish. Well, in the test case, when the testers checked the cornfield after using the machine, there was no longer any sign of pests. What's more, the process seemed to work equally well whether the amplifier was plugged in or not.

You are probably now feeling very much like a scientist—skeptical. The true, dedicated scientist, however, does not stop with saying, "Oh, yeah? Tell me another one!" Instead, he or she says, "Let's check this out."[3]

Where must the scientist begin? The standard model of the scientific method says that the first step is observation. Here, our observations (as well as our necessary generalization) are simply the description of the wish machine and the claims for its effectiveness. Perhaps we even have the device itself.

What is our hypothesis? We have two choices, one consistent with the claims for the device and one denying those claims: the wish machine always works, or the wish machine never works. Both are equally testable and equally falsifiable.

How do we test the hypothesis? Set up the wish machine, and perform the experiment of making a wish. If the wish comes true, the device works. If the wish does not come true, the device does not work.

Can it really be that simple? In essence, yes. But in fact, no.

Even if you do not believe that wishing can make something happen, sometimes wishes do come true by sheer coincidence. Therefore, even if the wish machine is as nonsensical as most people think it is, sometimes it will *seem* to work. We therefore need a way to shield against the misleading effects of coincidence.

Coincidence is not, of course, the only source of error we need to watch out for. For instance, there is a very human tendency to interpret events in such a way as to agree with our preexisting beliefs, or our prejudices. If we believe in wishes, we therefore need a way to guard against our willingness to interpret near misses as not quite misses at all. There is also a human tendency not to look for mistakes when the results agree with our prejudices. The cornfield, for instance, might not have been as badly infested as the testers said it was, or a farmer might have sprayed it with pesticide between checks, or the testers may have accidentally checked the wrong field. The point is that correlation does not necessarily reflect cause. In other words, although an event seems to occur as the result of another, there may be other factors at work that negate the relationship.

We also need to check whether or not the wish machine does indeed work equally well when the amplifier is unplugged as when it is plugged in, and then we must guard against the tendency to wish harder when we know that it is plugged in. Furthermore, we would like to know whether or not placing a photo between the copper plates makes any difference, and then we must guard against the tendency to wish harder when we know that the wish matches the photo.

Coincidence is easy to protect against. All that is necessary is to repeat the experiment enough times to be sure that we are not seeing flukes. This is one major purpose of replication. Our willingness to shade the results in our favor can be defeated by having another scientist judge the results of our wishing experiments. And our eagerness to overlook errors that produce favorable results can be defeated by taking great care to avoid any errors at all; peer reviewers also help by pointing out such problems.

Other sources of error are harder to avoid, but scientists have developed a number of helpful *control* techniques. One technique is called "blinding." In essence, blinding requires setting up the experiment in such a way that the critical aspects are hidden from either the test subjects, the scientist who is physically performing the experiment, or both. This helps to prevent individuals' expectations from influencing the outcome of the experiment.

In the pharmaceutical industry, blinding is used whenever a new drug is tested. The basic process goes like this: A number of patients with the affliction that the drug is supposed to affect are selected. Half of them— chosen randomly to avoid any unconscious bias that might put sicker patients in one group[4]—are given the drug. The others are given a dummy pill, or a sugar pill, also known as a *placebo*. In all other respects, the two groups are treated exactly the same.

Although, placebos are not supposed to have any effect on patients, they can sometimes have real medical effects, apparently because people tend to believe their doctors when they say that a pill will cure them. That is, when we put faith in our doctors, our minds do their best to bring our bodies into line with whatever the doctors tell us. This mind-over-body effect is called the "placebo effect." To guard against the placebo effect, experimenters employ either single-blind or double-blind techniques.

Single-Blind   With this approach, the researchers do not tell the patients what pill they are getting. The patients are therefore "blinded" to what is going on. Both placebo and drug then gain equal advantage from the placebo effect. If the drug seems to work better or worse than the placebo, then the researchers can be sure of a real difference between the two.

Double-Blind   If the researchers know what pill they are handing out, they can give subtle, unconscious cues that let the patients know whether they are receiving the drug or the placebo. The researchers may also interpret any changes in the symptoms of the patients who receive the drug as being caused by the drug. It is therefore best to keep the researchers in the dark too; and when both researchers and patients are blind to the truth, the experiment is said to be "double-blind." Drug trials often use pills that differ only in color or in the number on the bottle, and the code is not broken until all the test results are in. This way nobody knows who gets what until the knowledge can no longer make a difference.

Obviously, the double-blind approach can work only when there are human beings on both sides of the experiment, as experimenter and as experimental subject. When the object of the experiment is an inanimate object (such as the wish machine), only the single-blind approach is possible.

With suitable precautions against coincidence, self-delusion, wishful thinking, bias, and other sources of error, the wish machine could be convincingly tested. Yet, it cannot be perfectly tested, for perhaps it only works sometimes, such as when the aurora glows green over Copenhagen, in months without an *r*, or when certain people use it. It is impossible to rule out all the possibilities, although we can rule out enough to be pretty confident that the gadget is pure nonsense.

Similar precautions are essential in every scientific field, for the same sources of error lie in wait wherever experiments are done, and they serve very much the same function. However, no controls and no peer review system, no matter how elaborate, can completely protect a scientist—or science—from error. Here, as well as in the logical impossibility of proof (remember, experiments only fail to disprove) and science's dependence on the progressive growth of knowledge, lies the uncertainty that is the hallmark of science. Yet, it is also a hallmark of science that its methods guarantee that uncertainty will be reduced (not eliminated). Frauds and errors will be detected and corrected. Limited understandings of truth will be extended.

Those who bear this in mind will be better equipped to deal with issues of certainty and risk.

NOTES

1. Mesthene's essay, "The Role of Technology in Society," *Technology and Culture* (vol. 10, no. 4, 1969), is reprinted in A. H. Teich, ed., *Technology and the Future*, 6th ed. (St. Martin's Press, 1993).

2. McDermott's essay, "Technology: The Opiate of the Intellectuals," *The New York Review of Books* (July 31, 1969), is reprinted in A. H. Teich, ed., *Technology and the Future*, 6th ed. (St. Martin's Press, 1993).

3. Must we, really? After all, we can be quite sure that the wish machine does not work because, if it did, it would likely be on the market. Casinos would then be unable to make a profit for their backers, deadly diseases would be eradicated, and so on.

4. Or patients that are taller, shorter, male, female, homosexual, heterosexual, black, white—there is no telling what differences might affect the test results. Drug (and other) researchers therefore take great pains to be sure groups of experimental subjects are alike in every way but the one way being tested.

PART 1

The Place of Science and Technology in Society

The partnership between human society and science and technology is an uneasy one. Science and technology undoubtedly offer benefits, in both the short term and the long, but they also challenge accepted beliefs and present society with new worries.

The issues in this section deal with the best ways to obtain the benefits of science and technology, how to manage risk, the question of scientific misconduct, and the accessibility of advancing technology.

- Should Government Provide Funding for Basic Research?

- Are Worst-Case Estimates of Risk the Best Method for Making Environmental Decisions?

- Can Science Police Itself?

- Will the Information Revolution Benefit Everyone?

ISSUE 1

Should Government Provide Funding for Basic Research?

YES: Purnell Choppin, from "Basic Medical Research: Vital to Our Future," *Vital Speeches of the Day* (June 15, 1993)

NO: Barbara A. Mikulski, from "Science in the National Interest," *Science* (April 8, 1994)

ISSUE SUMMARY

YES: Purnell Choppin, the president of the Howard Hughes Medical Institute, argues that if society turns its back on basic research, it rejects both scientific progress and "part of the quest that makes us better human beings."

NO: Senator Barbara A. Mikulski (D-Maryland) argues that it is the place of science to lead to new ideas, new technologies, and new jobs, and that science funding must be seen as a public investment in the future.

What scientists do when they apply their methods is called *research*. Scientists who perform *basic research* seek no specific result. Basic research is motivated essentially by curiosity. It is the study of some aspect of nature for its own sake. In pursuing this study, basic researchers have revealed vast amounts of detail about the chemistry and function of genes, discovered ways to cut and splice genes, and learned how to insert into one organism genes from other organisms. They have revealed the structure of the atom and discovered radioactivity. And they have produced photographs of the surface of Mars.

Applied research is more mission-oriented. Scientists who conduct applied research seek answers to specific problems: they search for cures for diseases, methods for analyzing problems, and ways to control various phenomena. Many of the scientists who work for the government and industry are applied researchers. Among other things, applied researchers have taken the knowledge and techniques developed by basic researchers in genetics and molecular biology and have created the technology of genetic engineering. With this technology, they have made it possible to manufacture in quantity and relatively cheaply numerous chemicals for the treatment of diseases, and they are now trying to learn how to replace defective genes and how to equip organisms with new characteristics. This new industry has immense potential for growth and for impact on human welfare.

In addition to medicine, knowledge obtained through basic research has been applied in many other areas. For example, scientists have used the basic understanding of the atmosphere to improve weather forecasting; space research has yielded communications, weather, and earth-resource-survey satellites; and work on the behavior of electrons has led to the development of desktop computers. There are thousands of such examples.

The unexpected fruits—the practical applications—of basic research have been cited to justify steady growth in funding for this side of science ever since Vannevar Bush's 1945 report *Science, the Endless Frontier* (reprint, National Science Foundation, 1990). However, the search for justification is an ever-lasting struggle. For example, Warren Weaver, in "Fundamental Questions in Science," *Scientific American* (September 1953), expressed concern that the successes of applied science means the neglect of basic science. Today there is a movement to focus on "national goals" and "science in the national interest" and to emphasize applied research over basic research.

It is easy to see what drives the movement toward applied science: society has a host of problems that cry out for quick solutions. Yet, there is also a need for basic research, for basic research undeniably supplies a great many of the ideas, facts, and techniques that applied researchers use in their search for answers to problems. Basic researchers, of course, use the same ideas, facts, and techniques as they continue their probings into the way nature works.

Purnell Choppin is the President of the Howard Hughes Medical Institute, a private health research organization that channels hundreds of millions of dollars into basic medical research. In the following selection, he argues that if society puts too much emphasis on the applications of science and technology and fails to support vigorously basic research and education, then scientific, technological, and human progress will stagnate.

Many government decision makers, however, now see basic research as a luxury that society cannot afford because the payoff is not immediate, so-ciety has other needs that require funding, and the money is limited. This is the point made by Barbara A. Mikulski, chair of the Senate Appropria-tions Subcommittee on Veterans Affairs, Housing and Urban Development, and Independent Agencies. She sees a new mission of science in "strategic" research directed toward important national goals such as energy needs, in-ternational competitiveness, and climate change. Science funding, she says, is public investment in the future, and scientists need to let go of the idea that society has an obligation to support unlimited intellectual curiosity.

YES

Purnell Choppin

BASIC MEDICAL RESEARCH: VITAL TO OUR FUTURE

Delivered before the Commonwealth Club, Oakland, California, April 1, 1993

Several weeks ago, President Clinton visited the Bay Area to announce his new technology policy. It was not by happenstance that he did so here. The administration's new technology policy is designed to make the United States more competitive in high-tech fields such as computers, biotechnology, and advanced materials. President Clinton knows the high-tech horizon begins just beyond this room. Out of the windows to my right you can see some of the biotechnology companies in Emeryville and, further away, in South San Francisco. To our left lies Silicon Valley, a place whose name is synonymous with high technology.

Many of you may work in, or with, these companies. Apple. Intel. Chiron. Genentech. Alza. You know the list better than I do. I am not a business-man or a venture capitalist. I am a scientist who spent nearly three decades at The Rockefeller University in New York studying viruses and viral dis-eases. For the past several years, I have had the privilege of heading one of the world's great scientific organizations, the Howard Hughes Medical Insti-tute, or HHMI. UCSF [University of California, San Francisco], Stanford, and Berkeley are among the 53 research sites where our scientists are based. These three HHMI units employ 261 people, and expend nearly $29 million each year. We also support programs to improve the quality of science education in the Bay Area, as well as throughout the country.

In my talk today, I shall describe some of these activities. I hope you'll find them exciting. But, since most of you are not scientists, I also will try to put our activities, and those of other research organizations, into a broader context.

It is good news that the United States is getting more serious about high technology. That is where the future lies; we cannot maintain prosperity without it. But high technology flows from scientific advances. More effective drugs and faster computers are made possible by basic research in biology, physics, and other scientific fields. Not only does basic research produce the knowledge upon which technological progress is based, but the conduct of research also provides training for the next generation of scientists. Yet, despite its importance, basic research now faces some serious problems.

I am very pleased to discuss research before the Commonwealth Club as you celebrate your ninetieth birthday. The *San Francisco Chronicle* recently published excerpts from memorable speeches delivered to the club over the years. One of the very first was by a bank teller named Edward Berdick. Here's what he said in 1906 about a dangerous new invention— the automobile:

"The foul autoist is a greater menace to the best society ... than is the predatory highwayman."

I wonder what Mr. Berdick would say today about the automobile. I am sure he wouldn't like the traffic on the Bay Bridge. But he would have to concede that automobiles have changed our society profoundly and, on balance, for the better. When I was a boy in Louisiana, for a respiratory infection I would get a mustard plaster and for an intestinal problem, castor oil. Now we are treating patients with monoclonal antibodies and drugs produced by recombinant DNA techniques. The pace of change has been astonishing.

Nowhere has that pace accelerated faster than in biology. The life sciences are experiencing the same historic transformation that occurred earlier in this century in physics. Our understanding of living organisms has been totally recast in the four decades since Watson and Crick determined the structure of DNA. We have learned much about how our brains operate, what occurs within cells, and why people resist or succumb to diseases. We have produced an astonishing array of new drugs and diagnostic procedures, and have begun using gene therapy to treat some diseases. The biological revolution—and it truly is a revolution —is also changing the face of agriculture and other industries.

E. B. White once wrote, "I have occasionally had the exquisite thrill of putting my finger on a little capsule of truth and heard it give the faint squeak of mortality under my pressure." Today, we have the exquisite thrill of putting our fingers on new truths in biology almost every week. Some of nature's most wonderful secrets are within our grasp. The distinguished cell biologist George Palade has said that one must go back to the Italian Renaissance to find a comparable time of human creativity and imagination, and I agree with him.

The Howard Hughes Medical Institute is playing an important part in this process. Since the name Howard Hughes still conjures up an air of eccentricity and even mystery for many people, I shall take a few minutes to explain what our institute does.

HHMI was founded in 1953 when the aviator and industrialist spun off part of the Hughes Tool Company to create the Hughes Aircraft Company. He then gave the company, which was to become the country's fifth largest defense contractor, to a new medical institute bearing his name. For the first 25 years, the institute's contributions to medical research grew slowly, but in the mid-1970s the pace quickened. Then in 1984, a new board of distinguished trustees was appointed and, a year later, Hughes Aircraft was sold to General Motors for just over $5 billion. HHMI then became the largest private philanthropy in the country, and increased its research activities rapidly, about 7-fold in the past eight years. It also established a large grants program which is devoted to improving science education. Our budget for this year is $319 million.

HHMI is not a foundation. It is a medical research organization, or MRO. An MRO operates under different Treasury regulations than those governing private foundations like Ford or Rockefeller. We conduct research with our own employees in our own laboratories. We enter into long-term collaborative agreements with more than 50 universities, hospitals, and research centers throughout the United States. At Berkeley, for example, our investigators have laboratories at the university's new life sciences building addition. At Stanford, you'll find us at the medical school, and at UCSF along Parnassus Avenue. HHMI investigators are our employees but they continue as faculty members and good academic citizens of their host institutions, teaching classes, serving on faculty committees, and so forth. It is a complex arrangement but one that works well for everyone.

The whole of our far-flung institute is greater than the sum of its parts. Wonderful synergy emerges when we bring our investigators together from around the country, as we do regularly. It is like assembling a room full of academic Joe Montanas and watching them discuss what they have already accomplished and formulate ways to reach new scientific goals. The meetings often lead to productive collaborations. During the past year, for example, HHMI researchers at Duke University and the University of Michigan announced a new approach for stopping the AIDS virus from replicating once it infects T-cells of the immune system.

About a third of our 225 investigators work directly on specific diseases. Most carry out studies at a fundamental level. The goal is to produce knowledge that benefits humanity. We focus on five especially vibrant fields—cell biology and regulation, genetics, immunology, neuroscience, and structural biology. We identify the very best scientists, give them the resources they need, and set them loose, unencumbered by extensive paperwork or grant applications.

In return, we expect great science—and we get it. Our scientists include 39 members of the National Academy of Sciences. Just this past December Edwin Krebs, a Hughes investigator at the University of Washington who is now emeritus, became our fifth researcher to win the Nobel Prize. He was honored for a lifetime of distinguished research beginning with his co-discovery in the 1950s of protein phosphorylation.

Our largest contingent of investigators is here in California, with 28 in the Bay Area alone. Let me tell you about some of them. At Berkeley, Robert Tijan is among the world's experts on transcription, that is, how genes are expressed by turning the information in DNA into the proteins that carry out biological functions. By explaining the biochemistry of transcription, Bob's work could lead eventually to revolutionary new methods of treating diseases. Gerald Rubin, another investigator at Berkeley, is deciphering how the nervous system develops from the embryo to the adult. At Stanford, Uta Francke is searching for the genetic origin of Marfan syndrome, dwarfism, and other inherited diseases. Mark Davis is exploring the mechanism of immunity, knowledge that could help in the struggle against AIDS and other disorders. At UCSF, Y. W. Kan's pioneering work in human genetics led to many of the advances in diagnostic tests that we now use, as well as to the identification of genes involved in inherited diseases. Yuh Nung and Lily Jan, a husband-and-wife team, are exploring the molecular basis of learning and other functions within the brain.

I could have selected many other examples. During the past year our researchers across the country have made important discoveries involving tuberculosis, muscular dystrophy, Lyme disease, diabetes, and other major medical problems. In recent weeks they were among those announcing the discovery of the gene involved in amyotrophic lateral sclerosis, or Lou Gehrig's disease, and of the gene defect that underlies Huntington's disease, a fatal neurodegenerative illness.

Our activities and those of other research institutions are important not only medically, but also economically. Basic biological research is the foundation of biotechnology and related industries. Bioscience research has been especially important to the economy of northern California. According to one estimate, local bioscience firms hire more than 50,000 people and generate billions in revenue. Northern California's leadership in biotechnology would have been impossible without the presence of leading research universities and a well-educated labor force. Herbert Boyer, a founder of Genentech, and Stanley Cohen of Stanford wrote the historic scientific paper that showed the feasibility of DNA cloning. Boyer, a former Hughes investigator, spent much of his career as a biochemist at UCSF. Cetus, Chiron, Cal-

gene, and many other biotech firms also can trace their origins to Bay Area campuses. If basic research did not flourish locally, neither would the biotechnology industry.

Science requires a certain amount of faith. The secrets of nature cannot be churned out like widgets on an assembly line. They often reveal themselves serendipitously when we are patient and wise enough to discern them. Yet, with the country deeply in debt and struggling economically, one wonders whether Americans will be patient enough to await the payoff.

There is good reason to worry about this. Total funding for medical research and development in the United States has increased steadily in recent years but the increase is leveling off, and the relative proportion of funds from federal sources has decreased while that from industry has increased. The National Institutes of Health's share of total medical R&D funding dropped from 41 percent to 30 percent between 1979 and 1992. Other federal support declined from 19 percent to 11 percent during the same period. Four years ago, industrial funding on research exceeded federal spending for the first time. Industrial spending is not bad, of course. It is good. But companies spend much more on the "D"—development—than on the "R" —research. They need others to help with the fundamental science. Another important source of support has been the private, non-profit sector. But in recent years private foundations have increased their spending on basic research only modestly. All of the private not-for-profit foundations together spent $45 million less last year on biomedical research than the $281 million that the Hughes institute alone expended on basic research, and the figure does not include our grants program, which I'll discuss in a few moments.

I do not mean to minimize the generous support that Congress has provided to science in the past, nor to deny the severity of the current federal budget crisis. In many respects, science has fared well in recent years, although much more federal money has gone to military R&D than to basic science. I also think the administration's new technology policy deserves a lot of praise. It expands funding for the National Science Foundation and acknowledges explicitly the importance of basic science.

Nonetheless, the plan devotes barely more than a page to science while discussing at length proposals for a national network of manufacturing extension centers, a "clean car," a high-performance computing initiative, and other efforts. Since President Clinton was elected to create jobs and revive the economy, it is not surprising that the administration is focusing on applications. All of us want the economy revitalized. And I expect the administration will maintain support for basic research even while it emphasizes applications.

Why then do I and so many of my scientific colleagues feel uneasy? My concern is not with this administration. Rather, I worry what will happen to science over the long term if it is thought of as an adjunct to technology. Doing so puts science at risk. People who are unsophisticated about the linkage between science and technology may not understand that the two are increasingly inseparable, that you cannot abdicate in science and excel in technology. They may say, "Well, why not let the Japanese and the Germans carry the load in basic science for awhile while we get rich off the applications?" It is extremely important to note that the Japanese recognize that they cannot continue to rely on the strategy they used to win market share for automobiles, fax machines and VCRs. They have begun to increase their basic research effort significantly, especially in the life sciences. Japan recently took the lead in introducing new chemical entities of interest to the pharmaceutical industry. In 1988 and 1989, it introduced 24 such new entities while the United States introduced 13. Japan and Germany both spend more of their gross national product on non-defense research than we do.

It would be a terrible irony if the United States embraced Japan's old technology model just as the Japanese realize that to continue to win the economic battle in the 21st century they will have to emphasize basic research now. Such a U.S. course would lead to what many American corporations are experiencing when they put quarterly earnings before long-term planning—a slow but relentless decline. Are we in danger of going down such a path? Just ask any scientist how hard it is already to get an NIH grant. Or ask what further cutbacks at our universities would do to the vitality of basic research in this country.

Earlier, I mentioned George Palade's comparison of modern biological advances with the Italian Renaissance. He went on to note that the Italian city-states withered when they lost their leadership in navigation, nautical engineering and other areas of scientific innovation. They were content to ply Mediterranean trade lanes while the Portuguese, Spanish, English, and Dutch were exploring the world and reaping the rewards of that exploration. If you stop pushing the frontiers, you fall behind. That can happen to [the] U.S. Opportunity does not wait.

The Carnegie Commission on Science, Technology and Government reported recently that state of precollege mathematics and science education in our country poses "a chronic and serious threat to our nation's future." We are failing to attract enough of the brightest students to careers in science. This is especially true for minority students. According to the dean's office at Berkeley, African Americans comprised 12 percent of Cal's 1987 freshman class but only 4.5 percent of those enrolled in introductory biology. Can anyone guess what percentage African Americans comprised of those who finally got BA's in biology? The answer is 1.7 percent. Hispanic students comprised 16.5 percent of the same freshman class but got only 4.5 percent of the biology BA's.

The state of science education has to change, and soon. We cannot sustain a modern economy with a population that thinks gene splicing is something that Levi Strauss developed. Many of you may already have difficulty finding highly trained people to work in your laboratories and companies. Unless we improve math and science education dramatically, including reaching out to those who have been excluded in the past, things will get worse, not better.

In 1987 our institute launched a major effort to help reverse this situation. We provide grants to improve science education at all levels, from precollege through postgraduate training. Last year we awarded more than $50 million in grants. One grant went to Berkeley. Corey Goodman, one of our Hughes investigators, and his colleagues there are working to make biology more interesting for undergraduates. They want students to spend more time learning biology in the laboratory with their own eyes, ears, and hands. They are trying to remove barriers that prevent minority students from pursuing research careers. Some of the Hughes funds are used to enable work-study students to earn money by doing research in a lab instead of shelving books in the library. A Biology Scholars Program provides minority students with academic workshops, counseling, research opportunities, and a community of like-minded peers.

Another of our grants is supporting a remarkable program at Stanford that lets undergraduates learn first-hand what it means to be a research scientist. The students join a lab team and begin working on a project with graduate students, post-docs, and professors. They take apart cells and analyze DNA. They participate in original research and critique each other's work and writing up of results. Then the students propose projects of their own and compete for funds, just like someone trying to get an NIH grant. A faculty committee awards the best proposals some of the Hughes money. Stanford also sponsors symposia in which undergraduates present their research findings. By the time they graduate, many are hooked on research. The program also makes a special effort to reach out to minority students....

I have spoken with you today about the importance of basic medical research to our economy and quality of life. As I explained, we cannot build a future of silicon if we let the scientific foundation turn to sand. I also have spoken of the need to improve science education to ensure a steady stream of bright young minds into our laboratories, universities, and companies. The Howard Hughes Medical Institute is playing a major role both in pushing back the scientific frontiers and in training the next generation of researchers.

Einstein once said, "The important thing is not to stop questioning. Curiosity has its own reason for existing.... Never lose a holy curiosity." Unless our nation retains a holy curiosity, its future is clouded. If we turn our backs on basic research, we turn away not only from the high-tech horizon but also from part of the quest that makes us better human beings. And if we fail to bring the next generation along with us, we lose the reason for making the journey at all. The view outside these windows is grand, but the scientific landscape is even grander— if we have the vision to pursue it.

NO

Barbara A. Mikulski

SCIENCE IN THE NATIONAL INTEREST

Where will the United States of America be in science and technology in the year 2000? Where will we be in the year 2020? What do we need to do in order to get there, not only in terms of developing our intellectual capacity and enhancing and sustaining our research capacity, but also knowing the national goals that we will want to accomplish in the best interest of the United States of America?

I chair the subcommittee on appropriations called Veterans Affairs, Housing and Urban Development (HUD), and Independent Agencies. It's an $88-billion portfolio that oversees 25 different agencies. Outside of Senator Inouye's [D-Hawaii] subcommittee on defense, it has the largest amount of discretionary spending of any subcommittee in the federal appropriations process. Within the Appropriations Committee, the big three in terms of the amount of discretionary spending are Defense, my subcommittee, and Labor—Health and Human Services. I have the responsibility for funding the departments of Veterans Affairs and HUD, the National Space Agency, the Environmental Protection Agency (EPA), the Federal Emergency Management Agency, the National Science Foundation (NSF), and other agencies ranging from Jack Gibbon's Office on Science and Technology Policy to Arlington Cemetery, the Consumer Products Safety Commission, Selective Service, National Neighborhood Reinvestment, and many others. The four agencies that play a substantial role in funding of science are NASA, NSF, EPA, and the Department of Veterans Affairs, which has a substantial research budget in the area of applied and clinical life science research.

Congress first passes the President's [Clinton's] budget through the Budget Committee. The Budget Committee establishes something called the 602(a). This is the total amount of money we appropriators can spend without the Senate reaching a 60-vote supermajority to waive the Budget Act. Then, the Appropriations Committee chair divides the 602(a) among 13 subcommittees. We vie, we deal, and we duke it out to get something called the 602(b). That is the allocation that every subcommittee gets, and it varies according to our

From Barbara A. Mikulski, "Science in the National Interest," *Science,* vol. 264 (April 8, 1994), pp. 221–222. Copyright © 1994 by The American Association for the Advancement of Science. Reprinted by permission.

need. We then look at every agency that we need to fund, and we appropriate within the 602(b). The authorizing committees set the policy, but when it comes to the money, they are advisory to the Appropriations Committee.

The budget from the 602(b) is about $88 billion for my subcommittee. Thirty-six billion dollars out of this $88 billion immediately goes to the VA for the pensions, disability benefits, and so on, including $16 billion for veterans' health care. The remainder is used to fund the other agencies. We then establish priorities in the appropriations subcommittee, look for a synergistic and cumulative effect of what we do fund, and then work with others in other subcommittees to accomplish that.

So this is why the appropriators are essentially the investment brokers, or the bankers, for the federal budget. We are looking, particularly under the Clinton Administration, to make those public investments to achieve national dividends. We look at immediate, compelling, human needs of our society, but also the long-range needs of the United States of America.

* * *

In 1994, we are at a defining moment in American history. We have seen the collapse of Communism. We have seen the end of the Cold War. Yet we believe there is another war, and that is the war for America's economic future. With this president and vice president, we want to make sure that we aggressively claim the markets in the new world order, yet lay the groundwork that we will always, now and into the next century, continue to be an economic superpower. Our political, dynamic, democratic energy and our

ability to be a military superpower stems from our economics.

This new world order has profound repercussions for federal science policy. For the last half century—whether in high-energy physics or high-performance computing—federal science has grown, and largely been driven, by one overarching strategic objective, and that is America's national security. The largest funding for scientific research was strategically driven. It was driven by the Department of Defense. It was to make sure that we could win the Cold War and stop a nuclear holocaust from eclipsing this magical and wonderful planet Earth. Now, with the Berlin Wall coming down, so is the wall in research and development funds and science and scientific funding. We want that wall to come down. Just as we developed the smart weapons to win the Cold War, we want to be able to have the smart science and the smart technology to win the new wars in the economic arena.

This change, we know, has created a new crisis in the scientific community. It means that old assumptions about how to organize itself and how to spend increasingly limited dollars are really challenging scientists and engineers as they think about a new century of democracy. But it also means that the old funding that was relied upon, Department of Defense funding, has shrunk. Those who then say, "Why are we going into strategic research?" should remember that the basis of their funding in many of those agencies was defense-based or defense-linked. Unless we develop a new strategy that fits in with the realities of the new world order, I am concerned that science and science funding run the risk of being left out and left behind. And so will the United States of America.

* * *

There is a new mood in the Congress. There is an obsession with balancing the budget. There are those people in the U.S. Senate and in the House of Representatives who are what I call "cut-cruisers," the "budget hawks." They're out looking for pork, whether it's in honeybee research, a Lawrence Welk museum, or a Superconducting Super Collider. I do not put these items in the same category, but many of my colleagues do. Look what happened to the Super Collider. I voted to keep the Super Collider, and have consistently done that because of its importance in basic physics research. But my colleagues saw another situation. They saw that by one vote on their part, they could cut $8 billion from the budget and not keep one homeless person out of a shelter, not keep one veteran from having his disability benefits, and not keep one school child from having a school lunch program. The Super Collider represented what has happened in science. A wonderful scientific idea, funded with the best intentions, but gone awry. At every turn, there was another cost overrun, a technical complication, or the hubris of the people who ran it who refused to see the situation facing them. No one could adequately articulate how it fit into our national strategy.

Without a national strategy in science, and the will to see that this strategy gets implemented, federal science funding is sure to become a continuing target of opportunity for the narrow-minded cut-cruisers in Congress. Now how do we deal with this?

* * *

I believe we need to articulate a vision for where science is and where it is going throughout the federal government. People knew how important it was to win the Cold War. We now have to show how important it is to win the economic war. And that is why last year in my subcommittee I tried to elevate this debate by calling for a comprehensive reevaluation of how NSF does business. I was following on Walter Massey's report of the Commission for the Future of the NSF.

I believe there is a new paradigm emerging on how science is conducted and how it is organized. It is based upon the principle that science should lead to the new ideas that lead to the new technologies, which should lead to the new jobs, particularly in manufacturing. I believe that manufacturing is truly the engine of our economy and our industrial strength. Our efforts to generate manufacturing jobs must have a sense of urgency because as a nation the United States is losing ground, time, and opportunities. To regain this ground we have lost over the last two decades, we've got to seek new models of collaboration between the universities and the private sector. We must focus our science investments more strategically around national goals that are important to economic growth. We must train our scientists and engineers, whether they are undergraduates or Ph.D. candidates, so that they are ready to work in strategic areas in the private sector. And we must prepare our best and our brightest for the challenge of the uncertainties brought on by a new global market.

I like to go out and about and listen to what people are saying. First of all, I listen to students. I talk to kids majoring in physics, engineering, molecular biology, and a variety of other things. They do not know who's going to hire them. They know that they've been told: "Get out there and get these advanced degrees because it is the way of the future," and yet they are scared to death. They think there is a myth out there. They hear about how we continually need more of —and we could list every area of scientific exploration—and yet they wonder where are they going to work. The universities are concerned about their funding, but very often professors are more interested in producing other Ph.D.'s who are going to work in universities, rather than in a variety of opportunities in our society.

* * *

Looking at that situation and to promote the right change in the scientific community, I set a goal to follow on what President Clinton wanted in his budget, which was to ask that 60% of what NSF funds go for strategic research. And everybody's kind of vibrating over that. "What does she really mean?" and "Why did she say that?" I've gotten everything from accolades to rather tart, somewhat hysterical, criticism. By strategic research, I do not mean only applied research. I do not mean project-based research, like the tremendously interesting clean car initiative that the President has embarked upon. I mean investments in science that are focused around important national goals. Some of these have been identified in the Federal Coordinating Council for Science, Engineering, and Technology process: climate change, advanced manufacturing, biotechnology, and high-performance computing.

Strategic research does not mean that every NSF grant must result in six patents or four commercial licensing agreements.

Nor does it mean that every proposal must guarantee a private sector payoff in a number of years. That's not what I'm talking about at all. I am saying that we should spend more than half of our basic research dollars in areas that we have identified as strategic. And that our investments in science will become a new superhighway of ideas and technology to achieve those national goals.

I believe the best model for what I am talking about for strategic research is in the National Institutes of Health (NIH). NIH is grouped around strategic areas to treat and cure diseases and illness. It is crucial to our national well-being and it touches the day-to-day lives of the American people. NIH is not organized like a university. We do not have the National Institute for Molecular Biology; we have a National Cancer Institute, in which the most stunning research is going on in molecular biology and cellular biology, from the basic stuff of life itself all the way up to applied research. And the private sector then adds its value to that for biomedical products and pharmaceuticals, giving us a cornucopia of opportunities not only for the United States of America, but actually something to export around the world. It saves lives, it generates jobs, and it enhances our standing in the global market. When I'm talking about strategic research, that's what I mean. What are our national goals? And then what elements in the research community are needed to achieve these goals, from basic to more applied research? It is a continuum that I'm talking about to achieve those strategic goals.

I believe that science should continue to be the place where we do break new ground. And do what delights scientists and mesmerizes the world—the surprise of new discovery. When we look now at the reauthorization of the NSF, it is a way to think about how to organize it over time. Should we keep it organized as it is, or should it be organized as a series of institutes—in climate change or high-performance computing, for example? At the same time, we should not so bind ourselves that we cannot be nimble and agile and move where scientific opportunity takes us. So when we look at the NSF, we need to deal with these kinds of issues. The NSF has a great impact on every other scientific agency. The so-called "60% solution" is based on the Clinton Administration's budget request for the NSF in 1994. We didn't pick winners or losers; we just tried to lay out that framework.

* * *

Finally, as we begin to set out on a research agenda that has a strategic focus, we must build in rigorous milestones and evaluation of our efforts. In areas like manufacturing or high-performance computing, we need to ask ourselves: (i) what goals we seek to achieve; (ii) what are the specific benchmarks by which we can measure our progress in achieving these goals, and (iii) how do the federal investments we make parallel the priorities we have set in these areas. Federally funded scientists and engineers must be accountable to the public, to the Congress, and to the President. These measurable benchmarks will allow researchers to evaluate their own progress in concrete terms and to spot problem areas that need to be addressed. Concrete arguments will be much more effective than many of the vague, philosophical justifications for this funding that we have been hearing from the scientific community.

In terms of the future, we have to look at our funding as a public investment. Maybe not in an immediate practical application, because it does not work that way. If we try to make it work that way we will shortchange ourselves because the whole issue of discovery is you do not know where it will take you. But you do need a national goal.

* * *

There is something that has developed in our scientific community over the years, which is a sense of entitlement: that it is the job of the United States of America to fund every Ph.D. to pursue any area of intellectual curiosity. I believe that the very nature of a scientist is to be curious, and to be endlessly curious. That's the nature of why people go into science. And we want to continue to do that. But the United States of America needs to say to its scientific community, let's think of ourselves as one country and one community. Scientists are part of that. While you pursue individual excellence, join with us as one country in pursuing goals to be accomplished. It will not lead to you being intellectually stifled, but it will lead to us all moving together toward the same future. The science community needs to know that the taxpayers are asking where is their money going? And if the money is wisely spent, dealing with cost overruns and clearly setting objectives, they will back it. And I will be there to back it. And we will be able to do it.

POSTSCRIPT

Should Government Provide Funding for Basic Research?

Mikulski is by no means alone in calling for more emphasis on the applied side of science and technology. Congress as a whole killed the decade's biggest single basic research project, the superconducting supercollider that was already being built in Waxahachie, Texas, because the costs had risen well above the $10 billion mark and there were no concrete benefits to society in sight. Congress has also cut back the plans for the space station *Freedom* several times for very similar reasons. It also refused to cover the much smaller cost (about $10 million) of what has been called the most significant research project in human history: the search for extraterrestrial intelligence.

The emphasis on practicality extends even higher in the U.S. government. Early in 1993, the Clinton administration announced a research-and-development policy that focuses much more on developing high-tech projects such as the information superhighway—a state-of-the-art telecommunications network—than on basic research. Here, too, the thrust is toward commercial success, international competitiveness, more jobs, and increased prosperity. See Eliot Marshall's "R&D Policy That Emphasizes the 'D,' " *Science* (March 26, 1993). (The journal *Science* regularly carries news reports on science policy.)

A similar message has come from the Carnegie Commission on Science, Technology, and Government, which in September 1992 issued a report entitled *Enabling the Future: Linking Science and Technology to Societal Needs*. This report called for the development of a National Forum on Science and Technology Goals to help define, debate, focus, and articulate science and technology goals and to monitor the development and implementation of policies to achieve them. For a good discussion of this topic, see Gary Chapman, "The National Forum on Science and Technology Goals," *Communications of the ACM* (January 1994). Chapman, "a coordinator of the 21st Century Project, a national campaign to reorient U.S. science and technology policy in the post–Cold War era," strongly favors "new ... models that incorporate public participation, diversity, equity, and attention to national needs."

Choppin is not alone on his side of the issue either. When Howard E. Simmons, a senior science advisor for the DuPont chemical company and a member of the National Academy of Sciences, recently received the American Chemical Society's Priestley Medal, he spoke strongly in favor of basic research, emphasizing its value to long-term progress (see *Chemical & Engineering News*, March 14, 1994, pp. 27–31). Simmons also stressed that more attention must be paid to science education and that, from industry's perspective, basic research at the university level plays a crucial role in producing "bright young scientists, broadly trained, but solid in the fundamentals, whose curiosity about the world has been piqued."

In "Endangered Support of Basic Science," a short essay in the May 1994 issue of *Scientific American*, Victor F. Weisskopf, an emeritus professor of physics at the Massachusetts Institute of Technology, a Manhattan Project leader, and the director general of CERN (the European particle physics lab), writes, "Today we cannot afford the kind of lavish funding that basic science enjoyed during the decades following World War II." However, he goes on to say that society also cannot afford to abandon basic research: "Basic science . . . creates important educational, ethical and political values. It fosters a critical, antidogmatic spirit, a readiness to say, 'I was wrong,' and an idealistic inclination to do work where there is little financial gain. Basic science establishes a bond between humans and nature; it does not recognize industrial, national, racial and ideological barriers. . . . Science cannot flourish unless it is pursued for the sake of pure knowledge and insight."

ISSUE 2

Are Worst-Case Estimates of Risk the Best Method for Making Environmental Decisions?

YES: Robert Costanza and Laura Cornwell, from "The 4P Approach to Dealing With Scientific Uncertainty," *Environment* (November 1992)

NO: Wendy Cleland-Hamnett, from "The Role of Comparative Risk Analysis," *EPA Journal* (January–March 1993)

ISSUE SUMMARY

YES: Robert Costanza, a professor of environmental studies, and policy analyst Laura Cornwell argue that when uncertainty about potential future damage to health or the environment is high, those who are potentially responsible should be required to post a bond adequate to cover the costs associated with the worst possible results.

NO: Wendy Cleland-Hamnett, the acting deputy assistant administrator for policy, planning, and evaluation at the U.S. Environmental Protection Agency, insists that worst-case scenarios are far too unlikely to be used as the basis for policy.

Science and technology have helped provide the people of the modern world with access to a level of health, wealth, and consumer goods unparalleled in all of human history. Unfortunately, improved health has led to overpopulation, and the industrialization that has provided the wealth and consumer goods has resulted in extensive damage to the environment. In order to progress and to attain prosperity, society continually runs the risk of reducing the quality of life for future generations—possibly even destroying them. Some less sweeping risks to human health and the environment include medications that can have serious side effects; power plants that may pollute the air and aggravate respiratory diseases; and the possibility that the continued use of chlorofluorocarbon aerosol propellants and refrigerants will destroy the Earth's protective ozone layer and eventually lead to an epidemic of skin cancer.

Some risks are accepted because they have been around for a long time and people are used to them. New risks are generally found to be more alarming, and in this age of science and technology, society is surrounded by new risks. It is perhaps not too surprising that some people strive to reject such risks, even when they are small or unlikely or when they represent a trade-off against large benefits, simply because they are new. That is, many people do not approach risks realistically. Few people ever worry about the risks associated with population and prosperity. Most commuters rate the risks of driving a car fairly low, despite statistics indicating that far more people die in automobile accidents than (for instance) in airplane crashes. Rare risks, however, such as the chance of having a child with a serious birth defect or of getting cancer from cellular telephones or nuclear power plants, often rouse much greater concerns.

Most people do not seem to evaluate risks according to their odds. Rather, an activity is rated safer if the individual is perceived to be in control (as when driving a car) or if it is chosen voluntarily (as with people who choose to smoke). Activities are considered riskier when the possible damage is severe (such as death). Often, things that are not well understood are considered riskiest of all, no matter what the real dangers may be.

Life carries with it certain unavoidable risks. Some people insist that voluntarily adding any risk at all is intolerable. This is the idea behind the Delaney Clause, which forbids adding to food products any substance shown to cause cancer in any animal at any dose, even if the resulting increase in a consumer's chance of developing cancer is only one in many millions. (For a point/counterpoint discussion on the Delaney Clause, see Al Meyerhoff, "Let's Reform a Failed Food Safety Regime," and Clausen Ely, "An Obscure EPA Policy Is to Blame," *EPA Journal*, January/February/March 1993.)

One area in which people try to avoid all possible risk—or to hold someone accountable for unfortunate events—is vaccines. At one time, whooping cough, measles, diphtheria, and other childhood diseases killed many thousands of children every year in the United States alone. Vaccines have vastly reduced that toll. The first measles vaccine, for instance, hit the U.S. market in 1963 and within five years reduced the number of cases by 95 percent. Unfortunately, vaccines occasionally have had rare—sometimes fatal— side effects. The resulting lawsuits have led to multimillion-dollar damage awards, and concerns about liability have led many pharmaceutical companies to stop making vaccines, despite the existence of the National Vaccine Injury Compensation Program, a government effort to compensate victims without penalizing manufacturers.

Should society ban vaccines because of their risks? Surely not, for the risks they bear with them are many times less than the risks they avoid. But then, what should society's attitude be toward those risks or toward risk in general? In the following selections, Robert Costanza and Laura Cornwell argue in favor of the "precautionary polluter pays principle," which states that risk producers must pay in advance for the worst possible results from their activities. Wendy Cleland-Hamnett argues that policymakers must be realistic and make decisions based on more likely problems, not on unlikely worst cases.

YES

Robert Costanza and
Laura Cornwell

THE 4P APPROACH TO DEALING WITH SCIENTIFIC UNCERTAINTY

One often sees contradictory stories in the media from "reputable scientific sources" who claim, one day, that "Global warming will occur, and the results will be catastrophic unless something is done immediately," and, on another day, that "There is no direct evidence for global warming, and people should not waste money on something that may or may not happen." On yet another day, one hears that "Toxic chemical X causes cancer," followed on the next day by the statement that "Toxic chemical X occurs in too low a concentration in the environment to cause cancer." These seemingly contradictory statements from the scientific community send the social decisionmaking process into a tailspin. On the one hand, because scientists cannot agree on what is happening, should policymakers wait until better information is available before acting? On the other hand, if society fails to act, the situation may deteriorate rapidly and irreversibly. What are people to do in these all-too-common situations, and why has science failed to provide the certain and unbiased answers on which good policymaking depends? What is wrong with the link between science and policy, and how can it be improved? Is a different, nonregulatory approach needed for managing the environment?

There are several lines of thought in environmental science and economics about how to develop an effective approach to dealing with uncertainty. Two of the most renowned are the "precautionary principle," which has gained wide acceptance in international environmental circles, and the "polluter pays principle," which has long been advocated by environmental economists. Although both of these principles have gained wide acceptance in theory, practical applications have been severely hampered. One criticism is that, "though the precautionary principle provides a useful overall orientation, it is an insufficient basis for policy and largely lacks legal content." Large uncertainties about ecological damages also have caused applications of the polluter pays principle to founder on questions of "how much" and "when." However, an environmental deposit-refund or assurance bonding system could shift the burden of proof, incorporate uncertainty into what the

From Robert Costanza and Laura Cornwell, "The 4P Approach to Dealing With Scientific Uncertainty," *Environment*, vol. 34, no. 9 (November 1992), pp. 12–20. Copyright © 1992 by The Helen Dwight Reid Educational Foundation. Reprinted by permission of Heldref Publications, 1319 18th St., NW, Washington, DC 20036-1802. Notes omitted.

polluters pay for and when they pay it, and thus provide strong and effective economic incentives for both environmental precaution and technological innovation.

SCIENTIFIC UNCERTAINTY

One of the main reasons for the problems with current methods of environmental management is scientific uncertainty—not just its existence, but the radically different expectations and modes of operation that scientists and policymakers have developed to deal with it. To solve this problem, these differences must be exposed and understood, and better methods to incorporate uncertainty into policymaking and environmental management must be designed.

To understand the scope of the problem, it is necessary to differentiate between risk, which is an event with a known probability (sometimes referred to as statistical uncertainty), and true uncertainty, which is an event with an unknown probability (sometimes referred to as indeterminacy). For instance, every time you drive your car, you run the risk of having an accident because the probability of car accidents is known with very high certainty. The risk involved in driving is well known because there have been many car accidents with which to calculate the probabilities. These probabilities are known with enough certainty that they are used by insurance companies, for instance, to set rates that will assure those companies of a certain profit. There is little uncertainty about the possibility of car accidents. If you live near the disposal site of some newly synthesized toxic chemical, however, your health may be in jeopardy, but no one knows to what extent. Because no one knows the proba-bility of your getting cancer, for instance, or some other disease from this exposure, there is true uncertainty. Most important environmental problems suffer from true uncertainty, not merely risk.

Uncertainty may be thought of as a continuum ranging from zero for certain information to intermediate levels for information with statistical uncertainty and known probabilities (risk) to high levels for information with true uncertainty or indeterminacy. Risk assessment has become a central guiding principle at the U.S. Environmental Protection Agency (EPA) and other environmental management agencies, but true uncertainty has yet to be adequately incorporated into environmental protection strategies.

Scientists treat uncertainty as a given, a characteristic of all information that must be honestly acknowledged and communicated. Over the years, scientists have developed increasingly sophisticated methods to measure and communicate uncertainty arising from various causes. In general, however, scientists have uncovered more uncertainty rather than the absolute precision that the lay public often mistakenly associates with scientific results. Scientific inquiry can only set boundaries on the limits of knowledge. It can define the edges of the envelope of known possibilities, but often the envelope is very large, and the probabilities of what's inside (the known possibilities) actually occurring can be a complete mystery. For instance, scientists can describe the range of uncertainty about global warming and toxic chemicals and maybe say something about the relative probabilities of different outcomes, but, in most important cases, they cannot say which of the possible outcomes will occur with any degree of accuracy.

Current approaches to environmental management and policymaking, however, avoid uncertainty and gravitate to the edges of the scientific envelope. The reasons for this bias are clear. Policymakers want to make unambiguous, defensible decisions, which are often codified into laws and regulations. Although legislative language is often open to interpretation, regulations are much easier to write and enforce if they are stated in absolutely certain terms. For most of criminal law, the system works reasonably well. Either Cain killed his brother or he did not; the only question is whether there is enough evidence to demonstrate guilt beyond a reasonable doubt (with essentially zero uncertainty). Because the burden of proof is on the prosecution, it does little good to conclude that there was an 80-percent chance that Cain killed his brother. But many scientific studies come to just these kinds of conclusions. Science defines the envelope while the policy process gravitates to an edge—usually the edge that best advances the policymaker's political agenda. But to use science rationally to make policy, the whole envelope and all of its contents must be dealt with.

The problem is most severe for environmental regulation. Building on the legal traditions of criminal law, policymakers and environmental regulators desire certain information when designing environmental regulations. But much of environmental policy is based on scientific studies of the likely health, safety, and ecological consequences of human actions. Information gained from these studies is therefore only certain within the studies' epistemological and methodological limits. Regulators are increasingly confronted with decisionmaking outside the limits of scientific certainty, particularly with the recent shift in environmental concerns from visible, known pollution to more subtle threats, such as radon.

Problems arise when regulators ask scientists for answers to unanswerable questions. For example, the law may mandate that the regulatory agency devise safety standards for all known toxins when little or no information is available on the impacts of these chemicals. When trying to enforce the regulations after they are drafted, governments confront the problem of true uncertainty about the impacts. It is usually impossible to determine with any certainty if the local chemical company contributed to the death of some of the people in the vicinity of its toxic waste dump. Similarly, one cannot prove the connection between smoking and lung cancer in any direct, causal way, at least in the legal sense, but only as a statistical relationship. And of course, global warming may or may not happen after all.

Most environmental regulations, particularly those in the United States, demand certainty. When scientists are pressured to supply this nonexistent commodity, there is not only frustration and poor communication but also mixed messages in the media. Because of uncertainty, environmental issues are often manipulated by political and economic interest groups. Uncertainty about global warming is perhaps the most visible current example of this phenomenon.

The precautionary principle describes one theory of how the environmental regulatory community should deal with the problem of true uncertainty. The principle states that, rather than await certainty, regulators should act in anticipation of any potential environmental harm to prevent it. The precautionary principle is so frequently invoked in international environmental resolutions that it has come to be seen by some as a basic normative principle of international environmental law. But the principle offers no guidance as to what precautionary measures should be taken. It "implies the commitment of resources now to safeguard against the potentially adverse future outcomes of some decision" but does not say how many resources should be committed or which adverse future outcomes are most important.

Yet the size of the stakes is a primary determinant of how uncertainty is dealt with in the political arena. Normal applied science applies only under circumstances of low uncertainty and low stakes. Higher uncertainty or higher stakes result in a much more politicized decisionmaking environment. Moderate uncertainty or stakes correspond to "applied engineering" and "professional consultancy," which allow a good measure of judgment and opinion to deal with risk. Currently, however, there is no way to deal with either high stakes or high uncertainty, which require a new approach that could be called "post-normal" or "second-order" science. This "new" science is really just the application of the essence of the scientific method to new territory. The scientific method does not, in its basic form, imply anything about the precision of the results achieved. It does, however, imply a forum of free inquiry, without preconceived answers or agendas, aimed at determining the envelope of knowledge and the magnitude of ignorance.

Implementing second-order science requires a new approach to environmental protection, one that acknowledges the existence of true uncertainty rather than denying it and includes mechanisms to safeguard against potentially harmful effects but, at the same time, encourages the development of low-impact technologies and the reduction of uncertainty about impacts. The precautionary principle sets the stage for this approach, but the real challenge is to develop scientific methods to determine the potential costs of uncertainty and to adjust incentives so that the appropriate parties pay this cost of uncertainty and have appropriate incentives to reduce its detrimental effects. Without this adjustment, the full costs of environmental damage will continue to be left out of the accounting, and the hidden subsidies from society to those who profit from environmental degradation will continue to provide strong incentives to degrade the environment beyond sustainable levels.

DEALING WITH UNCERTAINTY

How should scientists and policymakers deal with the enormous uncertainty inherent in environmental issues? First, uncertainty should be accepted as a basic component of environmental decisionmaking at all levels and be better communicated. But environmental management should also change, and understanding of the link between ecological and economic systems must grow. Thus, economic and other incentives could be used more efficiently and effectively to achieve environmental goals.

The effort to integrate ecology and economics to improve environmental and economic management and to ensure long-term sustainability has become focused in the transdisciplinary field of ecological economics. This new field promises to permit a deeper understanding of the ecological functions and values that the precautionary principle is intended to protect and the development of more efficient and effective mechanisms to implement the principle. One goal of ecological economics is to estimate the long-term social and ecological costs and benefits of various human activities for comparison with the private short-term costs and benefits that are too often the only consideration in decisionmaking. To do this, the field must develop methods for the valuation of ecological damage based on a second-order scientific understanding of the functioning of linked ecological economic systems at several temporal and spatial scales. This understanding involves developing a description of the envelope of knowledge and the boundaries of ignorance about these interactions. For the purposes of pricing ecological functions and values for use with the precautionary principle, the edge of this envelope that describes the worst-case scenario, as far as ecological impacts are concerned, is the one of primary interest. Research focused on the "worst edge" should lead to much more effective use of science in anticipating and heading off problems.

For example, were worst-edge research the norm, scientists could easily have anticipated the greenhouse effect and taken steps to minimize its potential impacts. Indeed, the effect and humanity's potential impact on it were first described almost 100 years ago, but it remained a scientific curiosity until the 1980s, when enough data and models had been assembled to demonstrate that the effect was, in fact, likely to cause global warming. There is still much uncertainty about the magnitude of the warming and especially about its ultimate impacts, but science can do a very good job of anticipating potential problems if it focuses on that function rather than on demonstrating impacts that have already occurred. Current research should therefore focus on the worst edge of climatic and economic impacts that might result from releases of greenhouse gases, as well as on the range of uncertainty about these impacts and on ways to reduce the uncertainty.

Over the past two decades, there has been extensive discussion about the efficiency that theoretically can be achieved in environmental management through the use of market mechanisms. These mechanisms are designed to alter the pricing structure of the present market system to incorporate the long-term social and ecological costs of an economic agent's activities. Suggested incentive-based mechanisms include pollution taxes, tradable pollution-discharge permits, financial responsibility requirements, and deposit-refund systems.... Some new versions of these incentive-based alternatives should help policymakers deal in a precautionary way with the pervasive uncertainty inherent in environmental problems.

An innovative incentive-based instrument currently being researched to manage the environment for precaution under uncertainty is called a flexible environmental assurance bonding system. This variation of the deposit-refund system is designed to incorporate both known and uncertain environmental costs into the incentive system and to induce positive environmental technological innovation. It works by charging an economic agent directly for known environmental damages and levying an assurance bond equal to the current best estimate of the largest potential future environmental damages. The bond would be kept in an interest-bearing escrow account for a predetermined length of time.

In keeping with the precautionary principle, this system requires a commitment of resources up front to offset the potentially catastrophic future effects of current activity. Portions of the bond (plus interest) would be returned if and when the agent could demonstrate that the suspected worst-case damages had not occurred or would be less than was originally assessed. If damages did occur, portions of the bond would be used to rehabilitate or repair the environment and possibly to compensate injured parties. Funds tied up in bonds could still be used for other economic activities. The only cost would be the difference (plus or minus) between the interest on the bond and the return that could be earned by the business had it invested in other activities. On average, this difference would be minimal. In addition, the "forced savings" that the bond would require could actually improve overall economic performance in economies like that of the United States that chronically undersave.

By requiring the users of environmental resources to post a bond adequate to cover uncertain future environmental damages (with the possibility for refunds), the burden of proof and the cost of the uncertainty are shifted from the public to the resource user. At the same time, agents are not charged in any final way for uncertain future damages and can recover portions of their bond (with interest) in proportion to how much better their environmental performance is than the predicted worst-case scenario.

Deposit-refund systems are not a new concept; they have been successfully applied to a range of consumer, conservation, and environmental policy objectives. The most well-known examples are the systems for beverage containers and used lubricating oils that have proven to be quite effective and efficient.

Another precedent for environmental assurance bonds are the producer-paid performance bonds often required for federal, state, or local government construction work. For example, the Miller Act (40 U.S.C. 270), a 1935 federal statute, requires contractors performing construction work for the federal government to secure performance bonds. Performance bonds provide a contractual guarantee that the principal (the entity that is doing the work or providing the service) will perform in a designated way. Bonds are frequently required for construction work done in the private sector as well.

Performance bonds are frequently posted in the form of corporate surety bonds. Surety companies, which cosign these bonds, are licensed under various insurance laws and, under their charter, have legal authority to act as a financial guarantee for those posting the bond. The unrecoverable cost of this service is usually from one to five percent of the bond amount. However, under the Miller Act, any contract above a designated amount ($25,000 in the case of construction) can be backed by other types of securities, such as U.S. bonds or notes, in lieu of a bond guaranteed by a surety company. In this case, the contractor provides a duly executed power of attorney and an agreement authorizing collection on the bond or notes if the contractor defaults on the contract. If the contractor performs all of the obligations specified in the contract, the securities are returned to the contractor, and the usual cost of the surety is avoided.

Environmental assurance bonds would work in a similar manner, by providing a contractual guarantee that the principal would perform in an environmentally benign manner, but would be levied according to the best estimate of the largest potential future environmental damages. ...

The bond would be held until some or all of the uncertainty was removed. This would provide a strong incentive for principals to reduce the uncertainty about their environmental impacts as quickly as possible, either by funding independent research or by changing their processes to ones that are less damaging. The establishment of a quasi-judicial body would be necessary to resolve disputes about when and how much of the bonds should be refunded. This body would use the latest independent scientific information on the worst-case ecological damages that could result from a business's activities, but the burden of proof would fall on the economic agent that stands to gain from the activity, not on the public. EPA already has a protocol for worst-case analysis. In 1977, the U.S. Council on Environmental Quality required worst-case analysis for implementing the National Environmental Policy Act of 1969. This requirement forced EPA to consider the worst environmental consequences of an action when scientific uncertainty was involved.

One potential argument against the bond is that it would favor relatively large businesses that could afford to handle the financial responsibility of activities that are potentially hazardous to the environment. This is true, but it is exactly the desired effect, because businesses that cannot handle the financial responsibility should not be passing the cost of potential environmental damage on to the public. In the construction industry, the use of performance bonds would prevent small fly-by-night businesses from cutting corners and endangering the public to underbid responsible businesses.

This is not to say that small businesses would be eliminated; far from it. They could either band together to form associations to handle the financial responsibility for environmentally risky activities, or, preferably, they could change to more environmentally benign activities that did not require large assurance bonds. This encouragement of the development of new, environmentally benign technologies is one of the main attractions of the bonding system, and small, start-up businesses would certainly lead the way.

APPLYING THE "4P" APPROACH

Strong economic incentives would be provided by the proposed environmental assurance bond to reduce pollution, to research the true costs of environmentally damaging activities, and to develop innovative, cost-effective pollution control technologies. The bonding system extends the polluter pays principle to make the polluter pay for uncertainty as well. Thus is born the "precautionary polluter pays principle" (4P), which would allow a much more proactive approach to environmental problems because the bond would be paid up front, before the damage is done. By unleashing the creative resources of businesses, 4P would foster pollution prevention and the development of new, cleaner technologies (rather than merely cleanup). Because these technologies would be economically attractive in the short run, competition in the marketplace would lead to environmental improvement rather than degradation. The 4P approach would deal more appropriately with scientific uncertainty than do the current command-and-control systems.

The 4P approach has several potential applications. Three of them—growth management, toxic chemicals, and global warming—are high-stakes, high-uncertainty problems for which effective management mechanisms do not currently exist.

Traditional approaches to growth management have centered on zoning and other forms of land-use restrictions. Although the results of planning and zoning are better than totally uncontrolled growth, the approach leaves much to be desired, and one can certainly argue that most planning and zoning have not improved environmental conditions. 4P suggests a flexible impact bond system in addition to regional planning. A developer would post an initial impact bond that is large enough to cover the worst-case environmental and economic impacts of the proposed development. The developer would be refunded portions of the bond to the extent that the possible impacts did not occur. Innovative developers who designed projects with lower environmental impacts would be directly rewarded by refunds of their impact bonds. Developers who defaulted on their bonds would do poorly in economic competition with their more innovative competitors, and their bonds would be used to pay for whatever impacts they caused. Impact fees have been tried before, but, in most cases, they have been flat, inflexible, one-time fees that offered no incentive to developers to produce anything but the standard fare. They also generally covered only a small fraction of the real impacts of the development. A flexible impact bonding system would solve these problems and help manage growth in a rational yet flexible way, without taking the right to develop away but merely imposing the true costs of that growth on the parties that stand to gain from it while providing strong economic incentives for them to reduce their impacts to a minimum.

Another particularly difficult environmental management problem is the control of toxic chemicals from both point sources, such as factories, and nonpoint sources, such as agricultural and urban areas. Toxic chemicals can be damaging to ecosystems and human health in extremely low concentrations, and there is enormous uncertainty about their cumulative and individual impacts. The standard management approach is to develop lists of toxic chemicals and standards for their allowable concentrations in the environment. But because the list is so long (there are thousands of such chemicals in common use) and there is so much uncertainty about setting safe standards—as well as about who is producing and releasing what quantities of which chemicals and how the chemicals interact once they come in contact in the environment—this approach has not been very effective.

4P suggests a flexible toxic chemical bonding system. The bond would be sized according to the best current estimates of the worst-case damages from the release of the chemicals. Refunds would be based on the extent to which each potential polluter performed better than the worst case. This system would give polluters strong incentives to reduce their releases through recycling and more efficient use. Farmers could no longer afford to overuse agricultural chemicals just to be sure they were killing all pests. Industries could no longer afford to release new chemicals with poorly known impacts into the environment. Individual home owners would pay a high price for using potentially dangerous chemicals on their lawns and would be forced to find more environmentally benign alternatives, which, under the bonding system, would be relatively cheaper. This system would be designed to complement other regulatory schemes; would be self-policing and self-funding; and would provide strong incentives to correct environmental problems for which there are few good management alternatives.

Finally, the problem of global warming is probably the most severe current example of a high-stakes, high-uncertainty problem. A tax on carbon dioxide emissions has been proposed as an economic incentive to lessen this problem, but current ideas about the tax do not account for uncertainty. The 4P approach suggests that a bond for carbon dioxide emissions, with the size of the bond based on worst-case estimates of the magnitude of future damages, would work better than a tax, whose size would be based on much more uncertain estimates of what levels of emissions will not produce long-term problems. In this way, the efficiency advantages of economic incentives can be reaped without unduly penalizing current economic agents for the costs of unknown future damages.

There are several other potential applications of 4P. Any situation with large true uncertainty is a likely candidate, and these situations abound in today's world. To deal with these situations, scientific understanding must grow, and approaches to environmental management must change accordingly. Scientists can only define the envelope of ignorance. Given that envelope, policymakers should plan for the worst while providing incentives for firms to produce the best.

NO

Wendy Cleland-Hamnett

THE ROLE OF COMPARATIVE RISK ANALYSIS

EPA's support for using comparative risk analysis to help set the Agency's priorities has been no secret. Building on the lessons and insights gained in the 1988 *Unfinished Business* report, the Science Advisory Board's [SAB's] 1990 *Reducing Risk* report, and our experience in implementing strategic initiatives, we have seen how valuable it can be to have a grasp of the relative risk of various problems in narrowing our focus to the most important ones— especially as fiscal reality has dictated that we must.

Of course, other forces play critically important roles in directing policy, including statutory mandates, traditional considerations of costs and benefits, the state of technology, environmental equity, and, above all, public values and concerns. But comparative risk analysis, and its promise of objective, relevant, and even-handed guidance, has definitely "made it to the table" at EPA. The challenge for the Agency and its stakeholders will be in deciding the precise role it will play in delineating our priorities.

The particular ways we have tried to use relative risk and the conditions under which we operate are not universally understood. Some think risk ranking affects our entire budget, and some think it derives from a backroom dialogue with cloistered scientific gurus. Perhaps most often it is viewed as the only factor we intend to include in our decision making. It is important to note that we have never understood priority setting to be one dimensional, where comparative risk analysis is the last word. In *Reducing Risk*, the SAB made it clear that establishing the relative risks of different environmental problems was only "one tool" that could help make integrated and targeted national environmental policy a reality. It also stressed that the "dichotomy" that exists between the perceptions of the public and the "experts" on which risks are important "presents an enormous challenge to a pluralistic, democratic country."

As good as our intentions have been over the last few years, there is ample room for EPA to do a better job in meeting the challenge of piloting the

From Wendy Cleland-Hamnett, "The Role of Comparative Risk Analysis," *EPA Journal* (January– March 1993).

doctrine of risk through a democratic society. A quotation from Thomas Jefferson provides valuable insight:

I know of no safe depository of the ultimate powers of the society but the people themselves; and if we think them not enlightened enough to exercise their control with a wholesome discretion, the remedy is not to take it from them, but to inform their discretion.

This piece of wisdom implies, among other things, that a democratic government operates at its peril if it becomes so arrogant that it makes important decisions without informing, involving, and taking guidance from average citizens, and it should never underestimate the citizens' ability to understand. Jefferson is warning us not to lose touch. He is not recommending that all technical decisions of a government agency be made only through town meetings. But his statement is a persuasive argument for broader inclusion of the public in the basic decisions that determine the direction of all the policy minutiae that follows.

It is becoming clearer to those involved in this debate that risk-based decision making should be based on a synthesis of inputs broader and deeper than was envisioned in the past. Risk-based priority setting will be a major element of the kind of informed and effective dialogue that raises the quality of environmental action across the board, especially in the state and federal legislatures. To achieve this, though, we need a more participatory model of prioritization—a risk system much broader than the stereotypical one in which "experts" make their pronouncements about risks with clinical dispassion; one which is an organic part of a broad-based, decision-making process in which equity, social concerns, fis-

cal feasibility, technological innovation, and legislative mandates are fully considered alongside the science.

To ensure a proper place for comparative risk in developing environmental priorities, we must build the strongest possible foundation of individual risk assessments. I see three basic guiding principles in the building of that foundation. The first involves an early step in the risk assessment process, the characterization of risk. A memorandum on the subject issued in February 1992 provided that EPA needs to offer more useful information when characterizing a given risk—we need to give more accurate predictions than a single point estimate would allow, and we need to evaluate more realistic exposure situations than the unlikely worst-case scenarios sometimes used as the basis for policy. We must characterize individual risks using straightforward, consistent terminology identifying uncertainties and data gaps so that both experts and citizens can more easily compare one risk to another.

This challenge remains enormously important as more attention is focused on the need to take into account both hard science factors and societal elements in the comparison of risks. The question "What is really at stake here?" will need to be answered realistically and usefully, again and again, in terms that all can understand.

The second guiding principle is the need to bring varied expertise into the risk assessment process from the earliest stage. Our work in relative risk stands much less chance of acceptance if the common perception persists that assessments of specific risks emerge from a black box. Therefore, just as the whole enterprise of priority setting needs to be broadly inclusive, the work

TWO FACES OF RISK

The terms *risk assessment* and *comparative risk analysis* are sometimes confused. Actually, they have very different meanings.

Risk assessment, which in rudimentary form, at least, is older than EPA itself, is a complex process by which scientists determine the harm that an individual substance can inflict on human health or the environment. For human health risk assessment, the process takes place in a series of steps that begins by identifying the particular hazard(s) of the substance. Subsequent steps examine "dose-response" patterns and human exposure considerations,and the conclusion is a "risk characterization" that is both quantitative and qualitative. The risk characterization then becomes one of the factors considered in deciding whether and how the substance will be regulated.

Risk assessments are not infallible. For one thing, information on the effects of small amounts of a substance in the environment is often not available, and data from animal experiments must be extrapolated to humans. Such extrapolations cannot be made with absolute certainty.... [C]onsiderable research is being focused on improving the risk assessment process.

Unlike risk assessment, which for years has provided regulators the basis for deciding whether or not an individual substance needs to be controlled, **comparative risk analysis** and its derivative relative risk have arrived on the scene only recently. Very simply described, comparative risk analysis is a procedure for ranking environmental problems by their seriousness (relative risk) for the purpose of assigning them program priorities. Typically, teams of experts put together a list of problems then sort the problems by types of risk—cancer, noncancer health, materials damage, ecological effects, and so on. The experts rank the problems within each type by measuring them against such standards as the severity of effects, the likelihood of the problem occurring among those exposed, the number of people exposed, and the like. The relative risk of a problem is then used as a factor in determining what priority the problem should receive. Other factors include statutory mandates, public concern over the problem, and the economic and technological feasibility of controlling it.

Not unexpectedly, comparative risk analysis has its critics. As one skeptic asked in the pages of *EPA Journal* two years ago: "How does one compare a case of lung cancer in a retired petrochemical worker to the loss of cognitive function experienced by an urban child with lead poisoning? How do we make choices between habitat and health?" Nonetheless, in its September

Box continued on next page.

1990 report *Reducing Risk,* EPA's Science Advisory Board urged the Agency to order its priorities on the basis of reducing the most serious risks. The board argued, in part: "... There are heavy costs involved if society fails to set environmental priorities based on risk. If finite resources are expended on lower priority problems at the expense of higher priority risks, then society will face needlessly high risks. If priorities are established based on the greatest opportunities to reduce risk, total risk will be reduced in a more efficient way, lessening threats to both public health and local and global ecosystems...."

—Eds [of *EPA Journal*]

of our Agency professionals in working through the important issues of specific risks needs to be exposed to the critical eye of independent experts, peers, and colleagues in their fields. This both enhances the quality of the work and maximizes the number of people who understand what the work attempts to accomplish.

The Agency's existing peer review process should be expanded as far as possible into the earliest segments of the life cycle of our risk-related work, and active peer involvement in the characterization and assessment of individual risks should become standard procedure. We are implementing the recommendations made by the SAB and an independent panel in the March 1992 report *Credible Science, Credible Decisions* by establishing science advisors for the Administrator and Assistant Administrators, and I hope future administrations build on this collegial network.

We have also participated extensively in interagency organizations such as the Risk Assessment Working Group of the Federal Coordinating Council on Science Engineering and Technology (FCCSET), mindful that cross-pollinating expertise and real coordination on cross-cutting issues with other parts of the government can improve the quality of our work. This cooperation must continue and must extend not only to specific risk assessments but also to the important guidelines that are establishing the state of the art in process and methods for cancer, noncancer, and ecological risk end points.

The third guiding principle we must observe in building a foundation of credible risk assessment is the need for basic research and state-of-the-environment data. One of the most fundamental reasons for the controversy surrounding the uses of relative risk is the persistent belief that our risk assessments are based on default assumptions rather than on hard facts. Simply put, facts and hard conclusions from data are better than estimates based on extrapolations and interpolations. Facts are what our research operations must give our risk assessors if their work is to have dependable credibility at the priority-setting table. These facts can then be brought to life through advanced computer visualizations in geographic information systems, which will allow us to target risks and develop more meaningful geographic strategies.

Even if these principles are followed and our risk assessments become more widely accepted, there will remain major legislative barriers to the widespread use of relative risk, which makes it imperative that Congress be an integral part of the dialogue. As it stands now, EPA policy makers implementing risk-based priority setting can have an impact only at the margins of funding. The two funds set up for construction of wastewater treatment plants and the cleanup of abandoned hazardous waste sites under Superfund dwarf all other EPA spending areas, accounting in fiscal year (FY) 1990 for over 70 percent of the Agency's $6 billion budget. Only 16 percent of the full budget is allocated toward the higher risk areas identified by the SAB in *Reducing Risk.* In FY 1992, for example, indoor radon, indoor air, stratospheric ozone, and climate change accounted for a little more than 2 percent of our total budget, although they were listed by the SAB as high risk.

Adding to the pressure is spending for congressional projects: In FY 1993, Congress added about 100 specific items while approving an essentially flat budget from FY 1992. These new responsibilities have to be met at the expense of both existing Agency priorities and new initiatives. To be sure, there is not always a direct correlation between funding levels and results—[some] EPA programs... prove that rich results can be achieved through small budgetary investments. These budgetary facts do indicate, however, that comparative risk has a long way to go before it becomes a dominant element of priority setting at EPA.

Nevertheless, there are a number of things going on within EPA to prepare the way for a more inclusive and more credible role for comparative risk in pri-ority setting. The current dioxin reassessment..., sparked by net findings on the mechanisms of dioxin toxicity, has been widely praised as evidence that the Agency will practice what it preaches concerning dedication to good science and meaningful risk assessment, and has involved both extensive peer review and public participation. Agency professionals used the techniques of inclusion in the development of the forthcoming neurotoxicity and immunotoxicity guidelines, and EPA demonstrated its willingness to reach out to peers outside the Agency by involving a professional association; the Society for Risk Analysis, in issues associated with the cancer risk-assessment guidelines.

Successful development of an inclusive system of risk assessment at EPA in the future will require sustained attention to some very ambitious and large-scale initiatives. The principles in the February 1992 memorandum on risk characterization must be fully implemented. Development of information for EPA's computerized health risk-assessment database—the Integrated Risk Information System, or IRIS—is currently subject to very little peer review or public involvement, and this vulnerability must be addressed if we are to bring the credibility of the information up to par with the influence that this very important database has developed since it became public in 1988.

The Environmental Monitoring and Assessment Program, or EMAP, is a centerpiece of the Agency's enhanced focus on risks to the ecological health of regions and ecosystems. Yet the massive amounts of information gained from the environmental indicators it monitors form so broad a cut of cloth that there is a real challenge to link this information to new, concrete understandings about risk, and then to develop indicators that measure the progress of our prevention programs. And, in the wake of the June 1992 United Nations Conference on Environment and Development in Rio de Janeiro, risk assessment will necessarily be an international issue as well, and the Agency will have a direct stake in the attempt to build upon the work of the U.N.'s Organization for Economic Cooperation and Development in coordinating risk assessment activities by scientists and governments around the globe.

Government cannot do everything, and the question of which things matter the most is inevitable. Environmental decision making in a democracy is not a math problem. As a result, comparative risk will never be the only criterion for setting priorities. But if EPA's findings are built upon a foundation of good science and the public is fully informed and involved in the dialogue, then comparative risk will be an increasingly important factor. By building integrated strategies based upon solid facts, and by harnessing the power of communities and markets, I am absolutely confident EPA can stimulate entire new generations of clean production and give new expression to the concept of "sustainable development."

POSTSCRIPT

Are Worst-Case Estimates of Risk the Best Method for Making Environmental Decisions?

Many people involved in negotiating public acceptance of new technological ventures say that reducing ignorance or uncertainty is more useful than Costanza and Cornwell's "precautionary polluter pays principle." William J. Madia, in "Making the Right Choices," *Vital Speeches of the Day* (May 15, 1993), argues that education—informing the public about the nature of a venture and its genuine associated risks—tends to reduce fears. "The University of California at Berkeley," he says, "has started an exciting new program to teach risk-based decision making... in the public schools. [It] teaches young students to openly discuss risks on a comparative basis and deal with tradeoffs realistically."

Many others agree that education is crucial. The Institute of Electrical and Electronic Engineers (IEEE) even includes in its code of ethics the pledge that IEEE members will "improve the understanding of technology, its appropriate application, and potential consequences" (see Joseph R. Herkert, "Ethical Risk Assessment: Valuing Public Perceptions," *IEEE Technology and Society Magazine*, Spring 1994).

Public information efforts are now an essential part of all risk management programs. (For a discussion on the differences between risk assessment and risk management, see Dorothy E. Patton, "The ABCs of Risk Assessment," *EPA Journal*, January/February/March 1993.) Nevertheless, public perception of risk remains an important aspect of risk-as-issue, and most analysts agree that the public has a right to consent to the risks it confronts. On the other hand, according to Andreas Teuber, in "Justifying Risk," *Daedalus* (Fall 1990), "If we require actual consent to each and every risk of harm that is imposed, much of what we do in the course of our daily lives will have to be ruled out, since it will be impossible to obtain that consent."

Even given adequate efforts to provide information to the public, technological efforts are plagued by the negative public reactions captured in the acronyms NIMBY (Not In My Back Yard), NIMTOF (Not In My Term Of Office), and BANANA (Build Absolutely Nothing Anywhere Near Anything). Yet, M. Granger Morgan, in "Risk Analysis and Management," *Scientific American* (July 1993), argues, "If anyone should be faulted for the poor quality of responses to risk, it is probably not the public but rather risk managers in government and industry."

ISSUE 3

Can Science Police Itself?

YES: Howard K. Schachman, from "What Is Misconduct in Science?" *Science* (July 9, 1993)

NO: Donald E. Buzzelli, from "The Definition of Misconduct in Science: A View from NSF," *Science* (January 29, 1993)

ISSUE SUMMARY

YES: Howard K. Schachman, a research biochemist, argues that the phrase "other serious deviations from accepted research practices" should not be included in the definition of scientific misconduct because it is ambiguous, unfair to scientists, and potentially dangerous to science.

NO: Scientist Donald E. Buzzelli argues that it is essential to include the "other serious deviation" clause in the definition of scientific misconduct to cover cases that do not involve fabrication, falsification, or plagiarism.

Scientists make educated guesses, or hypotheses, as the first step toward figuring out how the universe works. However, most such guesses are wrong. The function of experiments is to replace the wrong guesses with correct ones.

It is normal for scientists to be wrong, at least until the experimental results are in. Yet, the normal procedures of scientific research can progress too slowly for the patience of some researchers, who therefore fake their results. For example, cancer researcher William Summerlin, eager to show his supervisor that the technique he had developed to transplant skin from a black mouse to a white mouse really worked, colored a white mouse with a black felt-tipped marker; he was caught when the ink rubbed off on a lab assistant's fingers. Other researchers, perhaps feeling the pressure to produce the results by which they are judged in the endless competition for research funding and promotion, have also faked data as well as plagiarized other scientists' reports and committed other dishonest acts.

Some people say that those who get caught in their misdeeds represent only the tip of the iceberg. Others say that fraudulent research and plagiarism are rare and that in any case it does not really matter because of the scientific ideal of "check it out," which guarantees that frauds will eventually be found out. Unfortunately, this guarantee is only theoretical. Researchers build reputations, receive promotions, and win research funding only for new investigations, not for repeating others' work, so very few experiments are ever repeated. Lies, once entered into the scientific literature, may remain to mislead future scientists.

Over the past two decades, many misconduct cases have come to light. Some have been very clear breaches of scientific ethics. Some have turned out to involve nothing more than sloppy record keeping or error. Congress has called for measures to detect and prevent scientific misconduct in order to curb the waste of federal research funds. However, many researchers have detected in the rhetoric a demand for guaranteed results. Some fear that if they spend years performing federally funded research that, through no fault of their own, fails to produce solutions to social problems, then the government will accuse them of taking the public's money without offering anything in return; that is, they will be accused of fraud.

Charges of misconduct have touched vital areas, such as AIDS research, and have even involved Nobel laureate researchers. The questions of what scientific misconduct is, how widespread it is, and what should be done about it have been much debated, and several government agencies have been established to receive and investigate complaints of misconduct. A "guilty" verdict may bar the offender from receiving federal grants for several years, but even a "not guilty" verdict can ruin an accused individual's career and—because of legal expenses—his or her bank account. Some of the debate has thus centered on how best to deal with charges of misconduct.

In 1992, the National Academy of Sciences (NAS) Panel on Scientific Responsibility and the Conduct of Research, Committee on Science, Engineering and Public Policy, published *Responsible Science: Ensuring the Integrity of the Research Process* (National Academy Press, 1992). The report said that scientific misconduct is a serious problem that warrants attention but that its definition should be limited to plagiarism and the making up of experimental data and results (fabrication and falsification). Mishandling of grant funds, sexual harassment of students and assistants, and reprisals against whistle-blowers, although serious matters, are not truly *scientific* misconduct and should be handled by the offenders' institutions or by the police. There is no need, said the report, for watchdog agencies such as the National Institutes of Health's (NIH's) Office of Research Integrity and the National Science Foundation's (NSF's) Office of Inspector General to include in their definitions of scientific misconduct a catchall phrase such as "other serious deviations from accepted research practices."

In the selections that follow, researcher Howard K. Schachman supports the NAS's view. He insists that the narrower definition of scientific misconduct is all that is necessary because scientists' offenses either fit that definition or should be handled by agencies other than the Office of Inspector General and its kin. In opposition, Donald E. Buzzelli of the NSF's Office of Inspector General argues in favor of the more open-ended definition of scientific misconduct, saying that it has worked well so far and that the NSF has safeguards against abuse.

YES

Howard K. Schachman

WHAT IS MISCONDUCT IN SCIENCE?

Answering the question posed in the title depends on one's perspective. One could focus on collegial behavior in an academic setting. In that case the discussion would be far-ranging and might include attempts to formulate ethical principles and guidelines for the conduct of research. It would examine complex problems involving the sharing of data and unusual materials, as well as authorship and publication practices. It would certainly include condemnation of egregious actions such as plagiarism and the fabrication and falsification of data and results. From such an examination one could formulate a definition of misconduct in science that would form the basis for governmental action leading potentially to debarment from federal support. Such a sanction, in effect, could lead to the termination of a career in science. For such an outcome a precise, rigorous, and unambiguous definition of misconduct in science is essential. Governmental oversight over the expenditure of taxpayers' money is legally mandated and clearly proper. It is obligatory for the National Science Foundation (NSF) and National Institutes of Health (NIH) to investigate allegations of fraudulent acts and to impose sanctions when guilt is demonstrated. In contrast, it is inappropriate, wasteful, and likely to be destructive to science for government agencies to delve into the styles of scientists and their behavioral patterns.

The definitions of misconduct in science currently used by governmental agencies unfortunately intermix these two different aims (1). In defining misconduct as fabrication, falsification, and plagiarism, NSF and NIH also include an open-ended phrase to encompass "other serious deviation from accepted practices in proposing, carrying out and reporting results." Because these definitions are overly broad and vague, it is appropriate to examine the history of congressional investigations of fraud in research and to consider a definition that is consistent with and responsive to the intent of Congress in establishing oversight of federal funds for scientific research.

Many scientists, like others in our society, are ambitious, self-serving, opportunistic, selfish, competitive, contentious, aggressive, and arrogant; but

From Howard K. Schachman, "What Is Misconduct in Science?" *Science*, vol. 261 (July 9, 1993), pp. 148–149, 183. Copyright © 1993 by The American Association for the Advancement of Science. Reprinted by permission.

that does not mean they are crooks. It is essential to distinguish between research fraud on the one hand and irritating and careless behavioral patterns of scientists, no matter how objectionable, on the other. We must distinguish between the crooks and the jerks (2). For the former we need (i) governmental oversight, (ii) a clear definition of those acts that are proscribed, (iii) adjudicatory machinery, (iv) due process, (v) protection of whistle-blowers, (vi) strong sanctions for the guilty, and (vii) full disclosure of conclusions in order to minimize repetition in other institutions. In contrast, such governmental intervention is inappropriate for concerns regarding errors in collecting and interpreting data, incompetence, poor laboratory procedures, selection of data, authorship practices, and multiple publications. These are matters for explicit dialog and education in universities and research institutions.

If we are to avoid the imposition of guidelines, rules, and regulations that may impede scientific research, it is essential to limit governmental action to fraud in science. A definition of misconduct in science that recognizes the dichotomy of roles and the need to "render, therefore, unto Caesar the things which are Caesar's..." will reduce the tension now existing between working scientists and government officials.

HOW "FRAUD IN SCIENCE" BECAME "MISCONDUCT IN SCIENCE"

In 1981 a subcommittee of Congress, under the chairmanship of Congressman Albert Gore, Jr., held hearings on fraud in biomedical research (3) in response to widespread reports of scientists falsifying their data. The cases cited dealt with fraud and plagiarism. One witness described how he falsified results of experiments that had not been performed. Another case, as described by the chairman, involved a researcher who "became entangled in a network of fraud and plagiarism, and a possible cover-up." Throughout these hearings the focus was on fabrication, falsification, and plagiarism.

When Congress passed the Health Research Extension Act in 1985, the legislation directed the secretary of the Department of Health and Human Services to

> require institutional applicants for NIH funds to review reports of fraud and report to the Secretary any investigation of suspected fraud which appears substantial.

The language focused on fraud, and the director of NIH was required to establish "a process for the prompt and appropriate response to information provided the Director... respecting scientific fraud."

Several years later, following increasing media coverage of several notorious cases of fabrication and falsification of data, the language was altered significantly when the Public Health Service (PHS) issued a proposed rule (4) entitled "Responsibilities of PHS Awardee and Applicant Institutions for Dealing with and Reporting Possible Misconduct in Science." In that proposed rule, "misconduct in science" was defined as

> (i) fabrication, falsification, plagiarism, deception or other practices that seriously deviate from those that are commonly accepted within the scientific community for proposing, conducting or reporting research; or (ii) material failure to comply with Federal requirements

that uniquely relate to the conduct of research.

Meanwhile, NSF issued final regulations under the title "Misconduct in Science and Engineering Education" that defined misconduct and also provided a safeguard for reprisals against whistle-blowers (5).

It was this transition from "fraud in science" to "misconduct in science" that led to apprehension among scientists. Some of the actions described in congressional hearings are labeled appropriately as fraud. Faking data is fraudulent. So is falsifying data. There is little confusion over the meaning of fraud. In contrast, "misconduct in science" means different things to different people. The change to "misconduct" instead of "fraud" was initiated and effected by lawyers and not by scientists. It was because of the legal burden of having to prove intent and injury to persons relying on fraudulent research that counsels for NSF and PHS wanted the change to misconduct (6). My concern is over vagueness of the term "misconduct in science" and how people with different orientations interpret various alleged abuses.

In formulations of the term "misconduct in science" there is agreement on fabrication, falsification, and plagiarism. Scientists have emphasized that "misconduct in science" does not include factors intrinsic to the process of science, such as error, conflicts in data, or differences in interpretation or judgments of data or experimental design (7). Particularly bothersome was inclusion of the phrase

other practices that seriously deviate from those that are commonly accepted within the scientific community for proposing, conducting or reporting research.

Not only is this language vague but it invites over-expansive interpretation. Also, its inclusion could discourage unorthodox, highly innovative approaches that lead to major advances in science. Brilliant, creative, pioneering research often deviates from that commonly accepted within the scientific community.

My apprehension over this open-ended, vague section of the definition is best illustrated by a case cited by the Office of Inspector General (OIG) of the NSF (8):

In November 1989, OIG received allegations of misconduct against the researcher. Our investigation involved conducting extensive interviews and collecting affidavits....

OIG determined that the researcher had been involved in 16 incidents of sexual misfeasance with female graduate and undergraduate students at the research site; on the way to the site; and in his home, car, and office. Many of these incidents were classifiable as sexual assaults. OIG further determined that these incidents were an integral part of this individual's performance as a researcher and research mentor and represented a serious deviation from accepted research practices. Therefore, they amounted to research misconduct under NSF regulations.

This is a preposterous and appalling application of the definition of scientific misconduct. The individual involved in this case, assuming the allegations were proven, should have been terminated by his institution for moral turpitude and the grant canceled accordingly. All of the grant funds should have been returned to the government by the institution that employed the individual. This case is an example of misconduct for which institutional and legal sanctions should have been imposed. But it is not misconduct in science. Having read the investigative report on this case, I am convinced that charges of sexual harassment as well as sexual abuse should have been filed. Buzzelli (1), however, reached an opposite conclusion, stating that "This case was not essentially a sexual harassment case, but sexual offenses were obviously at the heart of it. . . ."

DEFINING MISCONDUCT IN SCIENCE

In 1992 a panel convened by the National Academy of Sciences (NAS), National Academy of Engineering, and the Institute of Medicine released a report (9) that defined misconduct in science as

> fabrication, falsification, or plagiarism, in proposing, performing, or reporting research. Misconduct in science does not include errors of judgment; errors in the recording, selection, or analysis of data; differences in opinions involving the interpretation of data; or misconduct unrelated to the research process.

Fabrication is making up data or results. Falsification is changing data or results. Whereas plagiarism is described in the report as "using the ideas or words of another person without giving appropriate credit," Webster's *Seventh New Collegiate Dictionary* defines "plagiarize" as follows: "to steal and pass off as one's own (the ideas or words of another); to present as one's own an idea or product derived from an existing source." Because of the increasing focus on "intellectual property" in recent years, plagiarism is best defined as "misappropriation of intellectual property." Defined in this way, plagiarism not only encom-

passes those cases in which sentences or phrases are used without attribution but also includes unauthorized use of ideas, data, and interpretations obtained during the course of the grant review process or the review of scientific papers being considered for publication (10).

It is fabrication, falsification, and plagiarism that attracted the attention of the congressional committees, chaired by former Congressman Gore, Congressman John Dingell, and the late Congressman Ted Weiss (11). In the two most publicized cases that have dominated news disparaging the scientific community in the past few years, the initial charges were focused on these matters. Was the virus misappropriated? If so, a verdict of misconduct in science is correct. In the other case, it is important to know whether the experiments were done. If they were not, a verdict of misconduct is appropriate. One need not have a vague, open-ended phrase in the definition to adjudicate these cases. Reaching a verdict on grounds of fabrication, falsification, or plagiarism is difficult enough; there is no need to make the adjudication even more complex by considering spurious or vague charges as well.

RISKS OF AN OPEN-ENDED DEFINITION

Those who advocate the desirability of the clause "other serious deviation" have presented a variety of scenarios (1). One is tampering with research experiments. This, like sabotaging experiments and destroying animal quarters, is covered by other statutes and is, and should be, subject to sanctions. But we must face the fact that NSF could not impose sanctions on an individual who does not have an NSF grant even though that person tampers with or sabotages an experiment of an individual supported by NSF. Clearly, including such cases as misconduct in science leads to a morass. These are problems for local institutions and statutes dealing with vandalism. Invoking the "seriously deviates" clause to impose sanctions for such actions and labeling them misconduct in science is a great mistake (12).

Other examples, such as misrepresentations of one's qualifications and achievements in a grant application, are covered by falsification. The clause "seriously deviates" is also applied to reviewers of grant proposals who violate confidentiality and use materials in the proposals for their own purposes. This doubtless happens, and the cases should be investigated. If guilt is established, sanctions should be imposed. But one does not need an open-ended, vague, unclear phrase in the definition to encompass such egregious behavior. It is amply described as misappropriation of intellectual property and, therefore, encompassed in the definition as plagiarism.

The inclusion of ambiguous terms in the definition of misconduct in science potentially breaches an important principle of due process, the right to know in advance those activities that are proscribed. This principle is certainly violated by the view that " . . . you have to have a definition that covers situations that you can't even now conceive of" (13).

Although the word "misconduct" is now used in order to avoid legal ramifications of the word "fraud," it is nonetheless important to retain the original intent of Congress to focus on the role of government in investigating misconduct in science that is equivalent to "fraud which appears substantial." It is encouraging that the PHS Advisory Committee on Scientific Integrity has recently recommended a major change in the definition of misconduct in science now being used by the Office of Research Integrity. This proposal eliminates the phrase "other practices that seriously deviate from those that are commonly accepted within the scientific community" and moves closer to that proposed by the NAS panel (9, 14). Also, the PHS will no longer list in its ALERT system those individuals under investigation. This terrible practice of including names of individuals under investigation for misconduct in science has been abandoned; now names will be listed only if a finding of guilty has been reached. History is full of examples of governmental promulgations of laws expressed in broad, open-ended terms that were elastic enough to be stretched to cover any individual action that irritated some officials. In this century alone it was a major offense in some countries to publish scientific papers that seriously deviated from accepted practice. The enforcement of such strictures virtually destroyed major areas of science in those countries. We should not expose science in this country to similar risks.

NOTES

1. D. E. Buzzelli, *Science* **259,** 584 (1993).
2. C. K. Gunsalus, paper presented at the annual meeting of the American Association for the Advancement of Science, Chicago, IL, 6 February 1992, Symposium on Integrity and Misconduct in Science.
3. Hearings before the Subcommittee on Investigations and Oversight of the Committee on Science and Technology, U.S. House of Representatives, 97th Congress, 31 March to 1 April 1981.
4. Section 493 of the amended Public Health Service Act constitutes the Enabling

Act requiring the secretary of Health and Human Services to issue regulations requiring investigation of "alleged scientific fraud which appears substantial." This language is especially significant in terms of the wide variety of misdeeds now subject to investigation and imposition of sanctions by NSF and NIH. K. D. Hansen and B. C. Hansen [*FASEB J* 5, 2512 (1991)], in their critical analysis of "Scientific Fraud and the Public Health Service Act," emphasized that the amendment is clear on its face but there has been a tendency by the agencies to greatly expand the authority granted.

5. The current NSF definition of misconduct in science is: (i) fabrication, falsification, plagiarism, or other serious deviation from accepted practices in proposing, carrying out, or reporting results from activities funded by NSF or (ii) retaliation of any kind against a person who reported or provided information about suspected or alleged misconduct and who has not acted in bad faith (45 C.F.R. § 689).

6. R. M. Anderson, *Select Legal Provisions Regulating Scientific Misconduct in Federally Supported Research Papers* (AAAS—American Bar Association National Conference of Lawyers and Scientists Project on Scientific Fraud and Misconduct, Report on Workshop Number Three, American Association for the Advancement of Science, Washington, DC, 1989).

7. Testimony by H. K. Schachman before the Subcommittee on Investigations and Oversight of the Committee on Science, Space, and Technology, U.S. House of Representatives, 101st Congress, 28 June 1989.

8. Semiannual Report of the Office of Inspector General of the National Science Foundation, 1 April to 30 September 1990.

9. *Responsible Science: Ensuring the Integrity of the Research Process* (National Academy Press, Washington, DC, 1992), vol. 1.

10. Many of the cases of misconduct in science are described as plagiarism (First Annual Report of Scientific Misconduct Investigations Reviewed by Office of Scientific In-

tegrity Review, March 1989 to December 1990, of the Public Health Service; Semiannual Report of the Office of Inspector General of the National Science Foundation, No. 6, 1 October 1991 to 31 March 1992, and No. 7, 1 April 1992 to 30 September 1992). A definition of plagiarism as misappropriation of intellectual property would suffice for adjudicating the case at Michigan State University reported by E. Marshall [*Science* 259, 592 (1993)]. Based on the findings described by the independent panel (as reported in *Science*), the verdict of misconduct of science should have been attributed to plagiarism. There is no need to invoke the clause "a serious deviation from accepted practices."

11. In addition to the hearings in (3), a subcommittee of the Committee on Government Operations, House of Representatives, 100th Congress, held hearings on 11 and 12 April 1988 dealing with "Scientific Fraud and Misconduct and the Federal Response" under the chairmanship of the late Congressman Ted Weiss. On 12 April 1988, a hearing on "Fraud in NIH Grant Programs" was held by the Subcommittee on Oversight and Investigations of the Committee on Energy and Commerce, House of Representatives, 100th Congress, under the chairmanship of Congressman John D. Dingell. The Subcommittee on Human Resources and Intergovernmental Relations of the Committee on Government Operations of the U.S. House of Representatives, 100th Congress, held hearings on 29 September 1989, entitled "Federal Response to Misconduct in Science: Are Conflicts of Interest Hazardous to Our Health?" "Scientific Fraud" was the title of hearings of the Subcommittee on Oversight and Investigations of the Committee on Energy and Commerce of the U.S. House of Representatives, 101st Congress, 4 to 9 May 1989 and 30 April and 14 May 1990.

12. One might wonder whether a scientist who uses NSF funds to employ an illegal alien as a technician will be guilty of misconduct in science rather than of violating immigration and, perhaps, tax laws.

13. D. P. Hamilton, *Science* 255, 1345 (1992).

14. Eliminating this open-ended part of the definition will reduce the burdens on governmental officials, thereby facilitating their concentration on fraud of a substantial nature. Already the staff at ORI numbers about 50 people with an annual budget of $5 million.

15. This paper was presented in part at the 6th Annual Symposium of the Protein Society, San Diego, CA, 28 July 1992, and at the Sigma Xi Forum, "Ethics, Values, and the Promise of Science," San Francisco, CA, 25 to 26 February 1993.

NO

Donald E. Buzzelli

THE DEFINITION OF MISCONDUCT IN SCIENCE: A VIEW FROM NSF

In April 1992, a panel convened by the National Academy of Sciences issued its report on misconduct in science (1). At the end of its analysis, the report made 12 recommendations. Perhaps the most controversial of these recommendations concern the definition of misconduct that research institutions and government agencies should use when they deal with misconduct allegations. Since April, a number of science-related federal bodies and professional societies have been asked to endorse the report's recommendations. Funding agencies like the National Science Foundation (NSF) have been asked to adopt and implement them, especially the recommendations about the definition.

Some of these agencies, including NSF, already had considerable experience in handling misconduct cases. Because the Academy panel did not consult NSF about the definition, officials who work every day on misconduct cases as I do did not have the opportunity to contribute their thoughts and experience. Existing definitions can always be improved, and the report contains some useful ideas in this direction. Nevertheless, the changes the panel proposed in the definition are not helpful and in fact would hamper the ability of research institutions and federal agencies to deal with important cases of misconduct in science. Here, I will discuss the panel's recommendations. I will also try to explain NSF's definition and show how it was applied to an important and controversial case.

THE PANEL'S RECOMMENDATION

The panel unanimously recommended the removal of "ambiguous language such as the category 'other serious deviations from accepted research practices' currently included in regulatory definitions adopted by the Public Health Service and the National Science Foundation" (2). With less unanimity, it adopted a definition limited to "fabrication, falsification, or plagiarism, in proposing, performing, or reporting research" (1, p. 27). In other words,

From Donald E. Buzzelli, "The Definition of Misconduct in Science: A View from NSF," *Science*, vol. 259 (January 29, 1993), pp. 584–585, 647–648. Copyright © 1993 by The American Association for the Advancement of Science. Reprinted by permission. The views expressed are the author's and are not necessarily the positions of The Office of Inspector General, The National Science Board, or The National Science Foundation.

it proposed that nothing should replace the "other serious deviation" phrase (3). Finally, it recommended that research institutions and government agencies adopt a single, consistent definition of misconduct in science "based on" fabrication, falsification, and plagiarism (1, p. 147).

The panel's reason for proposing removal of the "other serious deviation" phrase was that (1, p. 27)

> the vagueness of this category has led to confusion about which actions constitute misconduct in science. In particular, the panel wishes to discourage the possibility that a misconduct complaint could be lodged against scientists based solely on their use of novel or unorthodox research methods.

Below, I will give some reasons for retaining language like "other serious deviation" in the definition of misconduct in science. The report gives no examples to show that confusion has occurred under the NSF definition in an actual case or that any scientists have been accused of misconduct under agency regulations because they were creative or unorthodox. The suggestion that NSF would bring such a case shows no understanding of NSF or of its misconduct procedures. The report does mention two cases in which NSF allegedly misused the "other serious deviation" phrase in a different way, by treating other kinds of misconduct as misconduct in science. These cases seem to be used as additional reasons for removing the "other serious deviation" phrase from the definition. I will take them up after discussing NSF's misconduct cases in general.

NSF'S MISCONDUCT CASES

NSF handles allegations of misconduct in science under regulations published in July 1987 and revised in May 1991. The Office of Inspector General (OIG) receives all cases that come to NSF's attention. Program officers are not informed of misconduct allegations that have been made against applicants for funding, and they may not take such allegations into consideration when processing proposals. If a case seems to require a full, formal investigation, OIG will usually allow the institution that employs the accused party to do it. The institution may make a finding of misconduct and impose its own sanction. OIG may accept the institution's investigation in lieu of an OIG investigation, may supplement the institution's investigation, or may even conduct a full investigation itself.

If OIG decides that a case seems to warrant a finding of misconduct and a sanction by NSF, it makes that recommendation to the deputy director of NSF. The deputy director arranges a hearing, if appropriate, and makes the adjudication. OIG investigates cases but cannot make findings of misconduct on behalf of NSF or impose sanctions. This is one of the protections that NSF regulations offer against abusive cases, such as the punishment of creative and unorthodox research as misconduct.

OIG was established in early 1989, so that it has over 3 years of experience in handling misconduct cases. Some numbers can be given to illustrate the case load, the types of cases received, and their resolution, but these numbers have little statistical value (4). From the formation of OIG in early 1989 to the end of June 1992, OIG added 124 (5) cases to its misconduct files. The number of cases rose rapidly at first but seems to be settling down to about 50 per year. Of the 124, approximately 70 have to do with intellectual property: plagiarism, theft of research ideas, or failure to give credit. One reason why there are so many cases of this type is that NSF program officers sometimes receive misconduct complaints from proposal reviewers and pass them on to OIG. Reviewers are especially likely to notice intellectual property problems. Although most of the misconduct cases that have received media attention involve the fabrication or misrepresentation of data, only about ten of NSF's cases are of this kind.

As of the end of July 1992, 67 of these 124 cases had been closed. Most of these were resolved without a formal investigation and did not lead to a formal finding of misconduct or a sanction. In some cases, preliminary inquiry showed that the allegation was not really about misconduct in science or that the offense that occurred was trivial. For example, a case involving a very small amount of plagiarism in a proposal may be resolved by OIG's clarifying what happened and having the applicant send a corrected proposal to NSF. In other cases, there was too little evidence to justify a full investigation or it was found that no NSF proposal or award was involved so that NSF had no jurisdiction in the matter.

Among the 67 closed cases, there were 8 in which NSF had jurisdiction and in which the university involved performed a formal investigation. Some of these cases began at the university, which then notified NSF. Others were sent to the university by NSF or another agency. Three of these investigations led to findings of misconduct by the institution, and all three were serious plagiarism cases. In a fourth case, involving data

falsification, OIG disagreed with the university's finding of no misconduct but did not pursue the matter because the subject of the investigation was a foreign citizen who had permanently left the country and was not likely to apply for federal grant funds in the future. Two major cases were investigated by OIG itself without a university investigation. One case came under the "other serious deviation" provision of the definition and is discussed below; the other involved possible noncompliance with guidelines for recombinant DNA research.

OIG has sent four cases to the Office of the Director of NSF with the recommendation that NSF make its own finding of misconduct and impose its own sanction. One was the "other serious deviation" case and the other three were plagiarism cases that had been investigated at universities. In all four cases, OIG recommended that the individual be debarred from receiving federal or NSF funds for a period of time. The director's office accepted the OIG recommendations, and the cases were resolved by debarment or voluntary agreements equivalent to debarment (6).

THE MAJOR "OTHER SERIOUS DEVIATION" CASE

Most of NSF's major cases have involved plagiarism, but one involved an "other serious deviation from accepted practices." This case deserves full discussion here because it illustrates the need for such a phrase in the definition of misconduct in science and also because the Academy report discusses it in a misleading way.

In late 1989, OIG began receiving complaints from women who had served as graduate teaching assistants in a field research project that had NSF funding. The complaints were against a senior researcher who had been taking teams of undergraduate students to a remote site in southern Mexico as part of a project in which they would observe and report on the behavior of a colony of primates. The project was supported by grants from NSF's Research Experiences for Undergraduates program. This program is intended to give active research experiences to undergraduate students, so that talented students can be attracted to research careers. The program especially tries to increase the participation of women in research.

In carrying out this project, the senior researcher was accused of a range of coercive sexual offenses against various female undergraduate students and teaching assistants, up to and including rape. These offenses occurred at and near the research site, in a private vehicle on the way to the site, and in the researcher's office, home, and car in the United States. He rationed out access to the research data and the computer on which they were stored and analyzed, as well as his own assistance, so that they were more available to those students who accepted his advances. He was also accused of threatening to blackball some of the graduate students in the professional community and to damage their careers if they reported his activities. For various reasons, this case has not been prosecuted under criminal or civil rights statutes.

OIG investigated the case itself instead of sending it to the subject's university because the university was not the grantee institution and had no involvement in the NSF grants under which this project was done. The grantee institution was a very small nonprofit institution that did not have professional staff members who were sufficiently distant from these grants and who had the expertise to conduct a difficult investigation that still had criminal implications. In any case, the researcher was no longer employed there.

The OIG investigation accumulated convincing evidence that the accusations were correct and that the subject showed a pattern of such behavior. OIG sent an investigation report to the Office of the Director of NSF with the recommendation that the subject be debarred from receiving any federal grant funds for 3 years. The case was also presented to other senior NSF management and to key members of the National Science Board, and all concurred in OIG's evaluation of it. The director's office raised the recommended term of debarment to 5 years and proposed that term to the subject. After negotiation, the subject waived his right to a hearing and agreed to a 5-year exclusion from federal support.

This was a genuine instance of misconduct in science. This case illustrates a "serious deviation from accepted practices" that is not falsification, fabrication, or plagiarism. The subject was never accused of any of those offenses. In fact, he was not accused of any kind of deception to a significant degree. For some, the only type of activity over and above falsification, fabrication, and plagiarism that might be considered misconduct in science would be some other kind of misrepresentation or deception (7). I will discuss the view the Academy panel took of the case and then I will try to explain why NSF acted as it did.

The Academy report maintains that this case was not misconduct in science but was rather what it calls "other misconduct" (1, pp. 82–83 and 86). The panel did not address the specifics of this case and perhaps did not know them (8). Instead, it treated the case as a generic instance of "sexual harassment" and argued in general that such cases are not misconduct in science. According to the report, sexual harassment is not misconduct in science because it is "not unique to the conduct of science, although [it] may occur in a laboratory or research environment." Rather, it is "subject to generally applicable legal and social penalties" and "should be handled by officials designated to implement personnel or equal opportunity regulations" (1, p. 29). Furthermore, the report continued, sexual harassment, sexual assault, and professional intimidation are not misconduct in science because they "do not require expert knowledge to resolve complaints" (1, p. 86; 9).

These general arguments have little validity. This case was not essentially a sexual harassment case, but sexual offenses were obviously at the heart of it. Such offenses can be misconduct in science, even though they are "not unique to the conduct of science." Plagiarism is also not unique to science, but it is universally regarded as misconduct in science when it occurs in a scientific setting. Similarly, the fact that there are other laws and regulations against sexual offenses would not always keep them from being misconduct in science: Even if laws were passed against fabricating data, the fabrication of data would still be misconduct in science. With regard to "expert knowledge," the amount required varies considerably from case to case. Thus, the need for expert knowledge in the resolution of misconduct cases is not a useful criterion for what is or is not misconduct in science.

Furthermore, the panel did not consider that NSF had to move to debar the subject. The government could not continue to be in the position of providing the funds and the opportunity for these activities. Even if this case had gone to court, NSF could not expect the courts or anyone else to protect the integrity of federal research funds. NSF had to do this itself, and only the misconduct regulation makes debarment possible in a case like this. Neither "personnel or equal opportunity regulations" nor "generally applicable legal and social penalties" are adequate to safeguard the integrity of federal funds.

The special features of this case distinguish it from a common sexual harassment case. The subject used his position as a research director and mentor to create opportunities to make impermissible sexual demands and even assaults on his students and teaching assistants. The students had to submit to these demands and assaults as a condition of receiving his services as a mentor. They were particularly dependent on him not only because he gave the final grades, but also because he was the only faculty member present at the isolated research site and the other places where these events occurred. These demands and assaults, plus the professional blackmail mentioned earlier, were an integral part of the subject's performance as a research mentor and director and ethically compromised that performance. Hence, they seriously deviated from the practices accepted in the scientific community.

I have argued that certain actions are misconduct in science whether or not they are subject to other penalties and whether or not they are unique to the conduct of science. I would suggest that the appropriate criterion should be whether those actions tend to do serious harm to science. The Academy report makes a similar point:

The distinguishing mark of misconduct in science, as opposed to other offenses, is that such actions "directly damage the integrity of the research process" (1, p. 28). The research process includes "the training and supervision of associates and students" (1, p. 18).

These considerations further help to explain NSF's treatment of this case. NSF would not treat a common sexual offense as misconduct in science, even if it occurred in a research setting. However, mentorship is an integral part of science, and science can be harmed by other actions besides issuing false data or stealing credit from one's peers: Science is harmed when students in a Research Experiences for Undergraduates project are taught to advance themselves by submitting to a research director's sexual demands.

OIG did not anticipate, much less seek, a case of this kind. There may be no case quite like it in the future. The important thing is that government agencies must not adopt a definition that is limited to the common run of cases so that they prevent themselves in advance from being able to deal with unexpected cases like this one. NSF's definition is "open-ended" for this reason.

OTHER EXAMPLES OF "OTHER SERIOUS DEVIATION"

Many allegations that come to OIG are about actions that do not fall under falsification, fabrication, or plagiarism. Except for the case just discussed, none of these cases has gone through the full process of investigation and adjudication. Hence, neither OIG nor NSF as a whole has made a decision that actions of these kinds would be genuine "other serious deviations." Still, among the cases OIG has received there are some strong candidates that deserve discussion. These examples again illustrate the need for a definition that goes beyond fabrication, falsification, and plagiarism.

One example of such a case involves tampering with research experiments. This would be another kind of misconduct in science that does not have to involve deception. The Academy panel criticized OIG for considering a case of this kind as misconduct in science. It reasoned that tampering is "other misconduct" rather than misconduct in science. Tampering, the report stated, is a form of vandalism or destruction of property, which again is not unique to the conduct of science and is subject to generally applicable legal and social penalties (1, p. 29, and p. 34, note 20).

There is actually a range of offenses that may fall under tampering. In some instances, tampering may consist of making adjustments to a colleague's experiment without that person's knowledge, so that bad data are obtained. It is difficult to see why falsifying one's own data is misconduct in science but falsifying a colleague's data is not. In other cases, the colleague's entire apparatus may be destroyed and removed. This clearly is vandalism, but arguably there would be enough harm to research in such a situation to justify opening a case of misconduct in science. The normal penalties for vandalism would not protect the integrity of federal research funds. Similarly, a colleague's cultures may be maliciously destroyed without the destruction of any equipment. This often could not be prosecuted as vandalism, but again I think scientists would agree that it violates ethical standards and departs from accepted practices in science.

Several other examples of "other serious deviation" can be suggested. Researchers often share cultures or reagents with colleagues in other laboratories. This may be done under an exclusionary agreement—for example, an agreement that the materials not be given to a third party or that they not be used for experiments that the originator wants to perform and publish. Violation of such an agreement arguably would be misconduct in science because such violation tends to discourage a practice of sharing that is fundamental to the process of research.

Another possible "other serious deviation" is misrepresentation in grant proposals or fellowship applications. An applicant may misrepresent his or her own qualifications and achievements or may misrepresent the institution's qualifications and programs. For example, untrue claims may be made about the institution's programs in support of minority students in order to encourage favorable consideration by the agency. This again is unethical and can be a serious deviation from the standards of the scientific community (10).

Finally, reviewers of grant proposals are instructed to keep the contents of the proposals and the opinions of other reviewers confidential. They are not supposed to use materials in the proposals for their own purposes. If these conditions are violated, harm is done to the whole process of submitting and reviewing proposals. Applicants may be afraid to write down and send in good ideas, and reviewers may feel they cannot be candid. Hence, violating the confidentiality of peer review seems to be an obvious instance of misconduct in science (11).

HOW TO INTERPRET NSF'S DEFINITION

Because the panel misunderstood the NSF definition, it may be useful if I explain my understanding of it. Far from being a worrisome add-on, the "other serious deviation from accepted practices" phrase is central to the NSF definition. This definition says, in effect, that misconduct in science is serious deviation from accepted practices. Falsification, fabrication, and plagiarism are mentioned as outstanding examples. Then the definition goes on to say that all "other" actions that similarly deviate from accepted practices are also misconduct in science.

However, I suggest that NSF, unlike the Academy panel, understands "deviation from accepted practices" in an ethical sense. The way to commit misconduct in science is to do something that scientists would recognize as deviating seriously from professional ethical standards. The panel evidently took "accepted practices" to mean accepted ways of doing experiments. Deviating from those does not ordinarily involve any ethical violation and has nothing to do with misconduct. Those who drafted the NSF definition obviously did not contemplate an interpretation that would make it misconduct in science just to do something novel or unorthodox (12).

The NSF definition does not attempt to give a full list of the practices that would violate professional standards in science. It might be very hard to draw up an exhaustive list, and standards might be found to vary from one branch of science to another. By referring to "accepted practices," the NSF definition points to the relevant scientific community as the authority for what is or is not misconduct.

Such a definition is heuristic rather than vague. It does not say whether each and every practice is or is not misconduct, but it points out where to look for the answer. The assumption is that working scientists, like the members of other professions, can and ought to know the standards of their profession and that in disputed cases representatives of the scientific community can agree on what those standards are. They should be able to do this without being given a complete list of the types of misconduct. Hence, misconduct can be recognized and dealt with under a heuristic definition like NSF's.

Some scientists may be willing to have their academic colleagues deal with misconduct in this heuristic way but may be less comfortable about a government agency doing so. This is not the place to discuss NSF's competence or public distrust of government. So far, no case has gone to adjudication at NSF that involved disagreement over whether an alleged activity would be misconduct in science. If that were to happen, I expect that a satisfactory method of consultation between the agency and the scientific community could and would be worked out.

CONCLUSION

NSF uses an open-ended definition that contains the phrase "other serious deviation from accepted practices." To date, this definition has worked successfully. One of its major advantages is that it leaves the agency the possibility of taking action when a case arises that is not on some short list of types of misconduct. It is legitimate to ask how NSF understands this definition, how it was applied in a major case, and what safeguards there are

against abuse. If the Academy panel had asked, it might have produced more helpful recommendations and might have advanced the discussion of this subject much more than it did. Those who work on misconduct cases will always need the guidance and insights of their colleagues in the broader scientific community. But those who wish to make useful policy recommendations also need the insights of those with day-to-day experience in this highly controversial area.

NOTES

1. National Academy of Sciences, Panel on Scientific Responsibility and the Conduct of Research, Committee on Science, Engineering, and Public Policy, *Responsible Science: Ensuring the Integrity of the Research Process* (National Academy Press, Washington, DC, 1992), vol. 1.

2. The Public Health Service definition is that "Misconduct" or "Misconduct in Science" means fabrication, falsification, plagiarism, or other practices that seriously deviate from those that are commonly accepted within the scientific community for proposing, conducting, or reporting research. It does not include honest error or honest differences in interpretations or judgments of data (45 C.F.R. § 50.102). The NSF definition is that "Misconduct" means (1) fabrication, falsification, plagiarism, or other serious deviation from accepted practices in proposing, carrying out, or reporting results from activities funded by NSF or (2) retaliation of any kind against a person who reported or provided information about suspected or alleged misconduct and who has not acted in bad faith [45 C.F.R. § 689.1(a)].

3. On the other hand, some panel members —majority, by some accounts—dissented and wanted to include other actions as misconduct under the Academy's definition. The report lists as examples "misuse of the peer-review system to penalize competitors,

deceptive selection of data or statistical analysis, or encouragement of trainees to practice misconduct in science" (1, p. 27). It goes on to say that "These issues deserve further consideration by the scientific research community to determine whether the panel's definition of misconduct in science is flexible enough to include all or most actions that directly damage the integrity of the research process and that were undertaken with the intent to deceive" (1, p. 28). Since this further discussion has not yet taken place, it seems premature to urge that agencies limit their definition to the three items on which all panel members could agree. By doing this, these agencies would preclude themselves from dealing with other situations, such as the ones just listed.

4. OIG receives complaints of many kinds that may involve various laws or regulations in various combinations. Some complaints are clearly about misconduct in science, but many are harder to classify. Most cases are concluded informally, without full investigation and adjudication, so that there may never be a decision about whether misconduct in science was involved. Universities also may resolve complaints against their students or faculty members without making it clear whether they are employing their misconduct-in-science regulations or some other disciplinary procedure. The result is that OIG's files contain some cases, including closed cases, that are not definitely classified as to whether they involve misconduct in science or not. Furthermore, the closed cases tend to be ones that were resolved quickly because it was easy to show that there was no misconduct. Some serious cases that require full investigation could not be closed quickly and remain open. Therefore, it is premature at this stage to draw any conclusions about what proportion of our cases will eventually lead to findings of misconduct or about what the distribution of those cases by type of misconduct will eventually be.

5. In fact, 131 were received, but 7 have been reclassified and transferred to other offices within OIG.

6. These cases are discussed more fully in OIG's series of semiannual reports to the Congress, which are available to the public. See, for example, OIG, *Semiannual Report to the Congress*, NSF, numbers 3 through 7.

7. This was the view of the Academy panel (1, pp. 28–29; 3). It was also apparently the view of the Public Health Service Advisory Committee on Scientific Integrity, which recommended the following definition at its June 1992 meeting: "Research fraud is defined as plagiarism; fabrication or intentional falsification of data, research procedures, or data analysis; or other deliberate misrepresentation in proposing, conducting, reporting or reviewing research"(Minutes of the Meeting of the Department of Health and Human Services, Public Health Service Advisory Committee on Scientific Integrity, 11–12 June 1992).

8. The available published information was too limited to permit a serious evaluation of this case. Under the Freedom of Information Act, the staff of the Academy panel requested and received a copy of OIG's investigation report, but I have not found any panel member who saw it. In any case, the arguments in the OIG investigation report are not addressed in the panel's report. The staff and panel also did not discuss the case with NSF.

9. A further argument, that these behaviors "should be governed by mechanisms that apply to all institutional members, not just those who receive government research awards" (1, p. 86), obviously applies to a grantee institution and not to a federal agency.

10. The fabrication of bibliographic material in research proposals is mentioned in the report, and the claim is made that the proposed definition covers it (1, p. 86). However, the proposed definition speaks only of the fabrication of data or results (1, pp. 27 and 47).

11. The Academy report characterizes the misuse of privileged information as plagiarism, which it defines as using the words or ideas of another person without giving appropriate credit (1, pp. 54–55). However, using privileged material without authorization is much different from using published material

and not giving credit. The privileged material is not supposed to be used at all, even if credit is given. NSF grant applicants, for instance, do not expect the ideas in their proposals to be used by everyone who is willing to give an acknowledgment. Hence, plagiarism is not a broad enough notion to cover this kind of misconduct.

12. An explanation of "other serious deviation" has been given by R. M. Anderson, one of the principal drafters of the NSF definition [*J. Law Technol.* **3**, 121 (1988), pp. 129–131].

POSTSCRIPT

Can Science Police Itself?

The "other serious deviations from accepted scientific practice" clause is still in federal definitions of scientific misconduct, although the National Academy of Sciences said in February 1994 that every offense other than plagiarism, falsification, and fabrication should be handled at the institutional level. The debate seems likely to continue.

An interesting question is, How common is scientific misconduct? In November 1993, social scientist Judith Swazey announced the results of a survey of graduate students and faculty at 99 U.S. campuses. Nine percent of the respondents said that they knew of cases of plagiarism; while 6 percent knew of falsified data. Nearly half the respondents in the fields of microbiology, chemistry, civil engineering, and sociology said that they knew of "questionable research practices," including sexual harassment, neglect of safety regulations, and financial conflict of interest. However, these statistics are misleading, for many respondents likely knew of the same cases.

In March 1994, Canadian researcher Roger Poisson confessed to falsifying data in a major study designed to learn whether radical mastectomy (removal of the breast) or lumpectomy (removal of just the tumor and surrounding tissue, not the entire breast) offered women with breast cancer a better chance of survival. The data had been collected years before and incorporated in reports telling women that lumpectomy was the better option. Poisson's confession put those reports and their conclusions into question, and although the study's directors belatedly reanalyzed the data (leaving out Poisson's contributions) and announced that the conclusions were the same, breast cancer patients remained skeptical.

In studies whose conclusions are not affected by the discovery of falsified data, the worst effect of the misconduct is the harm it does to patients' state of mind; that is, their confidence in the results of the study. But in studies whose conclusions *are* affected, the impact of misconduct can be far worse. Patients who choose a particular treatment for their disease because falsified data wrongly tell them that it is more likely than other treatments to save their lives decrease their chances of survival.

Some good articles discussing scientific fraud and the definition of scientific misconduct include: Faye Flam, "Misconduct: Views from the Trenches," *Science* (August 27, 1993); Brad Holland, "Scientific Fraud," *Omni* (June 1992); Charles Maechling, Jr., "The Laboratory Is Not a Courtroom," *Issues in Science and Technology* (Spring 1991); and David P. Hamilton, "A Shaky Consensus on Misconduct," *Science* (May 1, 1992).

ISSUE 4

Will the Information Revolution Benefit Everyone?

YES: Michael J. Mandel, from "The Digital Juggernaut," *Business Week* (The Information Revolution, 1994)

NO: Center for Media Education et al., from *Electronic Redlining* (Center for Media Education, 1994)

ISSUE SUMMARY

YES: Michael J. Mandel, an economics writer, argues that the telecommunications and information-processing industries will benefit the entire nation.

NO: The Center for Media Education et al. argue that plans for construction of the first portions of the information superhighway deliberately exclude minorities and the poor.

Do science and technology benefit everyone? Or do they benefit chiefly a technocratic elite and oppress the rest? Are they *fair* to minorities and the poor? These questions are worth asking because history assures us that although new technologies may offer humanity new and wondrous capabilities, and although they may make their inventors and developers rich, they may also harm and even destroy some populations of society. For example, the development of efficient stills and then of an industry devoted to producing cheap gin and rum made drunkenness and alcoholism serious social problems in eighteenth-century England. Railroads were a boon to farmers and ranchers, but they hastened the destruction of the Native American cultures. And the invention of the atomic bomb led to the destruction of Hiroshima and Nagasaki and to the deaths of hundreds of thousands of Japanese citizens in 1945.

In "Science, Technology, and Black Community Development," *The Black Scholar* (March/April 1984), Robert C. Johnson notes that some technologies have been especially damaging to blacks. Agricultural mechanization, for instance, drove blacks from small farms to the industrialized cities, where they felt useless, superfluous, and estranged from what Johnson calls the "Wonders of the White Man's Science and Technology." The result was destruction of community and family cohesiveness, crime, alcoholism, and marital break-up, among other things. Mass production of the automobile led to the movement of many high-paying jobs from the cities to the suburbs, thereby denying inner-city residents any hope of escape from poverty and creating ghettos.

Contemporary technologies hold threats of their own, according to Johnson. He asserts that he fears most new biomedical technologies: "Biogenetic manipulations, cloning, test-tube babies and the like bode ill for those of us who have been victims of forced sterilization, brutal castration, psychosurgery, aversion therapy, biased psychological testing, calculated syphilis experiments, persistent campaigns of birth and population control, and many other insidious and inhumane forms of so-called scientific research and human experimentation.... It is only natural and logical that ... we will be likely targets and victims of [genetic engineering]."

Johnson also notes that blacks develop more cancers than whites and tend to be exposed to more environmental pollutants. This has become an issue in its own right. "Environmental racism," as it is called, refers to the tendency of a white-dominated society to respond more slowly to environmental problems (such as toxic wastes) that afflict minority communities. It also includes the disproportionate hosting of landfills, toxic waste dumps, and noxious industries by minority communities. (See Robert D. Bullard, "Overcoming Racism in Environmental Decisionmaking," *Environment*, May 1994.)

What will happen with the latest technology—the information superhighway, or National Information Infrastructure (NII), which is being pushed vigorously by the Clinton administration? The intent of the NII is to facilitate the rapid flow of electronic data, including the flow in and out of the home, and thus to increase access to information, education, and entertainment for everyone who is hooked up to the system via computer, modem, and telephone or via interactive television. To help bring this technology into being, the Federal Communications Commission (FCC) in 1992 established a new policy called "video dialtone" to let telephone companies deliver not only telephone services but also video programming and computer services.

The advantages of the NII to those who already have or can afford to buy the necessary equipment—and who are comfortable working with the latest in technological gadgetry—are obvious. But what about the poor? What about minorities whose past limited access to education, training, and gadgetry has left them "technologically disadvantaged"?

In the following selections, Michael J. Mandel argues that, even though the computer and the telecommunications and information-processing industries may leave behind unskilled workers and those who simply cannot keep up with new technology, they will create jobs, lower unemployment, and bring urban services and amenities to rural areas, thus benefiting the entire nation. The Center for Media Education and other concerned organizations argue that current plans for the NII are flawed by discrimination and that the FCC should take steps to ensure that the benefits of the NII are not denied to minorities and the poor.

YES

Michael J. Mandel

THE DIGITAL JUGGERNAUT

In every era, there is a group of industries that sets the pace for the rest of the economy. A century ago, the railroads were America's growth engine. In the postwar decades, manufacturing was the key to U.S. prosperity. During the 1980s, the driving forces of expansion were booming service industries such as health care, legal services, and retailing: All told, during that decade, the service sector accounted for practically all of the growth in jobs and corporate profits. Economists began to speak of the U.S. shift from a manufacturing to a service economy.

Yet for all the vitality of services, many skeptics did not see how they could make the economy thrive over the long term. In fact, the shift seemed like a giant step backward, since service jobs paid lower wages on average than manufacturing and had significantly slower productivity growth. Moreover, services such as medical care and retailing were much harder to export than manufactured goods. The worry was that if the U.S. lost its manufacturing industries, it would have a difficult time selling enough services abroad to pay for its imports of cars, consumer electronics, and other goods.

Fear not: Like adolescence, the service economy has turned out to be a temporary stage. Far more than most people realize, economic growth is now being driven not by services, but by the computer, software, and telecommunications industries. Indeed, according to the Commerce Dept., business and consumer spending on high-tech equipment accounts for some 38% of economic growth since 1990.

What's more, government statistics underplay the evolution of the information economy. Industries that depend on processing and moving information—such as financial services and entertainment—are prospering. And companies in every industry are using information technology to reengineer themselves and become more competitive. In short, "the role of information is transforming the nature of economy," says Kenneth J. Arrow, a Nobel prizewinning economist at Stanford University.

In this regard, at least, the U.S. is leading the way for the rest of the world. Europe is deregulating its telecommunications industry in order to create jobs and stimulate development. Japan is mounting an intense effort to narrow the considerable edge the U.S. has built over the decade in personal-computer and network use. Even developing countries such as China, Hungary, and Thailand are investing heavily in state-of-the-art communications systems in an effort to leapfrog their way to prosperity.

America remains way ahead, however. And it's the place where the consequences of the new economy are first showing up. To a large degree, the news is turning out to be good. For one thing, unlike most services, information products such as software and entertainment can be easily exported. And whereas productivity in the service sector grew slowly, investment in information technology is boosting productivity across the economy.

Beyond that, the effect on work is less harmful than once feared. Far from becoming low-paid burger-flippers, the quintessential job of the service sector, many Americans are turning into computer jocks. Economic studies show that their wages are on the rise as a result. For example, earnings for male computer programmers have risen by 12% since 1990, compared with 6% for all male workers. For female computer programmers, the pay gains have been even bigger: a 21% rise since 1990, vs. 13% for all female workers.

The drawback is that along with the winners, there will temporarily be lots of losers. Higher productivity has led to big layoffs at many companies especially in the telecommunications industry. Elsewhere, meanwhile, advancing technology is favoring skilled workers over unskilled, increasing the inequality in wages.

For better or for worse, this transformation is occurring at an astonishing rate. Look at business investment. Measured in inflation-adjusted dollars, computers and other information technology now make up nearly half of all business spending on equipment—and that doesn't include the billions that companies spend on software and programmers each year. Meanwhile, business spending on industrial machinery, which traditionally has been the guts of manufacturing, has fallen as a share of equipment investment from 32% in 1975 to only 18% in 1993.

At the same time, information technology and services are helping to drive the continuing export boom. The aircraft industry is often held up as the shining star among U.S. exporters. Yet America's overseas sales of information-technology equipment in 1993 were $62 billion, far more than the $33 billion in overseas aircraft sales. The U.S. is also the world's largest exporter of software, a fact that doesn't show up in the government's numbers. In 1993, major U.S. software companies sold $2.5 billion worth of personal computer programs in Western Europe, Asia, and Latin America, according to the Software Publishers Assn. Microsoft Corp. alone derives some 55% of its revenues from overseas sales.

The U.S also is running a huge $3 billion trade surplus in computer-related services, such as data processing and information databases. It's nearly as easy now to send information to Europe or Japan as to the next state or across the hall. For example, Mead Data Central Inc., the company that runs Lexis and Nexis services, which contain legal news and general news respectively, also has databases on French and British law that lawyers in those countries use. The location of these databases: Dayton, Ohio.

Coming improvements in overseas communications will even make it possible to export such services as medical care. By this coming summer, doctors across sparsely populated South Dakota will be able to use a statewide telecommunications network to consult with specialists hundreds of miles away. The same expertise could be transmitted to Asia or Latin America just as easily. "The information economy can breed a healthy economy because a lot of its services are exportable," says George Bennett, chairman of Symmetrix, a technology consulting firm.

Two other positive byproducts of the Information Age are greater efficiency and lower prices. During much of the 1980s, economists worried that they could not find any impact of computers on productivity. But more recent research shows that investments in computers are worthwhile. Economists Erik Brynjolfsson and Lorin Hitt of the Massachusetts Institute of Technology surveyed 400 large companies to gauge the effect of technology on output per employee. They found that the return on investment in information systems exceeded 50%. "And most of these benefits are being passed on to consumers in the form of lower prices," says Brynjolfsson.

In fact, the productivity surge of the last two years—when nonfarm output per worker rose by 4.9%, its biggest two-year jump since 1976—may reflect the efforts of U.S. companies to finally take full advantage of the huge sums they've spent purchasing information technology. "If I put technology in and nothing changes, and then later a business gets in a crunch and discovers that it can cut out all the middle management, what made it possible?" asks Raymond Perry, chief information officer at Avon Products Inc. "Well, probably the technology did. It's just that

we weren't ready to take the people out until a later point in time."

Even the recent productivity numbers probably far understate the critical role of information technology and services in driving growth. To put it simply: Government statistics track goods and jobs, not flows of information. That means the U.S. has a large and vibrant "ghost economy" that traditional economic indicators don't measure. Take the communications sector, which includes the telephone, broadcasting, and cable industries. According to government figures, communications is only 3.1% of the economy, up from 2.8% in 1984, at the time of the AT&T divestiture. Over the same period, minutes of telephone use—a key number tracked by the Federal Communications Commission—has grown only slightly faster than the overall economy.

Yet a closer looks shows that the official statistics ignore many of the changes of the past decade. For one, a much greater percentage of the calls over the phone network are faxes and computer data going back and forth, rather than people talking. As much as 10% to 20% of the traffic across the AT&T long-distance network may be data, estimates Frank Ianna, the company's general manager for network services. That's up from 7% to 10% a few years ago. And because of time and language differences, about half of international calls are data, not voice.

These fax and computer messages pack a lot more data into a minute than they used to. Over the past few years, for example, the speed of a typical modem —which is used to transfer information between computers over phone lines— has quadrupled.

That means the amount of information being pumped through the system has gone through the roof. The point is this: If the output of the communications sector is measured in terms of data transferred instead of the number of minutes it's in use, it would show far more dramatic growth than the published numbers indicate.

Prices in the communications sector have also likely fallen much more sharply than the government numbers show. According to the Bureau of Labor Statistics, the producer price index for interstate telephone service has risen by 2.4% over the past five years. Yet this figure doesn't take into account the discount calling plans that most long-distance companies now offer. Nor does it adequately track the cost and use of leased lines. The BLS hopes to remedy some of these problems with a new index for telephone prices, perhaps by January.

The information economy also has a much larger productive capacity than the current government statistics indicate. For the moment, the main measure of how close the economy is to its maximum operating rate is the Federal Reserve's industrial capacity utilization number. While this includes utilities that sell electricity and natural gas, it leaves out telecommunications. That means there is no good measure of the amount of spare capacity in the U.S. telecom network. That's an important omission, since many businesses have become increasingly dependent on reliable—and widely available—communications services.

Even the investment boom of the past few years understates the true value of the spending on information technology. According to Commerce Dept. figures, investment in communications equipment has barely risen since 1990. What these numbers don't say is that for the same price, companies have been able to buy vastly more sophisticated switching gear and other telecommunications equipment, with new capabilities such as call forwarding.

Beyond those hidden by the measurement problems, there are some fundamental differences between the information economy and its predecessors. In the past, technological improvements such as railroads, auto plants, and steel mills required vast amounts of capital. But because the price of information technology continues to drop so quickly, companies can spend less to get healthy improvements in productivity and quality. Indeed, in recent years, the productivity of capital—defined as the amount of output produced per dollar of plant and equipment—has gone up for the first time in the postwar era. "As the U.S. becomes an information-oriented economy," says William Sterling, an economist at Merrill Lynch & Co., "you may have less need for capital than you have in the past."

For example, phone companies are able to boost the carrying capacity of their existing fiber-optic cables by simply upgrading the electronics at either end. That means they can add to capacity without having to go through the expensive process of digging up old cables and installing new ones.

Even connecting all of the nation's homes to the Information Superhighway may cost less than expected. In California, Pacific Telesis Group and AT&T are estimating that it will cost an average of $800 to wire each of 1.5 million homes with a combined fiber-optic/coaxial cable network that can carry the most advanced services. That compares with $1,600 for the electronics and labor needed to run a fiber cable all the way to the home. "The fiber-only estimates were scaring everybody off," says Robert Clark, vice-president for marketing and sales at

AT&T Network Systems. "We've been able to see another way of getting all the services."

If these lower estimates turn out to be right, it won't come as a total surprise: On a comparable basis, the price of information-technology equipment has dropped by 23% over the past five years, according to Commerce Dept. numbers. This trend, if it continues, will have important implications for interest rates. If companies need to borrow less money to finance their investment in high-tech equipment, that will keep overall rates lower than they would have been otherwise. And that will benefit homeowners, the government, and other borrowers.

Still, there's the matter of those losers from the shift to the information economy. At the top of the list are the workers who have lost their jobs as companies reengineer their businesses. The reduction in staff can be enormous. At USAir Inc., 650 people were once needed in the revenue accounting department. Now that much of the process has been automated, only 350 people are needed to do the work, says Senior Vice-President and CFO John W. Harper. And at many companies, the downsizing isn't over. "Where will all these people be employed?" asks Lester Thurow, an economics professor at MIT and former dean of the university's Sloan School of Management. "It's not at all obvious."

Ironically, some of the biggest staff reductions have come at computer and telephone companies, which are at the heart of the information economy. Competitive pressures play a role, but these cuts are being driven mainly by technological advances that let the phone companies, for example, do with fewer operators, maintenance people, and other workers. NYNEX Corp., which supplies local phone service in New England and New York, announced plans last January to pare its workforce by 22%, or 17,000 people, by the end of 1996. Overall, employment in the telephone and computer manufacturing industries has already dropped by 154,000 since 1988, with more cuts to come.

Also at sea in the information economy are unskilled workers and people who can't keep up with technology. Indeed, recent studies suggest a hefty payoff for workers who feel at home in the digital world. Princeton University economist Alan B. Krueger estimates that people who use computers at work earn 10% to 15% more than colleagues in similar occupations who do not use computers. Says Lawrence Katz, chief economist at the Labor Dept.: "There is very strong evidence that people who work with computers earn higher wages."

Still, even if some people are being left behind, the information economy is creating thousands of new businesses and jobs. For example, the Home Shopping Network—which sells jewelry and other merchandise on cable TV—has grown to employ some 5,000 people, up from 600 in 1985. At the other end of the spectrum are startups such as SandPoint Corp., a Cambridge (Mass.) maker of software that helps people track down information in databases. Over the past year, SandPoint has grown from 15 to 32 employees, and it's still expanding. Overall, the number of jobs in the software, data processing, and information retrieval industries has risen by 31% since 1988, and these industries now employ more people than the auto industry.

Besides creating jobs, the information economy may even make it a bit easier to match workers to existing jobs.

The Online Career Center, based in Indianapolis, provides job and resumé listings on the Internet. Since it went on-line in June, 1993, observes Director William Warren, it has become one of the most popular databases on the system, with 13,000 to 14,000 job openings listed and nearly as many resumés. Ultimately, nationwide listing services such as this could make labor markets more efficient and help lower unemployment.

The effects of the information economy are even reaching into rural areas by shifting development away from congested urban regions. With more and more parts of the country having access to high-capacity telecommunications, companies can now put jobs such as order-taking in remote locations without losing touch with the rest of the business. "What telecommunications allows you to do is put the right facilities with the right labor," notes Ken Kuhl, a consultant with Moran, Stahl & Boyer, a business relocation firm.

Technological advances will have an even more profound impact on the vitality of rural areas by bringing big-city services and amenities to small towns. For example, the telecommunications network operated by the state of South Dakota enables rural schools to offer Spanish classes via interactive TV— something they would never have been able to do on their own. The information revolution, says South Dakota Governor Walter D. Miller, "is going to change the face of South Dakota as much as rural electrification did."

That's an apt parallel. Just as the U.S. economy today would be unthinkable without electricity, so will tomorrow's economy be spurred by the free flow of information. Judging by the explosive growth of information technology so far, the juice is only starting to flow.

NO   Center for Media Education et al.

PETITION FOR RELIEF FROM UNJUST AND UNREASONABLE DISCRIMINATION IN THE DEPLOYMENT OF VIDEO DIALTONE FACILITIES

The introduction of video dialtone presages a new information age, and its widespread deployment has the potential to transform the way Americans live. Carrying video, audio, and data on two-way, high-capacity wires, video dialtone may supplant other traditional forms of data transmission—including telephone, cable television, and broadcasting—while adding previously unheard of services.

But such technological acceleration in the absence of sound policy governing its growth can leave damage in its wake. A nation whose economic life relies so heavily on information, and will to an even greater extent in the future, cannot afford a citizenry divided by its access to information. Inequitable access could widen the social, political and economic disparity between the wealthy and the poor. Already, traditional forms of communication, including newspapers and books, are increasingly converging into electronic formats. As switched, broadband networks like video dialtone replace older technologies, those who are not connected to the network will experience a severe information deficit. Almost inevitably, this lack of access will restrict the educational, employment, and political opportunities of the technologically disadvantaged, who, if the pattern of video dialtone proposals holds true, are likely to be the poor and/or minorities.

Surely, the public interest benefits of a national information infrastructure are dampened without universal service. Assuming that the [Federal Communications] Commission will achieve its objectives of nondiscriminatory access for programmers and universal service, the video dialtone platform could spur the development of an unrivaled array of programs and services. Potentially interactive, video dialtone may have its greatest applications in areas such as education and medicine, where services such as distance learning and remote medical diagnosis have been highly touted. Programming diversity and the increased inter-communication resulting from universal service

From Center for Media Education et al., "Petition for Relief from Unjust and Unreasonable Discrimination in the Deployment of Video Dialtone Facilities" (presented to The Federal Communications Commission, Washington, DC, May 23, 1994). Some notes omitted.

could benefit all Americans, regardless of race, ethnicity, or income, by helping ameliorate the differences that threaten to divide us while strengthening our social fabric.

Additionally, should interactivity become technologically and economically feasible, and the future predictions of some video dialtone proponents come to pass, universal video dialtone service could promote important First Amendment values by increasing participation in the democratic process. Accordingly, one's ability to participate in voting, school board meetings, local government, and other forms of public debate could be limited without access to advanced networks. This inability to participate is detrimental not only to those who find their speech muted, but to the rest who are never exposed to a full complement of ideas and viewpoints. Only universal service can ensure robust debate and equitable participation in our democracy, which includes both the right to receive information and the right to speak and be heard.

Universal service cannot occur overnight, which is why it is essential that video dialtone facilities are constructed and deployed to communities that are reasonably representative of the larger areas the local telephone companies serve. Petitioners believe it is now incumbent on the Commission to state emphatically that a consistent practice of excluding from service, or significantly delaying service to, poor and/or minority communities is anathema to the public interest and will not be tolerated.

Background

In 1987, the Commission began the process of reassessing its telephone company–cable television cross-ownership restrictions. At the time, local exchange carriers were prohibited from delivering video programming to the public in their telephone service areas, either directly or through an affiliate. Two years ago, the Commission modified its rules to allow local telephone companies to participate in the market for video delivery through video dialtone.

While determining that video dialtone deployment, in general, is in the public interest, the Commission stated that upon receiving video dialtone applications, it would more closely evaluate whether a particular proposal serves the public interest. The Commission has since accepted a number of § 214[1] applications for the construction and operation of video dialtone facilities. Five applications for the construction of facilities have already been approved and seventeen are pending. Companies filing applications include Bell Atlantic, U S WEST, Ameritech, and Pacific Bell. Most of the pending applications target larger metropolitan areas.

While examining the various applications, petitioners noticed a pattern in the proposals and maps provided by the companies. Specifically, telephone common carriers appear to be avoiding lower income areas and areas with a high concentration of minority residents in their service plans.

Petitioners engaged Dr. Mark Cooper, one of the country's leading experts in telecommunications economics and policy. He examined at least two applications from each of four Regional Bell Operating Companies.[2] Using a combination of data and maps provided by the applicant, telephone company marketing data, and census tract data, Dr. Cooper concluded that there is "a clear and systematic pattern of not serving some lower income areas, which turn out to be much more heavily minority areas."

Dr. Cooper found that in some situations, the unserved areas comprise a portion which is carved out of the center of a city. For example, the map of U S WEST's scheduled deployment in Denver depicts a large slice running through the center of the city where video dialtone facilities will not be initially constructed. Lower income and/or minority persons are heavily concentrated in the excluded area. This pattern suggests the conclusion that the poorest, minority, urban communities are being altogether bypassed.

Another pattern seems to consist of skipping entire counties. Counties with high income levels and lower minority concentrations appear to be the applicants' first choices. Examples of this include Orange County and South Bay, California, which are wealthier areas with a lower percentage of minorities than adjoining areas, and the Washington, D.C. metropolitan area, where Bell Atlantic is proposing to initially serve only certain Maryland and Virginia suburbs. In addition, deployment plans for Chicago exclude areas with the high concentrations of low-income and minority residents.

Redlining Is Inconsistent With the Goal of Universal Service in Telecommunications.

Section 1 of the Communications Act of 1934 created the Commission for the purpose of "regulating interstate and foreign commerce in communication by wire and radio so as to make available, so far as possible, to *all the people of the United States* a rapid, efficient, Nation-wide, and world-wide wire and radio communication service with adequate facilities at reasonable charges." (emphasis added)

This objective of universal service applies no less to video dialtone than to basic telephone service, and perhaps more so.[3] The goal has been oft-repeated by the Commission, and specifically with respect to video dialtone. Indeed, in its *Second Video Dialtone Order*, the Commission agreed that "encouraging universal service is an implicit goal of video dialtone" pursuant to the Commission's mandate under Section 1. So obvious was this objective that the Commission proclaimed it unnecessary to state it as an independent goal of its video dialtone regulatory framework.

Universal service is also a cornerstone of President Clinton's proposals for the National Information Infrastructure. One of the Administration's fundamental principles for telecommunications policy is "preserving and advancing universal service to avoid creating a society of information 'haves' and 'have nots'." The Administration supports making the advancement of universal service an explicit (rather than implicit) goal of Section 1 of the Communications Act. This definition would include making advanced services available to rural and urban lower income users.

Vice President Gore has stressed the Administration's strong commitment to universal service. Citing a newspaper headline which asked whether the information superhighway would detour the poor, Gore emphatically responded, "Not if I have anything to do about it." Gore said that all carriers must be required to contribute, "on an equitable and competitively neutral basis, to the preservation and advancement of universal service," with the Commission responsible for implementing the framework to accomplish this.

In a recent speech, Commission Chairman Reed E. Hundt echoed the importance of future interactive networks: "If these networks do not reach into every community and bring us together, they could end up dividing us further—leaving whole segments of our country without the skills and information necessary to prosper in our post-industrial economy."

Because of video dialtone's potential impact, universal service is an integral component of our future telecommunications policy. By not serving many lower-income and/or minority communities initially, video dialtone providers make it more unlikely that these communities will be served adequately in the future.

Redlining Violates the Nondiscrimination Clause of the Communications Act of 1934 and Is Inconsistent With the Public Interest.

Since it will take time to attain universal service, it is important that video dialtone networks are deployed and expanded on a nondiscriminatory basis. Indeed, Section 202(a) of the Communications Act prohibits unjust or unreasonable discrimination in the provision of communications facilities.[4]

Section 202(a) is violated by the "redlining" being practiced by the telephone common carriers on the basis of minority and/or income status. Petitioners believe that such discrimination on the basis of either minority or income status is facially unreasonable.

Not only is it unlawful for the applicants to discriminate in this manner, but such discrimination undermines the very purposes for which the Commission authorized video dialtone. In announcing its video dialtone rules, the Commission sought to achieve three public interest goals: (1) improving the national telecommunications infrastructure; (2) promoting a competitive video market in order to stimulate technological and service innovation, thereby benefitting consumers, video programmers, and other service providers; and (3) fostering the development of a greater diversity of video programming. These benefits are compromised if local telephone companies provide this technology in a discriminatory manner....

Conclusion

Petitioners ask the Commission to reiterate and enforce its policy goals of universal service and nondiscrimination with respect to video dialtone. Our goal is not to delay construction of advanced telecommunications networks. Rather, it is to ensure that the potential benefits of video dialtone will be available on an equitable basis. Ultimately, a commitment to universal service and nondiscriminatory deployment of video dialtone is a necessary pillar for constructing our national information infrastructure.

NOTES

1. 47 U.S.C. § 214(a) reads in part: "No carrier shall undertake the construction of a new line... unless and until there shall first have been obtained from the Commission a certificate that the present or future public convenience and necessity require or will require the construction... of such additional... line."

2. He examined applications from Ameritech (Indianapolis and Chicago areas), Bell Atlantic (Washington, D.C. area and Toms River, New Jersey), Pacific Bell (Orange County, South San Francisco Bay, and San Diego areas), and U S WEST (Denver and Portland areas).

3. Because of the wide range of applications expected, video dialtone is likely to become more essential than plain telephone service....

4. 47 U.S.C. § 202(a) makes it unlawful for any common carrier to:

make any unjust or unreasonable discrimination in... practices, classifications, regulations, facilities, or services for... communication service... or to make or give any undue or unreasonable preference or advantage to any particular person, class of persons, or locality,

or to subject any particular person, class of persons, or locality to any undue or unreasonable prejudice or disadvantage.

While cable television companies are not regulated as common carriers, they are also prohibited from denying service to "any group of potential residential cable subscribers because of the income of the residents of the local area in which such group resides." The Cable Communications Policy Act of 1984, § 621(a)(3), 47 U.S.C. § 541 (1991).

POSTSCRIPT

Will the Information Revolution Benefit Everyone?

Along with many other groups, the Center for Media Education is a member of the Telecommunications Policy Roundtable, which has formulated a framework to guide debate over whether and how the National Information Infrastructure (NII) will serve the public interest. Briefly, this framework states that the NII should support public applications such as education, libraries, public health, and delivery of government information and services; universal access (meaning minorities and the poor should not be excluded); and protection of basic rights such as privacy, freedom of speech, and intellectual property. See "Renewing the Commitment to a Public Interest Telecommunications Policy," *Communications of the ACM* (January 1994) and Fred W. Weingarten, "Public Interest and the NII," *Communications of the ACM* (March 1994).

The study of NII construction plans discussed by the Center for Media Education et al. is a natural extension of the Roundtable's interest in the issue. In a press release, Jeffrey Chester, executive director of the Center for Media Education, said that there was a clear pattern: "Low-income and minority neighborhoods are being systematically underrepresented in these plans," almost to the point of exclusion from the benefits of the technology. The Center for Media Education compared this exclusion to the now-outlawed practice of "redlining," by which banks once refused to grant mortgages to people in minority neighborhoods that were outlined on a map in red.

According to press reports, industry representatives have objected to charges of discrimination. Speaking for U S West, Inc., a Denver telephone company, Jerry Brown said, "We had to start building our network someplace. And it is being built in areas where there are customers we believe will use and buy the service. This is a business."

Jeffrey Chester, criticizing the business perspective, commented, "There have to be some rules—you can't just let the market determine who gets service and who doesn't." Raul H. Yzaguirre, president of the National Council of La Raza, agrees: "We want to make sure technology doesn't widen the gap between the rich and the poor."

Similar thoughts lie behind three bills that went before the House and Senate in May 1994. There is widespread agreement that universal access to the information superhighway is a worthy goal, but little agreement over how to pay for it. So far, the answer seems to be to refer the question to state regulators—how they handle the costs remains to be seen. See Laura Michaelis, "The Social Compact," *Congressional Quarterly* (May 14, 1994).

PART 2

The Environment

The search for understanding of the world has led scientists to some alarming conclusions about the hazards of population growth, the consequences of fossil fuel exhaustion, the possibility of ozone depletion, and the effects of increasing amounts of "greenhouse gases" in the atmosphere, among other things. The debates among scientists are generally over details and degrees of certainty. Many members of the general public, however, would rather believe that scientists are flat wrong about the existence of environmental hazards. Some steadfastly refuse to recognize potential future hazards and even accuse scientists of being environmentalist extremists who are out to destroy people's way of life.

In this section, researchers and analysts offer their projections for the future with regard to some of society's current environmental concerns.

■ Can the World Continue to Feed Billions
   of People?

■ Can the Sun Supply Our Energy Needs?

■ Is Ozone Depletion a Genuine Threat?

■ Should Society Be Concerned About
   Global Warming?

ISSUE 5

Can the World Continue to Feed Billions of People?

YES: David Norse, from "A New Strategy for Feeding a Crowded Planet," *Environment* (June 1992)

NO: K. O. Emery, from "Uncontrolled Growth of Human Populations, Geological Background, and Future Prospects," *Population and Environment: A Journal of Interdisciplinary Studies* (March 1994)

ISSUE SUMMARY

YES: Researcher David Norse argues that sustainable agriculture and greater equity in food distribution can ensure adequate food for a much greater human population than that which exists today.

NO: Marine geologist K. O. Emery asserts that if the population explosion is not reversed, then the population will grow beyond what the Earth's resources can accommodate, and the human species may become extinct.

In 1798, the British economist Thomas Malthus published his *Essay on the Principle of Population*. In it, he expressed alarm at the way the human population grew geometrically (a hockey-stick curve of increase) while agricultural productivity grew only arithmetically (a straight-line increase). It was obvious, he said, that the population must inevitably outstrip its food supply and experience famine. Contrary to the conventional wisdom of the time, Malthus argued, population growth was not necessarily a good thing. Indeed, it led inexorably to catastrophe.

For many years, Malthus was something of a laughingstock. The doom he forecast kept receding into the future as new lands were opened to agriculture, new agricultural technologies were developed, and new ways of preserving food were adopted, limiting the waste of spoilage. The food supply stayed ahead of population growth and seemed likely—to most observers —to continue to do so. Malthus's ideas were dismissed as irrelevant fantasies.

Yet, population continued to grow. In Malthus's time, there were about 1 billion human beings on Earth. By 1950—the year that Warren S. Thompson wrote that civilization would be endangered by the rapid growth of Asian and Latin American populations during the ensuing five decades ("Population," *Scientific American*, February 1950)—there were a little over 2.5 billion. In 1995, the tally will approach 5.8 billion people on Earth. Although global agricultural production has also increased, it has not kept up with rising demand, and, because of the loss of topsoil to erosion, the exhaustion of aquifers for irrigation water, and the high price of energy for making fertilizer (among other things), the prospect of improvement seems to many observers exceedingly slim. In fact, the statistics presented in *World Resources 1994–95* (Oxford University Press, 1994), a report of the World Resources Institute in collaboration with the United Nations Environment and Development Programmes, are positively frightening to many people.

Some people still laugh at Malthus and his forecasts of doom that two centuries never saw come to pass. Among his detractors is economist Julian Simon, who believes that more people on Earth means more talent available for solving problems and that humans can indeed find ways around all possible resource shortages (see his essay, "Life on Earth Is Getting Better, Not Worse," *The Futurist*, August 1983).

But more and more people—including some economists—are coming to believe that Malthus's error lay not in his prediction but in his timing. There is a growing consensus that Malthus was quite correct to say that a growing population must inevitably outrun its food supply; the only question is how long human ingenuity can stave off the day of reckoning.

How long can human ingenuity sustain the growing population? The World Resources Institute sets the global human population at about 8.5 billion in 2025. By 2050, the population is expected to hit 10 billion *and to be still rising;* some estimates peg the 2050 population at 12.5 billion. The United Nations expects that *if* human fertility can be controlled, the population may stabilize in the neighborhood of 11.5 billion by 2150.

Can the human race possibly survive that long? There are famines in the world *today.* Won't they grow far worse long before the population doubles—indeed, well before it hits the 10 billion (or more) mark in 2050? Not necessarily, says David Norse, a research associate for the Overseas Development Institute in London. He argues that with suitable attention to more ecologically sustainable agricultural practices and to better distribution of food supplies, the planet can support many more people. Although Norse admits that it will not be easy, he is optimistic that the productive capacity of agriculture can be increased and sustained.

K. O. Emery, of the Woods Hole Oceanographic Institution, is less optimistic. He maintains that Malthus was correct, and he argues that we must reduce and reverse human population growth to ensure the continued survival of the species.

YES

David Norse

A NEW STRATEGY FOR FEEDING A CROWDED PLANET

How many is too many? Is planet Earth really in danger of collapsing because of overpopulation? How valid is the recent joint statement by the U.S. National Academy of Sciences and the U.K. Royal Society that, "If current predictions of population growth prove accurate and pattern of human activity on the planet remain unchanged, science and technology may not be able to prevent either irreversible degradation of the environment or continued poverty for much of the world"?

Similar warnings were given by the British economist Thomas Malthus in 1798, when Earth's population was only about 1 billion; yet 5.3 billion people are now supported, albeit inadequately in many cases, by Earth's bounty. Malthus's warning of collapse was wrong because he had a static view of science and technology and of how they could compensate for the lack of land by raising agricultural productivity, for example, through irrigation and fertilization.

More recent assessments have taken account of technology to a greater or lesser extent. Some of them, however, surpassed Malthus's perception of the problem to introduce technology itself as an additional factor that could lead to collapse. For instance, such production inputs as mineral fertilizers and pesticides have been cited for causing environmental damage when they are applied incorrectly or excessively.

Earlier estimates of the maximum human population that Earth could support were methodologically weak and primarily concerned with the ratio of humans to land. More recent estimation techniques are more sophisticated and commonly use the concept of Earth's human-carrying capacity (or potential population-supporting capacity) to introduce agroecological and other factors into the analysis. The carrying capacity of a particular region is the maximum population of a given species that can be supported indefinitely, allowing for seasonal and random changes, without any degradation of the natural resource base that would diminish this maximum population in the future.

From David Norse, "A New Strategy for Feeding a Crowded Planet," *Environment*, vol. 34, no. 5 (June 1992), pp. 6–9, 11, 33–38. Copyright © 1992 by The Helen Dwight Reid Educational Foundation. Reprinted by permission of Heldref Publications, 1319 18th St., NW, Washington, DC 20036-1802. Notes omitted.

The concept was first used by ecologists and zoologists to describe the ability of natural ecosystems to support wildlife populations. If wildlife populations exceed the natural food supply available locally or through migration, population collapse is inevitable. But, whereas the carrying capacity of natural ecosystems is essentially static, that of managed agroecosystems is dynamic. A region's human-carrying capacity can be increased by raising land and labor productivity or through trade with better endowed regions.

Prior to about 1850, the world's human population could be fed, clothed, and otherwise supported by relatively limited modifications to natural ecosystems. Since then, however, and at an accelerating pace since about 1945, the food supply—and hence the carrying capacity—has become increasingly dependent on science-based agriculture and on external inputs of nonrenewable resources (notably fossil fuels and rock phosphate). Thus has arisen the critical question of sustainable agricultural development and the role of the United Nations Conference on Environment and Development (UNCED)... in effecting the necessary changes to achieve it.

... [E]ven a general assessment of the major threats to Earth's long-term carrying capacity reveals the need for a new strategy for sustainable agriculture.

Before addressing these issues, however, it should be stated that asking what the human-carrying capacity is or asking how many people can be fed is dodging the issue in two important respects. First, it is posing the problem as a supply problem stemming from the lack of production potential, whereas the demand problem is more serious and its analysis should take precedence over any theoretical estimates of carrying capacity. The 500 million to 1 billion people who go hungry each day do so because they are too poor to buy all of the food they need. Thus, the central issues should be the elimination of poverty, the resolution of the debt crisis, and the removal of developed countries' trade barriers that prevent developing countries and their people from raising their incomes. Second, the momentum of human population growth is so great and so insensitive to minor changes in mortality, migration, and fertility rates that world population will grow by some 3 billion between now and 2025, the year chosen as UNCED's development horizon, unless the AIDS pandemic goes out of control or unless socially unacceptable forms of family size limitation are adopted. Thus, the issue is not whether Earth can support a population of 8.6 billion or so in 2025—it will have to—but, rather, whether it can do so sustainably.

THE GLOBAL PICTURE

Almost 200 years have passed since Malthus first raised doubts about the global carrying capacity, and the global population has increased fivefold. Still, the debate continues, with estimates of carrying capacity ranging from 2 billion to 30 billion people. The issue was widely discussed in the aftermath of World War II and came back into prominence in the late 1960s and early 1970s, when various individuals and computer modeling groups, particularly those supported by the Club of Rome, argued that projected population growth, excessive demands on the natural resource base, and pollution would overburden the biosphere and cause its collapse. This was the basic message of the club's *The Limits to*

Growth [1972] report that shocked many people into examining the whole question of growth in a finite world. Other analysts, however, while not denying the seriousness of present population and pollution trends, have concluded that collapse is avoidable with relatively minor and equally realistic changes in the assumptions about the rate of technological growth (that is, faster), and about how prices and demand respond to scarcity of natural resources.

Dutch scientists belonging to one of the modeling groups set up by the Club of Rome produced the first comprehensive assessment of global carrying capacity. The scientists disaggregated the world's land resources into 222 broad soil regions with known climatic, vegetative, and topographic characteristics and irrigation potential. Maximum production potential per hectare was calculated in units of "cereal equivalents" for each of these soil regions and then summed to give a total maximum production of some 50 billion tonnes of cereal equivalent per year. However, this estimate is a theoretical maximum assuming the use of all of the land potentially suitable for farming (3.4 billion hectares compared with the 1.5 billion hectares that are currently farmed), no pests and diseases, no plant nutrient shortages, and no water constraints. Acknowledging that such assumptions are unrealistic, the scientists later applied a range of reduction factors for land availability, average attainable yields, seed requirements, storage losses, and so on to arrive at estimates of potential production of consumable grain. A comparison was also made between potential production using the full package of modern inputs and that from labor-oriented agriculture without the use of tractors, modern machines, pesticides, or fertilizers....

These output figures were roughly transformed into carrying capacity terms by assuming an average grain consumption of 800 kilograms per capita per year. The resulting global carrying capacities were 6.7 billion people for the modern system and 2.7 billion for the labor-oriented production system. It is interesting to compare these results with some other, back-of-the-envelope estimates. F. Baade, for example, assuming that the arable land area was between 2 billion and 3 billion hectares and that average yields could rise to 5 tonnes of cereal equivalent per hectare, estimated the potential carrying capacity at some 30 billion. No consideration was given to whether production could be sustained at this level; to whether all arable land would be used for agriculture; or to the increase in indirect demands for cereals as people switch to higher value but lower calorie-content foods when their income grows.

Roger Revelle and Bernard Gilland made assumptions similar to Baade's regarding potential crop yields, that is, about 5 tonnes of cereal equivalent per hectare. Revelle also assumed that much of the potentially arable land would be used for food production, whereas Gilland doubted whether the area available for sustainable agriculture would be much greater than the present one. At an average per-capita grain consumption of 800 kilograms per year, Baade's carrying capacity estimate becomes more than 18 billion, Revelle's becomes 14 billion, and Gilland's is 8.8 billion. These estimates exclude the output of rangelands, pastures, and fisheries, which could raise carrying capacity by more than 10 percent at the global level and by considerably more in certain regions....

LIMITATIONS TO THE CONCEPT

... [T]here are important limitations to the utility of the carrying capacity concept. As the saying goes, man does not live by bread alone, and people and countries are seldom entirely dependent on food production, agriculture, or their natural resource base for the means to ensure adequate access to basic needs. It is becoming increasingly clear, however, that at least part of this reduced dependence is a response to population pressures on the natural resource base. Poor farm families are diversifying their income sources to cope with population pressures and food production instability. Farmers may be able to meet their basic needs in a more sustainable way by producing export crops, for example, and buying their food requirements. Thus, in the Ivory Coast, oil palm production is four to five times more profitable than maize production. Moreover, oil palm cultivation is generally a more ecologically sound form of land use in tropical areas with high rainfall than is monocultural maize production.

Countries are seldom totally dependent on agriculture. Even in highly agrarian countries like Bangladesh, agriculture accounts for only 50 percent of the gross domestic product. At the other extreme, in countries like Switzerland and Singapore, the agricultural resource base no longer plays a significant role. As long as these countries use their capital bases well, the carrying capacity of their own lands will be of secondary importance. Thus, many of the critical countries identified by the FAO/IIASA study [on agroecological zones and their population-supporting capacity, completed in 1982 by the UN Food and Agriculture Organization (FAO) and the International Institute for Applied Systems Analysis (IIASA)] are not in danger of collapse because they can buy their way out of trouble, provided, of course, that the major food-exporting countries avoid serious land degradation and thus maintain their export potential.

... [A]ssuming that recent growth rates in technology continue, it appears that most countries have adequate land or other resources to carry their projected populations for 2025. Land and resources may even be sufficient over the very long term, when Earth's population is expected to stabilize at around 11 billion after about 2100, provided that the wasteful consumption patterns of the developed countries are not taken as the universal model and that satisfactory answers can be found to the following questions:

• Can agricultural production be increased fast enough to keep ahead of population growth?
• Will some of the carrying capacity potential be lost because of land degradation and other factors?
• What changes are required to shift from the present unsustainable development path?

PRODUCTION VS. POPULATION

Most carrying capacity studies make three major assumptions regarding the first question—namely that crop production will win the competition for land against livestock and forestry, and losses from urban and industrial development will not be serious; that crop yields can increase fast enough; and that food prices will not rise beyond people's ability to pay.

Historically, crop production has almost always won the competition for land. Increased desertification caused by crop production displaces livestock onto more and more marginal land and causes high rates of tropical deforestation, of which from one-half to two-thirds results from shifting cultivation. Competition for land from urban and industrial development, however, could become increasingly serious. Much of this development will involve the expansion of existing conurbations, which are often located on coastal plains and in river valleys with some of the best soils. Once these soils are built on, they are lost forever. Few of the developed countries had effective land-use policies to protect such soils before the 1960s and 1970s. It is not surprising, therefore, that many developing countries are finding it difficult to introduce the necessary policies, and so, nearly 300 million hectares—one-quarter of all highly arable land—are at risk.

The expansion of crop production through 2025 seems likely to cause the loss of some 180 million hectares of rangeland and forests, whose soils are only marginally suitable for annual crop production and need very careful management if degradation is to be avoided. Such losses are likely to have spill-over effects in terms of greater risks of overgrazing and intensification of the fuelwood crisis. Thus, it is vital for policymakers to focus on raising the productivity and employment requirements of the existing crop land so as to reduce the pressure for the cultivation of and migration onto these marginal lands.

Two facts cast doubt on whether it is possible for the rate of crop-yield increase to keep pace with population growth.

First, staple crop yields in many sub-Saharan countries have been essentially static for the past 10 years or more. The reasons are complex. In part, static yields stem from weak government policies that have failed to give adequate price incentives and infrastructural support to producers. But they also reflect the widespread lack of appropriate technologies and the failure of research systems to develop sustainable technologies that match the perceptions and resources of small farmers.

Second, although other regions have been more successful than sub-Saharan Africa at raising yields, there is growing concern that the future production potential may be insufficient. In parts of Asia, for example, experimental yields for irrigated wheat and rice fields seem to have reached a plateau. Maximum yields have been static for some 10 to 20 years. Meanwhile, average yields still fall well short of experimental yields and are unlikely to match them entirely, but there is still a yield gap to be closed. Thus, it seems possible that recent trends in yield growth will continue for another one or two decades. Thereafter, however, the evidence suggests that it will become increasingly difficult to prevent a slow decline in yield growth unless research achieves another shift on the production frontier. Whether advances in biotechnology will provide the solution is still an open question.

There remains the assumption regarding affordability. Current estimates of the number of malnourished people range from 500 million to 1 billion. The numbers are not expected to decline appreciably, at least in the mid term. By and large, people are malnourished because they are too poor to buy all of their needs. Purchasing power, however, has not been considered by a carrying capacity study conducted to date.

Projections suggest that future food prices will remain more or less constant in real terms for the next decade or so, as long as market mechanisms operate efficiently and the apparent crop yield ceiling is breached. If these projections are correct, the strains on carrying capacity will stem primarily from income growth. In the middle-income countries where people are consuming increasing amounts of livestock products, carrying capacity ceilings are already being breached because of the lack of grazing land and the greater cost-efficiency of raising dairy cattle, pigs, and poultry on feed grains. Many countries are currently or will soon be unable to produce these feed grains in adequate quantities. They will become increasingly dependent on feed grain imports, and part of the environmental costs of production will be transferred to exporting countries like the United States, Canada, Argentina, and Thailand.

THE EFFECTS OF SOIL DEGRADATION

... [T]here are other threats ... that cannot be dismissed, particularly those from land degradation and climate change. Over the past millennium, humanity has degraded about 2 billion hectares of land, though only a small proportion of this area is too degraded to remain in agricultural use. More recent estimates suggest that the present situation is much worse. For example, a recent study for the UN Environment Programme called the Global Assessment of Soil Degradation (GLASOD) concludes that people have degraded about 25 percent of the occupied land, and much of this

damage has been caused in the past 50 years. The most serious causes of degradation are water erosion through deforestation (43 percent), overgrazing (29 percent), and poor farming practices (24 percent). Population pressure on marginal lands plus mismanagement of the better soils may have accelerated land degradation over the past 20 years to reach some 5 million to 6 million hectares annually.

Much of this degradation has stripped the land of soil. The quantities involved are immense. The current rate of soil erosion in excess of new soil production has been estimated at some 23 billion tonnes per year. If the global soil reservoir is declining at about 0.7 percent annually, between 20 and 25 percent of the total could be lost by 2025.

These soil losses sound disastrous, but scientists and economists are unsure of their long-term implications. Estimating the consequences of this degradation for soil productivity and, hence, for human-carrying capacity is very difficult. There have been few well-conducted experiments on the relationship between soil degradation and crop yield losses, and most of them apply only to conditions in developed countries. Consequently, such estimations rely heavily on subjective judgements. Nonetheless, the GLASOD study concludes that some 295 million hectares are so degraded that restoration of the land to full productivity is beyond the normal means of a farmer but that these hectares could be restored with major investments. (There is, of course, substantial uncertainty about the cost of land restoration. The GLASOD estimates are based largely on formal project costs, but ... a number of NGO [nongovernmental organization] and community-based actions show that quite extreme degradation can be corrected profitably and at modest costs.) An even greater area—910 million hectares—is moderately degraded to the point that the original biotic functions are partly destroyed and agricultural productivity is greatly reduced. If these estimates are correct, human-carrying capacity has already been seriously undermined, and the present trend is for even greater damage in the future unless corrective actions are given much greater priority.

Substantiating evidence for this view comes from two other directions. Studies of soil nutrient balance in which rates of nutrient removal by crops, soil erosion, leaching, and other factors are set against nutrient inputs from natural soil processes, dust, rain, manures, and mineral fertilizers indicate that widespread soil nutrient mining is taking place, particularly in sub-Saharan Africa, where food production has failed to keep up with population growth for the past 20 years. This conclusion is supported by a number of other experiments that have compared declining yields and fertilizer response ratios over time. It appears that one of the consequences of nutrient mining has been unfertilized base yields. In areas of Ghana, Malawi, Kenya, and Java, for example, the base yields of cereals have been falling by 2 to 10 percent per year for the past 10 to 20 years. Such losses are clearly unsustainable over the long term. The reasons are complex. Contributing factors include nutrient mining, as well as physical and chemical damage to soil through erosion, loss of organic matter and soil moisture-holding capacity, and the buildup of soil pests and diseases caused by reduced fallows. Mineral fertilizers can compensate for such damage to a substantial degree, but they are too expensive for poor farmers or often simply unprofitable. And sometimes, mineral fertilizers are insufficient to restore fertility. Inputs of organic manures are required to achieve fertility, but the supply is commonly inadequate.

Attempts have been made to place these physical losses from land degradation in their national economic contexts. Recent estimates suggest that, if remedial action is not taken, Ghana could lose 7 percent of its gross national product because of land degradation and that Nigeria could lose more than 17 percent of its gross national product because of deforestation, soil degradation, water contamination, and other environmental problems over the long term. Again the message is clear: Land degradation at current rates will reduce carrying capacity both by lowering agricultural production potential and by lowering the ability of countries to import food.

These losses seem destined to be compounded by climate change. A scientific concensus has emerged during the past five years or so that the threat to food production is real, though the timing and regional pattern of climate change's impacts is still uncertain. Climate change could seriously threaten carrying capacity and sustainable agriculture in certain regions, though there may be both winners and losers from climate change. Some regions and countries may benefit from greater agricultural productivity because of temperature and rainfall increases and because of carbon dioxide's enhancement of plant growth.

Two major concerns are that some of the countries most at risk are already very vulnerable to food shortages and close to their human-carrying capacity if crop yields cannot be raised and that population pressure's negative impacts on the environment may increase both the intensity of and the land's vulnerability to climate change. In the case of some Sahelian countries, for example, the analog approach to impact analysis suggests that the potential human-carrying capacity from domestic agriculture could fall by some 30 percent if climate change causes a decline in rainfall similar to that experienced in the 1965 to 1985 drought.

A more recent analysis for Senegal that built on a carrying capacity model developed by the U.S. Geological Survey and on crop models from the Institut Senegalais de Recherche Agricole came to similar conclusions. Rain-fed production potential is projected to decrease 30 percent in spite of adaptive responses to climate change—a reduction equivalent to the food needs of 1 million to 2 million people. Related impact analyses focusing on maize production in Zimbabwe, where conditions are not so arid as in Senegal, have projected a smaller impact. Rain-fed yields should fall by less than 20 percent, in part because the positive effect of higher atmospheric carbon dioxide concentrations compensates partially for the negative impact of higher temperatures. What is more worrying, however, is the projected increase in the variability of rainfall and, hence, crop yield, which could seriously lower food security and increase the financial risk of using the mineral fertilizers essential for maintaining soil fertility.

A NEW STRATEGY

A new strategy is required that is the opposite in many respects to current policies. Present strategies tend to focus on four aspects of agricultural development —incentives, inputs, institutions, and infrastructures—and on the investments required by them and tend to give inade-

quate attention to sustainability. The new strategy should be more concerned with decentralized natural resource management by the farmers and communities that will ultimately decide the strategy's appropriateness and success. The strategy should therefore focus on local-level husbandry and development controlled by local community or user-based institutions, such as grazing associations and water-user groups, rather than on sophisticated institutional structures for national or regional land-use planning, for example, or for investment allocation. Of course, such structures do have an important role to play, provided that they are economically sustainable by the nations concerned and that they provide incentives rather than top-down directives for resource development and management. The issue is not top-down versus bottom-up; both approaches are needed, but they must be consistent with each other, and they must promote a convergence of national goals and local priorities.

The decentralization of decisionmaking can only lead to a socially desirable and sustainable allocation of productive and environmental resources if other requirements are met. For example, the responsibilities and entitlements of farmers and rural communities must also be decentralized through the clear allocation of property rights and environmental resources. User groups and similar bodies must have the power to raise revenues from resource users for operation, maintenance, and further development of those resources. Commodity prices must reflect as much as possible the full environmental costs of a given resource use, besides providing adequate incentives to producers. Once governments have provided the infrastructure to ensure market access and have set appropriate environmental standards and taxes on discharges to protect public goods, government intervention should be kept to a minimum so that markets can function efficiently.

The strategy should be built around four critical components of resource management—soil fertility management; integrated pest management; water management; and integrated crop, livestock, and tree management—and around their greater integration. Past efforts by public and private development organizations, however, have often followed a relatively uniform approach centered on encouraging the use of one or a limited number of purchased production inputs.

Many past conservation measures that have failed were not profitable, except possibly in the long term. Priority should be given to resource conservation actions that quickly raise productivity and farmers' incomes. Some of the required conservation techniques are already available. In many cases, however, new technologies must be developed for, or existing ones adapted to, specific ecological conditions. This development and adaptation will take several years, substantial research funding, and a change in research and extension techniques.

More emphasis is required on biological approaches to resource management, including

- biological (as opposed to engineering) approaches to soil and moisture conservation, such as maintaining continuous ground cover with live mulches;
- biological inputs to integrated pest management systems to minimize pesticide inputs; and
- biological sources of nitrogen to replace or, in most instances, to complement mineral sources (phosphorus and other nutrients commonly have to come from mineral sources).

This emphasis on biological approaches would not contradict efforts to promote the use of mineral fertilizers and other off-farm inputs. These will continue to be a prime contributor to increased agricultural production for the foreseeable future, but there are situations where such inputs are too costly and are therefore not a viable solution. In these situations, biological approaches can complement or substitute for off-farm inputs to reduce production costs and maximize environmental sustainability. It is this balance that the proposed strategy seeks to achieve.

The new strategy differs from past ones in that it addresses sustainability problems through their social and cultural determinants or through the institutional constraints that have previously blocked such approaches, rather than treating them as environmental problems to be addressed by technical solutions developed in isolation from the ultimate users. Consequently, it stresses the evolutionary approach in which changes in farming practices build on indigenous knowledge, rather than the prevailing step-wise or single-component approach, and focuses on improvements in both the levels and the stability of yields instead of just maximum yields. This evolutionary approach concentrates on highly informed but low-risk and low-cost measures to minimize the need for credit-demanding technologies involving extensive use of off-farm inputs that are more suited to large-scale farmers, but it does not ignore the needs of the latter nor the fact that such technologies can be equally suited to small farmers in very fertile areas. Large farms will continue to play a critical role in producing food for urban populations and other net food buyers and as major suppliers of export crops. Most farmers need better support regarding water supply management and integrated pest management and help in minimizing or preventing some of the environmental problems commonly associated with large-scale, intensive farming systems.

Three main conclusions can be drawn from this discussion. First, there are some grounds for optimism regarding humanity's ability to raise and sustain agriculture's carrying capacity at the global and regional levels. This optimism, however, is contingent on major policy changes regarding international equity and the ecological soundness of technological growth. It is difficult, however, to see how some countries can sustain their projected populations through agriculture or other economic activities. The pressure for international migration may therefore be substantial.

Second, and further tempering optimism, there are a number of uncertainties about the future that support the increasing calls for the adoption of the precautionary principle to provide "a scientifically sound basis for policies relating to complex systems that are so poorly understood that the consequences of dis-turbances cannot yet be predicted. According to this principle, highest priority should be given to reducing the two greatest disturbances to Planet Earth: the growth of human population and over-consumption of resources." These uncertainties include: the rate of deceleration in population growth, given that policy inaction could seriously delay the achievement of a stable population; the loss of arable land to urban development; the long-term consequences of soil degradation; the impacts of climate change; and the ability of science to continue to raise agricultural productivity.

Third, if the concept of carrying capacity is to be introduced more centrally into the debate on sustainable development, it has to be widened to embrace economic as well as environmental considerations and complemented by a new strategy for sustainable agriculture. Many poor farmers are forced to use unsustainable agricultural practices for a variety of institutional and economic reasons. In their struggle to satisfy current food needs, they have to place at risk the long-term carrying capacity of their land. Fine ecological words and appeals on behalf of future generations will not sway them unless the required changes in land management practices will also raise present-day household security.

NO

K. O. Emery

UNCONTROLLED GROWTH OF HUMAN POPULATIONS, GEOLOGICAL BACKGROUND, AND FUTURE PROSPECTS

GEOLOGICAL EVIDENCE OF ABRUPT CHANGES IN POPULATIONS

The geological record shows that animals that evolved in especially favorable environments proliferate until they reduce their environments to unfavorable levels by exhaustion of available food supplies, crowding, or accumulation of waste products. At that stage the animals face serious competition from successors that are hardier or more adaptable. Commonly, an environment undergoes periodic or episodic changes that at first may have little effect upon inhabitants, but after some longterm deterioration, similar changes can become unbearable for later and larger populations. Survivors then may die or emigrate. This sequence has occurred in the geological record of life on the Earth during at least the past 570 million years—after animals had begun to develop hard skeletal parts that could be preserved and later be collected and studied. Such fossil remains are used by geologists—paleontologists for determining relative ages of strata. Most useful are fossils of species whose numbers increased very rapidly, became widespread, reached high concentrations, and then suddenly disappeared never again to reappear. These are known as guide fossils, some of which are useful for dating strata within time ranges of less than a few million years.... Organisms that are more tolerant or hardier are useful to geologists only for dating strata having longer spans of habitation. A few organisms made so little demand upon their environments or represented so little competition to others which shared the same environment that their species have lived little changed for many tens or even hundreds of millions of years....

The history of *Homo sapiens* (beginning about 350,000 years ago, but especially during the past century) clearly parallels that of other animals which have inhabited less extensive regions of the Earth and have placed much smaller demands upon the Earth and its resources. Similarity of history suggests a likely similar future for humans, but one that can be accelerated because of the much greater effects of humans than of other animals on the environment, or delayed if humans can take measures to reduce their effects on the environment....

POPULATION EXPLOSION

An illustration of the situation which the human race is experiencing is that of potentially uncontrolled growth of bacteria. One tiny cell and its progeny are capable of doubling in less than a second. If sufficient food were available, one cell and its progeny theoretically could reproduce enough times to equal the mass of the entire Earth in less than two days. Growth of human populations, though much slower, also exhibits prodigious levels: about 10 million people 12,000 years ago, 300 million at the time of Christ, 1.7 billion in 1750, 2.5 billion in 1950, 5 billion in 1987, and perhaps 10 billion about the year 2050. Present doubling time is now only about 35 years, shorter than during the past and hopefully shorter than for the future. At this rate the world population would be about 43 billion in 2090. Hern likened this rapid growth and its many forms to growth of malignant tumors. Most of the present population increase is occurring in lesser-developed countries.

Restraint on geometric expansion during the ancient past was provided by the Four Horsemen of the Apocalypse: War, Famine, Pestilence, and Wild Beasts. These particular restraints now are limited, but not eliminated, by politically good-hearted but sometimes short-sighted means: United Nations' and developed nations' opposition to war (only moderately successful, as illustrated by

aftermaths to World War I—the 'War to End Wars'), transfer of food and money to chronically famine-stricken regions, and promotion of public health measures within densely-populated lesser-developed nations by industrial nations, churches, charitable organizations, and many individuals. The objective has been to reduce infant death rates and increase longevity of adults. Increased longevity is illustrated by a comparison of life expectancy in the United States of white males at birth: 38 years in 1850, 61 in 1935 when Social Security was designed, to 72 in 1988; for white females the expectancy was 40, 65, and 79 years, respectively. For all other males the life expectancy at birth in 1900, 1935, and 1988 was 33, 50, and 67, and for females 35, 53, and 75 years, respectively. Curiously, at the same time, governments of some industrial nations largely through religious and charitable motives promote increases in their own populations by providing income-tax credits for dependents, welfare support for children and mother-headed families, and widespread opposition to birth-control measures—especially to abortion that is the only recourse when contraceptives fail. Opposition in the United States included raising funds to oppose abortion rights in the courts and pro- and anti-abortion newspaper stories to influence election of congressmen; no attention was paid to effects of proliferating populations in these and other "pro-life" solicitations. During 1991 the United States' federally-funded prenatal and family-planning clinics were forbidden even to answer clients' questions about abortion! Only China has approached effective governmental control over birth rates, but its policies have become biased toward eliminating baby girls—a choice that is not approved in most other nations.

Measures that avoid uncontrolled increases in numbers of farm animals have long been taken by managers of live stock used for food, especially chickens and other fowls, pigs, sheep, and cows. These measures stem partly from economics: not to waste valuable food and not to produce more animals than can be used or sold. But they also are based upon recognition that animals, like plants, flourish best when given appropriate quantities of correct food, adequate space, selection for breeding, and adequate medial and other care. The same considerations are used for breeding of dogs and cats for domestic pets, horses for sport and show, various animals for zoos, and general wildlife—such as deer and rabbits whose numbers easily can outgrow food supplies and space, leading to their starvation. Similar thought is not being applied to human populations.

When farming and herding developed about 12,000 years ago, the increased food supply for humans led to increased commerce, shipping, writing, medicine, music, concern about existence after death, religion, and many other amenities that were difficult for nomadic gatherers and hunters to attain. During the twentieth century, migrations of small groups of people from lesser-developed industrial nations were followed by increases in stature, weight, life expectancy, and health of immigrant offspring made possible by availability of more and better food. Awareness of national differences in standards of living and in political treatments led to many desperate but nearly forgotten migrations centuries ago as well as during just the past few decades: the boat people from Vietnam, Cuba, and Haiti, flights past the Berlin Wall, and escapes from the People's Republic of China after the June 1989 event in Tiananmen Square [where students protesting for a more democratic government were massacred by Chinese soldiers]. Migrations for other reasons also have occurred, but most dramatic are those of escapes from shortages and repressions in the communist "peoples paradises" and from the rules of absolute dictators....

This background information is widely known, but the conclusion that it forces upon the human race is nearly completely avoided: that Malthus was correct—human population is certain to outrun the discovery, development, and distribution of resources required for sustaining that population: food, clothing, shelter, safety, and transport....

The annual rates of increase in populations now average from about 0.3% in Europe, through 2.9% in Africa, to 3.3% in southern Asia and South America. For individual nations the average rate of increase in populations ranges between 0.0 and about 4.0%—lower than the average birth rates of 1.0 to 5.1% largely because of high mortality of infants in poorer nations. In general, low birth rates, low rates of population increase, and high life expectancy occur in nations that have high percentages of literacy. Similarly, high gross national products (GNP) per capita and higher use of energy occur in nations having high literacy.... There is no clear relationship of population concentration per unit area with literacy, GNP/capita, or total national population. Because of this lack of relationship Le Bras saw no reason for alarm over future greatly increased human populations, but he did not consider the consequent increased demand for food, energy, metals, and other resources. Incidentally, the population of the largest city in nations is proportional to the total population of its nations—ranging near 10%; a possible increase in this ratio with time may indicate a general shift from farm to urban life.

Populations of lesser-developed nations have tried several different remedies for coping with their increased population relative to resources: asking for and receiving transfers of food and skills from industrialized nations (often almost immediately after becoming independent), increased migration to industrialized nations, and overexploitation of their environments. Tropical rain forests of Africa and South America now are being destroyed rapidly in attempts to convert unsuitable land areas to farming and herding, causing depletion of exportable timber and exhaustion of firewood, fossil-energy fuels, metals, and wild-animal products, as well as inadvertently and markedly reducing species diversity of animals. In the end, most such measures are considered likely to prove more harmful than beneficial and to further reduce capability of the lands to support indigeneous populations. Other examples of environmental destruction were initiated by industrial nations. They include the buildup of industrial gases in the atmosphere (the greenhouse heating effect), acid rain from some of the same gases, possible depletion of the ozone layer (by release of chlorofluorocarbons used in refrigeration and air-conditioning systems), continuing soil erosion, and widespread pollution of land, water, and atmosphere by wastes. Many of these effects of pollution may be removed in a self-healing and evolutionary treatment of the Earth ... if the rates of direct pollution can begin to be reduced by human populations.

THE DILEMMA

Is the human race capable of avoiding the cycles of drastically increased populations terminated by extinctions that have occurred for many species of animals during the geological past? Procreation is a private affair, but the results of too prolific procreation can affect the future of all humans on the Earth, and thus broad guidance may be needed for individuals who may be unaware of the cumulative effects of private actions or are unconcerned by them. Several main broad guidance systems should be considered here: religion, government controls, education, and culture. All are systems through which humans may be able to control their future—the teleological approach....

Government Controls
Government controls may have some potential for reducing population growth, but to-date most government efforts have been directed toward increasing populations in order to augment national military or industrial power, or to exhibit short-term concern for the welfare of children and their mothers.

What can the industrialized nations (that probably alone can understand the problems and perhaps solve them) do to avoid a serious sudden decrease of the proliferating human race because of progressive reduction in resources per capita? Unlimited acceptance of immigrants merely moves some offspring of more prolific populations of the world into regions having previously lesser rates of population increase, thereby expanding the problem. Transfer of more food and amenities from industrialized to lesser-developed nations must produce even faster increases in populations of the latter and ensure future increased difficulties. At present, the United States distributes an annual total of about $12 billion of food, credits, and/or military supplies among about two-third of the nations of the world, a total of $313 billion since 1945; additional such 'aid' is contributed by many other industrialized nations. In any event, these exchanges must increase the problems, and they eventually would produce a more homogeneous world with widespread life near the edge of poverty and starvation.

Wars of extermination are politically unthinkable, as illustrated by the world's reaction to the Nazi policy of eliminating Jews and other minorities in Europe before and during World War II. Education about the expected future might help, except that the literacy of populations in most lesser-developed nations is low. Certainly, many nations would view any restriction on growth of the have-nots as politically biased, and they would refuse to comply; however, without some solution that can change the trend of increasing world populations and decreasing world resources per capita, the human population of the entire world is heading toward catastrophe. A special and abrupt example can be a nuclear winter, when widespread nuclear warfare may produce so much dust and smoke as to resemble the great reduction of photosynthesis and extinction of many animal species that was produced probably by impact of a comet 65 million years ago.

Regional and global reductions of food supplies per capita have many causes: poor farming practices that increase rates of soil erosion, covering of farm and orchard land by expanding cities and proliferating highways to accommodate increasing human populations, exhaustion of water supplies by excessive use of water for sanitation and even growth of lawn in deserts (as in southern California), overfishing that has depleted stocks of desirable marine species (lobsters, sardines, tunas, whales, and even large sharks), septic and industrial pollution of coastal waters (reducing production of clams, oysters, and others), and pollution of freshwater bodies by wastes from wood-pulp production and other industries (diminishing trout, salmon, sturgeon, and others). Industrial and domestic pollution also has affected the air that is required by plants and animals, increasing the carbon dioxide content, possibly increasing the air temperature, producing smog from burning of fossil fuels in power plants, industry, and automobiles, and releasing sulfur compounds from the same sources followed by transportation in winds and rains to damage forests and acidify lakes, thereby reducing habitability for fish and other aquatic organisms. Land areas also are subject to despoliation by wasteful human practices—elimination of rain forests to produce quick profits in lumber-logging at rates enormously in excess of natural replacement, strip mining of coal without renewing original topography for other uses, mining of metals at depth followed by abandonment of mines and collapse of the ground surface, production and burial of increasing amounts of trash including radioactive and harmful chemical wastes, and worst of all from vindictiveness, as exemplified by the attempted destruction of about 700 producing oil wells leading to pollution of land, ocean, and air in Kuwait by the retreating Iraqi army during 1990–1991. This act had the additional effect of reducing future supplies of oil and gas needed for fuel and industrial feed stock in the face of decreasing rates of discovery of new petroleum resources, although it did not seriously affect world climate. Most of the wasteful actions have been permitted or caused by national governments through encouragement of policies by officials (politicians) usually intended to improve short-range conditions for their general publics....

Many town governments especially of England and northeastern United States long ago set aside plots of land as Commons to be used by citizens for free grazing of their live stock. Inevitably, the total number of live stock surpassed the carrying capacity of land, because the benefit of the "Commons" to each new individual live-stock owner exceeded the loss to individual former live-stock owners by the resulting decrease in carrying capacity of the Commons. This relationship (The Problem of the Commons) is a small illustration of the effect on the entire world of a drastic increase in the total human world population with a consequent decrease in the world's resources per capita and eventually in terms of absolute amounts of available resources. Much concern is now being expressed by the media, by politicians seeking re-election, and by well-meaning individuals and nations for alleviating both local and world-wide shortages of food and other resources, and for eliminating or reducing pollution within the air, land, and ocean, rather than for slowing or reversing the trend of increasing human population. In effect, this concern is associated with the results or symptoms of high population, but not with the root cause —the uncontrolled increase of population itself. Such a procedure is equivalent to a physician's treatment of a patient's fever rather than addressing the disease that caused the fever. Until the problem of uncontrolled population is solved, the

diminution of resources cannot be slowed except in ways that are only temporary and doomed to be overridden by new additions to the populations.

The dilemma for industrialized nations is that any action toward forcing lower rates of population increase in the world is most likely to be considered unfair and be politically unacceptable. Certainly, national governments cannot be expected to lead the way, in view of the short-term views that are characteristic of governments and their politicians. Democratic governments are not noted for their foresight nor for taking action until crises have arrived. On the other hand, inaction coupled with continued foreign aid is bound to accelerate the increasing world population in the face of declining resources, and thus inaction can cause catastrophic starving and conflict to arrive sooner rather than later. This is a classical "damned if we do and damned if we don't" situation in the face of steps that are needed to somehow forestall a future that is becoming increasingly evident. Opposition to restriction for continued population increase certainly would be so great that it cannot be overcome by either reason or persuasion. Moreover, the very thought of attempted government control of procreation is abhorrent and likely to be opposed by populations. Neither can force succeed in view of the already enormous population. What nation or coalition of nations can rightfully or reasonably claim to be the world's policeman? Is there any chance that governments of the world would agree? Would any religious organizations support the decision? What control can be applied other than sterilization? What kind of selection for sterilization could be applied, and could abuses of sterilization be avoided? Can demographics possibly cause a sort of automatic decrease in world population, as has occurred in some individual nations when prosperity increased, especially after resources per capita have further diminished? Does commercial interest in expanding sales to increased human population constitute an effective opposition to restriction of population growth? Would indefinite delay (the usual political approach) aid solution of the problem, or would it just permit the total population to become even more unmanageably huge? Is it possible that delay may allow time for discovery of massive new resources or use of energies as yet untapped? In the absence of population control, even such an unlikely discovery could allow the Earth to soon become a most uncomfortable abode for crowded humans. On the other hand, there may develop two competing systems, one allowing a minimum and the other a maximum ratio of population to energy. The system having the minimum ratio would concentrate efforts on ecological engineering and allow populations to enjoy a more satisfying existence.

Education

During recent decades many natural scientists and social scientists have recognized the progressive deterioration of the environment and have tried to obtain precise data on rates to aid understanding of the processes and aid prediction for the future.... Goodland seriously addressed the likelihood that the limit already has been reached, considering the huge demand placed by humans on Earth's biomass, the global warming, deterioration of the ozone shield, degradation of the land for agriculture, and reduction of diversity. Limitation to long-distance space travel that is exerted by the need to provide all fuel, food, and other necessities within the cargo of spacecraft is making the literate public aware of the similar limitation of the Earth to support its increasing number of human passengers. Efforts of national academies of science and of Nobel Laureates may begin to influence politics, as illustrated by the gathering of political leaders of the world at the United Nations Conference on Environmental Development at Rio de Janeiro during a few days of June 1992. Although increased efforts to improve literacy of the world's populations may be the route to long-term solution for many effects of overpopulation and overdemand for resources, these efforts may take so long to be effective that much further deterioration of the environment must be expected.

...[H]igher levels of literacy permit higher levels of education and corresponding greater enjoyment of life above the levels available to the average member of a nation. Unfortunately, in many nations the means of obtaining an education is limited by scarcity of teachers and schools and by high populations whose main aim is just to cope day by day. For these nations the route to prosperity is indeed long, and a reduction in rate of population increase may not soon be possible. Even in the most literate and prosperous of nations (including the United States) there are groups and individuals who for various reasons decide to drop out of available schools, thereby rejecting their future potential for progress with respect to others in their nation. Even at its best, education is a slow process especially for nations that have a long history of high population and low literacy. This means that much greater interest in education throughout the world cannot quickly reverse or slow the rapid increase of total world population and continued deterioration of the environment in which humans live. Perhaps the best hope is that increased literacy and broadening knowledge of the environment by national populations will persuade national governments to take actions to reduce both excessive populations and rates of environmental deterioration.

A further asset of increased literacy is the production of more scientists and engineers to attack problems of food and other resources for increasing populations. At present, the production of scientists and engineers is growing at a rate two or three times the rate of increase of total world population and even of the world labor force. This is positive for solution of environmental problems; although most production of scientists and engineers occurs in industrial nations, aspirants from lesser developed countries are attracted to these nations for professional education.

Culture

The term culture is a composite that includes many human activities or attributes, such as religion, government, and education; it is controlled by race, history, resource base, technological level, language, and others, and it changes with time and with geographical region. The growth rate of human populations is one of the attributes of culture, as shown by its change with time and with regional differences in birth rates, population growth, life expectancy, energy use, incomes, and population densities. The relation of these parameters with level of literacy indicates that education is an important factor limiting population growth. However, it is not the only control because population growth prior to a few hundred years ago was low, even though literacy then was less than now. Other factors, such as increased energy, food, medication, and mineral resources have significantly augmented standards of living and thus led to increased population. These changes were enhanced by transfer from industrial nations (which developed them) to lesser developed nations (where they had a greater effect because of long previous lower literacy and standard of living). The product was greater growth of populations in regions dominated by lesser-developed nations. Therefore, we can expect that continuing growth of populations in the latter nations is likely to lead to further increase in demands for food, space, and other resources and thus to increased conflict to obtain them.

...[T]here is only slow awakening of humans in all nations to the effects of vastly increasing total population and its demands for food and other resources. The human cultural organizations of religion, government, and education probably recognize the environmental results of the population explosion, but they fail to take the necessary steps to reduce and reverse it. Their failure is illustrated by the few results of the June 1992 Earth Summit conference at Rio de Janeiro. If the blindness continues, warfare and disease may do the job and reduce populations so that humans will follow the patterns of unthinking organisms that produced guide fossils during geological history.

POSTSCRIPT

Can the World Continue to Feed Billions of People?

The concept of "carrying capacity" is basic to the population issue. It is defined as the size of the population that the environment can support, or "carry," indefinitely, through good years and bad. It is not the population size that can prosper in good times alone, for any large population must suffer catastrophically when droughts, floods, or blights arrive or the climate warms or cools. Carrying capacity is thus a long-term concept, where "long term" means not decades or generations, nor even centuries, but millennia or more.

What is the Earth's carrying capacity for human beings? It is impossible to set a precise figure on the number of human beings the world can support for the long run, but in the Worldwatch Institute's *State of the World 1994* (W. W. Norton, 1994), Sandra Postel says, "As a result of our population size, consumption patterns, and technology choices, we have surpassed the planet's carrying capacity. This is plainly evident by the extent to which we are damaging and depleting natural capital" (including land and water). Gretchen C. Daily and Paul R. Ehrlich reach a very similar conclusion in "Population, Sustainability, and Earth's Carrying Capacity," *BioScience* (November 1992).

Later in the Worldwatch report, project director Lester Brown says, "As the nineties unfold, the world is facing a day of reckoning. Many knew that this time would come, that at some point the cumulative effects of environmental degradation and the limits of the earth's natural systems would start to restrict economic expansion." Brown goes on to say that the growth of food production is slowing, identifiable opportunities to expand food production are small, and the projected grain harvest for 2030—2.2 billion tons—would support a population of only 2.75 billion if everyone consumed the average U.S. citizen's diet (800 kilograms of grain or the equivalent per person per year [kg/person/year]), 5.5 billion if they consumed at Italy's level (400 kg/person/year), or 11 billion at India's consumption level (200 kg/person/year).

John Bongaarts is the director of the United Nations Population Council's Research Division. In "Can the Growing Human Population Feed Itself?" *Scientific American* (March 1994), he, like Norse, expresses optimism that "feeding a growing world population a diet that improves over time in quality and quantity is technologically feasible." However, in "Population Policy Options in the Developing World," *Science* (February 11, 1994), Bongaarts says that "large reductions in future population growth" are essential, especially in the developing nations, which have much higher population growth rates than the developed world.

At the 1994 annual meeting of the American Association for the Advancement of Science, Cornell University ecologist David Pimentel assured his audience that the prospects for the future are grim indeed. He claimed that if those of our children and grandchildren who are alive in the year 2100 are to have a comfortable standard of living, world population must fall to 2 billion or less; the alternative is "misery, poverty, disease, and starvation."

Few believe that the drastic reduction in world population that Pimentel endorses is possible without some massive disaster, natural or human. But there is a growing belief that population growth must be mightily restrained. In September 1994, the United Nations held its once-a-decade population conference. The action plan discussed included leveling off world population at a targeted 7.8 billion by 2050, instead of the projected 12.5 billion. See Margeurite Holloway, "Population Summit," *Scientific American* (June 1994).

Two books well worth attention are E. G. Nisbet's *Leaving Eden: To Protect and Manage the Earth* (Cambridge University Press, 1991) and Paul R. Ehrlich and Anne H. Ehrlich's *Healing the Planet: Strategies for Resolving the Environmental Crisis* (Addison Wesley, 1991), both of which hold out some hope that we can learn how to live within the means the Earth provides.

ISSUE 6

Can the Sun Supply Our Energy Needs?

YES: Christopher Flavin and Nicholas Lenssen, from "Here Comes the Sun," *World Watch* (September/October 1991)

NO: Chauncey Starr, Milton F. Searl, and Sy Alpert, from "Energy Sources: A Realistic Outlook," *Science* (May 15, 1992)

ISSUE SUMMARY

YES: Christopher Flavin and Nicholas Lenssen, researchers at the Worldwatch Institute, argue that the technology currently exists to meet most energy needs from renewable sources, with solar-generated hydrogen fulfilling the need for a portable fuel.

NO: Chauncey Starr, Milton F. Searl, and Sy Alpert, researchers at the Electric Power Research Institute, argue that renewable (solar) energy is limited particularly by its intermittency and lack of portability; thus, the hydrogen solution is of no practical interest.

A *renewable resource* is one whose supply is constantly replenished. Fresh water is one, for it is renewed as rapidly as the rain falls from the sky. Solar energy is another, for the Earth receives a new shipment every day.

It is possible to overuse a renewable resource by using it faster than it is renewed. The fresh water available for use includes not only the runoff from each day's rain but also past days' rain stored in underground aquifers that may have taken thousands of years to fill. If these reserves are drained for such uses as irrigation (as indeed is the case in many regions of the world), then their renewability is largely theoretical.

Oil, coal, and natural gas were once living organisms and therefore embody the solar energy those organisms captured when alive. They can therefore be called "reserves" of solar energy. However, considering that it took many millions of years to produce the Earth's stocks of fossil fuels and that people have been rapidly consuming them over the course of the past couple of centuries, in reality they must be called "nonrenewable." It will be a long, long time before the world forms new deposits of oil or coal.

The energy crisis that struck in the 1970s did not surprise everyone. A few people were aware that supplies of fossil fuels are finite and that if fossil fuels must be used to heat homes and power cars, then they must eventually run out. A few were also aware that as long as the United States and Canada remain dependent on other nations for much of their energy—North America in 1991 imported 61 percent of its liquid fuel and 53 percent of its total energy used—the countries are necessarily at the mercy of others who have their own interests at heart.

In 1973 an oil embargo imposed by the Organization of Petroleum Exporting Countries (OPEC) brought the same points to the attention of the general citizenry and their political representatives. Among the results was a massive effort to fund research into "energy independence," including ways to get oil from oil shales, to make oil from coal, to squeeze more oil from old oil wells, and to make renewable energy sources more acceptable.

The search for alternative energy sources led to many developments: the market for woodstoves boomed; small hydroelectric power plants were built along rivers where mills of the nineteenth century had left dams that could be reused; entrepreneurs generated electricity by burning sawmill waste and garbage; windmills sprouted like dandelions across the country; many people added energy-producing solar panels to the roofs of their houses; and cars, trucks, and buses were modified to run on hydrogen gas despite the danger of hydrogen's high flammability.

Then OPEC lost its political muscle: new, large oil fields were found; prices fell; and dependence on oil supplies seemed less chancy. As a result, the U.S. government decided it was a waste of money to fund alternative energy research. Research projects and demonstration plants were thus abandoned. However, there were some lasting benefits. For example, energy conservation —from increased building insulation to more efficient lightbulbs, refrigerators, and cars—became almost a cause and indeed reduced energy demand significantly. Photovoltaic cells, which utilize electromagnetic waves (such as those found in visible light) to generate electricity, became the power source for millions of hand-held calculators and other gadgets. And windmills were designed for greater efficiency and durability and were installed by utilities where the wind blew strong and steady.

The world remains enormously dependent on fossil fuels, and their supply remains finite. Can future energy crises far worse than the panics of the 1970s be avoided? Christopher Flavin and Nicholas Lenssen of the Worldwatch Institute say yes, maintaining that the technology currently exists to meet most of the world's energy needs from renewable sources, particularly solar-generated hydrogen. Chauncey Starr, Milton F. Searl, and Sy Alpert of the Electric Power Research Institute argue that renewable (solar) energy is too limited and that increases in energy efficiency and decreases in pollutant (including carbon dioxide) emissions will keep fossil fuels competitive well into the next century.

YES

Christopher Flavin and
Nicholas Lenssen

HERE COMES THE SUN

The technology exists today to produce most of our energy from the
sun, wind, and heat from the earth. Tapping these sources, though
will require a vigorous public commitment to push renewable energy into the mainstream.

Imagine an energy system that requires no oil, is immune to political events
in the Middle East, produces virtually no air pollution, generates no nuclear
waste, and yet is just as economical and versatile as today's.

Sound like a utopian dream? Hardly. Scientific and engineering breakthroughs now make it practical to begin producing our electricity, heating
our homes, and fueling our cars with renewable energy—the energy of the
sun, the winds, falling water, and the heat within the earth itself.

The conventional wisdom among government leaders, energy experts, and
the public at large is that we are stuck with dependence on fossil fuels—
whatever the cost in future oil crises, air pollution, or disrupted world climate.
But, with continuing advances in technology and improvements in efficiency
that make it possible to run the economy on reduced amounts of power, a
renewables-based economy is achievable within a few decades.

In California, the future has already begun to emerge. The state that always
seems to be a decade ahead of everyone else is once again ushering in a
new era. The current revolution is subtle, yet momentous. It's evident in
the spinning white wind turbines on the hills east of San Francisco and the
glinting mirrored solar-thermal troughs set in rows in the Mojave Desert.

Since the early 1980s, California has built no coal or nuclear power plants
and has been harnessing renewable energy and improving energy efficiency
with a vengeance. The state gets 42 percent of its electricity from renewable
resources, largely from hydropower, but also 12 percent from geothermal,
biomass, wind, and solar energy—virtually all of it developed in the past
decade.

But, for all its success, California's energy revolution is a bit one-dimension-
al. Its electricity system has been altered, but its cars and homes are still

From Christopher Flavin and Nicholas Lenssen, "Here Comes the Sun," *World Watch*
(September/October 1991). Copyright © 1991 by The Worldwatch Institute. Reprinted by
permission.

powered largely with fossil fuels. The next step is to find a way to run the whole economy on renewable energy sources.

The missing link is hydrogen—a clean-burning fuel easily produced using renewable power and conveyed by pipeline to cities and industries thousands of miles away. Hydrogen shows great promise as the new "currency" of a solar economy. It can be used to heat homes, cook food, power factories, and run automobiles. Moreover, the technologies to produce, move, and use hydrogen are already here in prototype form.

The challenge of creating a clean, efficient, solar-powered economy is essentially that of reducing the cost of the various constituents of a solar-hydrogen system—from the manufacturing costs of wind turbines to the efficiency of new automobiles.

Here, the pace of progress will be heavily influenced by government policies. The change will come slowly if governments continue to shower favors on fossil-fuel based energy sources. To encourage the adoption of alternative energy sources, policymakers will need to reduce subsidies, raise taxes on fossil fuels, increase research funding on new energy technologies, and provide incentives to private industry for renewable energy development.

POWER FROM THE SUN

Renewable resources now provide just 8 percent of the energy used in the United States, but government scientists estimate that renewables could supply the equivalent of 50 to 70 percent of current U.S. energy use by the year 2030 if the government got behind the effort. This estimate is based on the abundance of renewable resources and the technological advances made in tapping them since the mid-1970s.

Such improvements have reduced the cost of renewable energy technologies by 65 to 90 percent since 1980, a trend that is projected to continue through the 1990s. Increasingly, as governments begin to consider the full costs of fossil fuels (including air pollution and threats to national security), renewables look like a bargain.

Renewables' ability to go head-to-head with coal, oil, and nuclear power has credence even among some utility executives. Greg Rueger, senior vice president of California's Pacific Gas & Electric Company, the nation's largest utility, says "many renewable-generation options are technically feasible today, and with encouragement can prove to be fully cost-competitive ... within 10 years."

Solar energy probably will be the foundation of a sustainable energy economy, because sunlight is the most abundant renewable energy resource. Also, solar energy can be harnessed in an almost infinite variety of ways—from simple solar cookers now used in parts of India to gleaming solar collectors on rooftops in Beverly Hills.

Using sunlight to generate electricity has been a dream of scientists and energy planners since the early 1950s, when the first practical photovoltaic cell was invented. This device converts the sun's rays directly into electric current via a complex photoelectric process. Photovoltaic technology has advanced for four decades now, making it possible to convert a larger share of sunlight into electricity—as much as 14 percent in the most advanced prototype systems. Manufacturing costs also have fallen, making this technology a competitive energy source for some limited applications.

Photovoltaic solar cells are now widely used, for example, to power electronic calculators, remote telecommunications equipment, and electric lights and water pumps in Third World villages. These and dozens of other uses created a $500-million market for photovoltaics in 1990, with sales projected to double every five years. The 50 megawatts worth of cells produced in 1990, though, is only sufficient to power about 15,000 European or Japanese homes.

During the past two decades, the cost of photovoltaic power has fallen from $30 a kilowatt-hour to just 30 cents. (This figure is composed almost entirely of manufacturing costs, since solar power requires no fuel.) This is still four to six times the cost of power generation from fossil fuels, so further reductions are needed for solar power to be competitive with grid electricity. . . .

Photovoltaics are already the most economical way of delivering power to homes far from utility lines. This technology will soon become an economical way of providing supplementary utility power in rural areas, where the distance from power plants tends to cause a voltage reduction that is otherwise costly to remedy.

New applications will spur further cost reductions, which is likely to lead to widespread use of solar cells. As they become more compact and versatile, photovoltaic panels could be used as roofing material on individual homes, bringing about the ultimate decentralization of power generation. Around the same time, perhaps a decade from now, large solar power plants could begin to appear in the world's deserts—providing centralized power in the same way as do today's coal and nuclear plants.

Another source of centralized electricity is solar-thermal power, a technology already proving its viability in California's Mojave Desert. Luz International of Los Angeles has developed a solar-thermal system using large mirrored troughs to reflect the sun's rays onto an oil-filled tube, which in turn superheats water to produce the steam that drives an electricity-generating turbine.

Since the mid-1980s, Luz has installed 350 megawatts of solar systems across three square miles of southern California desert—enough to electrify 170,000 homes. The Luz systems turn 22 percent of incoming sunlight into electricity, which is higher than for any commercial photovoltaic system so far. And because they are of modular design, they can be built on a variety of scales.

Solar-thermal electricity is now produced for about 8 cents per kilowatt-hour, close to the cost of that from fossil fuels in California, where extensive pollution controls are required. However, because it relies on mirrored concentrators, solar-thermal power is only practical where there is intense, direct sunlight —conditions found only in arid regions.

Photovoltaics, which are much more effective in hazy or partly cloudy conditions and can be installed even on a very small scale on residential rooftops, are likely to become the more common power source in the long run. Still, both solar technologies will play important roles.

Contrary to what their critics charge, solar energy systems won't require unusually large areas of land to power the economies of tomorrow. In fact, they need less space to produce a megawatt of electricity than does coal-fired power when the land devoted to mining is factored in. One-quarter of U.S. electricity needs could be met by less than 6,000 square miles of solar "farms," according to the Electric Power Research Institute in Palo Alto, California, the research arm of the U.S. electric utility industry. That's about the area of Connecticut, or less than 8 percent of the land used by the U.S. military.

MORE RENEWABLE OPTIONS

Another form of renewable energy, wind power, can be captured by propeller-driven turbines mounted on towers in windy regions. Though wind power has a rich history in areas such as Holland and the American Great Plains, it has been taken seriously as a major energy source only since the late 1970s.

Technological advance in the design of wind turbines brought down the cost of wind electricity from more than $3.00 a kilowatt-hour in the early 1980s to the current average of just 80 cents. By the end of this decade, the cost of newer models is expected to be around 50 cents per kilowatt-hour, while the cost of coal-fired power will rise above 50 cents as a result of tightening pollution standards.

Most of the cost reductions for wind energy stem from experience gained in California, which has 15,000 wind machines producing about $200 million worth of electricity annually, enough to power all the homes in San Francisco. Denmark, the world's second-largest producer, received about 2 percent of its power from wind turbines in 1990—but still only about one-fifth of that produced in California.

Wind power could provide many countries with one-fifth or more of their electricity. Some of the most promising areas for wind energy are in North Africa, the western plains of the United States, and the trade wind belt around the tropics—including the Caribbean, Central America, and southeast Asia. In Europe, the largest wind farms will likely be placed on offshore platforms in the turbulent North and Baltic seas.

U.S. government studies show that one-quarter of the country's power could be provided by wind farms installed on the windiest 1.5 percent of the continental United States. A windy ridge in Minnesota, located less than 400 miles from Chicago, could provide one-quarter of the power the city now uses.

Most of the best land for wind power in the United States is grazing land in the western high plains—costing no more than $40 an acre. If "planted" in wind turbines, an acre of this land could generate $12,000 worth of electricity annually while cattle still graze below. One reason it's not being developed is that the region already has more electrical generating capacity than it can use.

Of course, any energy source has its drawbacks, and wind power development, with its rows of towering turbines, will need to be limited in scenic areas, particularly on coastlines. Further efforts are also needed to reduce the incidental bird kills that plague some wind farms....

Another potential source of power is geothermal energy—the heat from the earth's core. Already, El Salvador gets 40 percent of its electricity from the earth's natural heat, Nicaragua 28 percent, and Kenya 11 percent. Most Pacific Rim countries, as well as those along East Africa's Great Rift Valley and around the Mediterranean Sea, sit atop geothermal "hotspots." Virtually the entire country of Japan lies over an enormous heat source that one day could meet much of the country's energy needs.

Geothermal energy is not without its environmental drawbacks, including the underground sulfur it tends to release, and development will have to be limited in ecologically sensitive areas. However, this still leaves a vast resource potential, particularly as engineers develop techniques to drill deeper and deeper into the earth's crust.

THE HYDROGEN SOLUTION

If renewable energy is abundant and economical, then why isn't it being harvested on a larger scale? The answer stems in part from the difficulty of storing and moving energy from ephemeral, intermittent sources such as the sun and the wind. While oil can be moved from remote areas by tanker, and coal by barge, sunshine is hard to carry to far-off cities.

Electric power produced by renewable energy could be stored and transported to the user, but at some cost. Electric batteries are expensive, heavy, and must be recharged frequently. Power lines also are costly, generate potentially dangerous electromagnetic fields, and lose energy over long distances due to resistance in the lines. Nonetheless, extended transmission of electricity is already common: California, for example, relies on hydropower produced nearly 1,000 miles away in British Columbia.

Given the limits on moving electricity, it makes more sense to convert renewable power to a gaseous form that is cheap to transport and easy to store. Hydrogen is an almost completely clean-burning gas that can be used in place of petroleum, coal, or natural gas. It releases none of the carbon that leads to global warming. And it can be produced easily by running an electric current through water—a process known as electrolysis.

Hydrogen can be transported almost any distance with virtually no energy loss. Over distances greater than 400 miles, it costs about one-quarter as much as sending electricity through a wire. Gases are also less risky to move than any other form of energy—particularly compared with oil, which is frequently spilled in tanker accidents and during routine handling.

Hydrogen is much more readily stored than electricity—in a pressurized tank or in metal hydrides, metal powders that naturally absorb gaseous hydrogen and release it when heated. Years' worth of hydrogen could be stocked in depleted oil or gas wells in regions such as the U.S. Gulf Coast.

Moreover, hydrogen can provide the concentrated energy needed by factories and homes. It can be burned in lieu of natural gas to run restaurants, heat warehouses, and fuel a wide range of industrial processes. Around the home, new hydrogen-powered furnaces, stove burners, and water heaters can be developed that will be much more efficient than today's appliances.

The gas can also be used to produce electricity in small, modular generators that turn out heat and power for individual buildings. Such co-generating plants would produce far less pollution than today's power plants do in getting a similar amount of electricity to individual users. Hydrogen can be used to run automobiles, using either an internal combustion engine or, more efficiently, a fuel cell.

Eventually, hydrogen fuel could be even more prevalent than oil is today. The gas could become cost-competitive as a transportation fuel within the next two decades. Solar or wind-derived electricity at 5 cents per kilowatt-hour

—achievable by the late 1990s—could produce hydrogen that would sell at the pump for about the equivalent of a $3 gallon of gasoline. While this is more than Americans are now charged to fuel their cars, it is less than the price most Europeans pay.

The transition to hydrogen as a major energy source likely will be eased by the ability to mix hydrogen with natural gas up to a one-to-ten ratio with minimal alteration of the existing infrastructure of gas pipelines, furnaces, and burners. Thus, as natural gas reserves are gradually depleted and prices rise in the early part of the next century, hydrogen can gradually be worked into the mix.

THE GLOBAL SOLAR NETWORK

Solar energy—whether transmitted through electrical lines or used to produce hydrogen—could become the cornerstone of a new global energy economy. All of the world's major population centers are located within reach of sun- and wind-rich areas. The U.S. Southwest, for example, could supply much of the country either with electricity or hydrogen.

Although renewable energy sources are regionally concentrated, they are far less so than oil, where two-thirds of proven world reserves are found in the politically unstable Persian Gulf area.

Wherever renewable resources are abundant, hydrogen can be produced without pollution and shipped to distant markets: from the windy high plains of North America to the eastern seaboard; from the deserts of western China to the populous coastal plain; and from Australia's outback to its southern cities.

For Europe, solar-power plants could be built in southern Spain or in North Africa. From the latter, hydrogen would be transported along today's natural gas pipeline routes into Spain via the Strait of Gibraltar, or into Italy via Sicily. Within Europe, today's expanding pipelines and electrical networks would make it relatively easy to distribute the energy.

To the east, Kazakhstan and the other semi-arid Asian republics might supply much of the [former] Soviet Union's energy. In India, the sun-drenched Thar Desert in the northwest is within 1,000 miles of more than a half billion people. Electricity for China's expanding economy could be generated in the country's vast central and northwestern desert regions.

While pipelines must be sited to avoid ecological damage or accidents, their overall environmental impacts are minimal, especially where natural gas pipelines already exist, as between Wyoming or Oklahoma and the industrial Midwest and Northeast. The pipelines themselves will need to be modified or rebuilt to accommodate any shift to hydrogen, since the gas has properties that corrode some metals.

Germany leads the effort to develop solar-hydrogen systems. It has demonstration electrolysis projects powered by photovoltaic cells already operating in Germany and Saudi Arabia. Germany spends some $25 million annually on hydrogen research projects, according to Carl-Jochen Winter, a scientist with the German Aerospace Research Establishment (by contrast, the United States devotes less than $3 million). Experience in transporting hydrogen comes from a 120-mile pipeline in Germany that transports hydrogen produced from fossil fuels for use in industry.

GETTING THERE FROM HERE

In the end, major energy transitions tend to be driven by fundamental forces, either the evolution of new technology or problems facing society, such as population growth, resource depletion, or climate change. These forces, it can now be argued, are pushing the world toward a solar-hydrogen economy.

But the pace of change will inevitably be determined in part by government policies, most of which are now biased to favor today's energy systems. Will political leaders cling obstinately to the status quo or will they begin encouraging the development of new energy systems? In California, for example, it was a series of state policy changes made in the late 1970s and early 1980s that cleared the way for a new era.

Many state and local governments now encourage use of renewables through regulations and incentives. National governments are also moving toward new policies—under strong pressure from voters. Some European countries have raised gasoline taxes, other governments are taxing cars that pollute, and still more are forcing change via regulation. These are policies that work best in consort.

Higher taxes on fossil fuels is one way to accelerate the energy transition. The carbon taxes levied so far in countries such as the Netherlands and Sweden are an important step, but they haven't been set high enough to cause major shifts in the choice of energy technologies.

To make a real difference in energy habits, a carbon tax would have to be large enough to replace at least a quarter of today's taxes. One possibility is to lower income taxes as carbon taxes are raised. The voting public might accept higher taxes on gasoline, coal, and other fuels in exchange for more take-home pay.

Another approach that can level the playing field is including environmental costs within the electric-utility planning process. If environmental costs were added to construction costs in considering what kind of power plants to build, new coal-fired capacity would become economically unattractive compared with renewable energy sources.

The state of Nevada, for example, decided in early 1991 to tack on a hefty environmental charge when utilities license new coal-fired power plants. Part of the charge is for the potential costs of climate change, the rest is attributed to pollution costs, such as for the extra medical care required when air pollution damages people's lungs. As a result, the coal-based power that now dominates the state is likely to shift in the future to energy-efficiency programs, natural gas, geothermal heat, and sunshine.

National governments also can speed the transition to a sustainable energy future by providing modest incentives for the building of renewable energy systems. New energy technologies have in the past been subsidized by governments—hydropower and nuclear power are obvious examples. In this case, the subsidy can be justified due to the avoided environmental damage that results from renewable energy development. It is worth remembering that California state tax credits for renewable energy development helped spark the renewables boom of the early 1980s.

The U.S. Congress is now considering a subsidy for the generation of renewable electricity. An incentive of just 2 cents per kilowatt-hour—equivalent to about 25 percent of the average retail price of power in the United States—would be sufficient, according to market analysts, to spark a boom in renewable energy development. The cost to the taxpayer would be about $1 billion over five years—a fraction of 1 percent of the nation's annual power bill.

A re-orientation of research and development programs is also called for. In 1989, the leading industrial-country governments spent just 7 percent of their $7.3-billion in energy research funds on renewable technologies. Most of the rest went to nuclear energy and fossil fuels. Drastically trimming breeder-reactor and nuclear-fusion programs would free billions of dollars to accelerate the commercial development of new technologies.

Most countries still have a long way to go in reforming their outdated energy policies, but there is a new sense of urgency about future energy sources as the public reacts to the threats posed by greenhouse gases building in the atmosphere....

Some of the biggest obstacles blocking change in many countries are caused by the politicians who are captives of today's energy industries. The halls of the U.S. Congress, for example, are filled with lobbyists for powerful energy industries—ranging from oil to coal to nuclear power—and their policy agenda predominates. Ironically, while their political power remains intact, these industries have been automated and no longer provide many jobs. As more such positions are eliminated in the 1990s, the political position of these industries is likely to weaken.

In the end, the key to overcoming political barriers is to demonstrate that a solar economy would have major advantages over today's fossil fuel-based systems. California again provides a good example. It already has greatly reduced its fuel bills and begun to clear its skies as a result of the energy policy changes begun more than a decade ago.

As California's political leaders seem to understand, a solar future is just too attractive to be ignored. Indeed, a solar economy would be healthier and less vulnerable to oil price gyrations of the sort that have shaken the world in recent decades. And a solar future is the only practical energy future that would be environmentally sustainable—eliminating the greenhouse gases now threatening the planet's health.

NO

Chauncey Starr, Milton F. Searl, and Sy Alpert

ENERGY SOURCES:
A REALISTIC OUTLOOK

Projections to the middle of the next century indicate that unabated historical global energy trends would lead to an annual global energy demand about four times present levels, primarily due to population and economic growth. But extensive global conservation and energy-efficient systems might reduce this value by half. The cumulative effect of the coming half century's use may strain the world's low-cost resources, particularly oil. The future fuel mix is further complicated by the environmental thrust to reduce the global use of carbon-based fuels. The interaction of the principal factors influencing future energy resource and technology options are projected.

The energy supply mix of the coming century will depend on the magnitude of the demand growth for global energy, changing performance targets, and the technologies available to meet them....

The future adequacy of globally available fossil fuel resources will depend on the total societal costs of extracting and delivering such fuels and on their effectiveness in use to meet the broad performance objectives of energy systems. Projections of proven, probable, and speculative resources are often updated as new discoveries or extraction techniques are developed, but professional conservatism has often resulted in underestimating future resource expansion at acceptable costs. On a next century time scale, the traditional question is whether the cumulative effect of the increasing rate of depletion of these resources would result in a global constraint on energy systems, particularly on the future supply of liquid fuel for vehicles and airplanes. This question is technologically intriguing because of the now demonstrated large-scale convertibility of all fossil fuels to gas or liquid forms and the implications of the application of this technology as an option for a global source of liquid fuel derived from large coal resources.

The present global energy mix is likely to change substantially during the next century as a result of several factors. First, comparative scarcity

From Chauncey Starr, Milton F. Searl, and Sy Alpert, "Energy Sources: A Realistic Outlook," *Science*, vol. 256 (May 15, 1992), pp. 981–986. Copyright © 1992 by The American Association for the Advancement of Science. Reprinted by permission. References and notes omitted.

attributable either to resource or to political constraints may increase the relative price of the most convenient fossil fuel, oil; second, the growing costs of reducing environmental degradation will alter the cost competition among fuels; and third, the potential threat of global climate change may stimulate a shift from carbon-based fuels to nonfossil alternatives. A resource perspective for the next century involves speculation on future energy demand, likely competitive supply alternatives, and possible changes in energy systems and technologies. Such speculations are shaped by the long time periods required to develop new or improved energy technologies and to deploy them commercially. Although long-range projections are unavoidably judgmental and are dependent on present knowledge and experience, they permit the scoping of alternative trends and outcomes and thus help guide current strategies. A projected global energy supply mix based on such judgmental factors provides a conceptual basis for considering the factors discussed below, which are likely to shape future trends.

It is of particular interest that the availability of liquid fuels in the coming century and beyond is likely to be maintained as the rising cost of conventional oil brings into competition higher cost sources such as coal conversion, tar sands, and oil shale. This transition, initially based on the technologies described in this paper, should be under way by the middle of the century.

FUTURE ENERGY DEMAND

Two major trends determine global future end use energy demand, population growth and economic growth. The primary energy input depends on the efficiency of conversion to end use, as determined by the choice of technology. Thus, if a permanent increase in the real price of primary fuel is expected, there exists an incentive to invest in more efficient or alternative technologies. The range of future energy demand and supply outcomes based on plausible projections of these factors has been studied by Starr and Searl. Two bounding efficiencies were applied to current trends: (i) maintenance of current conversion efficiencies and (ii) a full conservation concept, which assumed reduction of the present trend by one-third of all electricity use and by half of all direct energy (nonelectric) use. This full conservation was judged to be the maximum amount of conservation that could foreseeably be implemented without inhibiting economic growth.

... By the year 2060, if present trends continue without modification, total energy demand is projected to increase 4.4 times and electricity demand is projected to increase 7.0 times the 1986 reference levels. If full conservation is accomplished, the total energy demand increase is reduced to 2.5 times and electricity demand is reduced to 4.7 times. Most of the anticipated increases are the result of the higher population and economic growth rates of the less developed countries. These large increases are the result of a global population increase of 1.95 times and an average per capita gross national product (GNP) increase of 2.8 times, for a combined product growth of 5.5 times. With the full conservation case, this implies that the efficiency of global economic productivity per unit of primary energy will be improved 2.2 times....

FUTURE SUPPLY: ARE FOSSIL FUELS A CONSTRAINT?

There is little likelihood that serious scarcity of fuels will develop during the next century on a global scale because of the intraconvertibility of coals, oil, and gas. The major uncertainties arise from the constantly changing economic competition among the various sources and the eventual effects of environmental constraints and increased costs arising from the need to minimize undesirable effluents of fuel use. The prevalent situation that many reserves are only proven for several decades is an artifact of prudent investment in development of a future inventory.... The proven fossil reserves are nearly twice that needed to meet the projected cumulative global demand. The specific resource factors for near-term oil and gas have been recently discussed in some detail, suggesting that low-cost oil will become scarcer after the next few decades. Of course, the speculative higher cost resources are uncertain but may be large. In fact, the real resource cost of energy is lower today than at the beginning of this century, even though the world's population has tripled and its economic output increased by an order of magnitude. Economic incentives and technology have historically overcome perceived resource limitations.

However, it is likely that real primary energy costs from the conventional oil and gas sources will eventually increase. The average cost of exploration and development of new oil fields has risen steadily. At some increasing price level, unconventional oil sources gradually become competitive but require large capital investments. For example, at an oil price of about $30 to $40 per barrel (1990 dollars), large high-cost oil resources (for example, tar sands) become economically viable. Even the direct use of oil shales in utility boilers becomes marginally economic. Such oil-bearing bodies are the energy equivalent of giant oil fields, sufficiently large to provide the liquid fuel needs of the next century but require much higher capital investment for the same flow rates. This would change the character of the liquid fuel production industry.

The most abundant fossil fuel is coal, representing about 90% of all known conventional fossil resources. Its convertibility to both liquid and gaseous hydrocarbons has been demonstrated. The production of complex hydrocarbons by coal conversion has been commercially deployed worldwide.... The famous Sasol plant in South Africa has been producing liquid transportation fuel for decades from indigenous coal. The true costs have been stated to be marginally competitive currently but would be more competitive at higher oil prices. In the past 6 years, a plant in New Zealand has demonstrated the feasibility of converting methane into gasoline with a large-scale zeolite process. Low-cost and large natural gas reserves discovered in some remote locations have stimulated the investment in on-site conversion of natural gas to liquid fuel, so as to economically ship the product to a distant transportation market. It is thus obvious that if the price of oil becomes sufficiently high, coal conversion to liquid fuel can enter the oil industry investment structure. Estimates for producing liquid fuel from coal or gas indicate that $50 to $60 billion over the next 30 to 40 years would be required to satisfy 5% of projected U.S. demand for transportation fuel. This should be compared with the present worldwide expenditure of the oil and gas companies of more than $50 billion annually for exploration and production, and the roughly $500 billion of annual crude oil sales.

A direct use of coal conversion to gas for the generation of electricity has already been demonstrated with the 100-MW integrated gasification combined cycle (IGCC) power plant at the cool water station of Southern California Edison. This is the cleanest coal-fueled technique developed.... The advanced cycles now have a marginally higher capital cost, but continuing development will eventually make them competitive, particularly because of environmental factors.

A major future improvement in the efficiency of fossil fuel-based electricity generation will come from the ongoing development of the fuel cell.... The molten carbonate fuel cell is the current focus of development.... If successful, the commercialization of the fuel cell would eventually decrease the electricity component of the global demand for coal to about two-thirds of that based on present power plant practice, reducing annual carbon emissions.

NONFOSSIL AND RENEWABLES: SIGNIFICANT OR MARGINAL?

The potential role of the nonfossil and renewables in the future global energy mix depends on their developing economic competitiveness. This category includes biomass, solar, wind, geothermal, and the two commercial electricity sources, hydro and nuclear. Only hydro and nuclear are significant contributors today, with hydro about 20% of global electricity and nuclear about 17%. There are practical upper bounds for the potential contri-

bution of the nonfossil and renewable sources summarized here.

Both the energy input to manufacture the renewables and their initial capital cost are the issues. A basic consideration is net energy output, or the output minus the energy input from other resources required for their manufacture. This is particularly relevant to biomass, where the energy input for their growth (for example, fertilizer and irrigation) and processing are substantial. Both factors determine the competitive lifetime cost per unit of delivered end-use energy. As yet, renewables such as solar, wind, and biomass have been able to penetrate only limited niche markets, with much uncertainty about their net energy contribution.

The economic issues for hydro and nuclear are understood the best out of the renewables. Both require about the same capital investment per plant—about twice that for a coal-based unit. Compared to coal, hydro has no fuel cost and a low maintenance and operating cost; nuclear has a low fuel cost and a high maintenance and operating cost. Depending on the treatment of capital costs, hydroelectricity is usually cheaper than coal. In the industrial countries, nuclear electricity is now generally competitive with coal. The upper limit for global hydro growth is about four times the present level. Nuclear is limited only by available capital and manufacturing facilities. Both are constrained by environmental considerations. Hydro expansion involves flooding large areas and altering river flows and probably will not grow significantly for environmental reasons. Nuclear, when operating as designed, has small environmental impact but faces serious public concerns about the risk of off-design accidental release of radioactivity from either the reactor or spent fuel, and thus, nuclear has high administrative penalties. This has stimulated the current engineering concentration on reducing the probability of such accidents. Nuclear growth depends on the future public perception of the comparative benefits, costs, and risks of alternative energy sources. Based on the comparative evaluations of tangible risks to public health, safety, and environment, nuclear appears to be a better choice than coal. The intangible risk comparisons are more uncertain. Historically, such perceptions have changed with time. A century ago oil was perceived as too inflammable to replace coal, retarding its use in naval vessels for decades. During the recent decades, large naval ships turned to nuclear power because of its fuel longevity. Similarly, public opinion may shift with the changing priorities of the issues—costs, pollution, safety, global warming, among others. In the meanwhile, nuclear is slowly expanding worldwide, now providing 17% of world electricity.

Biomass is an unusual case. Much of the population in the underdeveloped regions has historically depended on noncommercial biomass energy sources, such as wood, shrubs, agricultural wastes, and animal dung, because these required no capital, only labor. In the industrial world, wastes from the paper, pulp, and lumber industries are used as on-site fuel. Less than 2% of the global energy supply is estimated to be from such noncommercial sources. The true cost of the noncommercial sources in the underdeveloped world is speculative because they are not market priced. However, in labor-hours required for their collection, noncommercial sources are costly. If the economic growth of the underdeveloped countries continues, the shift of this labor pool to more economically productive activity will result in a corresponding shift from noncommercial to commercial fuels, probably petroleum products initially.

The concept of commercial biomass fuel production through managed agriculture and forestry has been studied in great detail. The production of ethanol from sugar cane in Brazil is a massive demonstration of this potential. Although it was initially undertaken for internal social and trade balance objectives, ethanol now appears embedded in that nation's structure and may continue for that reason. However, it does not appear to be economically competitive with petroleum products in a world market. From a net energy view, estimates range from marginal to providing about 20% more energy than it consumes. The tropical zone, including Brazil, is the optimum area for biomass production and provides the basis for the most optimistic estimates of managed forestry. As a feasible, although optimistic upper estimate, biomass might supply a fourth of the fuel for the electricity demand in 2060 with full conservation, provided that transmission to markets from such biomass plants is available. Hall *et al.* suggest a slightly more optimistic estimate of the potential. If reduction of carbon emission becomes a global priority, managed biomass deserves a high weighting because it will either recirculate atmospheric carbon or sequester it. This capability suggests that managed biomass (that is, forestry) be encouraged to sequester carbon rather than use it as a fuel, particularly because of its uncertain net energy contribution.

The key technological issue for solar and wind is epitomized by the windmill-driven old-fashioned well-water pump and tank (once common on farms). It represents the ideal theoretical arrangement —an intermittent source coupled to storage end use. Its only handicap was the catastrophic windless drought that occurs for extended periods almost every year. Windmills were abandoned when power lines became available for reliable electrical pumping. Analogously, solar sources face the uncertainty of heavy cloud cover and reduced output. Nevertheless, the immensity of the solar energy available both by direct radiation and from wind is such that, even with low-efficiency conversion systems of a few percent, it is seductively apparent that most of the future global energy needs could be met. The big barrier is the technical and economic feasibility of overcoming their intermittent nature with energy storage and the required expanded collectors.

Solar and wind have made minimal entries to the present energy structure. Several windmill demonstrations have been installed on utility systems. Subsidized solar generators are supplying electricity during the peak hours, which roughly coincide with the diurnal cycle. As yet, their competitiveness is marginal. Both direct thermal absorption and photovoltaic systems should improve with development. Both have high capital costs per unit of electricity, which will be multiplied many times if their intermittent nature is compensated by the addition of energy storage facilities. Unless a low-cost electricity storage device is developed, the large-scale participation of solar and wind sources will be limited to a 12% maximum of the total network capacity of fuel-based electrical systems. However, this is not inconsiderable. By the middle of the next century this limited fraction would be equivalent to about 60% of today's world electricity generation. Solar and wind in combination with batteries can today economically fill small power niches, such as remote signaling devices. This may establish a base for future improvements and growth.

Solar enthusiasts have suggested that solar electricity be used to dissociate water for the production of hydrogen as a transportation fuel. This would achieve the ideal system goal of energy storage, no carbon emissions or pollutants, and an eternal primary energy resource. Although scientifically sound, the practical barriers of economics and operable technologies are large. Many billions of cubic feet of pure hydrogen are routinely produced in the world's oil refineries, at costs that are a fraction of electrolytic hydrogen. Nevertheless, there are no indications that a transition from conventional end-use systems to hydrogen-based systems has been of practical interest. There are no developments now visible that are likely to remove these economic and technical barriers, although the obvious merits of hydrogen combustion producing only water as a byproduct provides a tantalizing target....

TECHNOLOGY TRANSITION—WHY DOES IT TAKE SO LONG?

In considering advanced energy systems that might supply future energy needs, many decades will be required for a significant transition from today's conventional systems. Only in a crisis is it feasible to compress research, development, demonstration, and deployment into a decade or less. This has been accomplished in wartime by overriding all normal priorities and economic constraints. The history of energy fuel transitions (wood-coal-oil) shows that in a peacetime commercial environment almost a half century is required to significantly shift fuel patterns.

A projection of modern industrial experience to the future of advanced coal technologies suggests the typical time sequence of energy research, development, demonstration, and deployment....

The long time required for these transitions has serious implications for global energy strategies. It is likely that this time scale of three to five decades for significant energy contribution will also apply to the renewables, with the eventual limitations already described. By the middle of the next century perhaps a third of the global electricity-generating capacity might be advanced technology, and by the end of the century most of it should be. In the industrial countries, the entry of advanced technologies is limited by the slow obsolescence of existing plants (with a usual lifetime of 40 years) and by the rate at which additional capacity is needed. At a typical long-term annual growth rate of 2%, it takes 35 years to double total capacity. For the undeveloped countries obsolescence is less an issue than the scarcity of capital and the avoidance of performance risk. Thus, they are likely to purchase only well-proven conventional plants. Nevertheless, they are in particular need of small and dispersed power growth, providing a special opportunity for small solar, wind, and conventional fossil-fueled units.

POSTSCRIPT

Can the Sun Supply Our Energy Needs?

Starr, Searl, and Alpert use a key phrase when they say that a shift to hydrogen fuel has not "been of practical interest." Perhaps the flow of energy from the sun to Earth *is* sufficient to meet the needs of society, and perhaps there are ways around the drawbacks, but as long as society can continue to use the physical infrastructure it has developed to deal with oil—even if this means, for instance, converting coal to a synthetic oil—nothing else will be "practical." The question really comes down to how long oil will remain a practical energy source.

How could a shift toward renewable sources of energy be achieved? The technology to use solar energy to produce liquid fuels other than hydrogen has been demonstrated (see Israel Dostrovsky, "Chemical Fuels from the Sun," *Scientific American*, December 1991). In addition, the prices of some renewable-energy technologies have been dropping steadily. Indeed, in the spring of 1994, United Solar Systems of Troy, Michigan, announced a form of photovoltaic cell that can convert to electricity enough of the sunlight hitting it (slightly more than 10 percent) and can be made cheaply enough that it will cut the cost of photovoltaic power in half. Also, wind energy now costs less than a dime per kilowatt-hour and is competitive with utility rates in many regions.

Yet, reduced cost is not enough. As noted in *World Resources 1994–95*, "Without leadership in developing and actively promoting advanced energy technologies ... it is unlikely that these technologies will be speedily adopted [by developing nations, which] do not command sufficient technical and financial resources to drive research and development, and they harbor institutional biases favoring conventional fossil fuel and hydroelectric approaches." The developed world must provide the technologies, furnish technical and financial assistance, and act as an exemplar by "adopting these technologies at home in the attempt to build and demonstrate model sustainable energy programs." To date, this leadership has been conspicuous mostly for its absence. See Dwight Holing, "America's Energy Plan: Missing in Action," *Amicus Journal* (Winter 1991).

To learn more about the use of hydrogen as a fuel, see Roger E. Billings's memoir *The Hydrogen World View* (American Academy of Science, 1991). Also useful are James J. MacKenzie, *Electric and Hydrogen Vehicles* (World Resources Institute, 1994), and Keith L. Kozloff and Roger C. Dower, *A New Power Base: Renewable Energy Policies for the Nineties and Beyond* (World Resources Institute, 1993).

ISSUE 7

Is Ozone Depletion a Genuine Threat?

YES: Mary H. Cooper, from "Ozone Depletion," *CQ Researcher* (April 3, 1992)

NO: James P. Hogan, from "Ozone Politics: They Call This Science?" *Omni* (June 1993)

ISSUE SUMMARY

YES: Mary H. Cooper, a staff writer for *CQ Researcher*, asserts that scientific findings in recent years indicate that the ozone layer is being depleted and that such depletion threatens the health of Earth's living organisms.

NO: James P. Hogan, a science fiction writer, maintains that reports of the ozone being destroyed by chlorofluorocarbons are politically motivated scare stories unsupported by any valid scientific evidence.

The debate about ozone depletion may offer a good example of how attempts to make life better may actually do great harm. The controversy can be traced back to early improvements on the refrigerator. The fluid in the cooling coils of early refrigerators was ammonia, which is both highly irritating and very toxic. Chlorofluorocarbons (CFCs) replaced ammonia in the 1930s because they were nontoxic, nonirritating, nonflammable, inexpensive, noncorrosive, and stable (that is, they did not have to be replaced periodically). They were ideal for the purpose, and later on they proved to be ideal for other purposes as well. Consequently, CFC production grew, and by 1974, over 800,000 metric tons of CFCs were being produced per year.

Around this time, however, Sherwood Rowland and Mario Molina, chemists at the University of California at Irvine, realized that those safe, stable chlorofluorocarbon molecules were stable enough to rise all the way into the stratosphere before they broke down. When the molecules did break down, the chemists said, they would release their chlorine component precisely where it could destroy stratospheric ozone. Two years later, the first solid evidence of CFC-induced damage to the ozone layer was reported. As a result, in 1978, the U.S. Environmental Protection Agency and Food and Drug Administration banned the use of CFCs in aerosol spray cans. In 1985, a roughly circular zone of greatly diminished ozone concentration— commonly called the "ozone hole"—was discovered over Antarctica. Since then, several key events have occurred that have firmly established ozone depletion as a worldwide concern: in 1987 the United States and 23 other countries signed the Montreal Protocol (promising to cut CFC use drastically); in 1991 the United Nations Environment Programme (UNEP) issued a report concluding that ozone depletion was a worldwide phenomenon; and in 1992 scientists from the National Aeronautics and Space Administration (NASA) reported alarmingly high levels of ozone-destroying chlorine monoxide in the stratosphere over the Northern Hemisphere, confirming the conclusions of the UNEP.

Why is news of the depleted ozone alarming? It has been known for many years that stratospheric ozone absorbs much of the ultraviolet (UV) light that comes to Earth from the sun (or "solar ultraviolet"). The small amount that reaches the Earth's surface stimulates the production of vitamin D in human skin, but it also causes sunburn, skin cancer, and cataracts, as well as other problems. An increase in solar UV at ground level would therefore pose a serious health threat to human beings. It would also threaten other living organisms, including crop plants.

As yet, there is no proof that ozone depletion is already causing health problems, but according to everything that scientists know or can calculate, it will. Furthermore, since CFCs can remain in the air for years, many believe that society cannot wait for the signs of damage to become incontrovertible before taking action because by then it will be too late to keep the damage from growing still worse for years.

Although the facts strongly suggest a connection between CFCs and the depletion of stratospheric ozone, science cannot prove beyond a doubt that CFCs are destroying the ozone. Despite the evidence, not everyone accepts as true the threat of CFCs and ozone depletion. Critics have denounced the "ozone scare" as a politically motivated scam, a conspiracy to provide monopoly control to companies that have patents on refrigerant alternatives to CFCs, a way to gain public funding for unnecessary research, and so on.

In the following selections, Mary H. Cooper provides a clear account of the discovery and nature of ozone depletion, and she asserts that the hazards of CFCs are real. James P. Hogan argues that any conclusions about the destruction of the ozone by CFCs are based on sloppy scientific procedures and misinterpretations of data, and he maintains that public fears about the ozone are perpetuated for political reasons.

YES

Mary H. Cooper

OZONE DEPLETION

Scientists at the National Aeronautics and Space Administration (NASA) hadn't planned to hold a news conference on February 3 [1992]. But, they decided at the last minute, their preliminary findings about Earth's upper atmosphere were too important to sit on. Earth's protective ozone layer,[1] they announced, was losing ozone much faster than anyone had predicted, exposing humans to higher amounts of harmful radiation.

Even more ominous, they said, it seemed likely that a highly depleted section of the ozone layer, known as a "hole," would develop over the Arctic, exposing populated areas of the Northern Hemisphere. A similar hole had first been observed over Antarctica in 1985.

The scientists based their startling announcement on new data collected over northern New England, eastern Canada and much of Europe and Asia. What their airborne instruments—carried aloft by a satellite and two high-flying planes—detected was the highest concentration of ozone-destroying chlorine monoxide ever measured in the atmosphere.

Chlorine monoxide is a derivative of an important family of synthetic chemicals that are known as chlorofluorocarbons (CFCs). They have enjoyed wide use for decades as coolants in refrigerators and air conditioners, propellants in aerosol spray cans, blowing agents in the manufacture of plastic and rubber foam products and as solvents in the production of electronic equipment.

Once released into the atmosphere, CFCs drift upward until they reach the ozone layer, which begins in the stratosphere. As long as they remain in their original molecular form, CFCs are harmless. But intense ultraviolet radiation can break the CFC molecule apart, producing chlorine monoxide and setting off a series of reactions that destroy ozone.

High levels of chlorine monoxide are alarming enough by themselves. But NASA's scientists found evidence of even more worrisome atmospheric problems: high levels of bromine monoxide. A byproduct of halons, man-made chemicals used in fire extinguishers, bromine monoxide is even more destructive than chlorine monoxide.

Michael Kurylo, NASA's program manager for the study, estimated that the two chemicals could destroy 1 to 2 percent of the ozone layer daily during brief periods of late winter. At that rate, as much as 40 percent of the ozone over populous areas of the Northern Hemisphere could be depleted by early spring, when ozone destruction ends each year. The resulting hole, scientists said, could be almost as serious as the one over Antarctica, where ozone depletion has been known to reach 50 percent.

In addition to high levels of ozone-destroying chlorine monoxide and bromine monoxide, the NASA team found reduced levels of nitrogen oxides, which protect ozone from the other two gases by converting them into harmless compounds before they have time to destroy ozone. The loss of nitrogen oxides, which scientists attribute to high levels of volcanic ash ejected into the stratosphere last summer during the eruption of Mount Pinatubo in the Philippines, diminishes the atmosphere's natural ability to recover from ozone depletion.

"The latest scientific findings indicate pretty clearly that the atmosphere all over the place, and not just in the polar regions, is nearly devoid of some of the constituents that protect ozone against depletion," says Michael Oppenheimer, senior scientist at the Environmental Defense Fund in New York City.

... [R]ecent findings are serious enough that several countries, including the United States, have taken new steps to slow ozone depletion. In 1987, for example, the main producers and consumers of CFCs and halons signed the Montreal Protocol, which mandated phasing out these destructive chemicals by the year 2000, or sooner. The phaseout was subsequently accelerated in 1990, and several signatories to the protocol have since committed themselves to beating the deadline....

How Dangerous Is Ozone Depletion?

Ozone-destroying chemicals are extremely stable, so they last in the atmosphere for many decades. That means that even if production of all CFCs and halons stopped today, the chemicals already in the atmosphere would go on destroying ozone well into the 21st century. And because large quantities of these chemicals are contained in existing air conditioners and refrigerators, from which they continue to escape through malfunction or intentional venting, it may be a century before the ozone layer has built itself back up.

Just how devastating widespread ozone depletion would be is not known. But a 1975 government study on the environmental effects of an all-out nuclear war—which scientists say would destroy much of the ozone layer—provided a chilling glimpse of the aftermath. Ozone depletion of 50 percent, the study postulated, "would cause [skin] blistering after one hour of exposure. This leads to the conclusion that outside daytime work in the Northern Hemisphere would require complete covering by protective clothing.... It would be very difficult to grow many (if any) food crops, and livestock would have to graze at dusk if there were any grass to eat."

The study speculated that a 25 to 30 percent depletion of stratospheric ozone —which NASA's findings indicate already may have occurred over parts of the Northern Hemisphere—would make it "difficult to imagine how survivors could carry out postwar recovery operations.

HOW OZONE-DEPLETING AGENTS ATTACK THE OZONE LAYER

Beginning in the stratosphere at an altitude of about 15 miles and extending up into the mesosphere, the 25-mile-wide ozone layer protects Earth by blocking out most of the sun's harmful ultraviolet light. Breakdown of ozone by chlorofluorocarbons and other chemicals allows harmful radiation to reach Earth.

1. Oxygen molecules in the stratosphere are transformed into ozone by solar ultraviolet (UV) radiation, which splits the oxygen molecule and releases highly reactive oxygen atoms. The free oxygen atoms then bind to oxygen molecules to form ozone molecules, which also are broken up by UV radiation. This continuous creation and destruction of oxygen and ozone occurs normally in the stratosphere.
2. Once certain chemicals, chiefly chlorofluorocarbons (CFCs), reach the ozone layer, UV radiation bombards the CFC molecule, breaking off an atom of chlorine.
3. The free chlorine atom attacks an ozone molecule, breaking off one of ozone's three oxygen atoms to form one chlorine monoxide molecule and leaving one oxygen molecule.
4. When the chlorine monoxide molecule encounters a free oxygen atom, produced during the natural mixing of oxygen and ozone, the oxygen atom breaks up the chlorine monoxide molecule and binds to its oxygen atom, forming a new oxygen molecule and leaving behind a free chlorine atom.
5. The newly freed chlorine atom can continue to destroy ozone molecules for many years. Oxygen molecules continue to break apart and form ozone, but this natural replenishing process is slowed in the presence of chlorine monoxide.
6. Because oxygen, unlike ozone, does not reflect UV radiation, the sun's potentially harmful UV rays penetrate the depleted areas of the ozone layer and reach Earth's surface.

Since the ozone hole opened over Antarctica in 1985, scientists have been assessing the impact of increased ultraviolet (UV) radiation on phytoplankton, the micro-organisms that make up the essential first link in the food chain that maintains all animal life in warm southern waters, including whales. Preliminary findings show that phytoplankton populations have dropped by up to 12 percent in areas where surface UV radiation has increased under the Antarctic ozone hole.

This is the first evidence outside the laboratory that links ozone depletion to damage of living organisms on Earth.

Excessive UV radiation is also thought to disrupt photosynthesis, the process by which green plants use the sun's radiant energy to produce carbohydrates. Ozone depletion could thus cause reduced yields in crops such as soybeans and rice, crops that are essential to feeding large parts of the Third World.

Ultraviolet radiation has long been known to cause health problems in animals, including cataracts in humans—the leading cause of blindness. The United Nations Environment Programme (UNEP), which was set up in 1972 to foster international cooperation in protecting the environment, predicts that ozone depletion will cause an additional 1.6 million cases per year.

There are also preliminary reports of widespread blindness among rabbits, sheep, horses and cattle in southern Chile, where high UV radiation exposure resulted from the ozone hole over Antarctica.

UNEP also foresees an annual increase of 300,000 cases of skin cancer, by the year 2000, particularly in Argentina and Australia, which have come under increased UV radiation. UNEP also estimates that a 10 percent depletion of the ozone layer would cause up to 26 percent more basal and squamous-cell skin cancers. The agency cites new evidence that UV radiation may also contribute to cancers of the lip and salivary glands.

Other studies project that a 10 percent increase in UV penetration would cause up to a 9 percent increase in the incidence of the more deadly malignant melanoma among light-skinned people, the group that is most vulnerable to this virulent form of cancer.

Ultraviolet radiation may also undermine the immune system's ability to ward off infectious diseases. This, says Margaret L. Kripke, an immunologist at the University of Texas' M. D. Anderson Cancer Center in Houston, is the biggest unknown health effect of UV radiation.

Animal experiments have indicated that UV radiation may reduce lymphocytes' ability to destroy certain microorganisms that enter the body through the skin, such as Leishmania, malaria, schistosoma and the leprosy bacillus.

Although it is not known whether UV radiation actually reduces human resistance to these agents, Kripke testified last fall, "infectious diseases constitute an enormous public health problem worldwide, and any factor that reduces immune defenses... is likely to have a devastating impact on human health."

Kripke's research was particularly ominous for sun worshipers. She found that commercial sunscreen preparations, which protect against sunburn and other damage to the skin from UV radiation, don't block the immunosuppressive effects of UV radiation. Similarly, skin pigmentation, which protects darker-skinned people from skin cancers that are prevalent among Caucasians, doesn't seem to protect the immune system from UV damage....

FIRST SIGNS OF TROUBLE

Even as industry was finding new uses for CFCs in the early 1970s, scientists were beginning to link them to ozone destruction. In 1974, Ralph Cicerone, then at the University of Michigan, and his colleague, Richard S. Stolarski, investigated the possible effects on stratospheric ozone of chlorine released by NASA rockets. They concluded that a single atom of chlorine would destroy many thousands of ozone molecules.

However, because the number of rockets passing through the ozone layer was small, and no other sources of chlorine at that altitude had been identified, their findings did not cause widespread alarm.

Findings reported later that year, however, showed that rocket engines were not the only source of chlorine in the stratosphere. Sherwood Rowland and Mario Molina at the University of California at Irvine decided to study CFCs after they are released into the atmosphere. They found that CFCs are so durable that they do not break down under the forces of solar radiation and precipitation in the lower atmosphere, but continue to float around in their original state for many years, eventually drifting upward into the stratosphere.

"What we did was to ask a question that hadn't been asked before: What is going to happen to the CFCs?" Rowland recalls. "The conclusion we came to was that nothing would happen quickly, but on the time scale of many decades CFCs would go away into the stratosphere and release chlorine atoms and then that the chlorine atoms would attack the ozone.... We concluded that there was danger to the ozone layer and... that we should quit putting CFCs into the atmosphere."

Not surprisingly, Rowland and Molina faced hostile reactions from the producers of CFCs when they published their results in 1974. "The public was probably more likely to believe it than the chemistry community," Rowland says. "Within the chemistry community then and still now there is a feeling that most environmental problems are really just public relations problems, that they are not real problems."

Rowland says the chemicals manufacturers set up the Committee on Atmospheric Science to discredit the two researchers' findings. Indeed, he adds that many critics dismissed their conclusions as "kooky. One of my favorites was an aerosol-propellant company that claimed [our results were] disinformation put out by the KGB."

But their data held up. In 1976, after a nationwide research effort involving NASA and the National Oceanic and Atmospheric Administration (NOAA), the National Academy of Sciences confirmed that CFC gases released into the atmosphere from spray cans were in fact damaging the ozone layer.

Two years later, after consumer boycotts had reduced the market for spray cans by almost two-thirds, the United States banned the use of CFCs as aerosol propellants in spray cans for most uses.

OZONE HOLE DISCOVERED

Although other industrial nations continued to produce and use CFCs for aerosol sprays and other purposes, the international scientific community continued the search for data on ozone depletion launched by Rowland and Molina. During the early 1980s, most research was confined to computer models of the atmosphere. Then, in 1985, British scientists discovered that ozone depletion had become so severe over a vast area of Antarctica that it amounted to a virtual "hole" in the ozone layer.

Still, resistance to the ozone-depletion theory remained so strong that the British team was refused additional government funding to continue their research. Ironically, they obtained backing instead from the U.S. Chemical Manufacturers Association, whose members had the most to lose from confirmation of Rowland and Molina's theory. Because of mounting pressure at home to find substitutes for CFCs, however, the American chemical industry wanted to resolve the issue once and for all before abandoning CFCs.

Meanwhile, Rowland and other scientists were learning more about ozone depletion and why the phenomenon was so strong over the Antarctic.

They discovered that CFCs are concentrated over the South Pole because of strong circular winds known as the "polar vortex," which sweep unimpeded over the flat, barren continent of Antarctica. The vortex gathers the destructive gases from the surrounding atmosphere into a wide funnel over Antarctica, where they remain isolated during the dark, frigid winter months.

Equally important, they found that as CFCs break down, the resulting chlorine monoxide clings to the ice crystals that form clouds in the stratosphere. These ice crystals provide the surfaces needed for the catalytic reaction in which chlorine breaks down ozone.

With the return of sunlight to Antarctica during September and October, the beginning of spring in the Southern Hemisphere, solar radiation acts as a catalyst enabling the chlorine monoxide produced by CFCs to destroy the surrounding ozone layer.

As the days lengthen, the air over Antarctica warms up, breaking up both the stratospheric ice clouds and the polar vortex. The destruction of ozone slows as the chlorine atoms are once again bound into harmless chlorine nitrate and hydrogen chloride molecules, and the hole disappears as the vortex dissipates, allowing ozone from the surrounding regions to fill the void.

The final confirmation of Rowland and Molina's theory linking CFCs to ozone depletion came in 1987, when NASA undertook a series of aerial tests over Antarctica. From inside the ozone hole, the NASA instruments detected high concentrations of chlorine monoxide.

Montreal Protocol Signed

International reaction to the proof that CFCs were destroying the ozone layer was swift. On Sept. 16, 1987, just nine months after formal negotiations began, 24 nations signed the Montreal Protocol on Substances That Deplete the Ozone Layer. The agreement garnered an unprecedented degree of international support for such a sweeping program to protect the environment: The ratifying nations accounted for 99 percent of the world's production of CFCs and 90 percent of their consumption.

The Montreal Protocol called for freezing halon emissions at 1986 levels by 1992; for halving CFC emissions by 1998; and halving CFC production and importation by 1999. To compensate for their low levels of production of ozone-depleting chemicals, developing nations were given an additional 10 years to meet these deadlines. By Jan. 1, 1989, the protocol had been ratified by enough countries to go into effect.

Richard Elliot Benedick, a Foreign Service officer who led the U.S. delegation in negotiating the Montreal Protocol, identifies several reasons for the treaty's overwhelming success. First, international cooperation among scientists allowed for the rapid discovery of CFCs' role in ozone depletion. Public opinion, which was then beginning to focus on environmental issues throughout the industrial world, was also quick to press governments to act. Negotiations were supported by the UNEP.

Benedick also credits the United States for its leading role in gaining support for the treaty. The United States was the first producer of ozone-depleting chemicals to restrict their production, he points out in his account of the negotiations surrounding the protocol.

In addition, Congress passed ozone-protection legislation as early as 1977, long before the governments of Western Europe responded at all.

The United States also was primarily responsible for the 1985 Vienna Convention for the Protection of the Ozone Layer, an agreement among the major CFC producers to collect additional data that led up to the Montreal Protocol.

"The U.S. government reflected its concerns over the fate of the ozone layer through stimulating and supporting both American and international scientific research," Benedick wrote. "Then, convinced of the dangers, it undertook extensive diplomatic and scientific initiatives to promote an ozone protection plan to other countries, many of which were initially hostile or indifferent to the idea."

The drafters of the Montreal Protocol also assured its success by making the agreement flexible. As such, it could be rapidly amended to reflect subsequent changes in environmental conditions or new findings. And new findings were soon to test the agreement's flexibility.

The ozone hole over Antarctica continued to appear each September and October after its initial discovery in 1985. In 1988, scientists were encouraged to find that the hole was not as big as before. But the following year, the ozone hole reappeared, covering more than 15 million square miles.

Arctic Expedition Launched

The same year, NASA and NOAA launched an airborne expedition to the Arctic to investigate whether conditions were ripe near the North Pole for another ozone hole. Because the Arctic terrain is not as flat as that of Antarctica—and because temperatures at the North Pole do not fall as low as they do at the South Pole—the polar vortex was found to be weaker in the north. But the scientists did find higher than expected concentrations of chlorine compounds and concluded that an ozone hole could easily develop.

Because more people live at far northern latitudes than in southern Chile, Argentina, Australia and New Zealand, which border the area exposed to UV radiation in the Southern Hemisphere, an ozone hole over the Arctic would pose far greater risks to human health.

Other research revealed a new potential source of ozone depletion in areas far from the polar regions. American chemists Susan Solomon and Dave Hoffman found that sulfate particles spewed into the stratosphere by strong volcanic eruptions could act in much the same way as ice crystals in polar stratospheric clouds by providing surfaces on which chlorine and bromine compounds can destroy ozone more efficiently than when they are floating free.

Studying the impact of volcanic ash in the aftermath of the 1982 eruption of El Chichon in Mexico, Solomon and Hoffman found that ozone concentrations over the middle latitudes were significantly depleted. They concluded that ozone depletion was likely following other major volcanic eruptions.

Although their research was limited to El Chichon, Solomon, a NOAA chemist in Boulder, Colo., says, "We found that similar processes could also take place on the liquid sulfuric acid and water particles that form following major volcanic eruptions."

The implications of Solomon and Hoffman's research are clear. While ice clouds form only over the polar regions, volcanic ash can travel anywhere. If volcanic ash does facilitate ozone depletion even in the absence of ice crystals, an ozone hole could open over any region on Earth.

In the summer of 1990, NASA reported that, globally, the ozone layer had been depleted by 2 to 3 percent over the previous two decades. It was also reported that the ozone layer had already begun to thin over the United States and other populated areas in the middle latitudes.

At the same time, the chemicals industry was quickly bringing into production substitutes for CFCs that are less damaging to the ozone layer. While not completely benign, these hydrochlorofluorocarbons, or HCFCs, were hailed as temporary substitutes for CFCs in many applications, particularly as coolants. Most important, the HCFCs and other substitute chemicals facilitated the rapid phaseout of CFCs.

Montreal Protocol nations were quick to respond to the news that ozone depletion was intensifying. In June 1990, in London, they amended the agreement to accelerate the phaseout of ozone-depleting chemicals. Under the new guidelines, all production and importation of CFCs and halons must stop by the year 2000. Other ozone-depleting agents, such as carbon tetrachloride and methyl chloroform, were added to the list of chemicals to be phased out of production. Developing countries still have an additional 10 years to meet the deadline. As a result of the new deadlines, chlorine pollution was expected by 2075 to fall below levels recorded prior to the first appearance of the ozone hole.

The amendments also addressed the special problems faced by developing nations. Although they produce few ozone-depleting chemicals, India, China and other countries have counted on introducing cheap refrigeration and air conditioning as part of their plans for modernization. They succeeded in convincing the industrial world to set up a fund to help them pay for the more expensive substitutes they will be forced to purchase, as well as information and equipment to help them produce environmentally sound refrigerators and air conditioners themselves.

Also in 1990, Congress passed the far-reaching Clean Air Act Amendments, which call for the complete phaseout of CFCs, halons and carbon tetrachloride by 2000, of methyl chloroform by 2002 and HCFCs by 2030. The law made the United States the first nation to legislate a ban on these chemicals. To reduce emissions of existing stores of ozone-depleting agents, the law called for regulations to require recycling of refrigerants and air-conditioning coolants. Finally, the new law mandated faster elimination of ozone-depleting substances if warranted by new scientific findings of damage to the ozone layer.

VAST AREA AT RISK

No sooner had the ink dried on the revisions to the Montreal Protocol than new information pointed to an even more dire situation. In October 1990, scientists found the lowest ozone levels ever recorded over Antarctica and discovered that the hole had stretched into southern Chile including Purna Arenas, a city of 100,000. There was also further evidence that parts of Australia had been exposed to high levels of UV radiation when bits of the ozone hole broke away as the polar vortex weakened and drifted northward from Antarctica.

On Oct. 22, the UNEP and the World Meteorological Organization announced that ozone depletion had begun to occur at the middle and high latitudes of both the Northern and the Southern Hemispheres in spring, summer and winter.

"Ozone depletion in the middle and high latitudes means that it covers almost all of North America, Europe, the Soviet Union, Australia, New Zealand and a sizable part of Latin America," said UNEP Director Mostafa K. Tolba. "The only area with no indication of change, that is, no visible reduction of ozone, is the tropical belt around the Earth."

European researchers, building on Solomon and Hoffman's volcano-ash findings, are now predicting that last year's eruption of Mount Pinatubo threatens to erode the ozone layer to dangerous levels over much of Europe this spring. Researchers participating in the 17-nation European Arctic Stratospheric Ozone Experiment based in northern Sweden have yet to complete their experiments. But they issued a recommendation in early February that governments in Northern Europe should take more urgent steps to protect the ozone layer.

The most recent signs of severe ozone loss were detected by NASA's Upper Atmosphere Research Satellite (UARS), launched last September [1991] to monitor the ozone layer and measure substances that destroy ozone. On Feb. 3, two months before the current study was scheduled for completion, NASA announced that the satellite had detected high levels of chlorine monoxide over Scandinavia and northern Eurasia, an area that includes London, Moscow and Amsterdam. The levels were comparable to concentrations found in the ozone hole over Antarctica.

NASA predicted that an ozone hole could open over the Northern Hemisphere this spring if chlorine monoxide levels remain high enough. Final results of the study are due in mid-April.

The bad news was not limited to the far north. NASA's satellite observations also showed ozone depletion over the tropics, which the agency suggested was due to plumes of ash from Mount Pinatubo. In addition, the satellite detected areas of low ozone across the western United States. These findings were confirmed by separate measurements taken in Boulder, Colo.

Confirming the satellite data were new findings from the NASA-led Airborne Arctic Stratospheric Expedition, which monitors ozone depletion from two specially equipped aircraft: the ER-2, a converted U-2 spy plane that gathers data at 70,000 feet, and the DC-8-72, a "flying lab" that operates at 41,000 feet. The expedition reported Feb. 3 that it had found even higher levels of chlorine monoxide than the satellite had over eastern Canada and northern New England. The readings—at 1.5 parts per billion by volume—surpass anything ever measured in either polar region.

"These findings have increased our concern that significant ozone loss will occur during any given winter over the Arctic in the next 10 years," scientists announced. "This is based on significant new data with improved instrumentation obtained with broader geographic and seasonal coverage and the knowledge that past release of CFCs will increase chlorine substantially in the stratosphere in the decade to come."

NOTES

1. The ozone layer is a 25-mile-wide band above the Earth with a high but uneven concentration of ozone gas. Starting at an altitude of about 15 miles, it shields humans and other organisms from the most harmful effects of the sun's ultraviolet (UV) radiation.

NO

James P. Hogan

OZONE POLITICS:
THEY CALL THIS SCIENCE?

Every age has its peculiar folly: some scheme, project, or fantasy into which it plunges, spurred on by the love of gain, the necessity of excitement, or the mere force of imitation.

—Charles Mackay
Extraordinary Popular Delusions and the Madness of Crowds, 1841

Earlier centuries saw witch-hunting hysteria, the Crusades, gold stampedes, and the South Sea Bubble. Periodically, societies are seized by collective delusions that take on lives of their own, where all facts are swept aside that fail to conform to the expectations of what has become a self-sustaining reality. Today we have the environmentalist mania reaching a crescendo over ozone.

Manmade chlorofluorocarbons, or CFCs, we're told, are eating away the ozone layer that shields us from ultraviolet radiation, and if we don't stop using them now deaths from skin cancer in the United States alone will rise by hundreds of thousands in the next half century. As a result, 80 nations are about to railroad through legislation to ban one of most beneficial substances ever discovered at a cost the public doesn't seem to comprehend but that will be staggering. It could mean having to replace today's refrigeration and air-conditioning equipment with more expensive types running on substitutes that are toxic, corrosive, flammable if sparked, less efficient, and generally reminiscent of the things people heaved sighs of relief to get rid of in the 1930s. And the domestic side will be only a small part. The food industry that we take for granted depends on refrigerated warehouses, trucks, and ships. So do supplies of drugs, medicines, and blood. Whole regions of the sunbelt states have prospered during the last 40 years because of the better living and working environments made possible by air conditioning. And to developing nations that rely completely on modern food-preservation methods, the effects will be devastating.

Now, I'd have to agree that the alternative of seeing the planet seared by lethal levels of radiation would make a pretty good justification for whatever drastic action is necessary to prevent it. The only problem is, there isn't one piece of solid, scientifically validated evidence to support the contention. The decisions being made are political, driven by media-friendly pressure groups wielding a power over public perceptions that is totally out of proportion to any scientific competence they possess. But when you ask the people who do have the competence to know—scientists who have specialized in the study of atmosphere and climate for years—a very different story emerges.

What they're saying, essentially, is that the whole notion of the ozone layer as something fixed and finite, to be eroded away at a faster or slower rate like shoe leather, is all wrong to begin with—it's simply not a depletable resource; that even if it were, the process by which CFCs are supposed to deplete it is highly speculative and has never been observed to take place; and even if it did, the effect would be trivial compared to what happens naturally. In short, there's no good reason for believing that human activity is having any significant effect at all.

To see why, let's start with the basics and take seashores as an analogy. Waves breaking along the coastline continually generate a belt of surf. The surf decomposes again, back into the ocean from where it came. The two processes are linked: Big waves on stormy days create more surf; the more surf there is to decay, the higher the rate at which it does so. The result is a balance between the rates of creation and destruction. Calmer days will see a general thinning of the surf line and possibly "holes" in more sheltered spots —but obviously the surf isn't something that runs out. Its supply is inexhaustible as long as oceans and shores exist.

In the same kind of way, ozone is all the time being created in the upper atmosphere—by sunshine, out of oxygen. A normal molecule of oxygen gas consists of two oxygen atoms joined together. High-energy ultraviolet radiation, known as UV-C, can split one of these molecules apart (a process known as photodissociation) into two free oxygen atoms. These can then attach to another molecule to form a three-atom species, which is ozone—produced mainly in the tropics above a 30-kilometer altitude where the ultraviolet flux is strongest. The ozone sinks and moves poleward to accumulate in lower-level reservoirs extending from 17 to 30 kilometers—the so-called ozone "layer."

Ozone is destroyed by chemical recombination back into normal oxygen—by reaction with nitrogen dioxide (produced in part by high-altitude cosmic rays), through ultraviolet dissociation by the same UV-C that creates ozone, and also by a less energetic band known as UV-B, which isn't absorbed in the higher regions. Every dissociation of an oxygen or ozone molecule absorbs an incoming UV-B photon, and that may be what gives this part of the atmosphere its ultraviolet screening ability.

Its height and thickness are not constant, but adjust automatically to accommodate variations in the incoming ultra-violet flux. When UV is stronger, it penetrates deeper before being absorbed; with weaker UV, penetration is less. Even if all the ozone were to suddenly vanish, there would still be 17 to 30 kilometers of hitherto untouched oxygen-rich atmosphere below, which would become available as a resource for new ozone creation, and the entire screening mechanism would promptly regenerate. As Robert Pease, professor emeritus of physical climatology at the University of California at Riverside, says, "Ozone in the atmosphere is not in finite supply." In other words, as in the case of surf with oceans and shores, it is inexhaustible for as long as sunshine and air continue to exist.

If ozone were depleting, UV intensity at the earth's surface would be increasing. In fact, actual measurements show that it has been decreasing—by as much as 8 percent in some places over the last decade.

Ordinarily, a scientific hypothesis that failed in its most elementary prediction would be dumped right there. But as Dr. Dixy Lee Ray—former governor of Washington state, chairman of the Atomic Energy Commission, and a scientist with the U.S. Bureau of Oceans and the University of Washington—put it: "There are fads in science. Scientists are capable of developing their own strange fixations, just like anyone else." Even though the physics makes it difficult to see how, the notion of something man-made destroying the ozone layer has always fascinated an apocalyptic few who have been seeking possible candidates for more than 40 years. According to Hugh Ellsaesser, guest scientist at the Atmospheric and Geophysical Sciences Division of the Lawrence Livermore National Laboratory, "There has been a small but concerted program to build the possibility of man destroying the ozone layer into a dire threat requiring governmental controls since the time of CIAP [Climatic Impact Assessment Program on the supersonic transport (SST), conducted in the early 1970s]."

In the 1950s, it was A-bomb testing; in the 1960s, the SST; in the 1970s, spacecraft launches and various chemicals from pesticides to fertilizers. All of these claimed threats to the destruction of the ozone layer were later discredited, and for a while, the controversy died out. Then, in 1985 and 1986, banner headlines blared that a huge ozone hole had been discovered in the Antarctic. This, it was proclaimed, confirmed the latest version of the threat.

In 1974, two chemists, Rowland and Molina at the University of California at Irvine, hypothesized that ozone might be attacked by CFCs—which had come into widespread use during the previous 20 years. Basically, they suggested that the same chemical inertness that makes CFCs noncorrosive, nontoxic, and ideal as a refrigerant would enable them to diffuse intact to the upper atmosphere. There, they would be dissociated by high-energy ultraviolet and release free atoms of chlorine. Chlorine will combine with one of the three oxygen atoms of an ozone molecule to produce chlorine monoxide and a normal two-molecule oxygen atom, thereby destroying the ozone molecule. The model becomes more insidious by postulating an additional chain of catalytic reactions via which the chlorine monoxide can be recycled back into free chlorine, hence evoking the specter of a single chlorine atom running amok in the stratosphere, gobbling up ozone molecules like Pac-Man.

Scary, vivid, sensational; perfect for activists seeking a cause, politicians in need of visibility; just what the media revel in. Unfortunately, however, it doesn't fit with a few vital facts. And if you claim to be talking about science, that's kind of important.

First, CFCs don't rise in significant amounts to where they need to be for UV-C photons to break them up. Because ozone absorbs heat directly from the sun's rays, the stratosphere exhibits a reverse temperature structure, or thermal "inversion"—it gets warmer with altitude rather than cooler. As Robert Pease points out, "This barrier greatly inhibits vertical air movements and the interchange of gases across the tropopause [the boundary between the lower atmosphere and the stratosphere], including CFCs. In the stratosphere, CFC gases decline rapidly and drop to only two percent of surface values by thirty kilometers of altitude. At the same time, less than two percent of the UV-C penetrates this deeply." Hence the number of CFC splittings is vastly lower than the original hypothesis assumes—for the same reason there aren't many marriages between Eskimos and Australian Aborigines: They don't mix very much.

For the UV photons that do make it, there are about 136 million oxygen molecules for them to collide with for every CFC—and every such reaction will create ozone, not destroy it. So even if we allow the big CFC molecule three times the chance of a small oxygen molecule of being hit, then 45 million ozone molecules will still be created for every CFC molecule that's broken up. Hardly a convincing disaster scenario, is it?

Ah, but what about the catalytic effect, whereby one chlorine atom can eat up thousands of ozone molecules? Doesn't that change the picture?

Not really. The catalysis argument depends on encounters between chlorine monoxide and free oxygen atoms. But the chances are much higher that a wandering free oxygen atom will find a molecule of normal oxygen rather than one of chlorine monoxide. So once again, probability favors ozone creation over ozone destruction.

At least 192 chemical reactions occur between substances in the upper stratosphere along with 48 different identifiable photochemical processes all linked through complex feedback mechanisms that are only partly understood. Selecting a few reactions brought about in a laboratory and claiming that this is what happens in the stratosphere (where it has never been measured) might be a way of getting to a predetermined conclusion. But it isn't science.

But surely it's been demonstrated! Hasn't a thousand times more chlorine been measured over the Antarctic than models say ought to be there?

Yes. High concentrations of chlorine—or to be exact, chlorine monoxide. But all chlorine atoms look alike. There is absolutely nothing to link the chlorine found over the Antarctic with CFCs from the other end of the world. What the purveyors of that story omitted to mention was that the measuring station at McMurdo Sound is located 15 kilometers downwind from Mount Erebus, an active volcano venting 100 to 200 tons of chlorine every day, and that in 1983 it averaged 1,000 tons per day. Mightn't that just have more to do with it than refrigerators in New York or air conditioners in Atlanta?

World CFC production is currently about 1.1 million tons annually—750,000 tons of which is chlorine. Twenty times as much comes from the passive outgassing of volcanoes. This can rise by a factor of ten with a single large eruption—for example that of Tambora in 1815, which pumped a minimum of 211 million tons straight into the atmosphere. Where are the records of all the cataclysmic effects that should presumably have followed from the consequent ozone depletion?

And on an even greater scale, 300 million tons of chlorine are contained in spray blown off the oceans every year. A single thunderstorm in the Amazon region can transport 200 million tons of air per hour into the atmosphere, containing 3 million tons of water vapor. On average 44,000 thunderstorms occur daily, mostly in the tropics. Even if we concede to the depletion theory and allow this mechanism to transport CFCs also, compared to what gets there naturally, the whiff of chlorine produced by all of human industry (and we're only talking about the leakage from it) is a snowflake in a blizzard.

Despite all that, isn't it still true that a hole has appeared in the last ten years and is getting bigger? What about that, then?

In 1985, a sharp, unpredicted decline was reported in the mean depth of ozone over Halley Bay, Antarctica. Although the phenomenon was limited to altitudes between 12 and 22 kilometers and the interior of a seasonal circulation of the polar jet stream known as the "polar vortex," it was all that the ozone-doomsday pushers needed. Without waiting for any scientific evaluation or consensus, they decided that this was the confirmation that the Rowland-Molina conjecture had been waiting for. The ominous term "ozone hole" was coined by a media machine well rehearsed in environmentalist politics, and anything the scientific community had to say has been drowned out.

Missing from the press and TV accounts, for instance, is that an unexpectedly low value in the Antarctic winter-spring ozone level was reported by the British scientist Gordon Dobson in 1956 —when CFCs were barely in use. In a 40-year history of ozone research written in 1968, he notes: "One of the most interesting results... which came out of the IGY [International Geophysical Year] was the discovery of the peculiar annual variation of ozone at Halley Bay." His first thought was that the result might have been due to faulty equipment or operator error. But when such possibilities were eliminated and the same thing happened the following year, he concluded: "It was clear that the winter vortex over the South Pole was maintained late into the spring and that this kept the ozone values low. When it suddenly broke up in November, both the ozone values and the stratosphere temperatures suddenly rose." A year after that, in 1958, a similar drop was reported by French scientists at the Antarctic observatory at Dumont d'Urville—larger than that causing all the hysteria today.

These measurements were on the edge of observational capability, especially in an environment such as the Antarctic, and most scientists regarded them with caution. After the 1985 "discovery," NASA reanalyzed its satellite data and found that it had been routinely throwing out low Antarctic ozone readings as "unreliable."

The real cause is slowly being unraveled, and while some correlation is evident with volcanic eruptions and sunspot cycles, the dominant factor appears to be the extreme Antarctic winter conditions, as Dobson originally suspected. The poleward transportation of ozone from its primary creation zones over the tropics does not penetrate into the polar vortex, where chemical depletion can't be replaced because of the lack of sunshine. Note that this is a localized minimum relative to the surrounding high-latitude reservoir regions, where global ozone is thickest. As Hugh Ellsaesser observes, "The ozone hole... leads only to spring values of ultraviolet flux over Antarctica... a factor of two less than those experienced every summer in North Dakota."

But isn't it getting bigger every year? And aren't the latest readings showing depletion elsewhere, too?

In April, 1991, EPA Administrator William Reilly announced that the ozone layer over North America was thinning twice as fast as expected and produced the figures for soaring deaths from skin cancer. This was based on readings from NASA's Nimbus-7 satellite. I talked to Dr. S. Fred Singer of the Washington-based Science and Environmental Policy Project, who developed the principle of UV backscatter that the ozone monitoring instrument aboard Nimbus-7 employs. "You simply cannot tell from one sunspot cycle," was his comment. "The data are too noisy. Scientists need at least one more cycle of satellite observations before they can establish a trend." In other words the trend exists in the eye of the determined beholder, not in any facts he beholds.

February 1992 saw a repeat performance when a NASA research aircraft detected high values of chlorine monoxide in the northern stratosphere. Not of CFCs; nor was there any evidence that ozone itself was actually being depleted, nor any mention that the Pinatubo volcano was active at the time. Yet almost as if on cue, the U.S. Senate passed an amendment only two days later calling for an accelerated phaseout of CFCs. (It's interesting to note that NASA's budget was under review at the time. After getting its increase, NASA has since conceded that perhaps the fears were premature.)

But apart from all that, yes, world mean-total ozone declined about 5 percent from 1979 to 1986. So what? From 1962 to 1979 it increased by $5\frac{1}{2}$ percent. And since 1986, it has been increasing again (although that part's left out of the story the public gets). On shorter time scales, it changes naturally all the time and from place to place, hence surface ultraviolet intensity is not constant and never was. It varies with latitude—for instance, how far north or south from the equator you are—with the seasons, and with solar activity. And it does so in amounts that are far greater than those causing all the fuss.

The whole doomsday case boils down to claiming that if something isn't done to curb CFCs, ultraviolet radiation will increase by 10 percent over the next 20 years. But from the poles to the equator, it increases naturally by a whopping factor of 50, or 5,000 percent, anyway! —equivalent to 1 percent for every six miles. Or to put it another way, a family moving from New York to Philadelphia would experience the same increase as is predicted by the worst-case depletion scenarios. Alternatively, they could live 1,500 feet higher in elevation—say, by moving to their summer cabin in the Catskills.

Superposed on this is a minimum 25-percent swing from summer to winter, and on top of that, a 10- to 12-year pattern that follows the sunspot cycle. Finally, there are irregular fluctuations caused by the effects of volcanic eruptions, electrical storms, and the like on atmospheric chemistry. Expecting to find some "natural" level that shouldn't be deviated from in all this is like trying to define sea level in a typhoon.

Skin cancer is increasing, nevertheless. Something must be causing it.

An increasing rate of UV-induced skin cancer means that more people are receiving more exposure than they ought to. It doesn't follow that the intensity of ultraviolet is increasing as it would if ozone were being depleted. (In fact, it's decreasing, as we saw earlier.) Other considerations explain the facts far better, such as that sun worship has become a fad among light-skinned people only in the last couple of generations, or the migrations in comparatively recent times of peoples into habitats for which they aren't adapted: for instance, the white population of Australia. (Native Australians have experienced no skin-cancer increase.)

Deaths from drowning increase as you get nearer the equator—not because the water becomes more lethal but because human behavior changes: Not many people go swimming in the Arctic. Nevertheless, when it comes to skin cancer, the National Academy of Sciences [NAS] has decided that only variation of UV matters. And from the measured ozone thinning from poles to equator and the change in zenith angle of the sun they determined that a 1-percent decrease in ozone equates to a 2-percent rise in skin cancer.

How you make a disaster scenario out of this, according to Ellsaesser, is to ignore the decline in surface UV actually measured over the last 15 years, ignore the reversal that shows ozone to have been increasing again since 1986, and extend the 1979–1986 slope as if it were going to continue for the next 40 years. Then, take the above formula as established fact and apply it to the entire U.S. population. Witness: According to the NAS report (1975), approximately 600,000 new cases of skin cancer occur annually. So, by the above, a 1-percent ozone decrease gives 12,000 more skin cancers. Projecting the 5-percent ozone

swing from the early 1980s through the next four decades gives 25 percent, hence a 50-percent rise in skin cancer, which works out at 300,000 new cases in the year 2030 A.D., or 7.5 million over the full period. Since the mortality rate is around 2.5 percent, this gives the EPA's "200,000 extra deaths in the United States alone." Voilà: Instant catastrophe.

As if this weren't flaky enough, it's possible that the lethal variety of skin cancer has little to do with UV exposure, anyway. The cancers that are caused by radiation are recognizable by their correlation with latitude and length of exposure to the sun and are relatively easily treated. The malignant melanoma form, which does kill, affects places like the soles of the feet as well as exposed areas, and there is more of it in Sweden than in Spain.

So, what's going on? What are publicly funded institutions that claim to be speaking science doing, waving readings known to be worthless (garbage in, gospel out?), faking data, pushing a cancer scare that contradicts fact, and force-feeding the public a line that basic physics says doesn't make sense? The only thing that comes through at all clearly is a determination to eliminate CFCs at any cost, whatever the facts, regardless of what scientists say.

Would it come as a complete surprise to learn that some very influential concerns stand to make a lot of money out of this? The patents on CFCs have recently run out, so anybody can now manufacture them without having to pay royalties. Sixty percent of the world CFC market is controlled by four companies who are already losing revenues and market share to rapidly growing chemicals industries in the Third World, notably Brazil, South Korea, and Taiwan. Some hold the patents on the only substitutes in sight, which will restore monopoly privileges once again if CFCs are outlawed. Mere coincidence?

Ultraviolet light has many beneficial effects as well as detrimental. For all any one knows, the increase that's being talked about could result in more overall good than harm. But research proposals to explore that side of things are turned down, while doomsayers line up for grants running into hundreds of millions. The race is on between chemicals manufacturers to come up with a better CFC substitute while equipment suppliers will be busy for years. Politicians are posturing as champions of the world, and the media are having a ball.

As Bob Holzknecht, a Florida engineer in the CFC industry for 20 years observes, "Nobody's interested in reality. Everyone who knows anything stands to gain. The public will end up paying through the nose, as always, but the public is unorganized and uninformed."

Good science will be the victim, too, of course. But science has a way of winning in the end. Today's superstitions can spread a million times faster than anything dreamed of by the doom prophets in days of old. But the same technologies which make that possible can also prove equally effective in putting them speedily to rest.

POSTSCRIPT

Is Ozone Depletion a Genuine Threat?

The critics of the "ozone scare" have made very little headway against the evidence. In November 1992 the Montreal Protocol was strengthened, and the deadline for ending production of CFCs was moved up by as much as nine years. By December 92 nations had ratified the treaty.

In March 1993 researchers reported a drop in Northern Hemisphere ozone concentrations that was worse than the one that kicked off the 1992 alarm discussed by Cooper. In April NASA researchers reported record thinning of the ozone layer worldwide. By autumn researchers had added that the 1993 ozone hole over the Antarctic was fully 15 percent worse than the one that had appeared the year before.

Some critics have suggested that the decline in ozone is a perfectly natural response to chlorine injected (as hydrochloric acid) into the atmosphere by volcanic eruptions or that volcanic chlorine could be making the problem worse than it would otherwise be. In the May 21, 1993, issue of *Science,* A. Tabazadeh and R. P. Turco reported calculations that indicate most volcanic chlorine would be removed from the sky by rain and ash long before it could reach the stratosphere. The August 27, 1993, issue of *Science* carried reports analyzing observations of stratospheric chlorine, ozone, and related chemistry and concluding that the ozone depletion mechanism depends on chlorine monoxide, not the hydrochloric acid found in volcanic eruptions. The conclusion, therefore, is that CFCs are the culprit.

Finally, in November 1993 James Kerr and Thomas McElroy of Canada's Atmospheric Environment Service answered critics who had been wondering why, if ozone depletion must lead to increased penetration of solar ultraviolet to the ground, no one had seen any sign of the increase outside Antarctica. Keer and McElroy reported that at a carefully studied Toronto site, the level of skin-damaging solar UV had increased more than 5 percent per year from 1989 to 1993.

For more reports on ozone depletion, see Richard S. Stolarski, "The Antarctic Ozone Hole," *Scientific American* (January 1988), and Owen B. Toon and Richard P. Turco, "Polar Stratospheric Clouds and Ozone Depletion," *Scientific American* (June 1991).

Two articles by critics of the "ozone scare" are Gary Taubes, "The Ozone Backlash," *Science* (June 11, 1993), and Ronald Bailey, "The Hole Story: The Science Behind the Scare," *Reason* (June 1992).

ISSUE 8

Should Society Be Concerned About Global Warming?

YES: Wallace S. Broecker, from "Global Warming on Trial," *Natural History* (April 1992)

NO: Wilfred Beckerman and Jesse Malkin, from "How Much Does Global Warming Matter?" *The Public Interest* (Winter 1994)

ISSUE SUMMARY

YES: Professor of geology Wallace S. Broecker argues that despite uncertainties about what causes climate change, the scientific consensus is that human-caused increases in the level of greenhouse gases in the atmosphere will indeed warm the world, with potentially serious consequences for human life.

NO: Economists Wilfred Beckerman and Jesse Malkin argue that global warming, if it even occurs, will not be catastrophic and warrants no immediate action; there are other worldwide concerns that are far more pressing.

Scientists have known for a century that carbon dioxide and other "greenhouse gases" (including water vapor, methane, and chlorofluorocarbons) help prevent heat from escaping the Earth. In fact, it is this "greenhouse effect" that keeps the Earth warm enough to support life. Yet, there can be too much of a good thing. Ever since the dawn of the industrial age, humans have been burning vast quantities of fossil fuels, releasing the carbon they contain as carbon dioxide. Because of this, some estimate that by the year 2050, the amount of carbon dioxide in the air will be double what it was in 1850. By 1982, the increase was apparent. Less than a decade later, many researchers were saying that the climate had already begun to warm. Now there is a strong consensus that the global climate will continue to warm. However, there is less agreement on just how much it will warm or what the impact of the warming will be on human (and other) life.

The June 1992 issue of *The Bulletin of the Atomic Scientists* carries two articles on the possible consequences of the greenhouse effect. In "Global Warming: The Worst Case," Jeremy Leggett says that although there are enormous uncertainties, a warmer climate will release more carbon dioxide, which will warm the climate even further. As a result, soil will grow dryer; forest fires will occur more frequently; and plant pests will thrive; and methane trapped in the world's seabeds will be released and will increase global warming much further— in effect, there will be a "runaway greenhouse effect." Leggett also hints at the possibility that the polar ice caps will melt and raise sea levels by hundreds of feet.

Taking the opposing view, in "Warming Theories Need Warning Label," S. Fred Singer emphasizes the uncertainties in the projections of global warming, their dependence on the accuracy of the computer models that generate them, and that improvements in the models have consistently shrunk the size of the predicted change. There will be no catastrophe, he argues, and money spent to ward off the climate warming would be better spent on "so many pressing—and real—problems in need of resources."

These scientists are not alone on their sides of the debate. In 1991, many scientists testified on "Global Climate Change and Greenhouse Emissions" before the House Subcommittee on Health and the Environment, Committee on Energy and Commerce. Some scientists maintained that the problem was real and potentially serious. Others asserted that they were not impressed by the data and computer models assembled to date. For instance, Sallie Baliunas, deputy director of the Mount Wilson Observatory and the chair of the Science Advisory Board at the George C. Marshall Institute in Washington, D.C., claimed that global warming in the next century will amount to no more than a few tenths of a degree, "indistinguishable from natural fluctuations in temperature."

It seems impossible for anyone to say with certainty just how severe the climate warming or its economic impact will be in the next century. Yet there are clues in the historical record. In the selections that follow, Wallace S. Broecker, a professor of geology at Columbia University's Lamont-Doherty Geological Observatory, notes that past climate coolings have been immensely disruptive. He argues that a cautious approach to the future warrants decreasing releases of greenhouse gases as much as possible to ward off potential disaster. On the other side, economics professor Wilfred Beckerman and economics writer Jesse Malkin deny that disaster is imminent from the accumulation of greenhouse gases, and they express certainty that humans can adapt to whatever changes may occur. They say that there are much better ways to spend money, such as on relieving world poverty, than in trying to ward off a nonproblem like global warming.

YES

Wallace S. Broecker

GLOBAL WARMING ON TRIAL

Jim Hansen, a climatologist at NASA's Goddard Space Institute, is convinced that the earth's temperature is rising and places the blame on the buildup of greenhouse gases in the atmosphere. Unconvinced, John Sununu, former White House chief of staff, doubts that the warming will be great enough to produce a serious threat and fears that measures to reduce the emissions would throw a wrench into the gears that drive the United States' troubled economy. During his three years at the White House, Sununu's view prevailed, ... [and now,] others continue to cast doubt on the reality of global warming....

The stakes in this debate are extremely high, for it pits society's short-term well-being against the future of all the planet's inhabitants. Our past transgressions have altered major portions of the earth's surface, but the effects have been limited. Now we can foresee the possibility that to satisfy the energy needs of an expanding human population, we will rapidly change the climate of the entire planet, with consequences for even the most remote and unspoiled regions of the globe.

The notion that certain gases could warm the planet is not new. In 1896 Svante Arrhenius, a Swedish chemist, resolved the longstanding question of how the earth's atmosphere could maintain the planet's relatively warm temperature when the oxygen and nitrogen that make up 99 percent of the atmosphere do not absorb any of the heat escaping as infrared radiation from the earth's surface into space. He discovered that even the small amounts of carbon dioxide in the atmosphere could absorb large amounts of heat. Furthermore, he reasoned that the burning of coal, oil, and natural gas could eventually release enough carbon dioxide to warm the earth.

Hansen and most other climatologists agree that enough greenhouse gases have accumulated in the atmosphere to make Arrhenius's prediction come true. Burning fossil fuels is not the only problem; a fifth of our emissions of carbon dioxide now come from clearing and burning forests. Scientists are also tracking a host of other greenhouse gases that emanate from a variety of human activities; the warming effect of methane, chlorofluorocarbons, and nitrous oxide combined equals that of carbon dioxide. Although the current

From Wallace S. Broecker, "Global Warming on Trial," *Natural History* (April 1992). Copyright © 1992 by The American Museum of Natural History. Reprinted by permission of *Natural History*.

warming from these gases may be difficult to detect against the background noise of natural climate variation, most climatologists are certain that as the gases continue to accumulate, increases in the earth's temperature will become evident even to skeptics.

The issue under debate has implications for our political and social behavior. It raises the question of whether we should renew efforts to curb population growth and reliance on fossil fuels. In other words, should the age of exponential growth initiated by the Industrial Revolution be brought to a close?

The battle lines for this particular skirmish are surprisingly well balanced. Those with concerns about global warming point to the recent report from the United Nation's Intergovernmental Plan on Climate Change, which suggests that with "business as usual," emissions of carbon dioxide by the year 2025 will be 25 percent greater than previously estimated. On the other side, the George C. Marshall Institute, a conservative think tank, published a report warning that without greenhouse gases to warm things up, the world would become cool in the next century....

If the reality of global warming were put on trial, each side would have trouble making its case. Jim Hansen's side could not prove beyond a reasonable doubt that carbon dioxide and the other greenhouse gases have warmed the planet. But neither could [the opposition] prove beyond a reasonable doubt that the warming expected from greenhouse gases has not occurred.

To see why each side would have difficulty proving its case, let us review the arguments that might be presented at such a hearing. The primary evidence would be the temperature records that have been kept by meteorologists since the 1850s. A number of independent analyses of these measurements have reached the same basic conclusions. Over the last century the planet has warmed about one degree. This warming was especially pronounced during the last decade, which had eight of the warmest years on record, with 1990 being the hottest. While [global warming critics] might question the adequacy of the geographic coverage of weather stations during the early part of the record and bicker a bit about whether the local warming produced by the growth of cities has biased some of the records, in the end they would concede that this record provides a reasonably good picture of the trend in the earth's temperature. [They] would then counter by asking, "Isn't it strange that between about 1940 and 1975 no warming occurred?" The Hansen group would have to admit that there is no widely accepted explanation for this leveling. [The opposition] would continue, "Isn't it true that roughly half the warming occurred before 1940, even though almost all the emissions of carbon dioxide and other greenhouse gases have taken place after this date?" Again the Hansen group would have to admit this to be the case.

At this point, a wise judge might pose the following question to both sides: "What do we know about the temperature fluctuations that occurred prior to the Industrial Revolution?" The aim of this question would be to determine what course the earth's temperature might have taken if the atmosphere had not been polluted with greenhouse gases. The answer by both sides would have to be that instead of remaining the same as it was in 1850, the planet's temperature would have undergone natural fluctuations, which could have been as large as the changes measured over the last one hundred years. Neither side, however, would be able to supply the judge with an acceptable estimate of what would have happened to the earth's temperature without the release of greenhouse gases.

Perhaps a longer record of the earth's climate would shed light on its natural variability. The climate prior to 1850 can be reconstructed from historical records of changing ice cover on mountaintops and on the sea. The earliest evidence of this type dates from the end of the tenth century A.D., when Eric the Red first sailed from Iceland to Greenland. Ship logs written between that time and 1190 indicate that sea ice was rarely seen along the Viking sailing routes. The temperature was warm enough that grain could be grown in Iceland. At the end of the twelfth century, however, conditions deteriorated, and sea ice appeared along the Viking sailing routes during the winters. By the midfourteenth century, these routes were forced far to the south because of the ice, and sometime in the late fifteenth century, ships were cut off altogether from Greenland and Iceland because of severe ice conditions. As temperatures dropped, people could no longer grow grain in Iceland. The Medieval Warm had given way to the Little Ice Age.

After 1600, records of sea-ice coverage around Iceland and of the extent of mountain glaciers in the Alps improved, giving us an even better idea of recent climate change. The glaciers attracted the attention of seventeenth-century tourists, including artists whose drawings and paintings document the position of a number of major Alpine glaciers. Modern measurements show that the leading edges of these glaciers fluctuated with temperature changes over the last century. Assuming that this correlation held true throughout the Little Ice Age, the historical evidence shows a long interval of glacier expansion, and thus cold climate, lasting until 1860. During the late 1800s, a widespread recession of Alpine glaciers heralded the end of Little Ice Age. Ridges of rock and earth bulldozed into position by the advancing ice still mark the point of maximum glacial progress into the valleys. (The glaciers are still shrinking; less than half of their 1860 volume remains.) The mild conditions that prevailed during the Medieval Warm did not return until this century.

The problem with all this evidence is that it represents only one region of the earth and is, in a sense, anecdotal. An informed judge might also challenge this evidence by pointing out that the northern Atlantic Ocean and its surrounding lands are warmed by powerful ocean currents, collectively known as the Great Conveyor, that transport heat away from the equator.... A temporary shutdown of this circulation 11,000 years ago brought about an 800-year cold period called the Younger Dryas, during which northern Europe was chilled by a whopping 12° F. Could the Little Ice Age have been brought about by a similar weakening of the Great Conveyor? If heat release from the northern Atlantic was the key factor, the Little Ice Age would have been restricted to the surrounding region, and the historical evidence from Iceland and the Alps could not be taken as an index of global temperatures.

Although records of similar duration and quality are not available from other parts of the world, we do have firm evidence that by 1850, mountain glaciers in some regions, such as New Zealand

and the Andes, reached down into valleys as far as they had at any time during the last 8,000 years. Furthermore, by 1870 these glaciers had also begun their retreat. This suggests that the Little Ice Age was indeed global in extent.

The global warming that caused the demise of the Little Ice Age confuses attempts to estimate how much of the last century's warming is natural and how much has been caused by pumping greenhouse gases into the atmosphere. [Warming critics] would pin as much of the blame as possible on the natural warming trend that ended the Little Ice Age, while Hansen's side would emphasize the role of the greenhouse gases. What is needed to resolve this dispute is a detailed, continuous temperature record that extends back beyond the Medieval Warm to see if cycles could be identified. By extending these cycles into the present century, scientists could estimate the course the earth's temperature would have taken in the absence of the Industrial Revolution.

I made such an attempt in 1975, at a time when the earth's temperature seemed to have remained almost constant since the mid-1940s. Puzzled scientists were asking, "Where's the expected greenhouse warming?" I looked for the answer in the only detailed long-term record then available, which came from a deep hole bored into northern Greenland's icecap at a place called Camp Century. In the 1950s, Willi Dansgaard, a Danish geochemist, had demonstrated that the ratio of heavy to light oxygen isotopes (18 neutrons to 16 neutrons per atom, respectively) in the snow falling in polar regions reflected the air temperature. Dansgaard made measurements of oxygen isotopes in different layers of the ice core; each represented the com-

pressed snowfall of an arctic year. His results served as a proxy for the changes in the mean annual temperature. Dansgaard and his colleagues analyzed the record to see if the temperature fluctuations were cyclic. They found indications of two cycles, one operating on an 80-year time scale and a weaker one operating on a 180-year time scale. (The Milankovitch cycles, caused by changes in the earth's orbit around the sun, operate on a much longer time scale. Ranging from 20,000 years upward, these cycles are thought to control the large swings between glacial and interglacial climates.)

I took Dansgaard's analysis a step further by extending his cyclic pattern into the future. When combined with the expected greenhouse warming, a most interesting result appeared. Temperatures leveled off during the 1940s and 1950s and dropped somewhat during the 1960s and 1970s. Then, in the 1980s, they began to rise sharply. If there is a natural eighty-year cycle and it was acting in conjunction with a greenhouse effect, I would explain the leveling of temperature after 1940 as follows: Dansgaard's eighty-year cycle would have produced a natural warming between 1895 and 1935 and a natural cooling from 1935 to 1975. The cooling in the second half of the cycle might have counterbalanced the fledgling greenhouse warming. After 1975, when the natural cycle turned once again, its warming effect would have been augmented by the ever stronger greenhouse phenomenon, producing a sharp upturn in temperature in the 1980s.

My exercise showed that the lack of warming between 1940 and 1975 could not be used to discount the possibility that the pollution we are pumping into the atmosphere will ultimately warm the globe. We cannot rule out this possibility until that time in the future when the predicted warming is so great that it can no longer be masked by natural temperature fluctuations. My projection suggested that a firm answer will not be available until the first decade of the next century.

While the Camp Century record seemed to provide a good method of determining how natural variations and increasing greenhouse gases were working in concert to produce the measured global temperatures, additional ice core data only created confusion. Oxygen isotope records from ice cores extracted from the Antarctica icecap and mountain glaciers in China and Peru do not follow the Camp Century ice core pattern. Even worse, oxygen isotope records from three additional Greenland ice cores differ significantly from one another and from the original Camp Century record. Perhaps the most disconcerting feature of these ice core records is that the Medieval Warm and Little Ice Age do not even stand out as major features. Local temperature variations could account for these discrepancies, but oxygen isotope ratios also depend on the season the snow falls and the source of the moisture. For these reasons, ice cores may provide good records of large changes, but the smaller ones we are looking for over the last several hundred years are obscured.

At this point, the judge would likely lose his patience and call a halt to this line of argument, saying, "While regional climate changes certainly occurred during the centuries preceding the Industrial Revolution, firm evidence for a coherent global pattern in these natural fluctuations is lacking." The judge might then suggest a different approach to settle the question of whether we are causing the earth to warm. What drives the

natural changes? If we could pin down the villain, then perhaps we could say more about how temperature would have changed in the absence of the Industrial Revolution. Witnesses would point to three such mechanisms. First, the sun's energy output may have changed. Second, large volcanic eruptions may have injected enough material into the stratosphere to reflect a substantial amount of solar radiation back into space, cooling the planet. Third, the operation of the ocean-atmosphere system may have changed internally, causing the earth's temperature to wander.

For several centuries astronomers have been observing the cycles of the sun and trying to link them with climate patterns on earth. Sunspots, caused by knots in the sun's magnetic field, undergo cyclic change, alternating between a maximum of spots in the Northern Hemisphere and then a maximum in the Southern Hemisphere. Between these peaks, the number of sunspots drops almost to zero. A complete solar cycle takes twenty-two years. With satellites, astronomers have been able to directly monitor the sun's energy output over the last cycles. Although the energy seems to dip slightly when sunspots disappear, the change seems too small to greatly alter the earth's temperature.

... [However,] between 1660 and 1720, sunspots disappeared altogether. Auroras, which are created when charged particles driven out from the sunspots enter the earth's upper atmosphere, were also absent from the skies during this period. Further, we know from measurements of carbon 14 in tree rings that this radioactive element, produced by cosmic rays bombarding the atmosphere, increased substantially during this time. Normally, charged particles streaming outward from sunspots create a magnetic shield that deflects cosmic rays away from the earth and the inner planets. From 1660 to 1720, this magnetic shield failed, permitting a larger number of cosmic rays to strike our atmosphere and form an unusually large number of radioactive carbon atoms.

From the record of radiocarbon locked up in tree rings, we can identify two even earlier periods of reduced sunspot activity: the Wolf sunspot minimum, from about 1260 to about 1320, and the Spörer sunspot minimum, from about 1400 to 1540. These three periods span a major portion of the Little Ice Age, but the last ended more than a hundred years before the Little Ice Age did—too long a time lag. This mismatch in timing and the small change in the sun's energy output (as measured by satellites over the last solar cycle) make a link between the Little Ice Age and the absence of sunspots unlikely. But the partial match prevents a firm rejection of the sun as a cause of the earth's natural temperature changes.

What about volcanic eruptions? Major volcanic eruptions occur roughly once per decade. Most have little effect on the climate, but occasionally an eruption blasts a large volume of sulfur dioxide high into the stratosphere. Within a month or two, the sulfur dioxide is transformed into droplets of sulfuric acid, which remain aloft in the stratosphere for a year or more. These tiny spheres reflect sunlight away from the earth, cooling the planet. Hansen and his colleagues predict that the recent eruption of Mount Pinatubo in the Philippines (which shot more sulfur dioxide into the upper atmosphere than any other eruption this century) will cool the planet about one degree Fahrenheit over the next two years.

Could the Little Ice Age have been caused by 500 years of intense volcanism releasing copious amounts of sulfur dioxide? This seems implausible, as the world's 100 or so major volcanoes erupt independently of one another and no mechanism exists that could cause them all to erupt with greater frequency. Therefore, the chance is slim that one long interval would be followed by a similar period of lesser activity.

Fortunately, a record is available in ice cores to check this assumption. When the droplets of sulfuric acid from a volcanic eruption drift down from the stratosphere, they are quickly incorporated into raindrops and snowflakes and carried to the earth's surface. So, in the years immediately following a major volcanic eruption, snow layers rich in sulfuric acid are deposited on all the world's icecaps. An ice core taken from the Dye 3 site in southern Greenland reveals that at about the time of the transition from the Medieval Warm to the Little Ice Age the acid content in the ice doubled. On the other hand, low acidity from 1750 to 1780 (during a time of cold weather) and the relatively high acidity from 1870 to 1920 (when the climate was warming) do not fit the pattern of climate change. Therefore, no strong correlation exists between the trends in volcanic sulfur dioxide and the trend in the earth's temperature.

The last of the three mechanisms that might account for the natural variations in the earth's temperature is a dramatic shift in the way the planet's ocean and wind currents operate. Of the three mechanisms, this one is the hardest to build a case around because we have only a rudimentary understanding of how the interacting elements of the earth's climate system might cause natural fluctuations in temperature. The only well-documented example of such a mechanism is the El Niño cycle, in which winds and ocean currents cause the temperatures of the surface waters of the eastern equatorial Pacific to alternate between warm and cold. The cycle was first noticed because of the severe drops in fish production along the west coast of South America during the warm episodes. Since the timing between these disruptive events ranges from three to seven years, scientists became interested in predicting their arrival. What emerged from these studies is that El Niño cycles are the product of a complex interaction between winds and ocean currents. The importance of this discovery to the global warming debate is that it raises the possibility that cycles involving larger-scale interactions between the atmosphere and oceans—over longer periods—may play an important role. If the earth's temperature is being pushed up and down by such an internal cycle, our chances of determining what would have happened in the absence of the extra greenhouse gases are indeed slim.

Again the judge would become restive and call a halt to this line of evidence as well. At this point he would likely dismiss the case and suggest that the litigants return a decade from now when additional evidence regarding the warming trend has accumulated.

[Warming critics] would deem this decision a victory, for it would provide an excuse to delay actions directed toward reductions in carbon dioxide emissions. On the other hand, Hansen could surely maintain that in the absence of proof that the world is not warming at the rate predicted by computer simulations, we should follow the standard applied to other environmental threats and rule on the side of caution. Instead of placing the burden of proof on the environmentalists, the proponents of "business as usual" should be obliged to prove that the unfettered release of greenhouse gases will *not* significantly warm the planet. And such proof does not exist; the balance of scientific opinion is that business as usual will alter the climate.

NO

**Wilfred Beckerman and
Jesse Malkin**

HOW MUCH DOES
GLOBAL WARMING MATTER?

More than a billion people in developing countries have no access to safe drinking water, and at least twice that many have no access to adequate sanitation. Consequently, between 1 and 1.5 billion people suffer from water-related diseases such as schistosomiasis, hookworm, and diarrhea. Infant mortality attributable to diarrhea is estimated to be about 5 million per year.

But the environmental problems that dominate the media, that are given the most attention by environmentalist pressure groups, and that capture the imagination of the public, are the melodramatic issues. The myth of "scarce resources" is one.... Another is global warming—"the highest-risk environmental problem the world faces today," according to Vice President Al Gore. The public is bombarded by television images showing the earth surrounded by a layer of "greenhouse gases" (GHGs) that allow the sun's energy to penetrate, but block much of the outgoing radiation from the earth's surface. These images are accompanied by dire predictions that we shall all frizzle up and that the world will become a desert—despite concurrent predictions that rainfall will increase and sea levels will rise. Such scenarios of global warming are much more exciting for the viewer than pictures showing that what the world's population needs most are more lavatories and better sewage systems.

* * *

The "consensus" opinion on climate change, as embodied in the 1990 report of the International Panel on Climate Change (IPCC), is that a doubling of equivalent carbon dioxide [CO_2] (an index that summarizes the effect of all man-made GHGs), is likely to occur within the next fifty years if nothing is done to reduce CO_2 emissions. Because of the time lags in the dynamics of climate change—notably those caused by the inertia introduced into the

From Wilfred Beckerman and Jesse Malkin, "How Much Does Global Warming Matter?" *The Public Interest*, no. 114 (Winter 1994), pp. 3–16. Copyright © 1994 by National Affairs, Inc. Reprinted by permission of the author.

system as a result of the absorption of carbon dioxide by the oceans—the temperature increase associated with this warming commitment would not be realized until approximately 2100. At that point, the global mean surface temperature is predicted to increase by between 2° and 5° Celsius.

This conclusion has not gone unquestioned. To be sure, the scientific work that has gone into climate modeling represents a major intellectual achievement. Yet it is widely recognized that these estimates have a wide margin of error and that there are still great gaps in our understanding of how the climate is determined. The IPCC report itself contains hundreds of pages of misgivings about the potential temperature increase, and many climatologists have expressed skepticism about the reliability of the global climate models that forecast significant warming.

For example, equivalent CO_2 levels have increased by over 40 percent during the past 100 years, yet the climate has not responded in the manner predicted by the models. Consider the following anomalies:

- The amount of global warming that has occurred over the past century—roughly .45°C—is at least a factor of two less than that predicted by the most sophisticated models.
- The Northern Hemisphere, which the models say should have warmed more rapidly than the Southern Hemisphere, is no warmer than it was a half century ago.
- The models say warming should occur as a result of GHG buildup, but most of the warming during the past 100 years occurred prior to World War II—*before* most of the GHGs were emitted.

Clearly a dose of skepticism is warranted. But let us suppose that the skeptics are wrong—suppose the earth's temperature does rise by somewhere between 2°C and 5°C. How damaging is this likely to be?

* * *

There is one simple piece of evidence, which does not require vast computerized models of the world's climate or economy (our understanding of both being extremely limited), and which does at least refute the widespread notion that the human race is some tender plant that can only survive in a narrow band of plus or minus 3°C. This is the present dispersion of the world's population throughout widely different temperature zones. For example, taking the average temperatures in the coldest month in the countries concerned, 32.3 percent of the world's population lives in a band of 0°C to 3°C, whereas 18.8 percent live in a band of 12°C to 15°C, and 14.6 percent live in a band of 24°C to 27°C. Furthermore, across the world as a whole there appears to be no correlation at all between average temperatures and income levels. ...

Of course, it will be argued that such cross-country comparisons do not adequately take into account the difficulty of adjusting to relatively rapid changes in temperature. There is some truth in this. But as the distinguished economist Thomas Schelling has observed, the sort of rapid climate changes experienced throughout history by vast migratory movements of population were far greater than those predicted to occur during the next century as a result of global warming. The human race has always been a highly adaptable species, and is likely to become increasingly so, since most of its adaptability comes from its accumulation of technical knowledge.

Similar back-of-the-envelope calculations show that, for the United States at least, global warming could hardly have a significant impact on national income. For the sector most likely to be affected is agriculture, which constitutes 2 percent of U.S. gross domestic product (GDP). Most other sectors of economic activity are not likely to be affected at all, and some, such as construction, will probably be favorably affected. So even if the net output of agriculture fell by 50 percent by the end of the next century, this is only a 1 percent reduction in GDP.

Anyway, the net effect on U.S. agriculture is more likely to be negligible. In the northern states, growing periods would be longer and there would be less disruption by frosts. Further, the predicted rise in carbon dioxide—the most important greenhouse gas leading to global warming—is actually good for plant growth. Authoritative estimates put the impact on the net output of U.S. agriculture at somewhere between plus and minus $10 billion. Even the worst end of this range, minus $10 billion, is a trivial part of a U.S. GDP of about $6 trillion.

Similar estimates for the world as a whole (which, as far as we know, were not done on the back of an envelope) also show that agricultural output in some countries will be favorably affected by global warming, whereas others will lose; and that, on balance, the net effect is likely to be negligible. Of course, the effects depend partly on how climate change affects the regional distribution of rainfall. But this is even more difficult to predict than is the global climate change.

All in all, such estimates as have been made of the overall effect of a doubling of the CO_2 concentration on the world economy suggest that world output would be reduced by about 1 or 2 percent. Suppose that these estimates are much too conservative—as they may well be given that the models on which they are based are extremely shaky. Suppose instead that world output would be reduced by 10 percent by the end of the next century below what it otherwise would be.

Well, what would it otherwise be? Over the whole period 1950 through 1985, the annual average compound rate of growth of world output *per head* has been 1.9 percent. Given that the rate of growth of world population is slowing down and that, at the same time, there has been a rapid increase in the proportion of the world's population receiving higher education or engaged in scientific research—the mainsprings of technical progress—there is good reason to believe that this growth rate will be at least maintained, if not increased. But suppose that it is only, say, 1.5 percent a year. This means that by the year 2093 world output per head will be 4.4 times as great as it is now. If global warming cuts world GDP by 10 percent, then instead of it being 4.4 times as great as it is now, it would be only 3.96 times as great. Would this be such a disaster? Would it justify imposing vast costs on the present generation rather than devoting more resources to helping developing countries overcome the environmental problems that they are facing today?

* * *

So far we have limited our discussion to the effect of global warming on agriculture, since this is the most vulnerable sector. But what about sea level rise, the other eco-catastrophe most frequently associated with global warming?

In 1980 scientists predicted that global warming would lead to a sea level rise of as much as 8 meters. In early 1989 the prevailing estimate was down to about 1 meter. By 1990 (as in the IPCC report) the predicted sea level rise was about 65 centimeters, and current authoritative estimates put it as low as about 30 cm by the end of the next century, assuming a 4°C rise in average temperature by then. (If one were to extrapolate from trends in these estimates, the sea level would be predicted to fall, with consequences for many seaside resorts that would be as serious as sea level rises!)

But even if sea levels did rise appreciably, the economic consequences would not be disastrous. A few years ago, when the sea level was still predicted to rise by 1 meter, the U.S. Environmental Protection Agency estimated that it would cost about $100 billion to protect U.S. cities by building sea walls. Applying a 1.5 percent a year annual growth rate to the present U.S. GDP of $6 trillion gives a GDP of $26.2 trillion in 2093; so as a fraction of GDP in the year 2093, the once-and-for-all capital cost of the sea walls would be about .38 percent. As a fraction of cumulative GDP over the whole of the next 100 years—the time during which the work would have to be carried out —the amounts involved are, of course, trivial.

What about the rest of the world? Estimates by William Cline of the Institute for International Economics, also assuming a 1 meter rise in the sea level and that the costs of sea walls for other threatened coastal cities are comparable to those of the U.S., show costs of adaptation, plus the value of land lost in coastal areas, of about $2 trillion. On the above assumption concerning the growth rate, world GDP in the year 2093 will be about $115 trillion—so the one-time capital cost of the sea walls would still be only about 1.7 percent of one year's GDP. As a fraction of cumulative GDP over the whole period it would still be negligible. Given that the latest predictions of the rise in the sea level are about one third of those assumed in these estimates and that a given reduction in the estimated sea level rise implies more than a proportionate reduction in the costs of adaptation or the damage done through land loss, the costs for the world as a whole would be insignificant even if the above estimates are way off.

Now that may be very well for the world as a whole, but it is little consolation to the people of Bangladesh, where 20 percent of the land could be lost under the sea with a 1 meter sea level rise. But leaving aside the falling trend in the estimate of sea level rises, suppose, purely for the sake of illustrating the logic of the choices to be made, that measures to prevent the climate change and the consequent sea level rise would cost the world community $20 trillion —i.e. ten times as much as the cost of protection against the rising sea level. It would clearly be in everyone's interest, including the Bangladeshis', to strike some sort of a deal. For example, instead of incurring $20 trillion in costs to prevent the climate change and the associated sea-level rise, the rich countries would do better to hand over, say, a quarter of the resulting economy—that is, $5 trillion— to the people who would suffer from the sea-level rise. The Bangladeshis would then gain $5 trillion to carry out work costing only $2 trillion, and the rest of the world still saves $15 trillion.

In other words, the course of action that is being urged by environmentalists —to prevent rising sea levels at any cost—would mean that the world is being asked to incur costs of $20 trillion —or whatever the cost would be—to prevent the Bangladeshis from suffering the effects of the sea level rise when there would be a much cheaper way of sparing them from these effects. Developed countries could, for example, help Bangladeshis move away from threatened coastal areas, diversify their economy, or take some other protective action. They might even consider making it easier for Bangladeshis to export goods and emigrate. The point is that adaptation should not be viewed as an impossibility. After all, over half the population of the Netherlands and virtually all the people in Amsterdam live below sea level.

If the estimates of the costs involved in significant reductions of CO_2 emissions referred to above are anywhere near reality, it is clear that the world and the Bangladeshis would be far better off if adaptive policies were taken rather than drastic action to prevent threatened rises in sea levels. In any event, since it is suspected that far more land is being lost to soil erosion than through climate change, there are policies that could be undertaken to reduce land loss without draconian cuts in carbon dioxide emissions.

* * *

But what would it cost to implement CO_2 cuts by the most economical means, and how would one do it? One view, espoused by the Clinton administration among others, is that cuts can be achieved at no cost whatsoever to the public or private sector. The White House insists that its "Climate Change Action Plan," a collection of mostly voluntary public-private partnerships which purports to stabilize greenhouse gas emissions at 1990 levels by 2000, will save the private sector $207 billion in reduced energy costs by 2010.

Most economists, however, believe the administration is relying on astonishingly optimistic assumptions about energy savings. The reason is simple: If energy-efficiency investments really yield such fantastic returns, businesses and individuals would undertake them without the government's push. To accept the administration's savings estimates, one would have to believe that firms are very stupid indeed.

As many disappointed environmentalists have noted, voluntary measures of the sort in Clinton's plan are likely to have only a very limited effect on greenhouse gas emissions. Deep cuts will require stronger government action, namely a carbon tax or a system of internationally tradable emissions permits.

Making a rapid transition to a less carbon-intensive economy would be painful, but just how much so is unclear. The uncertainties about the magnitude of the costs are as great, if not greater, than those embodied in the scientific models to predict climate change. Nobody can predict with much accuracy the future pattern of economic growth over the next century in a manner that enables one to say how much fossil fuel would be burned and hence how much needs to be done to reduce fossil fuel use by any given amount. Nor can anyone say with any degree of reliability how sensitive the consumption of fossil fuels is to different levels of carbon taxes. The impact of carbon taxes depends in large part on the degree to which carbon-free energy sources like nuclear, wind energy, and photovoltaics become cheaper and easier to use than their fossil rivals.

Finally, there is the huge question of what is done with the revenues raised by carbon taxes. If they are refunded to the economy in a way that merely changes the pattern of fuel use rather than exerting a depressive effect on the economy as a whole, the effect could well be favorable. For example, there is a strong case for reducing government subsidies to the coal and oil industries apart from any considerations about global warming. If the savings from the elimination of those subsidies were used to pursue growth-enhancing policies, so much the better. If, on the other hand, carbon taxes were used to fund extra entitlements or low-return government "investment" programs, the effect would more likely be negative. A tax on a basic input to the economy, which is what fossil fuels are, could have a far more serious impact than other taxes such as those that are levied on different items of consumer expenditure, such as cigarettes or beer.

Vast computerized models tend to blind people with science and impress grant-giving institutions. Most of them produce a maximum amount of statistical "results" with a minimum input of ideas or insight. The estimates that they churn out of the cost of measures designed to cut CO_2 emissions are highly uncertain. Inevitably, different models lead to widely different results. But for what they are worth, it seems that the cost of freezing CO_2 emissions at 1990 levels would be somewhere in the region of 2 percent of output per year in advanced industrial countries and perhaps twice that in developing countries, which have fewer financial and technological resources with which to adapt. To put that in perspective, 2 percent of current U.S. GDP is about $120 billion. The large magnitude of the costs is not surprising since, again, it seems obvious—even without the aid of any sophisticated computerized models —that, if carried out quickly, a drastic cut in the use of fossil fuels would cause severe economic disruption.

* * *

The above discussion of the damage that might be done by a doubling of present concentrations of carbon in the atmosphere considers only the costs over a 100-year period. Some economists have pointed out that there is no reason to confine the analysis to a single century. Fossil fuels will probably continue to be used well after the year 2100, so it is likely that there will be greater atmospheric build-up of CO_2 and more global warming than that indicated by the century-long models. William Cline, for example, has shown that over a period of three centuries, atmospheric concentration of CO_2 might increase eight-fold and temperatures might rise 10°C to 13°C or more unless action is taken to reduce carbon dioxide emissions. This, he argues, could lead to a reduction of world GDP on the order of 10 percent.

Of course, the further one projects into the future the more uncertain the already shaky projections become. There have been vast technological changes in energy use in the last century. And these will probably be dwarfed by the changes that will take place in the next three centuries, during which an incomparably greater number of people will be engaged in technological and scientific research all over the world. Hence, nobody can suppose that the world of the 23rd century will bear much resemblance to the world that we know today. It is most unlikely that energy will still be produced on a large scale by the use of dirty and polluting substances such as coal.

One need only look at the past to see how difficult it is to make predictions over hundreds of years. Who could have predicted three centuries ago that sources of power would shift from wind, water, and wood to coal, oil, natural gas, and nuclear energy? Who could have imagined that modern gas-fired, combined-cycle power plants would be about ten times as energy efficient as power stations built at the beginning of the century, or that the thermal efficiency of steam engines would be about forty times that of the earliest engines, or that the most advanced fluorescent lights would be 900 times more energy efficient than the original kerosene lamp?

And progress is now being made in developing viable forms of renewable energy that emit no carbon at all. These include the photovoltaic cells that convert sunlight directly into storable electricity. They are regarded as having great promise for local power generation in developing countries. During the past twenty years the cost of photovoltaic-generated electricity has fallen from about $60 per kilowatt hour to about 30–50 cents, and is expected to fall to about 12–16 cents within the next few years as a result of further efficiency improvements that are already in the pipeline. Industry analysts say costs could go as low as 6 cents per kilowatt hour by 2020, little more than the price of electricity from a coal-fired station.

Similarly, the cost of wind-generated electricity has dropped from 50 cents per kilowatt hour in 1975, to 25 cents in 1980, to 7–9 cents in the best locations today. A new wind turbine under development is expected to bring costs down to 5 cents or less. The U.S. Department of Energy projects that over the next twenty years, costs in moderately windy sites could fall to 3.5 cents per kilowatt hour. Wind power's contribution will ultimately be limited by the number of suitable sites. The German Future Energies Forum, an energy research group, estimates that wind power can meet no more than 15 percent of the world's energy requirements.

Then there is always the possibility of a breakthrough in geothermal, solar thermal, hydrogen fuel, or nuclear fusion technology. It is impossible to determine the ultimate potential of technologies that are barely off the drawing board, but it would be foolishly pessimistic to assume that none of these carbon-free technologies will ever become cost-competitive with fossil fuels.

Even without any significant recourse to the many forms of renewable energy under investigation, there have been major reductions in the ratio of both energy use and carbon emissions to GDP. For example, from 1950 to 1985 the rate of growth of CO_2 emissions in the US was 1.9 percent a year, compared with a growth of GDP of 3.2 percent a year. This means that there was a 1.3 percent a year fall in carbon emissions per unit of GDP over the period 1950–1985. This is accounted for by a 0.8 percent a year decline in the rate of energy use per unit of output and a 0.5 percent a year decline in the rate of CO_2 emissions per unit of energy.

Cline does not make explicit his assumptions concerning these two influences on the growth of CO_2 emissions in his predictions. But based on his projections of GDP growth and CO_2 emissions, it is possible to work out what assumption is implied. It appears that he is assuming that the carbon emissions per unit of GDP will fall by only about 0.7 percent a year in the latter half of the twenty-first century—i.e. only about half the rate of decline in the U.S. between 1950 and 1985. Further, his estimates imply that the ratio of carbon emissions to GDP will fall even more slowly thereafter, and will actually rise during the last 75 years of the period covered in his projections.

Cline also assumes that every carbon dioxide molecule released into the atmosphere stays there for the duration of his three-century model. Calculating the effective lifespan of carbon dioxide is complex because CO_2 molecules are constantly exchanged between the atmosphere, the oceans, and the biosphere. Yet according to the IPCC Scientific Assessment, the "lifetime" associated with an individual CO_2 surge is only 50 to 200 years.

Adjusting Cline's assumptions yields dramatic changes. If we assume (a) that CO_2 molecules have an average lifespan of 100 years in the atmosphere and (b) that the amount of carbon emissions per unit of GDP declines 1.3 percent a year, both the CO_2 build-up and the warming projections become far less ominous. Instead of Cline's assumed eight-fold increase in carbon dioxide, there would be only about a one-and-a-half-fold increase. And the temperature increase resulting from this carbon buildup falls from between 10°C and 13°C to just 2°C. Even allowing for a generous margin of error, it would seem that Cline's projections are terribly pessimistic.

* * *

Assessing carbon abatement measures requires the comparison of costs and benefits over very long periods of time. This raises an important question: How is a benefit enjoyed in many years' time to be compared with a benefit enjoyed immediately? Most people would be unwilling to exchange $1.00 for, say, only $1.02 in one year's time—even if the $1.02 were indexed for inflation.

The need to discount the future at some rate of interest implies that the benefits in two or three centuries' time of abating GHG emissions now would have to be astronomic to justify significant current sacrifices. In fact, for almost any discount rate at all, what happens in the twenty-third century is of almost no importance. For example, if future costs and benefits are discounted at 2 percent a year—which is well below what most people would expect to earn on their investments, even net of tax and inflation—$1 of cost or benefit in 200 years' time would have a present value today of only 1.9 cents. In other words, if the damage done by global warming in 200 years' time were to be $1,000 billion, it would not be worthwhile taking steps to avoid it if the cost of doing so today would be greater than $19 billion. If a more conventional discount rate were used—say, 6 percent— it would not be worthwhile taking steps to avoid $1,000 billion of damage in 200 years' time if the cost of doing so today exceeded only $8.7 million.

People discount the future for two types of reasons. First, many people simply prefer to consume resources now rather than in the future. This "time preference" generally arises from any of three motives, namely (a) the risk that one might not survive to reap the future rewards for sacrifice of consumption today; (b) an expectation that future consumption levels will be higher (combined with the usual assumption of diminishing marginal utility of consumption), and (c) "pure" time preference—e.g., sheer impatience, or lack of imagination.

But even an individual who had no *basic* time preference whatsoever—who had no worry that her investment might not pay off, who did not expect to be richer, and was not impatient—would still not lend $1 now for $1 next year (leaving aside personal motivations, such as helping out a friend). The reason for this is that she would know that any old fool can get a better rate of return on the market. She would lend, therefore, up to the point where *at the margin* the rate of return she could get on her savings and investments would be equal to the relative valuation she places on consumption today as against consumption tomorrow. The same principle applies—with a few adjustments—to society.

In other words, the use of a discount rate in allocating investments today between alternative uses does not reflect any tendency by economists to attach less value, per se, to future *welfare*. On the contrary, a unit of *welfare* in 200 years' time is given the same value as a unit of welfare today. But, if technological progress and economic growth continue, a unit of *consumption* in 200 years' time will give a smaller unit of welfare than it does today. Taking account of the discount rate when choosing between projects is a technique designed to maximize welfare over the whole time period regarded as relevant. To invest in some environmental project that yields only, say, a 1 percent rate of return, when there are alternative projects around that will yield, say, 5 percent, would leave future generations much worse off than they could otherwise have been.

The simple answer, therefore, to the criticism that, by discounting, one is being unfair to future generations is this: If, Heaven forbid, there were some leap in medical science so that we all now expected to live for 300 years, *we would still use the discount rate in our savings and investment decisions.* So, as a result of our doing so today (when we do not expect to survive for centuries), future generations are left no worse off than we would be if it were us who were to be alive in 200 years' time, not them. Hence, it is absurd to argue that we are somehow or other being unfair to them.

In short, the widespread environmentalist attack on the validity of time preference is a vast red herring. What matters is the rate of technological progress and economic growth that one can expect to take place. As we have argued, there are good reasons for expecting this to be as rapid in the future as in the past. Of course, if it is expected to slow down to zero, or become negative—which is not beyond the bounds of possibility—one should adopt a zero or negative discount rate for later years. But a case should be laid out for such a prediction. The "immorality" of time preference has nothing to do with it.

*   *   *

Global warming may be a problem, but it is no cause for undue alarm or drastic action. There is plenty of time to improve our understanding of the science and scrap policies that encourage economically inefficient uses of fossil fuels. It does not justify diverting vast amounts of time, energy, and funds from more urgent environmental problems, particularly those in developing countries. Nor does it justify a massive diversion of resources from high-yield projects in the private sector. We are not on the edge of an abyss and the human race is not facing destruction from the accumulation of greenhouse gases. There is far less danger of the human race being wiped out on account of the conflict between Man and the Environment than on account of the conflict between Man and Man (or Woman and Woman). Global warming is far more glamorous and telegenic, of course, than the need for better toilets and drains in the Third World. But if we truly care about the welfare of our fellow world citizens, it is these kinds of environmental issues upon which we must focus our attention.

POSTSCRIPT

Should Society Be Concerned About Global Warming?

In 1992 the United Nations Conference on Environment and Development in Rio de Janeiro was held. High on the agenda was the issue of global warming, but despite widespread concern and calls for reductions in carbon dioxide releases, the United States refused to consider rigid deadlines or set quotas. The Bush administration felt that the uncertainties were too great and that the economic costs of cutting back on carbon dioxide emissions might well be greater than the costs of letting the climate warm.

The change of presidents in January 1993 brought a change in policy. In October 1993, the Clinton administration announced a "Climate Change Action Plan" that called for stabilizing carbon dioxide releases by such measures as planting trees (which remove carbon dioxide from the air) and promoting energy efficiency in hopes of pushing the full impact of climate warming a few years into the future. At the same time, however, James Kasting of Pennsylvania State University and James Walker of the University of Michigan warned that if one looks a little further into the future than the next century, the prospects look much more frightening. By 2100, they said, the amount of carbon dioxide in the atmosphere will reach double its preindustrial level. By the 2200s it could be 7.6 times the preindustrial level. Correspondingly, they predict, global warming in the twenty-first century will be worse than anyone is currently forecasting.

By the spring of 1994, climate analysts were already reporting a worldwide pattern of more extreme fluctuations in the weather—more and stronger droughts, floods, and storms, for example—and noting that the number of catastrophic windstorms had increased from 8 in the 1960s to 14 in the 1970s to 29 in the 1980s. This is consistent with the claims of climate modelers that warming the global climate puts more energy into storm systems and increases both the variability and the severity of the weather.

For some earlier reports on increases in carbon dioxide in the atmosphere and warming trends, see Roger Revelle, "Carbon Dioxide and World Climate," *Scientific American* (August 1982), and Philip D. Jones and Tom M. L. Wigley, "Global Warming Trends," *Scientific American* (August 1990). For further reading on global warming, see William D. Nordhaus, "Expert Opinion on Climatic Change," *American Scientist* (January–February 1994), and John Byrne, Constantine Hadjilambrinos, and Subodh Wagle, "Distributing Costs of Global Climate Change," *IEEE Technology and Society Magazine* (Spring 1994).

PART 3

The Cutting Edge of Technology

Many interesting controversies arise in connection with technologies that are so new that they often sound more like science fiction than fact. Some examples are technologies that allow the exploration of both outer space and the ocean depths, devices that search for extraterrestrial life, and advances in computer intelligences. Such advances offer capabilities undreamt of in earlier ages, and they raise genuine, important questions about what it is to be a human being, the limits on human freedom in a technological age, and the place of humanity in the broader universe. They also raise the questions of how society should respond: Should we accept the new devices and abilities offered by scientists and engineers? Or should we reject them?

- Should the Goals of the U.S. Space Program Include Manned Exploration of Space?

- Is It Worthwhile to Continue the Search for Extraterrestrial Life?

- Should Law Enforcement Agencies Be Permitted to Eavesdrop on Computer Communications?

- Will It Be Possible to Build a Computer That Can Think?

ISSUE 9

Should the Goals of the U.S. Space Program Include Manned Exploration of Space?

YES: Doug Beason, from "America's Blueprint for Mars: The Report of the Synthesis Group," *Analog Science Fiction and Fact* (Mid-December 1992)

NO: David Callahan, from "A Fork in the Road to Space," *Technology Review* (August/September 1993)

ISSUE SUMMARY

YES: Associate professor of physics Doug Beason argues that a U.S. government program oriented to the manned space exploration of Mars would provide an invigorating, economy-stimulating focus for the nation.

NO: David Callahan, a foreign-policy analyst, argues that fiscal realities will keep the space program's focus closer to Earth and force greater reliance on automated (unmanned) missions.

The dream of conquering space has a long history. The pioneers of rocketry —the Russian Konstantin Tsiolkovsky (1857–1935) and the American Robert H. Goddard (1882–1945)—both dreamed of exploring other worlds, although neither lived long enough to see the first artificial satellite, the Soviet Sputnik, go up in 1957. That success sparked a race between America and the Soviet Union to be the first to achieve each step in the progression of space exploration. The next steps were to put dogs (the Soviet Laika was the first), monkeys, chimps, and finally human beings into orbit. Communications, weather, and spy satellites were then designed and launched. And on July 20, 1969, the U.S. Apollo program landed the first men on the moon (see Buzz Aldrin and Malcolm McConnell, *Men from Earth*, Bantam Books, 1989).

There were a few more Apollo moon landings, but not many. The United States had achieved its main political goal of beating the Soviets to the moon and, in the minds of the government, demonstrated American superiority. Thereafter, the United States was content to send automated spacecraft (operated by robots) off to observe Venus, Mars, and the rings of Saturn; to land on Mars and study its soil; and even to carry recordings of Earth's sights and sounds past the distant edge of the solar system, perhaps to be retrieved by intelligent life from other worlds. (Those recordings are attached to the Voyager spacecraft, launched in 1977; if you wish a copy, it was advertised in February 1994 as a combination of CD, CD-ROM, and book, *Murmurs of Earth: The Voyager Interstellar Record*, available from Time-Warner Interactive Group, 2210 Olive Avenue, Burbank, CA 91506.)

Humans have not left near-Earth orbit for two decades, even though the technology of space travel has continued to develop. The Soviets even have a small space station in orbit now. The American equivalent, Skylab, fell to Earth in 1979 and has not been replaced. However, the National Aeronautics and Space Administration (NASA) does have the space shuttle, which is able to lift crews of a few men and women into space for a few days at a time, where they perform experiments and launch satellites. The task that earns these crews the greatest publicity is satellite repair, as in December 1993, when astronauts were sent into orbit to correct the problems suffered by the Hubble Space Telescope, which was launched into orbit in April 1990. The repair or emergency-response value of such crews is often used to argue against relying totally on automated space missions.

Why has human space exploration gone no further? One reason is that robots are now extremely capable; indeed, James A. Van Allen has called them more appropriate for the task than humans (see "Space Science, Space Technology and the Space Station," *Scientific American*, January 1986). Although some robot spacecraft have failed partially or completely, there have been many grand successes that have added enormously to mankind's knowledge of the Earth and other planets.

Another reason for the reduction in human space travel seems to be the fear that astronauts will die in space. This point was emphasized by the explosion of the space shuttle *Challenger* upon takeoff in January 1986, which killed seven astronauts and froze the entire shuttle program for over two and a half years. Still another reason is money: Lifting robotic explorers into space is expensive, but lifting people into space—along with all the food, water, air, and other supplies necessary to keep them alive for the duration of a mission —is much more expensive. And there are many people in government and elsewhere who believe that there are numerous better ways to spend the money on Earth.

Physicist Doug Beason was a member of the Synthesis Group of the White House Science Office during the Bush administration. The group was given the task of finding the best way to go to Mars, and it concluded that the benefits of such a mission would be much greater than simply getting to Mars; additional benefits would include job creation, investment in science and technology, and stimulated innovation. In the following selections, Beason outlines the requirements for the manned exploration of Mars and argues that although manned space exploration may have high costs, it also has many benefits for society on Earth. National security and foreign policy analyst David Callahan stresses that space is still expensive. He argues that society must make choices and that those choices should not include "a high-profile piloted component" to the space program.

YES
Doug Beason

AMERICA'S BLUEPRINT FOR MARS: THE REPORT OF THE SYNTHESIS GROUP

On July 20, 1989, on the steps of the National Air and Space Museum, President George Bush gave a speech commemorating the 20th anniversary of the landing of the first men on the Moon. In this speech he outlined an exhilarating national goal—for humans to return to the Moon, this time to stay, and then to go to Mars *and beyond*. This marked the first time since John F. Kennedy's speech that America was challenged to "go where no man has gone before."

For all intents and purposes, the nation had pulled out of exploring space at the end of the Apollo era. Human presence was limited to a mere few hundred kilometers from the surface of the Earth.

However, if properly instituted, this new challenge could define a renaissance for exploring the Universe.

In response to Bush's speech, NASA [National Aeronautics and Space Administration] conducted a "90 Day Study" that laid the groundwork for achieving the president's goal. The next step was taken by Vice President Quayle, as head of the National Space Council. Determined not to continue business as usual, he directed NASA to establish the Outreach Program to "cast nets widely" for new approaches to accomplish SEI, the Space Exploration Initiative. The Outreach Program was initiated as a nationwide hunt for the best ideas on how to send humans to Mars, cheaper, faster, smarter.

Astronaut Tom Stafford—*Gemini* pilot, *Apollo X* commander (where he brought the lunar module to within kilometers of the lunar surface) and pilot of the *Apollo/Soyuz* mission—was asked by the vice president to establish a *Synthesis Group*, responsible for pulling the Outreach program together. Stafford assembled a group of 46 experts hailing from all walks of life—academia, industry and government—after receiving nominations for his group from industry heads, cabinet officials, and professional societies. He also included 23 senior members consisting of internationally acknowledged space leaders, ranging from a former secretary of the Air Force, to the designer of the *Mercury*, *Gemini* and *Apollo* spacecraft. Once convened, the Synthesis Group was tasked to achieve three goals: to analyze and

From Doug Beason, "America's Blueprint for Mars: The Report of the Synthesis Group," *Analog Science Fiction and Fact*, vol. 112, no. 15 (Mid-December 1992). Copyright © 1992 by Doug Beason. Reprinted by permission.

synthesize the thousands of Outreach responses, to recommend two or more significantly different architectures for the Space Exploration Initiative, and to identify technological priorities and early milestones to land humans on Mars.

The Synthesis Group report has been widely distributed, briefed to Congress, and its ramifications are still being debated throughout academia, industry, and government. The report provides a vision of America's future in the exploration of space. This article will concentrate on the rationale of why specific recommendations were made and how they will affect America's space program.

The crux of the Space Exploration Initiative is to pursue the peaceful application of high technology. With a goal of reaching Mars, this will inspire and invigorate generations to come. And when combined with technical spin-offs, the increase in scientific knowledge will add to reestablishing national leadership.... [T]he Synthesis Group has ... drawn up blueprints for invigorating the nation, just as *Apollo* did in the sixties.

But before the results of the Synthesis Group are presented, two questions brought by critics should be addressed: why bother exploring space, and why now?

The obvious answer is that SEI provides a focus not only for our space efforts, but for the nation as a whole. It allows us to invest in our nation's scientific and technological base, creating new job opportunities and markets; arguing to go to space for "Teflon and Tang" simply won't hack it anymore.

More directly, SEI provides the chance to reorient our GNP [gross national product] from being fueled by the military-industrial complex to being based on that of a space-faring nation. This is especially critical during these post-Cold War days, where America needs a stimulating national goal on which to base its economy.

SEI has the opportunity to facilitate the commercialization of space and promote space-based industries, products, and services. In fact, one of the architectures developed by the Synthesis Group concentrates on using space resources for just these purposes.

Further, SEI allows for advancing technological innovation. This means spurring new technologies with terrestrial and commercial applications. This in turn will inspire interest in science and engineering.

The consequence of investing in space is to radically increase our knowledge of the Universe. This will help us better understand the origin of the Universe, planets and perhaps life itself.

These are all good reasons for establishing a space exploration policy. But still the question remains, why should America do this now? Why can't we wait until times are "better," economically as well as socially? After all, it's pretty hard to justify sending a few people to Mars when there are plenty of people hurting right here at home.

Part of the reason has already been given—SEI is a fundamental way to ensure that those better times will come. It's more than just sending people to another planet. Rather than simply dumping money into the hands of bureaucrats, "experts" in redistributing wealth, it provides for a systematic way to rebuild America's infrastructure. In the 1940s, after World War II, America invested in the future of its past adversaries, Germany and Japan, through vehicles such as the Marshall Plan and MacArthur accords. Some may say that looking back, this was not such a bright idea, but there is no doubt of the success these programs have had in rebuilding those nations' infrastructure.

America is in a similar situation today. But this time we have the chance to invest in *ourselves*, to rebuild the very backbone that defines our nation's economic strength.

And there are other compelling reasons.

The SEI is more than an exploration program; it embodies the essence of a new social paradigm and it is therefore constructed without limits. This is different from saying that "no end is in sight." Rather than having a closed goal of only getting humans to Mars and ending the program there, SEI uses education as a basic priority to bring out the very best in our nation, and to hold the future open for our children. It is forward-looking and will focus technologies to allow this social effort to succeed. (Compare this to what happened to the *Apollo* program: once we got to the Moon, the public lost interest and the space program went downhill.)

The SEI provides a focus to the entire space program. Just as *Apollo* succeeded in the 1960s, SEI can unify our future goals in space.

The Moon and Mars are the first elements of an exploration program. The Moon provides a natural platform for astronomy, planetary science, and even as a resource for materials and energy. Since it's only 240,000 miles away from Earth, it's a logical first step for getting to Mars. With a surface area of 14.6 million square miles—roughly that of Africa—it provides a unique test bed for checking out equipment and procedures while being only three days away.

In addition to the fact that Mars might someday be a habitable colony, the opportunities to explore this pristine planet can reveal myriad facts about Earth—through geologic evolution, how the atmosphere and climate has changed over time, and even by searching for fossil life. This would be perhaps the most far reaching discovery of all: if true life is found to have existed on Mars, the societal implication back on Earth will have enormous ramifications.

The mere task of getting to Mars is much harder than simply fielding a test bed on the Moon and then rocketing out to the fourth planet. The differences between the Moon and Mars are vast. Everything from the presence of an atmosphere to radio delay times of up to 40 minutes will bring unique challenges. As such, any architecture for SEI must be diverse, robust, and flexible.

To define the architectures, the Synthesis Group established the concept of *Waypoints*—specific objectives to be achieved on the surface of the Moon or Mars. The architectures were then comprised of a linear combination of these Waypoints. This allowed the group to configure a set of architectures that gives policy makers a wide choice in how they accomplish SEI's goals. . . .

Architecture 1: Mars Exploration

This architecture is the classic "flags and footprints" mission. It achieves the basic SEI goal of landing humans on Mars by 2014. In addition, its main strengths include exploring Mars and accomplishing good science. In this and the following architectures, the human missions are preceeded by a cargo mission. The philosophy of splitting up the cargo and human missions is called a "split sprint" concept. That is, the cargo is sent on an energy efficient (minimum energy) Hohmann transfer orbit, taking as long as 1,000 days to reach Mars. Since there are no humans on board, there is no reason to minimize transit time. Once the cargo ship has successfully been inserted into an orbit around Mars, then a fast, or "sprint" mission with humans may be launched to rendezvous with the cargo ship. The human mission is thus relieved from carrying the enormous amount of fuel and supplies needed for a Martian descent. . . .

Expeditionary missions will precede any permanent outpost on Mars. Timelines for this architecture are to land the first 5 person mission on the Moon in 2005 for a stay of 14 Earth days. . . .

Architecture 2: Science Emphasis for Moon and Mars

This architecture takes full advantage of the Moon and Mars to increase our knowledge of the Universe. It consists of a balanced science program and emphasizes exploration.

Pressurized lunar rovers, especially fitted for long duration missions of up to two weeks, can roam 50 kilometers from base, increasing to 100 kilometers on later missions. Mini-telerobotic prospectors, perhaps piloted with virtual presence technology, can greatly add to the exploration. On the lunar surface, these prospectors may even be commanded from Earth. The 2.5 second round trip light delay is not enough to preclude direct interaction with Earth researchers. On the other hand, on Mars the light delay will run from 10 to 40 *minutes* each way, depending on the relative positions of the planets. This will result in a radical change of command and control philosophy. No longer will the astronauts be required to clear every activity with mission control. Emergencies won't wait for light delays.

As an example of the science program, an optical interferometer on the Moon with arms kilometers in length may be able to achieve resolutions on the order of a microarcsecond—over a hundred thousand times greater than what the Hubble telescope was designed to resolve. With resolutions this small, it is not only possible to detect Earth-sized planets orbiting nearby star systems, but to make interferometric studies of those planets' atmospheres (for example, we can tell if the atmosphere holds oxygen and other life-bearing constituents).

Compared to the Earth there is a *million times* less seismic activity on the Moon. The Moon is thus a near perfect place to put sensitive astronomical equipment such as the optical interferometer.

… All in all, if SEI develops as an ongoing program, the science return could be (sorry!) astronomical.

Timelines for this architecture are to land the first 5 person mission on the Moon in 2003 for a stay of 14 Earth days. Several additional lunar missions with increasingly complex astronomical equipment are planned with longer stays, until a training mission for the Mars flight occurs in 2008. A 600-day Mars mission, the first of several, is planned for 2014.

Architecture 3: Moon to Stay and Mars Exploration

Along with sending humans to Mars, this architecture fulfills the president's goal of establishing a permanent, albeit initially small, human presence on the Moon. More importantly, this is the architecture that will expand mankind's presence in the Universe. It's the first step in setting up a self-sufficient colony.

As with the other architectures, the lunar colony will use the Moon as a test bed for exploring Mars, putting into operation as many Mars systems as possible. In addition, it will accomplish a small amount of science and exploration on the lunar surface.

The main thrust of Architecture 3 is still to explore Mars by making a concerted effort to study geological features, search for fossil life, and to make a detailed study of Mars. But the most exciting aspect of this architecture is that if humans are ever going to go to the stars, if they are ever going to take that first step in colonizing the planets, *this* is the way to go. This doesn't mean that the other architectures won't result in colonies—rather, this is the architecture that explicitly states that as a goal.

Timelines for this architecture are to land the first 5 person mission on the Moon in 2004 and set up a man-tended site for a period of 14 Earth days. Additional lunar missions are planned, increasing the number of inhabitants to 18 with a yearly rotation of 6 crew members. As in the other architectures, a training mission for the Mars flight is planned with a 600-day Mars mission in 2014.

Architecture 4: Space Resource Utilization
This architecture emphasizes the maximum, early use of extraterrestrial resources to support exploration. The ultimate goal is to explore the Moon and Mars while solving such problems on Earth as the greenhouse effect, depletion of the ozone layer, and the dwindling supply of finite (and "dirty") energy sources. This architecture will allow us to meet our energy problems head-on.

The Moon could provide energy for the Earth in the form of helium-3—a fusion energy source created in the Sun, swept away by the solar wind and absorbed into the lunar regolith

(dirt).... [A]llowing time to gear up for full-scale helium-3 mining, this fits in well with the Department of Energy's forecast of having a working commercial fusion reactor by 2025. An estimated 25 metric tons of helium-3 per year is needed to supply the entire world's energy demand.

In addition to mining helium-3, solar cells manufactured on the lunar surface for use in space would be cheaper than lifting the cells off Earth. This results from the need to overcome Earth's gravity well and lift the solar cells into low-Earth-orbit. Lunar regolith could also provide volatiles for propellant, oxygen, water, and even building material for use on the Moon or in space.

The initial plan for this architecture is to demonstrate that it's feasible to process regolith and extract volatiles....

Timelines for this architecture are to land the first 5 person mission on the Moon in 2003 for a stay of 14 Earth days. Additional lunar missions are planned, increasing to 180 day stays in which a demonstration mining plant is working on the lunar surface. A 600 day Mars mission is planned for 2016, allowing time to accomplish the lunar mining goals....

CONCLUSIONS

Since the Synthesis Group report has been released, NASA has appointed Dr. Mike Griffin, formerly Deputy Director for Technology of the Strategic Defense Initiative and a long-time space researcher, to head up the Exploration Office. Dr. Griffin has assembled an impressive team of space experts and is aggressively pursuing a program based on the recommendations of the Synthesis Group. Further, the president has established a multi-agency organization to accomplish the SEI. The Departments of Energy and Defense are joining NASA in pursuing this national goal.

The president has stated that the long-term goals for space exploration are the Space Exploration Initiative. The nation is truly at a threshold—and not a crossroads. A crossroads implies that there exist more than one choice that the nation can make if it is going to flourish; a *threshold* correctly suggests that *there is no other choice.*

The Synthesis Group's vision for the 21st century includes a strong relation between science, technology, and manned and unmanned exploration. This vision compliments NASA's current Mission to Planet Earth and bases its success upon excellence in education. The Synthesis Group believes this initiative should be the centerpiece of the nation's space program.

More importantly, they believe that the nation can't afford *not* to do it. As the group so often stated during their year-long tenure: "We must make the decision to either lead, follow, or get out of the way."

The bottom line is that if we're going to survive, we *must* go down this path.

NO

David Callahan

A FORK IN THE ROAD TO SPACE

Thirty-five years ago, in the wake of the first Sputnik [a series of artificial Earth satellites, the launching of which ushered in the space age], a group of top White House scientists issued a report on the future of U.S. space exploration. Although the challenges of space travel were then only barely comprehended, the report, entitled *Introduction to Outer Space*, predicted steady progress in placing human beings in orbit, sending piloted craft to the moon, and exploring Mars and other planets. The United States has since made spectacular strides toward realizing all those dreams.

Today, however, President Bill Clinton confronts a space effort in trouble. Fiscally, there are tough questions about whether the National Aeronautics and Space Administration [NASA] will have the resources to pay for all the projects it now has in the pipeline. More broadly, many critics believe that the space program has lost its direction, and wonder whether an ambitious space program has become an unaffordable luxury in this age of towering deficits and worsening social ills.

Most immediately, NASA faces strong resistance to its central program, the proposed space station, which Congress has come close to canceling two years in a row. On June 17, President Clinton approved a revised version of the space station, shrinking its size and cutting its costs, which the General Accounting Office (GAO) had estimated at a hefty $40 billion to deploy and $78 billion to operate into the twenty-first century. Clinton had already announced, in early April, that NASA would collaborate with Russia in the station project. Although numerous technical and political uncertainties surround such a proposition, this step has the potential to further reduce the space station's cost through the use of Russian hardware like the *Mir* space station and the 20-story Energia rocket. U.S.-Russian cooperation on the station could also represent a paradigm shift in the way the world conducts its space activities, with the two largest spacefaring nations finally putting aside political differences to pool their resources.

But neither redesign nor the new partnership with Russia is certain to save the space station program. Some on Capitol Hill say the station will still be unaffordable, and they question the benefits of a permanent U.S. presence in

From David Callahan, "A Fork in the Road to Space," *Technology Review* (August/September 1993). Copyright © 1993 by *Technology Review*. Reprinted by permission of the author.

space. (On June 23, the House came within one vote of canceling the station program.) A greater appreciation of the dangers of piloted spaceflight in the wake of the 1986 *Challenger* accident has compounded doubts about NASA's plans.

Despite these problems, there remains a determined commitment in many quarters to continuing a high-profile piloted space program. At the grassroots level, legions of "space buffs" believe fervently in America's destiny to explore space. In Washington, space funding is vigorously promoted by the powerful aerospace lobby, legislators whose constituents benefit from space spending, and NASA itself, which has historically been adept at public relations.

The space coalition also counts among its allies a number of top political leaders, including Vice-President Al Gore, formerly chair of the Senate Subcommittee on Science, Space, and Technology. The United States cannot afford to ignore current domestic problems, Gore said last year, but nor can it abandon a long-term investment in space.

As steward of this investment, President Clinton must reconcile ambitious goals with limited means. According to estimates by the GAO, there is a significant gap between the cost of NASA's planned programs and the level of funding the agency can expect from Congress over the next five years. Despite recent efforts by NASA to close this gap through various cost-saving measures, it may no longer be possible to avoid hard choices among major space policy priorities.

Two distinct paths are clearly discernible: under one, piloted space exploration in close cooperation with Russia would reign as NASA's top priority, and the space station would serve as the flag-ship of this effort. But according to GAO analyses, pursuing this vision—even assuming significant savings from the redesign of the space station and a partnership with Russia—would probably drain funds from a range of important space science projects.

Under the alternative path, NASA would engage in a far-reaching retrenchment and curtail its piloted space exploration plans. While few analysts have spelled out what the U.S. space program might look like without a major piloted component, several changes would seem inevitable. The space station would be canceled, shuttle flights would be scaled back, and NASA would defer indefinitely the long-standing dream of placing human beings permanently in space and sending them to Mars and beyond. In the years ahead, NASA would continue its popular space science programs while giving new prominence to programs for studying global environmental problems and to research efforts in technology with commercial applications. Instead of selling itself as the agency that is spearheading humankind's exploration of the heavens, NASA would play up its role in improving life on planet earth and enhancing U.S. industrial competitiveness.

Faced with tough political choices, Bill Clinton has often sought to find a middle way. His effort to keep the space station alive with a less costly design is typical of this penchant for compromise. However, as Clinton faces the fork in the road of American space policy, he may have little choice but to pick one direction or the other.

NASA'S FUNDING CRUNCH

The Bush years were good to NASA. In July 1989, six months after taking office, Bush declared that the United States should build a permanent base on the moon and journey to Mars early in the next century. He reestablished the defunct White House National Space Council and gave Vice-President Dan Quayle, as head of that body, free rein to push a vigorous space policy at the highest levels of government. At NASA, a new Office of Exploration was created to plan for America's eventual return to the moon and trip to Mars. NASA's budget climbed from $9 billion in 1988 to $14 billion in 1991.

On the surface, a second golden age of U.S. space exploration appeared to be at hand as the 1990s dawned—arriving just in time, some thought, to offset concerns about America's declining global status. "We must lead in space if we are to lead on earth," declared Bush. "I am fully committed to the peaceful exploration of near and far space. I am convinced this is not only an adventure but a responsibility, and one we shirk at our peril."

But fiscal reality cut short the second golden age before it even began. In 1990, NASA officials were counting on annual budget increases of up to 10 percent in real dollars through the end of the decade. Yet within a year, most budget experts had come to believe that NASA funding would barely keep up with inflation during the 1990s. Through 1991 and 1992, policy analysts and lawmakers alike warned that NASA was failing to adjust to these new fiscal conditions and that its vision of the future was untenable. In March 1992, GAO analyst Neal P. Curtin estimated that NASA's planned five-year program would require $92.4 billion in spending through fiscal year 1997. For this to be achieved, said Curtin, the agency's budget would have to grow significantly each year to over $21 billion by fiscal 1997. "There appears to be a serious mismatch between NASA's program plans and the budget resources that seem likely to be available," he said.

Sometime last year, the ticking sound from NASA's budgetary time bomb reached the ears of its new administrator, Daniel Goldin. Since taking office, Goldin has acknowledged the magnitude of the crunch his agency faces. In an effort to find savings, Goldin has pitted "Blue Teams" of program managers against "Red Teams" of in-house program critics. According to NASA, these competing teams have already found ways to cut future program costs by 17 percent.

Other savings are also projected. Since last year, NASA has cut planned outlays for the Earth Observing System [EOS] program during the remainder of this decade from $11 billion to $8 billion. EOS, a proposed system of satellites for studying climate change and ozone depletion and monitoring rainforests and deserts, is the centerpiece of NASA's Mission to Planet Earth, which, as now envisioned, is a comprehensive effort to observe from space the environmental impact of human activities. NASA also promises to save nearly $2 billion by better managing the space shuttle program over the next five years, and has reduced funding for the National Aerospace Plane, a passenger craft that would be able to fly into orbit without using a booster rocket. Finally, NASA expects substantial savings through the 1990s from restructuring the space station and cooperating with Russia. Goldin has stated that achieving these savings is crucial if NASA is to adequately fund its other priorities.

Although space analysts at the GAO acknowledge NASA's efforts at belt tightening, they see little improvement in the basic budgetary problem. Last year, when Congress approved a NASA budget of $14.3 billion, legislators warned the space agency not to expect more than 3 to 5 percent annual growth. Heeding that warning, NASA this year requested only $14.7 billion for fiscal 1994. In all likelihood, NASA will receive no more than $75 billion over the next five years. But recent cost cutting notwithstanding, NASA is still trying to juggle too many programs. "Even if they got $80 billion over five years, they still wouldn't be able to carry out their plans," says one GAO space analyst. "They'd still leave their major programs limping and bleeding."

NASA's fiscal predicament may actually be worse than the overall budget estimates indicate. A GAO report released in January pointed out NASA's habit of underestimating costs. Of 29 major programs over the last 15 years, the report concluded, 22 exceeded NASA's projections. The median cost increase for the offending programs was 77 percent. "If there is substantial growth in program cost beyond what is planned, which has historically been the case, the funding gap will be ever wider," says a GAO analyst who worked on the latest report. Thus, for all of NASA's effort to adjust to fiscal reality, it may be running in place. Even if the agency's budget keeps up with inflation over the next five years, new and more substantial cuts in its program plans seem unavoidable.

THE CASE FOR AN ORBITAL OUTPOST

By far the most widely discussed option for reducing NASA spending is to cancel the space station. Although the redesign has cut the station's construction and operating costs by an estimated $27 billion, the program remains hugely expensive. NASA plans to spend over $2 billion annually on the program over the next five years, and up to $16.5 billion through the year 2001.

To proponents, the space station is well worth its cost. The case for a permanent U.S. presence in space is manifold, based partly on claims about the scientific, medical, and commercial benefits that a station could yield, and partly on the inspirational arguments long invoked to justify piloted space projects. The station "is essential for advancing the human exploration of space and will lead to discoveries we cannot yet fully appreciate or comprehend," said a top NASA official, Arnold Aldrich, last year. "By exploring the effect of microgravity in fields such as biotechnology, materials science, and combustion science, we hope to discover the role gravity plays in the growth of living cells, the formation of crystallizing solids, and combustion processes. By exploring the long-term effects of microgravity on living systems, we hope to discover how gravity has affected the evolution of life on our planet. Development of effective countermeasures to the changes caused by microgravity will enable humans to live and work productively in space and to apply this knowledge to the advancement of health care on earth."

This last point, on the potential medical benefits of space research, is among the most often emphasized—and most controversial—arguments in favor of building the station. Bernadine Healy, director of the National Institutes of Health under President Bush, argued last year that medical research in space could provide insights into such problems as cardiovascular disease, osteoporosis (loss of bone minerals), muscle atrophy, inner ear disturbances, and the consequences of radiation exposure. As Ronald Merrell of the University of Texas Health Science Center explained, "space-based research offers us a totally different approach to understanding these processes. We can study the body's gravity sensors and test the pulse and pressures of the cardiovascular system under entirely different conditions than here on the ground. We are able to look at the neurosensory system from a completely different perspective and we can watch the metabolism and the way fluids and bones respond, in a process that cannot be duplicated in any other setting."

Supporters also see the space station as essential to preserving the U.S. aerospace industry, and point to the huge numbers of high-quality jobs the program is creating. During the presidential campaign, Al Gore called the aerospace industry "our last surviving crown jewel" of technological innovation that has not been eclipsed by foreign competition. "The space station will serve as an anchor for the aerospace industry, particularly during a time when high-skilled defense workers are being displaced by cutbacks. Any effort to cancel this program will be opposed, because taking such a course would only exacerbate an already difficult situation."

The economic case for the space station resonates not just with executive branch officials eager to aid America's high-tech sector but also with members of Congress. The program is expected eventually to employ 75,000 people. Perhaps not accidentally, NASA has spread contracts over 37 states and hundreds of congressional districts.

The space station doesn't just keep today's engineers and scientists employed, say enthusiasts: high-profile NASA projects help inspire the engi-

neers and scientists of tomorrow. "Too many children believe that they can't 'do' science or that math is 'too hard,'" Administrator Goldin remarked last year. "However, these same students are fascinated by space subjects, especially astronauts." Inspirational programs like the space station, said Goldin, help to "ensure a sufficient talent pool to meet the competitive challenges of the twenty-first century." Rep. F. James Sensenbrenner, Jr. (R-Wis.), has put it more bluntly: "If we should neglect the space program we are going to see fewer and fewer students going into math and science, and we are going to pay the price for that, maybe not next year, but in the decades ahead."

NASA officials not only emphasize the benefits of the program that will be felt on earth but also stress that it is essential for furthering America's exploration agenda. The station will both prepare astronauts for the long stays in space that a Mars flight would entail and serve as an orbital staging site for such a mission....

THE SPACE STATION IN TROUBLE

Despite lofty arguments in its favor, the space station is under assault from all directions. Critics pursue two lines of attack: one, that it is unaffordable, whatever its value; and two, that its value is in fact wildly exaggerated.

"Quite simply, our government does not have the resources to fund a program as all-consuming as the space station while attempting to support a vast array of smaller but equally important space science and technology development programs," Sen. Ernest Hollings (D-S.C.) remarked last year. "I am one of those enthusiasts with the fire in the eyes and fire in the belly for space," said Hollings, who chairs the Commerce, Science, and Transportation Committee. "But I live in the real world."

If one accepts that something has got to give in NASA's budget, the question then becomes where to make the cuts. Nobody wants to cut deeply into NASA's other major project of the coming decade, Mission to Planet Earth, because of a widespread consensus that it will provide crucial data on environmental problems. Other reductions in space science spending—which accounts for some 20 percent of the NASA budget and includes such popular programs as the Hubble space telescope and the Magellan robotic mission to Venus—are also not palatable. In late 1990 a special advisory committee on space policy chaired by aerospace expert Norman Augustine expressed the view of many policy experts when it recommended that space science should have top priority in NASA's budget. It is this endeavor, stated the committee's final report, "that enables basic discovery and understanding that uncovers the fundamental knowledge of our own planet to improve the quality of life for all people on earth, and that stimulates the education of the scientists needed for the future."

Yet NASA's enthusiasm for the space station has already begun to bite into space science. In putting together its 1993 budget request, the agency was forced to cancel or cut back several science programs such as the Comet Rendezvous/Asteroid Flyby robotic expedition. More such cutbacks may lie down the road as NASA begins to deploy the space station in the late 1990s and the program's annual costs rise. Under current plans, this ramp-up will occur at the same time that the expensive Earth Observing System program is slated to

reach its funding peak. As one environmental lobbyist has observed, the basic problem with NASA's budgetary plans is that it has two growing children and "food enough for only one."

The space station simply cannot stand on its merits, say many critics. Medical researchers have been vocal in countering promises of health-related breakthroughs on the station. "It is extremely difficult to imagine how the conditions of space, such as low gravity, could possibly add significantly to our understanding of normal growth, cancer, AIDS, or any other disease of man or other organisms on the planet," argued biologist Maxine Singer, president of the Carnegie Institution, in congressional testimony last year. Singer stressed that biomedical experiments require carefully controlled environments and immense attention to detail. A cramped and busy space station is not the place for such research.

Another witness, Veronica Catanese, co-chair for public policy of the American Federation for Clinical Research, told Congress: "NASA's life science research proposals are not bad science. They are just not good enough to be ranked above the existing programs of the National Institutes of Health and the Veterans Administration, which are seriously underfunded."

Investigators in other areas, such as materials research, have also criticized NASA's scientific claims. "To date no examples have been found of materials that are worthy of manufacture in space," concluded a 1991 study of the Space Studies Board of the National Research Council. "Unless and until such examples are found, space manufacturing should not be used as a rationale for this program."

Even some space station advocates who believe in the program's medical and commercial utility worry about the obstacles to doing sustained laboratory work in space. "An orbiting manned platform would be an ideal place to conduct sophisticated biological and pharmaceutical research," says Jeffrey Manber, senior adviser to the Space Studies Institute, a private organization in Princeton, N.J. "But we need routine transportation" to fulfill the strict, long-term schedules that such research entails....

Amid all the arguments about the space station's scientific and economic merits, it is easy to forget about the grander dream that underpins the project. Nobody disagrees that a space station would be needed to prepare for an eventual trip to Mars, and analysts like John Pike believe Russian help makes this dream considerably more realistic. Yet station critics see a big problem: if Congress is already balking at the high cost of the space program, chances are slim that it will, in the foreseeable future, cough up hundreds of billions of dollars for a piloted mission to Mars.

A NEW SPACE POLICY?

During the presidential campaign, Clinton and Gore pledged to push ahead with the space station. But even with administration backing, the program, which has only narrowly survived in Congress over the past two years, will continue to be vulnerable....

Ironically, too, NASA's redesign of the station may actually erode support for the program, since a smaller, less capable station will be harder to justify on medical and scientific grounds. Even before the new design was announced in June, long-time supporters of the station, such as House Science Committee Chair George E. Brown, Jr. (D-Calif.), were warning that a scaled-back station might be doomed in Congress. Some observers have even suggested that the White House's real aim in ordering the redesign was to set the stage for killing the station.

Whether or not this is true, a softening of White House support could be fatal to the station's prospects. Former congressman Leon Panetta, Clinton's director of the Office of Management and Budget, has long been skeptical of NASA's long-range plans. As Panetta and other deficit hawks continue the search for budget cuts, NASA could look like an attractive target. Given Clinton's direct campaign pledge to keep the station and now Russia's involvement in the project, it is unlikely that the White house itself would ax the space station program. But as space policy expert Pike notes, a failure by the White House to invest "political capital" in keeping the program alive could give opponents in Congress an opening. Indeed, Clinton's statement in February that he would not impede congressional debate on the program suggests that there may be limits to the political capital he is willing to expend.

The future of U.S. space policy would look fundamentally different in the absence of plans to deploy the station. Since the late 1960s, space analysts have worried that without an inspirational piloted component, the whole space program could be in jeopardy. "Politically, there are a lot of people who are uncomfortable with accepting the responsibility for halting the American piloted spaceflight program," notes Pike. It is felt that in the wake of such a move NASA's "whole house of cards would come tumbling down." The White House will not take such a prospect lightly. "Do Bill Clinton and Al Gore want to go down in the history books as the president and vice-president who shut down the space program?" Pike asks rhetorically.

Yet this fear may be exaggerated. Even without a human presence, NASA would continue to pursue ambitious space science projects that fire the public's imagination by producing new information about the solar system and the universe. A U.S. space policy without a major piloted component could also be harnessed to at least two ideas that are central to the Clinton administration's long-term thinking: technological competitiveness and environmental protection.

Proposals for sharpening NASA's commercial relevance are already emerging. In February, for example, the Clinton administration announced that money saved by restructuring the space station would be transferred into NASA's aeronautical programs in an effort to keep U.S. aviation strong. And in May, an internal NASA report by analyst Charles D. Pellerin, Jr., said that to survive, the agency must move away from exploration for its own sake and concentrate on fostering new technologies and commercial opportunities. NASA Administrator Goldin reportedly received this advice with enthusiasm.

Many in Congress, while opposing the space station, support the general idea that funding NASA is one way to help sustain a robust high-tech sector. This goal, of course, is very different from NASA's traditional mission of exploring space. But by making a case that such research and development spending is a good investment, the Clinton administration can build political support for a space program that lacks a high-profile piloted component.

Emphasizing NASA's environmental mission can do even more to safeguard the agency's future. During a Senate hearing two years ago, Vice-President Gore argued that the agency's political future will hinge on whether it can help humankind deal with global environmental degradation. He said that NASA must clearly make this issue its top priority.

If the space station were canceled, the environmental mission would become NASA's most expensive and visible undertaking. Mission to Planet Earth could serve as a sturdy cornerstone for the space program into the next century. And a "green" NASA could continue to inspire scientific interest among young people.

NASA's most glamorous days might then have passed, but its greatest contribution to life on earth could be made in the years to come.

POSTSCRIPT

Should the Goals of the U.S. Space Program Include Manned Exploration of Space?

Parts of Beason's original report, which were edited out for brevity, included a call for the development of a Heavy Lift Launch Vehicle (HLLV) to reduce the cost and difficulty of getting materials into orbit. Such a cargo vehicle has been discussed for years as a supplement to the space shuttle, with a great deal of emphasis on its value for constructing space stations as well as interplanetary spaceships. However, an HLLV has never been approved, and it seems very unlikely that NASA will be able to find funds for any major new launch system that would replace or supplement the space shuttle as well as make a mission to Mars possible.

In August and September 1993 a new technology was introduced in the United States—the Delta Clipper DC-X, which boasted vertical-takeoff-and-landing capabilities and total reusability. See G. Harry Stine, "The Rooster Crows at White Sands," *Analog* (May 1994), for a report on the test flight. In October 1993, however, immediately after the DC-X's successful test-flight, the Defense Department canceled its funding. Fortunately for the program, as reported in the February 7, 1994, issue of *Aviation Week and Space Technology*, NASA was able to find $1 million to pay for some further testing.

If this new spaceship is able to continue development successfully, it may help change the outlook of the space program a few years from now. However, funding shortages seem likely to continue, largely because problems on Earth (environmental and other) seem to need money more urgently than do space exploration projects.

Early in 1994 the prospect for a renewal of manned space exploration (much less a trip to Mars) seemed fainter than ever. NASA's budget request to Congress forecast a 10 percent per year decline in space science funding through 1996. Major new missions—manned or unmanned—were slated to become rare events. See Christopher Anderson, "The Coming Crunch for Space Science," *Science* (February 18, 1994).

The reason for NASA's shrinking budget is that efforts to reduce the federal deficit have forced government agencies to trim back programs to free up funds for new programs. The resulting funding cuts are eliminating numerous once-planned missions and seriously hampering efforts to analyze data from spacecraft already in space. Money that is available is flowing toward programs such as Mission to Planet Earth, which focuses on Earth and its environmental problems, not toward programs that propose to study the distant reaches of the solar system. As Wesley Huntress, NASA's associate administrator for space science, said, "If we're going to be serious about the agency's budget as a whole remaining flat, and if Mission to Planet Earth is going to grow, something has to give. In this budget projection, that's space science."

The space station may also suffer. Indeed, it is apparently in worse trouble than Callahan notes. In April 1994 the station's cost was quoted as $28 billion, and the projected cost savings from Russian participation in the project were cut in half, prompting some to fear that the space station—and even the space shuttle—could be scrapped. See James R. Asker, "NASA's Budget Woes Will Threaten Station," *Aviation Week and Space Technology* (March 14, 1994).

It is worth noting that manned space exploration is not the only kind of manned exploration in trouble. Marine scientists are currently arguing over whether the best way to explore the ocean floor is with manned submersibles such as *Alvin*, which has served well for three decades and earned considerable fame with the public for making photographs of the sunken *Titanic* possible (see *National Geographic*, December 1985, December 1986, and October 1987), or with robots such as *Jason*, which photographed the wreck of the *Lusitania* (see *National Geographic*, April 1994). Arguments against manned exploration, here as in space, include both safety and expense. See John Travis, "Deep-Sea Debate Pits Alvin Against Jason," *Science* (March 12, 1993).

ISSUE 10

Is It Worthwhile to Continue the Search for Extraterrestrial Life?

YES: Frank Drake and Dava Sobel, from *Is Anyone Out There? The Scientific Search for Extraterrestrial Intelligence* (Delacorte Press, 1992)

NO: Richard G. Teske, from "Is This the E.T. to Whom I Am Speaking?" *Discover* (May 1993)

ISSUE SUMMARY

YES: Professor of astronomy Frank Drake and science writer Dava Sobel argue that the search for radio signals from extraterrestrial civilizations has only just begun and that scientists must continue to search because contact will eventually occur.

NO: Professor of astronomy Richard G. Teske asserts that Earth's history is so unique that it is highly unlikely that there are any beings outside of the planet with the technological capability to send signals that scientists on Earth can receive.

In the 1960s and early 1970s the business of listening to the radio whispers of the stars and hoping to pick up signals emanating from some alien civilization was still new. Few scientists held visions equal to Frank Drake, one of the pioneers of the search for extraterrestrial intelligence (SETI) field. Drake and scientists like him utilize radio telescopes—a radio receiver–antenna combination—to scan radio frequencies (channels) for signal patterns that would indicate that the signal was transmitted by an intelligent being. In his early days, Drake worked with relatively small and weak telescopes out of listening posts that he had established in Green Bank, West Virginia, and Arecibo, Puerto Rico. (See Carl Sagan and Frank Drake, "The Search for Extraterrestrial Intelligence," *Scientific American*, May 1975.)

There have been more than 50 searches for extraterrestrial radio signals since 1960. The earliest ones were very limited. Later searches have been more ambitious, culminating in the 10-year program known as the High Resolution Microwave Survey (HRMS). The HRMS, which began on Columbus Day of 1992, uses several radio telescopes and massive computers to scan 15 million radio frequencies per second. This has been the most massive SETI to date and the one with the greatest hope of success.

At the outset, many people thought—and many still think—that SETI has about as much scientific relevance as searches for Loch Ness Monsters and

Abominable Snowmen. However, to Drake and his colleagues, it seemed inevitable that with so many stars in the sky, there must be other worlds with life upon them, and some of that life must be intelligent and have a suitable technology and the desire to search for alien life too.

Writing about SETI in the September–October 1991 issue of *The Humanist*, physicist Shawn Carlson compares visiting the National Shrine of the Immaculate Conception in Washington, D.C., to looking up at the stars and "wondering if, in all [the] vastness [of the starry sky], there is anybody out there looking in our direction.... [A]re there planets like ours peopled with creatures like us staring into their skies and wondering about the possibilities of life on other worlds, perhaps even trying to contact it?" That is, SETI arouses in its devotees an almost religious sense of mystery and awe, a craving for contact with the *other*. Success would open up a universe of possibilities, add immensely to human knowledge, and perhaps even provide solutions to problems that our interstellar neighbors have already defeated.

SETI also arouses strong objections, perhaps partly because it challenges human uniqueness. Many scientists have objected that life-bearing worlds such as Earth must be exceedingly rare because the conditions that make them suitable for life as we know it—composition and temperature—are so narrowly defined. Others have objected that there is no reason whatsoever to expect that evolution would produce intelligence more than once or that, if it did, the species would be similar enough to humans to allow communication. Still others say that even if intelligent life is common, technology may not be so common, or technology may occupy such a brief period in the life of an intelligent species that there is virtually no chance that it would coincide with Earth scientists' current search. Whatever their reasons, SETI detractors agree that listening for extraterrestrial signals is a waste of time and money.

In the selections that follow, Drake and science writer Dava Sobel discuss Drake's first search for messages from distant stars (Project Ozma). Today's technology, the authors note, has made it possible to duplicate all of Ozma's work in a fraction of a second, making it that much more probable that Earth will soon make contact with extraterrestrials. Richard G. Teske, a professor of astronomy at the University of Michigan, represents the pessimistic view, arguing that the evolutionary processes of Earth that have supplied humans with the raw materials of technology are too unlikely to have been repeated elsewhere.

YES   Frank Drake and Dava Sobel

NO GREATER DISCOVERY

My scientific colleagues raise their eyebrows when I speculate on the appearance of extraterrestrials. But about 99.9 percent of them agree wholeheartedly that other intelligent life-forms do exist—and furthermore that there may be large populations of them throughout our galaxy and beyond.

Personally, I find nothing more tantalizing than the thought that radio messages from alien civilizations in space are passing through our offices and homes, right now, like a whisper we can't quite hear. In fact, we have the technology to detect such signals *today*, if only we knew where to point our radio telescopes, and the right frequency for listening.

I have been scanning the stars in search of extraterrestrial intelligence (an activity now abbreviated as SETI, and pronounced *SET-ee*) for more than thirty years. I engineered the first such effort in 1959, at the National Radio Astronomy Observatory in Green Bank, West Virginia. I named it "Project Ozma," after a land far away, difficult to reach, and populated by strange and exotic beings. I used what would now be considered crude equipment to listen for signals from two nearby, Sunlike stars. It took two months to complete the job. With the marvelous technological advances we have made in the intervening years, we could repeat the whole of Project Ozma today in a fraction of a second. We could scan for signals from a *million* stars or more at a time, at distances of at least a *thousand* light-years from Earth....

Until the late 1980s, the fact that we had not yet found another civilization, despite continued global efforts and better equipment, simply meant we had not looked long enough or hard enough. No knowledgeable person was disappointed by our inability to detect alien intelligence, as this in no way proved that extraterrestrials did not exist. Rather, our failure simply confirmed that our efforts were puny in relation to the enormity of the task —somewhat like hunting for a needle in a cosmic haystack of inconceivable size. The way we were going about it, with our small-scale attempts, was like looking for the needle by strolling past the haystack every now and then. We weren't embarked on a search that had any real chance of success.

Then many people began to grasp the nature and scope of the challenge, the consequent investment required to succeed, and the importance of success

From Frank Drake and Dava Sobel, *Is Anyone Out There? The Scientific Search for Extraterrestrial Intelligence* (Delacorte Press, 1992). Copyright © 1992 by Frank Drake and Dava Sobel. Reprinted by permission of Dell Books, a division of Bantam Doubleday Dell Publishing Group, Inc. Notes omitted.

to all humanity. They pushed relentlessly for a serious search. And won. The National Aeronautics and Space Administration (NASA) committed $100 million to a formal SETI mission spanning the decade of the 1990s, making the work a priority for the space agency and guaranteeing that coveted telescope time will be devoted to the search.

Now, after all our efforts over the past three decades, I am standing with my colleagues at last on the brink of discovery.... I see a pressing need to prepare thinking adults for the outcome of the present search activity—the imminent detection of signals from an extraterrestrial civilization. This discovery, which I fully expect to witness before the year 2000, will profoundly change the world....

I want to show that we need not be afraid of interstellar contact, for unlike the primitive civilizations on Earth that were overpowered by more advanced technological societies, we cannot be exploited or enslaved. The extraterrestrials aren't going to come and eat us; they are too far away to pose a threat. Even back-and-forth conversation with them is highly unlikely, since radio signals, traveling at the speed of light, take *years* to reach the nearest stars, and many *millennia* to get to the farthest ones, where advanced civilizations may reside. But one-way communication is a different story. Just as our radio and television transmissions leak out into space, carrying the news of our existence far and wide, so similar information from the planets of other stars has no doubt been quietly arriving at Earth for perhaps billions of years. Even more exciting is the likelihood of *intentional* messages beamed to Earth for our particular benefit. As we know from our own

efforts at composing for a pangalactic audience, reams of information about a planet's culture, history, and technology —the entire thirty-seven-volume set, if you will, of the "Encyclopedia Galactica" —could be transmitted (and received) easily and cheaply.

As a scientist, I'm driven by curiosity, of course. I want to know what's out there. But as a human being, I persevere in this pursuit because SETI promises answers to our most profound questions about who we are and where we stand in the universe. SETI is at once the most technical of scientific subjects, and also the most human. Every tactical problem in the search endeavor rests on some age-old philosophical conundrum: *Where did we come from? Are we unique? What does it mean to he a human being? ...*

* * *

[W]e have only just begun to search.

So many individuals I meet seem to think that we have already searched the sky completely and continuously over the past thirty years. The deed is done, they assume. And since we found nothing out there, to search further is to beat a dead horse. But in fact, the combinations of frequencies and places to look have hardly been touched.

In my historical analysis; the search for extraterrestrial intelligence divides itself into four eras. The first dates back at least three thousand years, to the time when people started contemplating the universe....

I trace the start of the second era to the coming of the Copernican Revolution in the sixteenth century. That was when astronomers such as Kepler and Galileo, who used a real telescope, recognized that some of the other objects in the Solar System were planets similar to the

Earth. Scientific observations could now support the philosophical argument in favor of other life in the cosmos—and perhaps even within the Solar System....

The third era began in 1959–60, when scientists first employed quantitative measures to compute the strength of possible signs of life crossing interstellar space. In other words, we made precise calculations of the detectability of alien signals, and acted on them. Projects —beginning with [Cornell physics professors Philip] Morrison and [Giuseppe] Cocconi's proposal to search for radio waves and my strategy for Project Ozma —sprang from a greater knowledge of the universe and a real sense of the numbers involved. For the first time, SETI embodied philosophical, qualitative, *and* quantitative elements. Scientists conducted some sixty "third era" extraterrestrial searches in the 1960s, 1970s, and 1980s. Most of these, however, were low-budget productions, done with leftover funds in borrowed time on equipment built for other purposes.

The fourth era, which starts now, is not only quantitative, it is also, finally, *thorough*. The projects of the 1990s represent the most exhaustive probing to date of the cosmic haystack. Here I am referring especially to the NASA SETI project....

My involvement in SETI activities has actually increased over the years, because SETI itself has grown so much. It occupies more people than ever before, and demands more of their time. Jill Tarter, for example, is the first astronomer to work full-time as a SETI scientist. When she isn't fully engaged in her role as project scientist, the senior scientific position in the NASA SETI project, she is in Washington, explaining the project to congressional representatives. Paul

Horowitz runs a close second in activity. Despite his teaching duties at Harvard, Paul has had one search or another in progress since 1977. In some years he devotes nearly 100 percent of his time to these efforts—masterminding a new project and then personally soldering the thousands of joints that hold the equipment together....

I finally got my turn to meet Paul in 1977, when he was already a full professor of physics at Harvard....

A short time later,... Paul accepted a 1981–82 NASA Ames fellowship, which enabled him to work on SETI at the Ames Research Center and at Stanford University. He joined the Ames-Stanford group trying to create a SETI machine that could analyze a huge number of separate channels—128,000 of them, more than anyone had ever been able to monitor simultaneously....

The sheer number of channels in this multichannel analyzer was a big advance in itself, but Paul also made the components portable, so they could be packed up in three small boxes and hand-carried to any observatory, anywhere in the world. The system, which he dubbed "Suitcase SETI," traveled first to Arecibo [Ionospheric Observatory in northern Puerto Rico, home of the largest radio telescope ever built]. After examining 250 stars with it, Paul took it back to Harvard in 1983. He hooked it up to the same telescope I had partially built and calibrated in my student days —the one I had used to observe the Pleiades for my doctoral thesis. Suitcase SETI's rambling days were over at that point. Portable though it was, it never ventured out of Harvard's Oak Ridge Observatory again, A new name, Project Sentinel, recognized the fact that Paul's multichannel analyzer was now connected to a dedicated telescope, with funding from The Planetary Society to run a permanent SETI facility.

In time, Sentinel begat "META-SETI" —the Megachannel ExtraTerrestrial Assay—which boosted the number of channels from 128,000 to more than 8 million.... Paul needed the extra channels, he said, to respond to a new concept put forward by Phil Morrison, who had reminded him in a letter that everything in the universe is in motion....

Intelligent radio signals from distant civilizations could [therefore] be expected to arrive shifted in frequency, just as the starlight from distant suns is shifted toward the red or the blue end of the optical spectrum by stellar motions. There was no way to predict which way a signal's frequency would shift without knowing how its home star was moving. Thus a message transmitted on the hydrogen frequency could wind up far above or far below that frequency by the time it reached a radio telescope on Earth.

With META, Paul could scrutinize myriad frequencies in the vicinity of the hydrogen line and sift through them, narrow bandwidth by narrow bandwidth, on millions of channels at once to detect the displaced signals.

In 1991 Paul set up a second META, also financed by The Planetary Society, called META II, in the Southern Hemisphere, at the Instituto Argentino de Radioastronomia in Villa Elisa, Argentina. This allowed Argentinian astronomers led by Raul Colombo to observe the portion of the southern sky that's not visible from Cambridge. META II opened up very important new regions of the Milky Way as well as a clear line of sight to the two galaxies that are the Milky Way's nearest neighbors: the Magellanic Clouds. Now, with META and META

II thriving, Paul is already dreaming of BETA. This would be a new system ("It'll be *betta* than META," he promises), with one hundred million channels.

Paul has obviously done more searching, with more sensitivity, than anybody who preceded him, so it shouldn't be too surprising to learn that he's actually heard things through his systems. Indeed, Paul has records of about sixty signals that are all excellent candidates for being the real thing. But Paul's searches run themselves, automatically. By the time he recognizes the candidates in the recorded data, hours or days later, it's too late to check them. Looking for them later proves fruitless, as they are no longer where they were. No doubt the civilizations are still there—if that's what made the signal—but they've stopped talking, at least for the moment.... If only Paul's strategy included a human operator who could double-check the signals on the spot! However, Paul has severe budget constraints, and I know that he can't afford to pay someone to sit there through the long nights and wait.

The new NASA SETI Microwave Observing Project will change all that, because I'll be sitting there myself. Or Jill will, or some other radio astronomer who will be able to react immediately to chase down a candidate signal the moment it appears. This project, which has been in various stages of planning and development since 1978, is just now beginning its methodical hunt. Because of its great power and sensitivity, it outstrips all previous search activities combined. Three days' operation can accomplish more than was done in the preceding three decades. Indeed, it gives me a strange chill to acknowledge that it takes this new setup only one one-hundredth of a second to duplicate what

Project Ozma did in its full two hundred hours....

What does NASA SETI have that no other search had? The short answer is "everything." It has everything that early searches had, and everything we could think of that had never been done before.

Like Ozma, NASA SETI scrutinizes a group of relatively close, Sun-like stars for signs of intelligent life. But where Ozma had only two targets, NASA SETI has one thousand. This much more extensive "targeted search," however, is still only half the mission. The other half is an "all-sky survey" that repeatedly scans the whole grand volume of outer space for alien signals from any star, anywhere. Our dual search strategy deals with two alternate possibilities for our cosmic neighbors: Either the easiest aliens to detect are right nearby (targeted search), or they are very far away but very bright (all-sky survey and targeted search).

Like the Ohio State project, NASA SETI is an ongoing endeavor that will run for years. But unlike the low-cost efforts that preceded it, this project fought for and won a total of more than $100 million in federal funding. While other searches started up and faded out without so much as a nod from NASA, this one enjoys the same position as a mission to send a small spacecraft to another planet. Mission status means that SETI is supported all through NASA management, right up to the topmost level.

Like META and META II, NASA SETI spans the globe and the heavens. It utilizes at least five telescopes—at Arecibo, Green Bank, the Observatoire de Nançy in France, the Goldstone Tracking Station in California, and an identical NASA tracking station at Tidbinbilla, Australia.

It is the first truly global cooperative effort to search for interstellar signals.

Unlike ... Suitcase SETI, NASA SETI is no backseat or part-time visitor. It constitutes the largest single program running at Arecibo and will soon dominate a fully dedicated telescope at Green Bank. It employs more than one hundred people, including a rotating team of radio astronomers who stand ready to respond to candidate signals in real time.

Most American searches until now have sought narrow-band signals on magic frequencies, such as the hydrogen line. We call them "magic" because they seem to have some real rationale for being logical channels of communication. Part of their magic is that they occupy quiet regions of the electromagnetic spectrum. What's more, the hydrogen line, considered the most magical frequency of all, is such a fertile field for making general discoveries in radio astronomy that scientists of all civilizations probably keep close tabs on it. Thus, a signal on that particular frequency should have the greatest chance of being detected. The hydrogen line is the frequency Morrison and Cocconi suggested in their original paper, and the actual frequency searched in Project Ozma....

Magic frequencies have special appeal, but even human beings disagree as to which ones are best.... The point is, any search based on a magic frequency assumes first of all that extraterrestrials are broadcasting on a chosen frequency, and furthermore that we can know what that frequency is.

The NASA SETI project makes no such assumptions. It scans most of the frequencies in the waterhole that penetrate the Earth's atmosphere. This means we'll have a much greater chance than ever before to detect a message, whether the aliens choose a frequency for convenience' sake or some numerology of their own. Our new equipment frees us from the need to select just one or two frequencies from among the vast field of possibilities....

META set a world's record with 8 million channels, but NASA SETI has 28 million. At the core of its hardware is a device called a multichannel spectrum analyzer (MCSA in NASA's beloved alphabet soup), which divides the incoming radio noise into 14 million narrowband channels. The MCSA also combines the signals from several adjacent channels to create another 14 million broader bandwidths, just in case the extraterrestrials use them.

The MCSA relies on ultra-advanced software to make sense out of the millions of data points pouring in every second. Software analyzes the data, looking for patterns that reveal intelligence—and that could not possibly be intercepted as fast or as well by human intelligence. The human operator, whose presence is so important to me, steps in *after* computers sound the alarm that a candidate signal has just been detected....

In the course of gushing about the great power of NASA SETI compared to any and all of its predecessors, I've dropped several huge numbers, referring to everything from frequencies and sensitivities to dollars and cents. That said, do I really need one more quantitative comparison to make my point? Would it really clarify things further to say that NASA SETI is a ten-millionfold improvement over past efforts? Maybe not. Maybe the more important thing to say now is that the magnitude of our current efforts creates so much promise that we find ourselves contemplating what we should do when

we actually receive signal evidence of extraterrestrial life. When and how do we inform the people of Earth?

John Billingham [a former aerospace physician with England's Royal Air Force] has probably given more thought to this delicious dilemma than anyone else. Working with other members of the SETI committee of the International Academy of Astronautics (IAA), he has drawn up a "Declaration of Principles Concerning Activities Following the Detection of Extraterrestrial Intelligence." It lists all the steps to be taken to verify the authenticity of a signal and inform the proper authorities that extraterrestrial word has been heard,

This document has been approved or endorsed by every major, international, professional space society, including the IAA, the International Institute of Space Law, the Committee on Space Research, Commission 51 of the International Astronomical Union, and Commission J of the Union Radio Scientifique Internationale. In essence, Billingham's protocol says, *Make sure you've got something; then tell EVERYBODY.*

I've spoken at some length about how one goes about checking a candidate signal for authenticity—how to establish extraterrestrial origin, and how the special hallmarks of artificiality can distinguish a signal as being of intelligent design. But to announce to the world at large that you've made the greatest discovery in the history of astronomy—perhaps in history, period—takes an even wider margin of certainty.

On the NASA SETI project, you probably can't ask another observatory to help you verify your findings. If the long-awaited signal is intercepted at Arecibo, and it is weak, which is the most likely possibility, then no other observatory in the world could make the desired verification. This is because Arecibo has the greatest collecting area of any telescope, as well as the Gregorian feed and other specialized equipment. Even the other participants in NASA SETI, in France and Australia, will not match Arecibo's wide range of frequency coverage. And if the signal did fall within their frequency range, they might lack the sensitivity to hear it. Arecibo is so much more sensitive than the others—ever so much more capable of picking a faint, fragile *"We are here!"* out of a welter of cosmic noise.

In lieu of interobservatory checks and balances, the people at Arecibo (I hope I'm one of them when this happens) will have to spend several days checking and rechecking their data, locating the signal, if possible, a second, third, and fourth time rather than risk setting off a false alarm. After several days, however, repeated observations would build up a chink-free wall of evidence that would justify going public....

Hard upon detection of an intelligent signal, there follows the delicate matter of a reply to the civilization that sent it. I've thought a lot, of course, about what to say in that happy situation. I have waited a lifetime for the opportunity, and the waiting has not diminished my confidence or my enthusiasm. I can't be specific about it, though, because when you really think about it, the only answer to the question "What do you say?" is "It depends."

It depends on the nature of the signal and what it's telling us. It depends on the world's reaction. It depends on the distance the message traveled, because we couldn't establish true dialogue with civilizations far removed from us— only lengthy monologues, crossing each other eternally in the interstellar mail. It depends on whether we can understand it. Certainly no stock reply, prepared in advance and stashed in someone's file cabinet, could match more than one of the infinite possibilities for the message's content. Certainly any reply should be crafted on a worldwide basis, and only after lengthy deliberation by knowledgeable individuals.

I have a recurring dream in which we receive our much-anticipated intelligent signal from across the Galaxy. The signal is unambiguous. It repeats over and over, allowing us to get a fix on its source, some twenty thousand light-years away. The signal is... apparently dense with information content. It is so full of noise, however, that we can't extract any information from it. And so we know only that another civilization exists. We cannot decipher the message itself.

If this dream becomes real, such documented detection of alien signals will, of course, be big news in itself. It will be a call to action, too, beckoning us to do whatever is required—build a much larger radio-telescope system, for example—to obtain information about that civilization, to learn whatever secrets the extraterrestrials will share with us.

Indeed, our response to a message from an alien civilization may thus be a response to the *situation* instead of an actual reply to the senders. We will tell the world at large what has happened, and that we're taking the next step by building better equipment to understand the message we've received. How I would love to have to go to Congress with a budget request for that project. I don't imagine I'd encounter much opposition....

I do not wonder *whether* this will happen. My only question is *When?*

The silence we have heard so far is not in any way significant. We still have not looked long enough or hard enough. We've not explored a large enough chunk of the cosmic haystack. I could speculate that "they" are watching us to see if we are worth talking to. Or perhaps the ethic exists among them that rules, "There is no free lunch in the Galaxy." If we want to join the community of advanced civilizations, we must work as hard as they must. Perhaps they will send a signal that can be detected only if we put as much effort into receiving it as they put into transmitting it. NASA SETI is the beginning of the first truly meaningful effort to demonstrate the sincerity of our intentions.

Thus, the lesson we have learned from all our previous searching is that the greatest discovery is not a simple one to make. If there were once cockeyed optimists in the SETI endeavor, there aren't any now. In a way, I am glad. The priceless benefits of knowledge and experience that will accrue from interstellar contact should not come too easily. To appreciate them, we should expect to devote a substantial portion of our resources, our assets, our intellectual vigor, and our patience. We should be willing to sweat and crawl and wait.

The goal is not beyond us. It is within our grasp.

NO

Richard G. Teske

IS THIS THE E.T. TO WHOM
I AM SPEAKING?

Those who have seen the movie *E.T.* will remember that as the little extraterrestrial lies near death amid the bedlam of a makeshift medical center, an amazed scientist rushes in exclaiming, "He's got DNA! He's got DNA!" Why "he"? Why "DNA"? We know almost nothing about how alien life might begin and evolve. We are totally ignorant about whether sex is essential for the creation of a race of advanced beings. We are unable to say for sure if DNA or a similar complex genetic material is a requirement for intelligence. Despite this ignorance—or because of it—radio astronomers involved in NASA's Search for Extraterrestrial Intelligence (SETI) are now listening intently for broadcasts from the stars. They listen in hopes of hearing the signal of another civilization. Hope, in this case, springs from something called the principle of humility: Surely, among the billions of stellar systems in the billions of galaxies that fill our universe, Earth's ability to support intelligent life isn't unique. The universe is too vast, and we're not that special—something else is probably out there. It's just a matter of our finding it, or of its finding us.

I don't agree. I think it's unlikely that an intelligent being from outer space will communicate with us. And I think this not because of any insight into life's origins, molecular structure, and evolution but because of some very basic issues of technology.

I start with an assumption: any extraterrestrial that we might hear has to use metal. Radio antennas and rockets are fabricated of massive metal structures because of that material's strength, electrical conductivity, and other properties. The science and technology that have to lie behind the making of such hardware imply a culture possessing vast industrial talents. In turn this demands planetary natural resources aplenty, especially metallic ores—the raw materials for the technical infrastructure.

We now have a good idea how the useful ores of our own planet were made. Surprisingly, this information indicates that planets with mineral riches may be as hard to find as the forty-niners' mother lode. Even more surprisingly, it means the odds are *against* E.T.'s having the resources to build an

From Richard G. Teske, "Is This the E.T. to Whom I Am Speaking?" *Discover* (May 1993).

interstellar phone, no matter how favorably you calculate the odds of the alien's existence.

Let's take a close look at those odds. Alien existence is usually estimated with a famous equation first suggested by astronomer Frank Drake. The calculation begins with a guess at the number of planets in the galaxy: There are some 400 billion stars in the Milky Way, and astronomers believe that planets are fairly common, perhaps orbiting around one star in 10. That's 40 billion stars with planets. If each star has 10 planets (similar to our solar system), that's 400 billion planets.

After that, certain probabilities that go into the equation are roughed out using the humility principle. There are various opinions about how high or low those probabilities should be set; I'll use values that fall somewhere on the optimistic side. To estimate the number of potentially habitable planets, we can say that because in our solar system only Earth and perhaps Mars have ever qualified as fit places to live, the likelihood of habitable planets existing in other planetary systems is roughly 2 in 10—say, 80 billion planets. What are the odds that one of these habitable planets will actually develop life? Again using the local evidence of Earth and Mars, we can set this value at 1/2. So the result is 40 billion planets with life.

How many shelter *intelligent* life? There's really no way to determine this. Some people arbitrarily set the odds at 1/100. But if we want to be as generous as possible, we can argue that the one planet we know of with life also has intelligent creatures, and thus we can set the probability at 1. That leaves us with anywhere from 400 million to 40 billion planets teeming with intelligent life.

But how many of those are capable of the highly technical achievement of radio communication between the stars? We now need to estimate the probability that intelligent creatures can create the necessary technology and decide to make use of it. SETI advocates often set the value between 1/10 and 1/5, again using the local evidence and the principle of humility. They point out that on Earth there have been a number of independently developed civilizations. But only one—modern Western European—has indeed created a high level of technology. Depending on just how they count the number of past civilizations, SETI supporters reason that one out of five or seven or maybe ten other planetary civilizations will develop the tools of interstellar contact. At any rate, we are left with between 40 million and 8 billion communicating civilizations.

This number can be, and usually is, reduced far further—sometimes down to mere thousands—even by SETI's most dedicated proponents. They factor in such things as the average life of a planet and the life of any single civilization on it —after all, what we are interested in is the possibility of communicating with other intelligent beings *right now,* and it does us little good if some alien signal is going to miss our attempts to detect it by millions of years.

But we don't have to focus on these last steps. Let's consider only the assumption above, that one out of five or ten civilizations will be able to develop the technology necessary for interstellar communication. It is precisely here that recent strides in understanding the origins of Earth's natural wealth require a different, and more pessimistic, calculation. Let us, as the SETI advocates do, look at the local evidence. When a planet like Earth forms, most of the high-density materials such as iron and nickel sink to the center of the molten sphere. But some of this material is left behind in the mantle, where it is widely scattered in small amounts. If something hadn't happened on Earth to bring it to the surface and concentrate it in significant quantities, metallic material would have remained unavailable to the creatures who inherited the planet, no matter how intelligent they became.

What happened was this: Starting about 3.8 billion years ago, according to geologists, lavas rich in iron and magnesium erupted cataclysmically from the seafloor. Chemical reactions of the magma with materials dissolved by the seawater resulted in deposition of metal-enriched sediments. Later the sediments were remelted and modified by rumbling, ongoing volcanism, which further enriched and concentrated metal ores deposited on the sea bottom.

On our planet this sea bottom moves. Its crustal plates unroll from midocean ridges like hug conveyor belts. Floating upon them are thick, lighter, nearly permanent continents, rafting back and forth. The conveyor belts of ocean bottom eventually dive under the edges of the buoyant continents at areas called subduction zones. As this crust slides beneath the continents, it sinks down into the mantle, where metal-rich sediments are heated and rise to the surface, becoming part of mountain ranges. The heat generated by this activity also promotes volcanoes, and the erupting lavas further concentrate the metals.

The existence and near permanence of continents is an important ingredient in making metal ores available to us. Had the earliest sea-bottom ore deposits been carried beneath the continents and lost altogether, there would be fewer re-sources for us to recover. Instead, and to our great good fortune, some primitive oceanic deposits were incorporated into the long-surviving continents, where further chemical and physical modification and concentration could take place. There the ores were stored over billion-year intervals.

Circulation of water in Earth's crust is essential in making ores, too. On the continents as well as beneath the seafloor, water gurgles into the rocks through cracks and fractures that may let it percolate miles deep. The groundwater or seawater contains dissolved salts, acids, or bases that promote chemical reactions between rock and fluid. Metals are dissolved and transported to other regions, often quite far away, where further chemical reactions release them, precipitating the metallic materials and thus creating ores. For example, midcontinental ore deposits in the Mississippi Valley were brought there by groundwater circulating from the ancient Appalachian Mountains almost half a continent away.

A planet's atmosphere also plays an important role in metal accumulation. According to geologist George Brimhall of the University of California at Berkeley, the gases interact with crustal rocks, creating a chemical environment that has a decisive effect on the kinds of metals that can be dissolved and concentrated. For example, when free oxygen is absent, iron separates from other substances easily, and so the iron particles can settle together on the ocean bottom, creating large iron deposits. In the presence of free oxygen, however, iron combines stubbornly with it, becomes insoluble, and stays locked up as dispersed iron in the rocks.

* * *

Remarkably, our atmosphere has provided both kinds of environment, each for about half Earth's lifetime. The most recent of the known major iron ore deposits are roughly 1.6 to 1.9 billion years old, suggesting that that period was the transition time, and prior to it Earth's atmosphere had little or no free oxygen. Why did such a transition occur? Most scientists believe our oxygen atmosphere is the product of biological activity, that the transition took place when one-celled ancestors of green plants learned the lesson of photosynthesis and began taking in carbon dioxide and releasing oxygen.

Although the arrival of free oxygen ended a long period of transport and deposition of iron, it led to a period of greater mobility for many other metals that, unlike iron, dissolve more easily when oxygen abounds. The transition thus paved the way for deposition of new kinds of ores such as uranium, copper, lead, and zinc. Concentration of these materials—used today for fission bombs, pennies, and water pipes—continued to be driven at a snail's pace by the thrust and collision of moving crustal plates, while ongoing circulation of crustal waters continued to be essential in emplacing Earth's bounty.

Of course, making these ores is only part of what's needed. They don't do us any good if we can't get at them. They have to be close to the surface. Therefore their availability often depends upon their being uncovered by erosion and weathering. Yet if erosion goes too far, the ores may be modified and dispersed—and wasted. It's a truly delicate balance.

So much for our planet. A brief tour through the solar system gives us an idea of just how rare each of these processes is, and how much rarer still is their combination. For this examination, let's look at just the four planets of the inner solar system, plus our moon. The other planets have followed different paths of development since their assembly, and I believe that if our own history is any guide, they are unlikely to have significant ore deposits. In any case, we simply don't yet know enough about them to judge.

Mercury and the moon never accumulated dense atmospheres nor abundant surface waters, and they show no signs of the moving crustal plates that drive the machinery of ore deposition on Earth. On Venus there seem to be a few small continentlike areas, and it is probable that these rest upon a soft, hot interior like that of Earth. But scientists think the crust is too thick and stiff for plate movements. Water was lost very early because it stayed up in the atmosphere, where the sun's rays could slice apart vast numbers of water molecules and quickly let free hydrogen escape to space in massive amounts. Some of the atmospheric water may also have been lost when it reacted with the crust, with the oxygen combining with rocks and the light hydrogen escaping. Either way, the absence of sufficient water to transport dissolved metals, together with the absence of moving crustal plates, means there's little chance that the goddess of beauty can be a goddess of metallic wealth.

Mars shows no widespread evidence of moving crustal plates, either. Because of its smaller size, Mars had less inner heat than Earth and so had volcanism that was wimpy by comparison. As a result, less water and fewer gases emerged from its crust and interior. Moreover, release of the gases petered out at an early time, so that as hydrogen was lost in space the water from which it came was not replaced. Spacecraft imagery of Mars' surface shows undeniable evidence that water was once present, but the pictures of floodplains and gullies also indicate that aquatic circulation was violent and short-lived, with floods and torrents that ended during the planet's middle age. This is not the kind of continuing process that produced our planet's plenitude.

None of this activity—plate movements on Mars and Venus, continents on Venus, early Martian water—exhibits the musical humming of Earth's planetary engine. The crucial issue is whether the processes of ore deposition are orchestrated elsewhere by nature as harmoniously as here at home. It's possible these different factors are somehow physically linked like Siamese quadruplets, so that if you have one you'll also have others. I believe, however, the evidence from Venus and Mars indicates that these factors are indeed independent. Yet they all need to operate together and in the right way. In the solar system only Earth is so blessed, suggesting that delicate balances may be but rarely achieved.

Remember that factor in the Drake equation that expresses the probability that intelligent beings will develop the technology and taste for interstellar communication? Recall that it's often given a value of 1/10 or 1/5, based on Earth's civilizations. But the evidence of the solar system yields a much lower number.

* * *

How many planets have the attributes necessary for metal-based technology? (The processes that give rise to this are independent of habitability, so it is fair for us to consider the four inner planets plus our moon, and not just habitable Earth and Mars.) On only 1 in 5 of these objects (Earth) do long-lasting crustal plate movements occur. On 1 in 5 of them do we find an ongoing hydrologic cycle. On just 1 in 5 of them did the atmosphere gain enough free oxygen for a long enough time so that deposition of a great range of metal ores could take place. And on 1 in 5 do we have large and long-lasting areas of buoyant continents to store resources in. If I am correct in viewing these as independent processes, we would calculate their joint probability by multiplying the individual probabilities: $1/5 \times 1/5 \times 1/5 \times 1/5 = 1/625$.

But the sample in the solar system surely does not include all possible planetary examples. Suppose we knew of five more objects unlike Earth. With them included among the present five and in the spirit of unlinked processes, we would calculate a joint probability of $1/10 \times 1/10 \times 1/10 \times 1/10 = 1/10,000$. Notice the predicted probability diminishes rapidly as more examples of impotent planets are included. I think we still haven't seen all possible kinds of planets and that the value of the probability can go lower still.

Am I being too harsh, too pessimistic? If we were to find more examples of potent planets, of course, the odds would go the other way. But I actually think I'm being overly *generous*. In our arithmetic we have not yet assessed such "delicate balances" as how long an atmosphere needs to have free oxygen, and how much it needs, to create industrial-strength ore deposits of all kinds. We haven't examined the fine balance between deposition and erosion, nor estimated how many nearly permanent, floating continents are desirable. My guess is that if we knew enough about these matters right now, we would come up with an extraordinarily low value for that key number in the Drake equation.

It is safe to predict that life indeed does exist elsewhere. It's probably safe to predict that some of that life is intelligent. But the rare and delicate balance of geology and chemistry that led to technology on Earth leads me to predict that there may be few or no technologically competent civilizations in the galaxy other than ourselves. I wish SETI all the success in the world, or in any world, for contact would be a truly exciting, absolutely marvelous discovery. But there may not be any calls from E.T. to listen for after all.

POSTSCRIPT

Is It Worthwhile to Continue the Search for Extraterrestrial Life?

The modern, high-tech version of SETI, the High Resolution Microwave Survey (HRMS), almost never came to pass. As Donald Tarter of the International Space University writes, in "Treading on the Edge: Practicing Safe Science With SETI," *Skeptical Inquirer* (Spring 1993), "SETI's recent history has been one of fighting for scientific respect and then fighting for funding.... SETI has been so frequently ridiculed and singled out as [a program that could be eliminated by budget-cutting congressional members] that officially SETI no longer exists." He then notes that, shortly before NASA began its current search for extraterrestrial intelligence, the name was changed to HRMS.

However, the name change did not solve the problem. A year after HRMS was born, the budget was cut. By October 12, 1993, the $1 million a month needed to sustain it had been eliminated from the budget by a House-Senate conference committee. In support of the cut, Senator Richard H. Bryan (D-Nevada) said, "The Great Martian Chase may finally come to an end. As of today, millions have been spent and we have yet to bag a single little green fellow. Not a single martian has said 'take me to your leader,' and not a single flying saucer has applied for FAA approval." See Seth Shostak, "The New Search for Intelligent Life," *Mercury* (September–October 1993).

It was not the sort of arguments raised by critics such as Teske that defeated HRMS; it was image. SETI smacked too much of science fiction and Hollywood. It might not be terribly expensive—the cost of a single space shuttle flight could pay SETI's bills for several years—but whatever it cost seemed to the budget cutters pure waste when compared to the many other programs and problems requiring funds.

Politicians were not the only ones who reacted in this way. Harvard biologist Ernst Mayr reacted to a review of Drake and Sobel's book *Is Anyone Out There?* by saying, "I find it astounding ... that such a highly dubious endeavor is supported by NASA in this time of appalling federal debt" (*Science*, March 12, 1993, p. 1522–1523).

Yet, SETI was not dead. Many scientists—including nonastronomers such as David M. Raup of the University of Chicago's Department of Geophysical Sciences and Committee on Evolutionary Biology—disagree with those who believe that humans are probably alone in the universe and who say that the search for intelligent extraterrestrials is not worth the effort. So do many nonscientists. By January 1994, Jill Tarter, former head of NASA's HRMS (and no relation to the Donald Tarter mentioned above), and the private SETI Institute had gained promises of $4.4 million from prominent business leaders in California's computer industry. "They're in it for the adventure. They have vision," said Seth Shostak, a SETI Institute scientist (*Science*, January 28, 1994).

Renamed Project Phoenix, the HRMS still requires several more millions of dollars even to operate at a reduced level, which would involve searching 1,000 nearby stars for radio signals instead of the entire sky. However, the fund-raising efforts so far have been successful enough to keep SETI's devotees optimistic. For its part, NASA is allowing crucial HRMS equipment to remain on loan to the SETI Institute. Furthermore, new technology, which allows SETI equipment to be attached to radio telescopes working on other projects, also helps bring the costs down.

ISSUE 11

Should Law Enforcement Agencies Be Permitted to Eavesdrop on Computer Communications?

YES: Dorothy E. Denning, from "To Tap or Not to Tap," *Communications of the ACM* (March 1993)

NO: Mike Godwin, from "A Chip Over My Shoulder: The Problems With Clipper," *Internet World* (July 1994)

ISSUE SUMMARY

YES: Professor of computer science Dorothy E. Denning holds that law enforcement agencies have a legitimate interest in ensuring access to private communications, even if this means regulating the use of secret codes.

NO: Mike Godwin, staff counsel for the Electronic Frontier Foundation, a group of people who are concerned with civil liberties in connection with computers, argues that the individual's right to privacy must take precedence over the government's power to intrude, even at the risk of diminished national security.

The U.S. Bill of Rights established the right of private citizens to be secure against unreasonable searches and seizures. "Unreasonable" has come to mean "without a search warrant" for physical searches of homes and offices and "without a court order" for interceptions of mail and wiretaps of phone conversations.

Private citizens who—for whatever reason—do not wish to have their communications with others shared with law enforcement and security agencies have long sought ways to preserve their privacy. One solution has been secret codes. Encryption (encoding) schemes range from the use of prearranged phrases on the phone to elaborate transformations of written passages. A simple example would be cryptograms—puzzles in which a familiar quote is coded by substituting one letter for another letter throughout.

U.S. government agencies such as the Federal Bureau of Investigation (FBI), Central Intelligence Agency (CIA), and National Security Agency (NSA) have developed considerable expertise at breaking codes. This skill is commonly used to gain evidence of crime and to intercept diplomatic and military messages.

Government code-breaking expertise was threatened in the 1970s, when university researchers realized that computers made it possible to create virtually unbreakable codes. Many people welcomed this development, for it offered ways to guarantee privacy and to protect both corporate and private secrets. Law enforcement and national security agencies did not welcome it, however; they feared that the new encryption technologies would allow terrorists, drug runners, racketeers, and spies to operate with less fear of detection than ever before.

Not long after, as David Banisar of Computer Professionals for Social Responsibility (CPSR) writes in "Battle for Control of Encryption Technology," *IEEE Software* (July 1993), the NSA "claimed exclusive control over encryption development and attempted to prevent the National Science Foundation from providing grants to mathematicians who wished to study encryption." Since then, the NSA has tried to use the Patent Secrecy Act to classify patents and suppress consumer devices that incorporate encryption technology. It has also used the Export Administration Act to prohibit the export of encryption technology to other countries, even those that have equal or better technologies on the market already. Finally, the NSA has developed its own encryption techniques—with "holes" that allow those who know what those holes are to break the codes quickly and easily—and has tried to pressure others to use them.

While coding capabilities were changing, communications technology was also changing, shifting from easily tappable copper wires to fiber optics, and from analog (which mimics voice vibrations) to digital (which encodes them). The Department of Justice therefore sought legislation to require that the makers and providers of communications products and services ensure that their products remain tappable. In September 1992, the Clinton administration submitted the Digital Telephony Act to Congress, a piece of legislation that would prevent advancing technology from limiting the government's ability to legally intercept communications.

This is the basic shape of the debate: the U.S. government insists that private citizens do not have the right to act in such a way that they cannot be watched, supervised, and punished if the government deems it necessary. The CPSR, the Electronic Frontier Foundation (EFF), and numerous other groups and individuals insist equally strenuously that the right to privacy must come first.

In the following selections, Dorothy E. Denning defends the government's position as it stood immediately after the Digital Telephony Act was proposed. She argues that controlling the use and strength of secret codes is a natural extension of the act. Mike Godwin focuses on the proposed "Clipper chip," a computer chip designed by the NSA that would become the standard encryption device for everyone, but which also could be decoded at will by the government. He argues that people should be free to use whatever codes they wish to use and that they should be allowed to regulate their own privacy.

YES

Dorothy E. Denning

TO TAP OR NOT TO TAP

Under current U.S. law, the government is authorized to intercept the wire, electronic, or oral communications of a criminal subject by obtaining a special court order which has been designed by Congress and approved by the Supreme Court. When served with a court order, service providers and operators are obligated under statute to assist in the execution of a court-authorized tap or microphone installation. To obtain this order, Congress and the Supreme Court have specified that law enforcement must demonstrate there is probable cause to believe the subject under investigation is committing some specific, serious felony and communications concerning the offense will be obtained through the intercepts. Before issuing a court order, a judge must review a lengthy affidavit that sets forth all the evidence and agree with the assertions contained therein. The affidavit must also demonstrate other investigative techniques have been tried without success, or won't work, or would be too dangerous. In the decade from 1982 to 1991, state and federal agencies conducted 7,467 taps, leading to 19,259 convictions so far. Convictions resulting from interceptions conducted in the last few years are still accumulating, as trials regarding those subjects are held.

The ability of law enforcement to draw on this investigative tool is now at risk. Methods that have been used to intercept analogue voice communications carried over copper wires do not work with many of the new digital-based technologies and services such as ISDN (Integrated Services Digital Network), fiber optic transmissions, and the increasing number of mobile telecommunication networks and architectures. Although it is technically feasible to intercept digital communications, not all systems have been designed or equipped to meet the intercept requirements of law enforcement. According to the FBI, numerous court orders have not been sought, executed, or fully carried out because of technological problems. To address these problems, the Department of Justice is seeking digital telephony legislation to require the service providers and operators to meet their statutory assistance requirements by maintaining the capability to intercept particular communications, permitting law enforcement to perform its monitoring function at a remote government monitoring facility in real time.

From Dorothy E. Denning, "To Tap or Not to Tap," *Communications of the ACM,* vol. 36, no. 3 (March 1993). Copyright © 1993 by The Association for Computing Machinery, Inc. Reprinted by permission. Acknowledgments and references omitted.

The proposed legislation has stimulated a lively debate. Much of the debate has focused on concerns that the proposal, if enacted, could hold back technology, jeopardize security and privacy, make U.S. products noncompetitive, burden the country with unjustifiable and unnecessary costs, and ultimately fail to meet the stated objectives if criminals encrypt their communications.

This article presents the case for the proposed digital telephony legislation and responds to the preceding concerns. Although the digital telephony proposal does not address encryption, the possibility of regulating cryptography will be discussed following the section on the proposed legislation.

THE DIGITAL TELEPHONY PROPOSAL

To ensure law enforcement's continued ability to conduct court-authorized taps, the administration, at the bequest of the Department of Justice and the FBI, proposed digital telephony legislation. The version submitted to Congress in September 1992 would require providers of electronic communications services and private branch exchange (PBX) operators to ensure that the government's ability to lawfully intercept communications is not curtailed or prevented entirely by the introduction of advanced technology. Service providers would be responsible for providing the government, in real time, the communication signals of the individual(s) named in a court order so the signals could be transferred to a remote government monitoring facility, without detection by the subject, and without degradation of service. Providers of services within the public switched network would be given 18 months to comply

and PBX operators three years. The Attorney General would have the authority to grant exceptions and waivers and seek civil penalties and injunctive relief to enforce the provisions. A fine of up to $10,000 a day could be levied for noncompliance. Government systems would be exempt on the grounds that law enforcement has the necessary cooperation to access the premises. The proposal is strongly supported as a critical public safety measure by state and local law enforcement (who conduct the majority of wiretaps), the National Association of Attorney Generals, the National Association of District Attorneys, and numerous law enforcement associations.

Although the proposed legislation does not expand the authority of the government to lawfully acquire the contents of communications, it arguably places greater constraints and demands on service providers and operators. The current law (Title 18, U.S. Code, Section 2518(4)) states that service providers are required to furnish the responsible law enforcement official with all information, facilities, and technical assistance necessary to perform the intercept unobtrusively and with a minimum of interference. It does not say explicitly that providers must build and use systems that ensure timely interception is possible. This is not surprising, since the emerging technological advances and attendant difficulties would not have been anticipated in 1968 when the legislation was enacted, but it leaves open to interpretation the meaning of the word "assist" and the exact requirements placed on service providers and operators in today's digital world.

When the FBI first encountered the intercept problems, they attempted to educate the telecommunications industry concerning the problems. They sought voluntary cooperation and a commitment to address the problems. But after meeting with industry officials for more than two years, they concluded that industry was not committed to resolving the problems without a mandate and that legislation was necessary to clarify the responsibilities of service providers and operators, to ensure that all providers and operators comply, and to provide a mechanism whereby industry could justify the development costs. Legislation would ensure all service providers remain on the same competitive "level playing field."

The proposed digital telephony legislation was not introduced in the last (1992) session of Congress because time ran out. Meanwhile, the FBI is continuing its discussions with industry through two technical committees, one with representatives from the telecommunications industry, the other with representatives from the computer industry, and many companies are working hard to meet law enforcement's needs.

The following sections address major concerns that have been expressed by some computer scientists, civil libertarians, and people in the telecommunications industry. Many of these concerns are articulated in a white paper issued by the Electronic Frontier Foundation (EFF) on behalf of an *ad hoc* coalition of representatives from industry and public interest groups, including AT&T, IBM, and ACLU.

Technology Advancement

Concern 1: The proposal would hold back technology and stymie innovation. Some people are concerned that requiring technology modifications to support taps would prevent full use of new technologies. Janlori Goldman of the ACLU has called this a "dumbing down" and stated that "if the government wants to engage in surveillance, it must bear the burden of keeping pace with new developments."

I see no technological reason why any of the new technologies, including digital technologies, cannot support an intercept capability. In many cases the intercept capability would likely parallel or draw on the maintenance and security features used by the telephone companies to ensure their systems are functioning properly and are not abused. At the very least, the intercept capability can be programmed into the switches where the bit stream for a connection must be isolated anyway so that it can be routed to its correct destination (for interception, a duplicate copy of the bit stream can be routed to a remote government monitoring facility). But whereas this modification would be relatively straightforward for the service providers to make, it would be impossible for the government to do on its own since it lacks access to the switches. Also, because of the complexities of switches and switch software, the government has no desire to engage in self help and interject itself into the arena of networks or central office switching and thereby perhaps inadvertently disrupt service on a widespread basis.

Another reason for not asking the government to implement its own surveillance mechanisms is that the providers can do so surgically, and hence less intrusively. For example, where ISDN or bundled fiber optic transmissions are involved, service providers can isolate an individual communications channel, whereas the government might have to intercept everything traveling over a line or link supporting simultaneous transmission of multiple, commingled communications in order to extract the desired channel. The FBI has stated that law enforcement does not want access to the communications of anyone outside the ambit of the court order.

In short, the digital telephony proposal would not require the communications industry to "dumb down" technology. Rather, it would require industry to use technology to make networks *smarter*.

Security and Privacy

Concern 2: Providing an intercept capability would jeopardize security and privacy, first because the remote monitoring capability would make the systems vulnerable to attack, and second because the intercept capability itself would introduce a new vulnerability into the systems. The first part of this concern relating to the remote monitoring capability seems to have arisen from a misinterpretation of the requirement for remote monitoring. Sec. 2. (1) of the proposed bill states that "Providers of electronic communication services and private branch exchange operators shall provide... the capacity for the government to intercept wire and electronic communications when authorized by law:... (4) at a government monitoring facility remote from the target facility and remote from the system of the electronic communication services provider or private branch exchange operator." Some people have mistakenly interpreted this as a requirement for law enforcement to be able to electronically, and independently, enter a computer switch from a remote location to initiate a tap. If this were the case, then an unauthorized person might be able to come in through the connection and tap into a line.

The FBI has made it clear they are not asking for the capability to initiate taps in this fashion, but rather for a tap initiated by the service provider to be routed to a predefined remote location over a leased line. In the specification of the requirements for the government monitoring facility, the proposal states: "Normally, the government leases a line from the electronic communication services provider's or private branch exchange operator's switch to another location owned or operated by the government.... The legislation does not establish any independent 'dial-up' authority by which criminal law enforcement agencies could effectuate interceptions without the affirmative assistance of the providers or operators. The providers and operators will continue to make the necessary interconnections or issue the necessary switch program instructions to effectuate an interception." Indeed, the requirement set forth in the legislation memorializes long-standing practice and procedure. Since the connection to a remote government monitoring facility would support an outgoing data stream only, it could not be used to break into a switch and, therefore, does not impose any new or additional danger to the security of the systems and the privacy of the people who rely on them for their communications.

This misinterpretation of the remote monitoring requirement also led to a concern that law enforcement would abuse the wiretapping capability and surreptitiously perform unauthorized taps. Because the only people who would have access to the systems for activating a tap would be employees of the service providers, who have been strict about requiring court orders, the possibility of law enforcement performing unauthorized taps seems even less likely than with present technology.

The second part of the concern, that the intercept capability itself could introduce a new vulnerability, is at least potentially more serious. If the intercept capability is programmed into the switches and an authorized person can break into a switch, then that person might be able to eavesdrop on a line or find out if a particular line is being tapped. Indeed, "hackers" have broken into poorly protected computer switches and eavesdropped on lines. But the switches can and must be designed and operated to prevent such break-ins independent of any intercept capabilities. Security is essential not only to protect against unlawful eavesdropping but to ensure reliable service and protect against other types of abuses. The administration, the Department of Justice, and the FBI all are strong advocates for security in telecommunications networks.

To protect against possible abuses by employees of the service providers, access to the software for activating an intercept should be minimized and well-protected through appropriate authentication mechanisms and access controls. The intercept control software might be left off the system and installed in an isolated partition only when needed prior to executing an authorized tap. With newer, advanced technology and proper overall security measures, it should be possible to provide greater protection against abuse than is presently provided.

Competitiveness

Concern 3: Implementing the intercept requirements could harm the competitiveness of U.S. products in the global market. This concern, which arose in conjunction with the preceding concerns about holding back technology and security, is based on an assumption that it would take U.S. companies longer to bring their products to market, and other countries would not want to buy products that increased the vulnerability of their systems. However, because the products can be designed to operate with a high level of security and because other governments (many of which run or oversee their nation's telecommunications networks) might desire similar features in their telecommunications systems, the digital telephony proposal would be competition-neutral. In fact, several other countries have expressed an interest in obtaining such products. U.S. companies could have a competitive advantage if they take the lead now, and indeed might be at a disadvantage if they fail to act and companies outside the U.S. do. Under the proposed legislation, foreign communications companies would have to comply with the U.S. law and standards if they seek to provide service in the U.S., thereby preventing any unfair competition in this country.

Cost and Benefits

Concern 4: The cost could be enormous and is not obviously justifiable by the perceived benefits. The cost of compliance is a major concern. The existing law states that service providers and operators shall be compensated for "expenses" incurred in assisting with a tap. The proposed law leaves open who would bear the capital expenses of modifications and engineering costs required to maintain the intercept capability.

The FBI, in consultation with industry, has estimated the cumulative costs for a switched-based software solution to be in the range $150 to $250 million, and the maximum development costs to be $300 million or approximately 1.5% of the telecommunications industry's yearly acquisition budget of $22 billion. These costs, however, are highly speculative and actual costs could be considerably lower if the service providers pursue a combination nonswitch/switch-based solution. In addition, whatever the costs, they likely would be amortized over several years. Some people have suggested the government should pay the costs, but a privately funded approach is more likely to encourage market forces to bring forth the most cost-effective solutions. In either case, this is a societal cost that will be paid for one way or the other by the citizenry to ensure effective law enforcement and the public safety.

The benefits derived from the use of electronic surveillance are difficult to quantify. Because wiretapping has been used infrequently (less than 1,000 taps per year), some people have argued it is not essential—that crimes could be solved by other means that would be less costly. But by law, wiretapping can only be used when normal investigative procedures have been tried and have failed or when they appear unlikely to succeed or too dangerous. Also, according to the FBI, many serious crimes can *only* be solved or prevented by electronic surveillance.

According to the FBI, electronic surveillance has been essential in preventing serious and often violent criminal activities including organized crime, drug trafficking, extortion, terrorism, kidnapping, and murder. While the benefits to society of preventing such crimes and saving human lives are incalculable, the economic benefits alone are estimated to be billions of dollars per year. During the period from 1985 to 1991, court-ordered electronic surveillance conducted just by the FBI led to 7,324 convictions, almost $300 million in fines being levied, over $750 million in recoveries, restitutions, and court-ordered forfeitures, and close to $2 billion in prevented potential economic loss. Since the FBI conducts fewer than one-third of all intercepts, the total benefits derived from electronic surveillance by all law enforcement agencies is considerably higher.

One area where electronic surveillance has played a major role is in combatting organized crime. In 1986, the President's Commission on Organized Crime estimated that organized crime reduces the output of the U.S. economy by $18.2 billion a year (1986 dollars), costs workers 414,000 jobs, raises consumer prices by 0.3%, and lowers per capita personal income by $77.22 (1986 dollars). Although the impact of law enforcement's successful investigations of organized crime on these losses has not been thoroughly studied, in 1988 David Williams of the Office of Special Investigations, General Accounting Office, testified before U.S. Senate hearings on organized crime that "Evidence gathered through electronic surveillance... has had a devastating impact on organized crime." According to the FBI, the hierarchy of organized crime has been neutralized or destabilized through the use of electronic surveillance, and 30 years of successes would be reversed if the ability to conduct court-authorized electronic surveillance was lost.

Almost two-thirds of all court orders for electronic surveillance are used to fight the war on drugs, and electronic surveillance has been critical in identifying and then dismantling major drug trafficking organizations. Although the benefits of these operations are difficult to quantify, their impact on the economy and people's lives is potentially enormous. In 1988, the Public Health Service estimated the health, labor, and crime costs of drug abuse at $58.3 billion. The FBI estimates the war on drugs and its continuing legacy of violent street crime in the form of near daily drive-by murders would be substantially, if not totally, lost if law enforcement were to lose its capability for electronic surveillance.

Electronic surveillance has been used to investigate aggravated governmental fraud and corruption. A recent military-procurement fraud case ("Ill-Wind") involving persons in the Department of Defense and defense contractors has so far led to 59 convictions and nearly $250 million in fines, restitutions, and recoveries ordered.

The use of electronic surveillance has successfully prevented several terrorist attacks, including the bombing of a foreign consulate in the U.S., a rocket attack against a U.S. ally, and the acquisition of a surface-to-air missile that was to be used in an act that likely would have led to numerous deaths. By intercepting voice, fax, and communications on a local bulletin board system, the FBI prevented the proposed kidnapping and murder of a young child for the purpose of making a "snuff murder" film. Wiretapping also has been used to obtain evidence against hackers who broke into computer systems. This case illustrates how wiretapping, which is popularly regarded as an antiprivacy tool, actually helps protect the privacy and proprietary interests of law-abiding citizens by helping to convict those who violate those interests.

Aside from preventing and solving serious crime, wiretapping yields evidence that is considerably more reliable than that obtained by many other methods such as informants, and is less dangerous for law enforcement officials than breaking and entering to install bugs in homes or offices. It is critical in those situations where the crime leaders are not present at the places where the illegal transactions take place, as is the case with major drug cartels directed by distant drug chieftains.

The societal and economic benefits of authorized electronic surveillance will increase as telecommunication services and facilities continue to expand and electronic commerce comes into widespread use, bringing with it more possibilities for fraud and other types of crimes.

Some people are troubled that citizens would have to pay for the wiretapping capability, possibly through their phone bills. In an open letter to several congressional committees, Joseph Truitt wrote: "What an insult—to be forced to pay for the privilege of being tapped!" However, through tax revenues and telephone company security office budgets, law enforcement has always been able to carry out investigations and conduct electronic surveillance, and unless a person is the subject of a court order, that person will not be paying to be intercepted. As citizens, we have always paid for law enforcement, knowing fully well that it will be used against us if we ever engage in criminal activities. This is one of the costs of protecting society from people who do not respect the laws. One could equally say: "What an insult—to be forced to pay for the privilege of being arrested!"

Compliance

Concern 5: It is unclear who must comply with the proposed legislation and what compliance means. The EFF expressed a concern that the proposal was overly broad, covering "just about everyone" including businesses, universities, and other organizations owning local and wide area networks; providers of electronic mail and information services such as Prodigy and Compuserve; operators of networks such as the Internet; and owners of computer bulletin boards. They raised questions about the conditions under which exemptions might be granted and the requirements for compliance. An earlier report published by the General Accounting Office also asked for greater clarity about what is meant by full compliance, for example, response time for executing a court order.

In response, the FBI points out the existing legislation already imposes an assistance obligation on electronic communication service providers that includes all of the foregoing named service entities, and that the reason the requirements are stated in generic terms is because historically these have sufficed and law enforcement's requirements, including those for a timely response, have been met. With respect to exemptions, the proposed legislation states that the attorney general may grant exemptions for whole classes of systems where no serious criminal activity is likely to take place, for example, hospital telephone systems, and grant waivers for providers and operators who cannot comply or need additional time. The FBI has also indicated that interceptions would normally be sought at a point close to the target, such that intranetwork interceptions would be very infrequent generally, and that information networks such as Compuserve and Prodigy would likely be considered for exemption. Although the proposed legislation allows for stiff fines, the legislative history background materials state that "this provision is not expected to be used."

CRYPTOGRAPHY

It is now possible to purchase at reasonable cost a telephone security device that encrypts communications and to acquire software that encrypts data transmitted over computer networks. Even if law enforcement retains its capability to intercept communications, this capability ultimately could be diminished if criminals begin to hide their communications through encryption and law enforcement is unable to obtain access to the "plaintext" or unscrambled communications. If encryption becomes cheap and ubiquitous, this could pose a serious threat to effective law enforcement and hence to the public's safety.

The digital telephony proposal does not address encryption, leaving open the question of how best to deal with it. Currently, the use of cryptography in this country is unregulated, though export of the technology is regulated. Cryptography is regulated in some of the major European countries. This section explores the possibility of regulating cryptography use....

Possible Approaches
In order to assess whether cryptography can or should be regulated, we need some idea of how it might be done. Our knowledge of available options is quite limited, however, since the possibility of regulating cryptography in the U.S. has thus far received little public discussion. The following three possibilities are offered as a starting point for discussion:

Weak Cryptography. This approach would require cryptographic systems to be sufficiently weak so that the government could break them, preferably in real time since timeliness is crucial for preventing many crimes such as murder and terrorist attacks. While weak cryptography would offer adequate protection against most eavesdropping when the consequences of disclosure are not particularly damaging, it could be unacceptable in many contexts such as protecting corporate communications that are seriously threatened by industrial espionage.

However, it is worth noting the general migration from analog to digital communications *itself* provides a high level of protection in the area of telecommunications, since such communications are only understandable with the aid of very sophisticated technology unlike the relative ease with which eavesdroppers can understand analog intercepts. Thus, it is not obvious that most individuals and organizations would either need or demand strong encryption, especially since most do not use any form of encryption at present. However, since history shows that methods which are secure today may be blown apart tomorrow, this may not be a dependable long-term solution.

Escrowed Private Keys. Ron Rivest has proposed using high-security encryption with "escrowed secret keys." Each user would be required to register his or her secret key with an independent trustee, and cryptographic products would be designed to operate only with keys that are certified as being properly escrowed. The trustee could be some neutral entity such as the U.S. Postal Service, a bank, or the clerks of the federal courts. It would be extremely difficult to subvert the system since someone would need the cooperation of the telecommunications provider (to get the communication stream) and the trustee (to get the key), both of which would require a court order.

Additional protection can be obtained by distributing the power of the trustee. For example, two trustees could be used, and the keys could be stored with the first trustee encrypted under a key known only to the second. Alternatively, using Silvio Micali's "fair public-key cryptography," each user's private key could be split into, say, five pieces, and each piece given to a different trustee. The splitting is done in such a way that all five pieces are required to reconstruct the original key, but each one can be independently verified, and the set of five can be verified as a whole without putting them all together.

In order to implement an approach based on escrowed keys, methods would be needed for registering and changing keys that belong to individuals and organizations and for gaining access to the transient "session keys" that are used to encrypt actual communications. Key registration might be incorporated into the sale and licensing of cryptographic products. To facilitate law enforcement's access to session keys, the protocols used to distribute or negotiate session keys during the start of a communications could be standardized. Once law enforcement has acquired the private keys on a given line, they would then be able to acquire the session keys by intercepting the key initialization protocol.

One drawback to this approach is the overhead and bureaucracy associated with key registration. Another is that it is limited to cryptographic systems that require more-or-less permanent private keys. Although some such as the RSA public-key cryptosystem fit this description, others do not.

Direct Access to Session Keys. Ultimately a session key is needed to decrypt a communications stream, and this approach would give the service provider direct access to the session key when an intercept has been established in response to a court order. The service provider can then make the session key available to law enforcement along with the communications stream.

One way of making the session key available to the provider is for the provider to participate in the protocol used to set up the key. For example, the following three-way extension of the Diffie-Hellman public-key distribution protocol could be used to establish a session key that would be known only to the two communicants and the service provider: Each party independently generates a random exponent x and computes $y = g^x \bmod p$ for a given g and prime p. All three parties then pass their value of y to the right (imagine they are in a circle). Next, using the received value of y, they compute $z = y^x \bmod p$ and pass it to the right. Finally, using the received value of z, they compute the shared session key $k = z^x \bmod p$, which will be the value g raised to all three exponents. An eavesdropper, who sees only the values of y and z, cannot compute k because he or she will lack the requisite exponent.

If a court order has been issued and an intercept activated, the component or module operating on behalf of the service provider would pass the key on to the remote government monitoring facility before destroying it. Obviously, this component would have to be designed with great care in order to ensure that keys are not improperly disclosed and they are immediately destroyed when no intercept has been activated.

This approach has the advantage over the preceding ones of allowing the use of a strong cryptosystem while not requiring the use and registration of permanent keys. It has the disadvantage of requiring the service provider to be brought into the loop during the key negotiation protocol, which might also be difficult or costly to implement.

The cost of regulating the use of cryptography following either of these last two approaches is unknown. A feasibility study would be needed to examine the requirements in greater detail and estimate the costs.

Protecting Privacy and Proprietary Interests

The last two approaches suggest that it is possible to regulate cryptography without compromising the privacy and proprietary interests of the citizens. Some people have argued, however, that the citizens have a right to *absolute* communications secrecy from everyone, including the government, under all circumstances, and that requiring people to make the plaintext of their encrypted communications available to the government directly or indirectly would be tantamount to forbidding them from having a private conversation in a secret place or using an obscure foreign language, or making them carry a microphone. These absolutist positions, however, contort the concept of privacy and do not represent valid analogies.

Our laws, as embodied in the Constitution and Bill of Rights, common law, tort law, and legislation, reflect a *social contract* that strikes a balance between our rights to privacy and to an orderly society. This contract does not grant us absolute privacy in all areas. For example, whereas we are protected against *un-*

reasonable searches and seizures by the Fourth Amendment, we are not immune from searches and seizures when there is probable cause we have committed a crime and a judge has issued a warrant. When Congress enacted wiretapping legislation and the Supreme Court ruled that wiretapping with a warrant was permitted, law enforcement was empowered to intercept communications, whether they were encrypted or not. Now that encryption is becoming an issue, it would seem appropriate for Congress to set an encryption policy.

Viewed narrowly, cryptography offers the possibility for absolute communications protection or privacy that is not available to us in any other area of our lives. Our physical beings are constantly at risk, and our premises, cars, safes, and lockers can be illegally broken into or lawfully searched. We live with this risk and indeed benefit from it whenever we lock ourselves out of our homes, cars, and so forth. It is unclear that we need an absolute level of protection or privacy for our communications surpassing the levels in other areas of our lives. Indeed, our speech in many regards and areas is already subject to balanced regulation (e.g., slander, libel, obscenity, falsely yelling "fire" in a theater).

Although illegal eavesdropping poses a threat to corporate security, the communications network is not the weak link. Employees and former employees have posed a bigger threat. If companies themselves do not regulate cryptography, their employees would have a means of transmitting company secrets outside the company with impunity and without detection. The military procurement fraud case mentioned earlier was solved only because law enforcement was able to tap the communications of a Pentagon employee. Thus, corporate security is not necessarily best served by an encryption system that offers absolute secrecy to its employees.

Competitiveness

Some people have argued that regulating cryptography in this country would harm the competitiveness of U.S. products overseas. No other country would want to buy products based on weak encryption algorithms or with built-in mechanisms for registering private keys or making session keys available to the service providers.

As with the basic intercept capability issue, it is not only conceivable but likely that other countries will be interested in products that allow their governments to decrypt communications when authorized by law. Foreign governments, for example, would be loathe to see terrorists operate and communicate in their country with impunity behind the shield of absolutely secure cryptographic devices. U.S. companies could take the lead in developing products that meet the security needs of customers and the legitimate needs of law enforcement and governments abroad.

Enforcing Cryptography Regulation

Many people have voiced a concern that criminals would violate cryptography regulations and use cryptosystems that the government could not decrypt, thereby also obtaining an absolute privacy beyond that of law-abiding citizens. This is typically expressed as "if encryption is outlawed, only outlaws will have encryption." Because products are being designed, sold, and given away in the absence of any regulation, this outcome is indeed possible.

Cryptography can be embedded in a device such as a secure phone or security device attached to a standard phone that encrypts communications transmitted between phones (or fax machines), or it can be embedded in software packages or modules that run on computers and encrypt the communications transmitted over computer networks. It seems easier to regulate and control telephone encryption devices than software. For example, if an approach based on escrowed keys is adopted, then the keys embedded in the products could be given to one or more trustees at the time of sale, and the products could be designed so the keys could not be changed without bringing the product in for service or negotiating a new key with a trustee on-line. Similarly, if an approach based on direct access to session keys is adopted, a suitable key negotiation protocol could be built into the products. Although criminals could develop their own noncompliant products, it is likely that most criminals would use commercial off-the-shelf products rather than developing their own.

Software encryption, performed on personal computers or servers, could be much more difficult to regulate, especially since strong cryptographic methods have been distributed through networks such as the Internet and cryptographic algorithms can be implemented by any competent programmer. But enforcing cryptography regulations on software may be less critical for law enforcement since electronic surveillance has typically focused on telephone calls or conversations. Thus, it would be a mistake to make the difficulty of controlling software encryption an excuse for not regulating cryptography.

Although it would be practically impossible to prevent the use of noncompli-ant products, the work factor required to acquire and use these products may be sufficiently high to deter their use. But even if they are used, if there is probable cause that a person is involved with some serious crime and a warrant is issued for that person's communications, then legislation could also provide grounds for arresting that person if he or she violated the laws governing cryptography as a separate offense. However, it would be important to not lose sight of the purpose of cryptography regulation and to not expend resources enforcing it for its own sake.

If private encryption is allowed to proceed without some reasonable accommodation, it will logically lead to situations in which someone is arrested outright when probable cause for a criminal act is demonstrated. This could lead to premature cessation of investigations where critical evidence would not be obtained.

CONCLUSIONS

Granger Morgan has observed that controversy over the proposed digital telephony legislation is symbolic of a broader set of conflicts arising from several competing national interests: individual privacy, security for organizations, effective domestic law enforcement, effective international intelligence-gathering, and secure worldwide reliable communications. Because the balance among these becomes hardwired into the design of our telecommunications system, it is difficult to adjust the balance in response to changing world conditions and changing values. Technology has been drifting in a direction that could shift the balance away from effective law enforcement and intelligence-gathering toward absolute individual privacy and corporate security. Since the consequences of doing so would pose a serious threat to society, I am not content to let this happen without careful consideration and public discussion.

With respect to wiretapping, we can take the steps necessary to ensure law enforcement's continued ability to intercept and interpret electronic communications when authorized by court order, or let this capability gradually fade away as new technologies are deployed and cryptographic products become widely available. The consequence of this choice will affect our personal safety, our right to live in a society where lawlessness is not tolerated, and the ability of law enforcement to prevent serious and often violent criminal activity.

While the societal and economic benefits that would come from the proposed digital telephony legislation are difficult to quantify, the economic benefits of maintaining effective law enforcement through its capability of conducting authorized intercepts are estimated to be in the billions and many lives would likely be saved. These benefits are likely to increase with the growth in telecommunications. By comparison, the cumulative costs of complying with the proposed digital telephony legislation are roughly estimated to be in the range of $150 to $250 million. Although the benefits might not be fully realized if the intercept capability would, as has been suggested, thwart technological progress, compromise security and privacy, or harm competitiveness, these are unlikely outcomes as discussed in this article. Indeed, effective law enforcement is crucial for protecting the privacy of law-abiding citizens and the business interests of companies.

If we fail to enact legislation that will ensure a continued capability for court-ordered electronic surveillance, we cannot be guaranteed that all service providers will provide this capability voluntarily. Systems fielded without an adequate provision for court-ordered intercepts would become sanctuaries for criminality wherein organized crime leaders, drug dealers, terrorists, and other criminals could conspire and act with impunity. Eventually, we could find ourselves with an increase in major crimes against society, a greatly diminished capacity to fight them, and no timely solution.

Less is known about the implications of regulating cryptography since no specific legislative or other proposal has been seriously considered. Although government regulation of cryptography may be somewhat cumbersome and subject to evasion, we should give it full consideration. Regulated encryption would provide considerably greater security and privacy than no encryption, which has been the norm for most personal and corporate communications. We must balance our competing interests in a way that ensures effective law enforcement and intelligence gathering, while protecting individual privacy and corporate security.

NO

Mike Godwin

A CHIP OVER MY SHOULDER: THE PROBLEMS WITH CLIPPER

Your government is deeply troubled by the possibility that you can keep a secret.

Or, to put it more precisely, the government is disturbed by the prospect of widespread powerful encryption tools in individual hands. Once you can keep your communications and data truly secret, officials worry, the value of wiretapping, an important law-enforcement and intelligence tool, will evaporate.

It's unclear whether the government's arguments are valid. But regardless of whether they are, the government's latest efforts to prevent us from adopting powerful and uncrackable encryption technologies raise serious questions about personal liberty, the role of government, and the possibility of privacy in the 21st century.

If you're not already familiar with these efforts, here's an update. The Clinton Administration has embarked on an ambitious plan to prevent a mass market for uncrackable encryption from arising. The first step in this plan has already been announced: the Administration has called for the entire federal government to adopt the Clipper Chip—an encryption standard with a "back door"—for communications and data security. In addition, the government has declared its intention to use every legal method short of outright prohibition to discourage alternative forms of encryption technology.

"Just what is this Clipper Chip?" you may be wondering. The short answer is: the chip is an encryption device, developed to National Security Agency specs, that keeps your communications and data secret from everyone... except the government.

To understand how the chip works, you need to look at what officials call its "key escrow encryption method." Designed by a private company called Mykotronix and manufactured by VLSI Technology, the chip uses an NSA-developed algorithm called "Skipjack," which, by all accounts so far, is a remarkably powerful algorithm. But the chip also includes the "feature" that its primary encryption key can be divided up mathematically into two "partial keys." The government proposes that each partial key be held by

From Mike Godwin, "A Chip Over My Shoulder: The Problems With Clipper," *Internet World* (July 1994). Copyright © 1994 by Mike Godwin. Reprinted by permission.

a separate government agency—the Administration has picked the Department of the Treasury and the National Institute of Standards and Technology (NIST) —from which the keys can be retrieved when government officials obtain a wiretap order.

The NSA and the FBI love this idea. With the Clipper Chip in your phone or computer, they believe, you have the power to keep your information private from crooks and industrial spies and anyone else who wants to pry—except of course for law enforcement and the NSA. Law enforcement and intelligence agencies would be barred from seeking those escrowed keys in the absence of legal authorization, normally a court order. "And of course you needn't worry about us," say government officials. "We're here to protect you."

CHIPS OFF THE NEW BLOCK

The current initiative has been a long time coming. It was in April of last year the Clinton Administration first announced Clipper—the announcement was met with a public outcry from civil-liberties and industry groups. Civil libertarians were concerned about the government's insistence on its need to prevent citizens from having access to truly unbreachable privacy technologies. Computer and telecom industry leaders worried about a standard that might crush a potentially vital market in such technologies. At first the Administration expressed a willingness to listen. The Digital Privacy and Security Working Group, a coalition of industry and public-interest organizations headed by the Electronic Frontier Foundation, outlined its objections and expressed the hope of engaging in talks with the Administration about the issue.

In early February of this year, however, the Clinton Administration and various agencies announced to the world that, in spite of the grave misgivings of civil-liberties and industry groups, it would be proposing the Clipper Chip's encryption scheme as a new Federal Information Processing standard (FIPS). The standard, stresses the government, will be entirely "voluntary"—but the government plans to use export-control laws and other methods to frustrate the market for any competitive form of encryption technology.

Current export-control laws restrict the sales in foreign countries of encryption hardware and software. The laws have not been entirely effective in keeping commercial encryption technologies out of foreign hands—it's possible these days to buy encryption products in Moscow, for example. But the laws do succeed in deterring the American software industry from developing powerful and easy-to-use encryption products, since any company that does so is denied the right to sell the product on the global market.

Still, if Clipper is voluntary, you may ask, what does it matter to *individuals* what standard the government adopts? The government also adopted the ADA programming language, after all, yet there are still people programming in all sorts of languages, from BASIC to C++. The answer is simple—"freedom of choice" is meaningful only if there are real choices. The government's export-control strategy is designed to make sure that there aren't any choices. If commercial software companies aren't allowed to sell encryption to the world market, they're unlikely to develop strong, easy-to-use alternatives to Clipper. And that means individuals won't have access to alternatives.

Now, it's perfectly possible, in theory, to thwart the government-approved Clipper scheme by using a non-commercial encryption application, such as PGP, to pre-encrypt your messages before sending them through Clipper-equipped devices. But PGP and other products, because of their slowness or difficulty, are never likely to expand beyond the circle of hobbyists that enthusiastically support them. For encryption products to give rise to a genuine consumer market, they have to be quick and almost transparently easy to use.

The government knows this, which is why their focus is on nipping (clipping?) the commercial encryption software market in the bud. It's the commercial market that really matters.

THE GOVERNMENT'S SIDE

When asked to substantiate the need for Clipper, or the threat of unbreakable encryption, the government often talks about crime prevention. As a practical matter, however, wiretaps are almost always used *after* crimes are committed—to gather evidence about the individuals the government already suspects to have been involved in a crime. So, the hypothetical cases involving nuclear terrorism or murder-kidnappings aren't really convincing—it's the rare case in which a wiretap prevents a crime from occurring. As a practical matter, the single most important asset to law enforcement is not wiretaps but informants. And nothing about unbreakable encryption poses the risk that informants are going to disappear.

One of the more rational statements of the government's case for Clipper comes from my friend Trotter Hardy, a law professor at William and Mary, who writes:

> "The government's argument, I take it, is that the benefit is law enforcement. That strikes me as at least as great a benefit as minimum wage laws; perhaps more, since it protects everybody (at least in theory), whereas [minimum] wage laws primarily benefit their recipients. Maybe EPA regs are the better analogy: everybody gets reduced pollution; with Clipper, everybody gets reduced criminal activity. Is that not a reasonable trade-off?"

But the problem is that the government refuses to be forthcoming as to what kind of trade-off we're talking about. According to government statistics, there are fewer than 1,000 state and federal law-enforcement wiretaps per year, and only a minority of these wiretaps leads to convictions. Yet we are being asked to abandon the chance for true privacy and to risk billions of dollars in trade losses when there has never been shown to be any crime associated with uncrackable encryption whatsoever. And we're also being asked to believe that the kind of criminals who are smart enough to use encryption are dumb enough to choose the one kind of encryption that the government is guaranteed to be able to crack.

Moreover, there are fundamental political issues at stake. This country was founded on a principle of restraints on government. A system in which the privacy of our communications is contingent on the good faith of the government, which holds all the encryption keys, flies in the face of what we have been taught to believe about the structure of government and the importance of individual liberty.

In short, the government fails to make its case in two separate ways—pragmatically and philosophically.

Trotter goes on to write:

"... I don't think the government cares whether an accountant in India can password protect a spreadsheet. I would guess that even Clipper or DES [the government's current Digital Encryption Standard] or whatever would be more than enough protection for such a person. I think the government cares that it be able to detect foreign intelligence that is relevant to US security or interests. I am not sure where I come out on the question, but at the very least it seems to me that the government is reasonable in this desire."

Yet there are some premises here that need to be questioned. Do we really suppose that "foreign intelligence" is dependent on the American software industry to develop its encryption tools? Public-key encryption and DES are already available worldwide, yet Microsoft can't export software that contains either form of encryption.

No, the real issue is that, to the extent that a mass market arises for encryption products, it makes the NSA's job more difficult, and it may at some future time make some investigations more difficult as well.

When asked to quantify the problem, however, the government invariably begs off. Instead, government spokespeople say, "Well, how would you feel if there were a murder-kidnapping that we couldn't solve because of encryption?" To which my answer is, "Well, I'd feel about the same way that I'd feel if there were a murder-kidnapping that couldn't be solved because of the privilege against self-incrimination."

Which is to say, I understand that limits on government power entail a loss in efficiency of law-enforcement investigations and intelligence-agency operations. Nevertheless, there is a fundamental choice we have to make about what kind of society we want to live in. Open societies, and societies that allow individual privacy, are *less safe*. But we have been taught to value liberty more highly than safety, and I think that's a lesson well-learned.

WAGERING AGAINST THE UNTHINKABLE

What's more, we need to be able to engage in rational risk assessment, and that's something that the government resists. Instead, the government subscribes to the reasoning of Pascal's Wager. Pascal, you may recall, argued that the rational man is a Christian, even if the chances that Christianity is true are small. His reasoning is quasi-mathematical—even if the chances of Christianity's truth are small, the consequences of choosing not to be a Christian are (if that choice is incorrect) infinitely terrible. Eternal torment, demons, flames, the whole works.

This is precisely the way that the government talks about nuclear terrorism and murder-kidnappings. When asked what the probability is of a) a nuclear terrorist, who b) decides to use encryption, and c) manages otherwise to thwart counterterrorist efforts, they'll answer "What does it matter what the probability is? Even one case is too much to risk!

But we can't live in a society that defines its approach to civil liberties in terms of infinitely bad but low-probability events. Open societies are risky. Individual freedom and privacy are risky. If we are to make a mature commitment to an open society, we have to acknowledge those risks up front, and reaffirm our willingness to endure them.

We face a choice now. After a century of technological development that has eroded our ability to keep our personal lives private, we finally possess, thanks to cheap computing power and advances in cryptography, the ability to take privacy into our own hands and make our own decisions about how much we want, and how well to protect it.

This prospect is frightening to a government that has come to rely on its ability to reach into our private lives when it sees the need to do so. But I have faith that our society is not dependent on our government's right to mandate disclosure of our personal records and private communications—that a mature society can tolerate a large degree of personal privacy and autonomy.

It's a faith I hope you share.

POSTSCRIPT

Should Law Enforcement Agencies Be Permitted to Eavesdrop on Computer Communications?

One month after Denning's essay appeared, the government shifted the emphasis of the debate from the Digital Telephony Act to encryption by the Clipper chip, which is discussed by Godwin.

The Clinton administration has proposed that the Clipper chip be part of every computer that the government buys, and it is exerting pressure to ensure that the chip is the only encryption device anyone uses. Critics have objected that this amounts to giving law enforcement agencies, who hold the decoding "key" to Clipper, a spare set of keys to one's house so they can walk in at any time they wish. Critics do not trust that the authorization procedures will operate as intended (that is, that a government agency will go through the process of gaining a court order, for example, before using the key), that unauthorized persons will not gain access to the key, or that computer hackers will not find a way to exploit Clipper's built-in vulnerability. Conservative columnist William Safire, in the *New York Times* (February 15, 1994), writes of "the brave new world of snooperware" that promises to leave "the individual citizen standing naked to the nosy bureaucrat," and he states that "no self-respecting vice overlord or terrorist," only honest Americans and dopey crooks, would fall for Clipper.

Proponents answer that Clipper's guaranteed tappability is essential for protecting public safety and national security. It is worth noting, however, that traditional wiretaps account for a very small proportion of total arrests.

Intriguingly, the May 7, 1994, issue of *Science News* reports that mathematicians and computer scientists have found new and faster ways to factor the large numbers on which Clipper-type codes depend. Because this development means that government security agents (and others) will be able to crack private codes, it promises to make tappability guarantees unnecessary and to make encryption a less-than-dependable way to protect secrets.

For now, however, Clipper is required in government-purchased computers and communication devices. So far, it has not been well accepted at all outside the government. The debate has raged through the pages of science, computer, and news magazines, as well as the Internet—the national and international computer network on which computer-related (as well as many other) matters are discussed—and it shows no signs of quieting. Two good articles on the topic are Salvatore Salamone, "Clinton's Clipper: Can It Keep a Secret?" *Data Communications* (August 1993), and John Perry Barlow, "A

Plain Text on Crypto Policy," *Communications of the ACM* (November 1993). A number of related issues are also discussed in Bruce Sterling's *The Hacker Crackdown: Law and Disorder on the Electronic Frontier* (Bantam Books, 1992).

It is worth noting that the issue of *Communications of the ACM* in which the Denning piece appears (March 1993) also contains several pages of responses from people who are concerned about the Digital Telephony Act, including one from Godwin.

If you have access to the Internet, you can obtain copies of many documents related to the Clipper chip controversy, courtesy of the Electronic Frontier Foundation (EFF). They are available via anonymous ftp (file transfer protocol) or via WWW (World Wide Web). The foundation may be reached at electronic mail address mnemonic@eff.org.

ISSUE 12

Will It Be Possible to Build a Computer That Can Think?

YES: Hans Moravec, from "The Universal Robot," in *Vision-21: Interdisciplinary Science and Engineering in the Era of Cyberspace* (National Aeronautics and Space Administration, 1993)

NO: John R. Searle, from "Is the Brain's Mind a Computer Program?" *Scientific American* (January 1990)

ISSUE SUMMARY

YES: Research scientist Hans Moravec describes the necessary steps in what he considers to be the inevitable development of computers that match and even exceed human intelligence.

NO: Professor of philosophy John R. Searle argues that a crucial difference between artificial (machine) intelligence and human intelligence—that humans attach meaning to the symbols they manipulate while computers cannot—makes it impossible to create a computer that can think.

The first primitive digital computers were instantly dubbed "thinking machines" because they were able to perform functions—initially only arithmetic—that had always been considered part of the uniquely human ability to think. Some critics of the "thinking machine" label, however, objected that arithmetic is so much simpler than, say, poetry or philosophy (after all, it is only a matter of following a few simple rules) that computers were not thinking at all. Thinking, they said, is for humans only. In fact, if a machine can do it, then it cannot possibly be real thinking.

In 1950, Alan Turing, an English mathematician and logician, devised a test to determine whether or not a machine was intelligent. Turing's test entailed whether or not one could converse with a person and with a computer (through a teletype so that neither could be seen nor could the human be heard) and, after a suitable period, tell which was which. If the computer could pass for an intelligent conversationalist, Turing felt, then it would have to be considered intelligent.

Over the next two decades, computer scientists learned how to program their machines to play games such as chess, solve mathematical theorems, parse sentences (break them down into their grammatical components), and perform a number of other tasks that had once been thought doable by thinking humans only. In most cases the machines were not as good at these tasks as humans, but many artificial intelligence (AI) researchers believed it was only a matter of time before the machines matched and even exceeded their creators.

The closest any machine has come to passing the Turing test may have been in the early 1970s, when Kenneth Mark Colby, then a Stanford University psychiatrist and computer scientist, programmed a computer to imitate the conversational style of paranoid humans. This was much easier than programming a computer to imitate a nonparanoid human's conversational style because paranoid individuals tend to be very rigid and predictable in their responses. When Colby had psychiatrists interview the programmed computer and a human paranoid (through a teletype, per Turing's criteria), only half could correctly distinguish between computer and human. That is, the computer did indeed come close to passing the Turing test. On the other hand, it was not trying to pass as an average human being, whose thought processes are far freer and more flexible than those of a paranoid person.

Will a computer ever be able to imitate a normal human being? And if it can, will that mean it is really "thinking" or really "intelligent"? Many computer scientists believe it is still just a matter of time before a computer passes the Turing test with flying colors and that that machine will be truly intelligent. Indeed, many even say that the human mind is nothing more than a program that runs on a biological machine.

Others argue that machines cannot have emotions or appreciate beauty and that computers cannot be self-aware or conscious, no matter how intelligent they may seem to an interrogator. They therefore can never be intelligent in a human way.

Hans Moravec, director of the Mobile Robot Laboratory at Carnegie Mellon University, strongly believes that true artificial intelligence can be achieved. It will require computers that are much more powerful than any that exist today, he predicts, and the process of achieving intelligence will involve a series of evolutionary stages.

In contrast, John R. Searle, professor of philosophy at the University of California, Berkeley, argues that although humans *can* be regarded as biological machines, there are essential differences between natural and artificial intelligence. Furthermore, he objects to the idea that the human mind is nothing more than a computer program.

YES

Hans Moravec

THE UNIVERSAL ROBOT

Abstract. Our artifacts are getting smarter, and a loose parallel with the evolution of animal intelligence suggests one future course for them. Computerless industrial machinery exhibits the behavioral flexibility of single-celled organisms. Today's best computer-controlled robots are like the simpler invertebrates. A thousand-fold increase in computer power in the next decade should make possible machines with reptile-like sensory and motor competence. Properly configured, such robots could do in the physical world what personal computers now do in the world of data—act on our behalf as literal-minded slaves. Growing computer power over the next half-century will allow this reptile stage to be surpassed, in stages producing robots that learn like mammals, model their world like primates and eventually reason like humans. Depending on your point of view, humanity will then have produced a worthy successor, or transcended some of its inherited limitations and so transformed itself into something quite new.

INTRODUCTION: STATE OF THE ART

Instincts which predispose the nature and quantity of work we enjoy probably evolved during the 100,000 years our ancestors lived as hunter-gatherers. Less than 10,000 years ago the agricultural revolution made life more stable, and richer in goods and information. But, paradoxically, it requires more human labor to support an agricultural society than a primitive one, and the work is of a different, "unnatural" kind, out of step with the old instincts. The effort to avoid this work has resulted in domestication of animals, slavery and the industrial revolution. But many jobs must still be done by hand, engendering for hundreds of years the fantasy of an intelligent but soulless being that can tirelessly dispatch the drudgery. Only in this century have electronic sensors and computers given machines the ability to sense their world and to think about it, and so offered a way to fulfill the wish.

From National Aeronautics and Space Administration. Office of Management. Scientific and Technical Information Program. *Vision-21: Interdisciplinary Science and Engineering in the Era of Cyberspace.* (NASA Conference Publication 10129; 1993). References omitted.

As in fables, the unexpected side effects of robot slaves are likely to dominate the resulting story. Most significantly, these perfect slaves will continue to develop, and will not long remain soulless. As they increase in competence they will have occasion to make more and more autonomous decisions, and so will slowly develop a volition and purposes of their own. At the same time they will become indispensable. Our minds were evolved to store the skills and memories of a stone-age life, not the enormous complexity that has developed in the last ten thousand years. We've kept up, after a fashion, through a series of social inventions—social stratification and division of labor, memory aids like poetry and schooling, written records, stored outside the body, and recently machines that can do some of our thinking entirely without us. The portion of absolutely essential human activity that takes place outside of human bodies and minds has been steadily increasing. Hard working intelligent machines may complete the trend.

Serious attempts to build thinking machines began after the second world war. One line of research, called Cybernetics, used simple electronic circuitry to mimic small nervous systems, and produced machines that could learn to recognize simple patterns, and turtle-like robots that found their way to lighted recharging hutches. An entirely different approach, named Artificial Intelligence (AI), attempted to duplicate rational human thought in the large computers that appeared after the war. By 1965, these computers ran programs that proved theorems in logic and geometry, solved calculus problems and played good games of checkers. In the early 1970s, AI research groups at MIT (the Massachusetts Insti-

tute of Technology) and Stanford University attached television cameras and robot arms to their computers, so their "thinking" programs could begin to collect their information directly from the real world.

What a shock! While the pure reasoning programs did their jobs about as well and about as fast as college freshmen, the best robot control programs took hours to find and pick up a few blocks on a table. Often these robots failed completely, giving a performance much worse than a six month old child. This disparity between programs that reason and programs that perceive and act in the real world holds to this day. In recent years Carnegie Mellon University produced two desk-sized computers that can play chess at grandmaster level, within the top 100 players in the world, when given their moves on a keyboard. But present-day robotics could produce only a complex and unreliable machine for finding and moving normal chess pieces.

In hindsight it seems that, in an absolute sense, reasoning is much easier than perceiving and acting—a position not hard to rationalize in evolutionary terms. The survival of human beings (and their ancestors) has depended for hundreds of millions of years on seeing and moving in the physical world, and in that competition large parts of their brains have become efficiently organized for the task. But we didn't appreciate this monumental skill because it is shared by every human being and most animals—it is commonplace. On the other hand, rational thinking, as in chess, is a newly acquired skill, perhaps less than one hundred thousand years old. The parts of our brain devoted to it are not well organized, and, in an absolute sense, we're not very good at it. But until recently we had no competition to show us up.

By comparing the edge and motion detecting circuitry in the four layers of nerve cells in the retina, the best understood major circuit in the human nervous system, with similar processes developed for "computer vision" systems that allow robots in research and industry to see, I've estimated that it would take a billion computations per second (the power of a world-leading Cray 2 supercomputer) to produce the same results at the same speed as a human retina. By extrapolation, to emulate a whole brain takes ten trillion arithmetic operations per second, or ten thousand Crays worth. This is for operations our nervous systems do extremely efficiently and well.

Arithmetic provides an example at the other extreme. In 1989 a new computer was tested for a few months with a program that computed the number pi to more than one billion decimal places. By contrast, the largest unaided manual computation of pi was 707 digits by William Shanks in 1873. It took him several years, and because of a mistake every digit past the 527th was wrong! In arithmetic, today's average computers are one million times more powerful than human beings. In very narrow areas of rational thought (like playing chess or proving theorems) they are about the same. And in perception and control of movement in the complex real world, and related areas of common-sense knowledge and intuitive and visual problem solving, today's average computers are a million times less capable.

The deficit is evident even in pure problem solving AI programs. To this day, AI programs exhibit no shred of common sense—a medical diagnosis program, for instance, may prescribe an an-

tibiotic when presented a broken bicycle because it lacks a model of people, diseases or bicycles. Yet these programs, on existing computers, would be overwhelmed were they to be bloated with the details of everyday life, since each new fact can interact with the others in an astronomical "combinatorial explosion." [A ten year project called Cyc at the Microelectronics and Computer Consortium in Austin, Texas, is attempting to build just such a common-sense data base. They estimate the final result will contain over one hundred million logic sentences about everyday objects and actions.]

Machines have a lot of catching up to do. On the other hand, for most of the century, machine calculation has been improving a thousandfold every twenty years, and there are basic developments in research labs that can sustain this for at least several decades more. In less than fifty years computer hardware should be powerful enough to match, and exceed, even the well-developed parts of human intelligence. But what about the software that would be required to give these powerful machines the ability to perceive, intuit and think as well as humans? The Cybernetic approach that attempts to directly imitate nervous systems is very slow, partly because examining a working brain in detail is a very tedious process. New instruments may change that in the future. The AI approach has successfully imitated some aspects of rational thought, but that seems to be only about one millionth of the problem. I feel that the fastest progress on the hardest problems will come from a third approach, the newer field of robotics, the construction of systems that must see and move in the physical world. Robotics research is imitating the evolution of animal minds, adding capabilities to machines a few at a time, so that the resulting sequence of machine behaviors resembles the capabilities of animals with increasingly complex nervous systems. This effort to build intelligence from the bottom up is helped by biological peeks at the "back of the book"—at the neuronal, structural, and behavioral features of animals and humans.

The best robots today are controlled by computers which are just powerful enough to simulate the nervous system of an insect, cost as much as houses, and so find only a few profitable niches in society (among them, spray painting and spot welding cars and assembling electronics). But those few applications are encouraging research that is slowly providing a base for a huge future growth. Robot evolution in the direction of full intelligence will greatly accelerate, I believe, in about a decade when the mass-produced general purpose, universal robot becomes possible. These machines will do in the physical world what personal computers do in the world of data—act on our behalf as literal-minded slaves.

THE DUMB ROBOT (ca. 2000–2010)

To be useful in many tasks, the first generation of universal robots should navigate efficiently over flat ground and reliably and safely over rough terrain and stairs, be able to manipulate most objects, and to find them in the nearby world. There are beginnings of solutions today. In the 1980s Hitachi of Japan developed a mobility system of five steerable wheels, each on its own telescoping stalk that allows it to accommodate to rises and dips in uneven terrain, and to climb stairs, by raising one wheel at a time while standing stably on the other four. My laboratory at Carnegie Mellon University in Pittsburgh has developed a navigation method that enables a robot equipped with sonar range measuring devices and television cameras to build probabilistic maps of its surroundings to determine its location and plan routes. An elegant three-fingered mechanical hand at the Massachusetts Institute of Technology can hold and orient bolts and eggs and manipulate a string in a humanlike fashion. A system called 3DPO from SRI International in Menlo Park, California, can find a desired part in a jumble seen by a special range-finding camera. The slow operation of these systems suggests one other element needed for the universal robot, namely a computer about one thousand times as powerful as those found on desks and in robots today. Such machines, able to do one billion computations per second, would provide robots approximately the brain power of a reptile, and the personality of a washing machine.

Universal robots will find their first uses in factories, where they will be cheaper and more versatile than the older generation of robots they replace. Eventually they will become cheap enough for some households, extending the reach of personal computers from a few tasks in the data world to many in the physical world. . . .

LEARNING (2010–2020)

Useful though they will be, the first generation of universal robots will be rigid slaves to simple programs. If the machine bangs its elbow while chopping beef in your kitchen making Stroganoff, you will have to find another place for the robot to do its work, or beg the software manufacturer for a fix. Second generation robots with more powerful computers will be able to host a more flexible kind of program able to adjust itself by a kind of conditioned learning. First generation programs will consist primarily of sequences of the type "Do step A, then B, then C...." The programs for the second generation will read "Do step A1 or A2 or A3... then B1 or B2 or B3... then C1 or C2 or C3...." In the Beef Stroganoff example, A1 might be to chop with the right hand of the robot, while A2 is to use the left hand. Each alternative in the program has a "weight," a number that indicates the desirability of using it rather than one of the other branches. The machine also contains a "pain" system, a series of programs that look out for problems, such as collisions, and respond by reducing the weights of recently invoked branches, and a "pleasure" system that increases the relevant weights when good conditions, such as well charged batteries or a task efficiently completed, are detected. As the robot bangs its elbow repeatedly in your kitchen, it gradually learns to use its other hand (as well as adapting to its surroundings in a thousand other ways). A program with many alternatives at each step, whose pain and pleasure systems are arranged to produce a pleasure signal on hearing the word "good" and a pain message on hearing "bad" could be slowly trained to do new tasks, like a small mammal. A particular suite of pain- and pleasure-producing programs interacting with a robot's individual environment would subtly shape its behavior and give it a distinct character.

IMAGERY (2020–2030)

Adaptive robots will find jobs everywhere, and the hardware and software industry that supports them could become the largest on earth. But teaching them new tasks, whether by writing programs or through punishment and reward, will be very tedious. This deficiency will lead to a portentous innovation, a software world-modeler (requiring another big increase in computer power), that allows the robot to simulate its immediate surroundings and its own actions within them, and thus to think about its tasks before acting. Before making Beef Stroganoff in your kitchen, the new robot would simulate the task many times. Each time its simulated elbow bangs the simulated cabinet, the software would update the learning weights just as if the collision had physically happened. After many such mental run-throughs the robot would be well trained, so that when it finally cooks for real, it does it correctly. The simulation can be used in many other ways. After a job, the robot can run though its previous actions, and try variations on them to improve future performance. A robot might even be configured to invent some of its own programs by means of a simpler program that can detect how nearly a sequence of robot actions achieves a desired task. This training program would, in repeated simulations, provide the "good" and "bad" indications needed to condition a general learning program like the one of the previous section.

It will take a large community of patient researchers to build good simulators. A robot entering a new room must include vast amounts of not directly perceived prior knowledge in its simulation, such as the expected shapes and probable contents of kitchen counters and the effect of (and force needed for) turning faucet knobs. It needs instinctive motor-perceptual knowledge about the world that took millions of years of evolution to install in us, that tells us instinctively when a height is dangerous, how hard to throw a stone, or if the animal facing us is a threat. Robots that incorporate it may be as smart as monkeys.

REASONING (2030–2040)

In the decades while the "bottom-up" evolution of robots is transferring the perceptual and motor faculties of human beings into machinery, the conventional Artificial Intelligence industry will be perfecting the mechanization of reasoning. Since today's programs already match human beings in some areas, those of 40 years from now, running on computers a million times as fast as today's, should be quite superhuman. Today's reasoning programs work from small amounts of clear and correct information prepared by human beings. Data from robot sensors such as cameras is much too voluminous and too noisy for them to use. But a good robot simulator will contain neatly organized data about the robot and its world. For instance, if a knife is on a countertop, or if the robot is holding a cup. A robot with a simulator can be married to a reasoning program to produce a machine with most of the abilities of a human being. The combination will create beings that in some ways resemble us, but in others are like nothing the world has seen before.

FIRST GENERATION TECHNICALITIES

Both industrial robot manipulators and the research effort to build "smart" robots are twenty five years old. Universal robots will require at least another decade of development, but some of their ele-

ments can be guessed from the experience so far. One consideration is weight. Mobile robots built to work in human sized spaces today weigh too many hundreds of pounds. This dangerously large mass has three major components: batteries, actuators and structure. Lead-acid batteries able to drive a mobile robot for a day contribute about one third of the weight. But nickel-cadmium aircraft batteries weigh half as much, and newer lithium batteries can be half again as light. Electric motors are efficient and precisely controllable, but standard motors are heavy and require equally heavy reducing gears. Ultrastrong permanent magnets can halve the weight and generate high torque without gears. Robot structure has been primarily aluminum. Its weight contribution can be cut by a factor of four by substituting composite materials containing superstrength fibers of graphite, aramid or the new material Spectra. These innovations could be combined to make a robot with roughly the size, weight, strength and endurance of a human.

The first generation robot will probably move on wheels. Legged robots have advantages on complicated terrain, but they consume too much power. A simple wheeled robot would be confined to areas of flat ground, but if each wheel had a controlled suspension with about a meter of travel, the robot could slowly lift its wheels as needed to negotiate rough ground and stairs. The manipulation system will consist of two or more arms ending in dexterous manipulators. There are several designs in the research labs today, but the most elegant is probably that of the so-called Stanford-JPL hand (mentioned above, now found at MIT), which has three fingers each with three controlled joints.

The robot's travels would be greatly aided if it could continuously pinpoint its location, perhaps by noting the delay from a handful of small synchronized transmitters distributed in its environment. This approach is used in some terrestrial and satellite navigation systems. The robot will also require a sense of its immediate surroundings, to find doors, detect obstacles and track objects in its workspace. Research laboratories, including my own, have experimented with techniques that do this with data from television cameras, scanning lasers, sonar transducers, infrared proximity sensors and contact sensors. A more precise sensory system will be needed to find particular work objects in clutter. The most successful methods to date start with three dimensional data from special cameras and laser arrangements that directly measure distance as well as lateral position. The robot will thus probably contain a wide angle sensor for general spatial awareness, and a precise, narrow angle, three dimensional imaging system to find particular objects it will grasp.

Research experience to date suggests that to navigate, visually locate objects, and plan and control arm motions, the first universal robots will require a billion operations per second of computer power. The 1980s have witnessed a number of well publicized fads that claim to be solutions to the artificial intelligence or robot control problem. Expert systems, the Prolog logical inference language, neural nets, fuzzy logic and massive parallelism have all had their spot in the limelight. The common element that I note in these pronouncements is the sudden enthusiasm of groups of researchers experienced in some area of computer science for applying their methods to the robotics problems of perceiving and act-ing in the physical world. Invariably each approach produces some simple showcase demonstrations, then bogs down on real problems. This pattern is no surprise to those with a background in the twenty five year research robotics effort.

Making a machine to see, hear or act reliably in the raw physical world is much, much more difficult than naive intuition leads us to believe....

MIND CHILDREN (2050+)

The fourth robot generation and its successors, with human perceptual and motor abilities and superior reasoning powers, could replace human beings in every essential task. In principle, our society could continue to operate increasingly well without us, with machines running the companies and doing the research as well as performing the productive work. Since machines can be designed to work well in outer space, production could move to the greater resources of the solar system, leaving behind a nature preserve subsidized from space. Meek humans would inherit the earth, but rapidly evolving machines would expand into the rest of the universe.

This development can be viewed as a very natural one. Human beings have two forms of heredity, one the traditional biological kind, passed on strands of DNA, the other cultural, passed from mind to mind by example, language, books and recently machines. At present the two are inextricably linked, but the cultural part is evolving very rapidly, and gradually assuming functions once the province of our biology. In terms of information content, our cultural side is already by far the larger part of us. The fully intelligent robot marks the point where our cultural side can exist on its own, free of biological limits. Intelligent machines, which are evolving among us, learning our skills, sharing our goals, and being shaped by our values, can be viewed as our children, the children of our minds. With them our biological heritage is not lost. It will be safely stored in libraries at least; however its importance will be greatly diminished.

What about life back on the preserve? For some of us the thought of being grandly upstaged by our artificial progeny will be disappointing, and life may seem pointless if we are fated to spend it staring stupidly at our ultra-intelligent progeny as they try to describe their ever more spectacular discoveries in baby-talk that we can understand. Is there any way individual humans might join the adventure?

You've just been wheeled into the operating room. A robot brain surgeon is in attendance, a computer waits nearby. Your skull, but not your brain, is anesthetized. You are fully conscious. The robot surgeon opens your brain case and places a hand on the brain's surface. This unusual hand bristles with microscopic machinery, and a cable connects it to the computer at your side. Instruments in the hand scan the first few millimeters of brain surface. These measurements, and a comprehensive understanding of human neural architecture, allow the surgeon to write a program that models the behavior of the uppermost layer of the scanned brain tissue. This program is installed in a small portion of the waiting computer and activated. Electrodes in the hand supply the simulation with the appropriate inputs from your brain, and can inject signals from the simulation. You and the surgeon compare the signals it produces with the original ones. They flash by very fast, but any discrepancies are highlighted on a display screen. The surgeon fine-tunes the simulation until the correspondence is nearly perfect. As soon as you are satisfied, the simulation output is activated. The brain layer is now impotent—it receives inputs and reacts as before but its output is ignored. Microscopic manipulators on the hand's surface excise this superfluous tissue and pass them to an aspirator, where they are drawn away.

The surgeon's hand sinks a fraction of a millimeter deeper into your brain, instantly compensating its measurements and signals for the changed position. The process is repeated for the next layer, and soon a second simulation resides in the computer, communicating with the first and with the remaining brain tissue. Layer after layer the brain is simulated, then excavated. Eventually your skull is empty, and the surgeon's hand rests deep in your brainstem. Though you have not lost consciousness, or even your train of thought, your mind has been removed from the brain and transferred to a machine. In a final, disorienting step the surgeon lifts its hand. Your suddenly abandoned body dies. For a moment you experience only quiet and dark. Then, once again, you can open your eyes. Your perspective has shifted. The computer simulation has been disconnected from the cable leading to the surgeon's hand and reconnected to a shiny new body of the style, color, and material of your choice. Your metamorphosis is complete.

Your new mind has a control labeled "speed." It had been set at 1, to keep the simulations synchronized with the old brain, but now you change it to 10,000, allowing you to communicate, react, and think ten thousand times faster. You now seem to have hours to respond to situations that previously seemed instantaneous. You have time, during the fall of a dropped object, to research the advantages and disadvantages of trying to catch it, perhaps to solve its differential equations of motion. When your old biological friends speak with you, their sentences take hours—you have plenty of time to think about the conversations, but they try your patience. Boredom is a mental alarm that keeps you from wasting your time in profitless activity, but if it acts too soon or too aggressively it limits your attention span, and thus your intelligence. With help from the machines, you change your mind-program to retard the onset of boredom. Having done that, you will find yourself comfortably working on long problems with sidetracks upon sidetracks. In fact, your thoughts routinely become so involved that you need an increase in your memory. These are but the first of many changes. Soon your friends complain that you have become more like the machines than the biological human you once were. That's life.

NO

John R. Searle

IS THE BRAIN'S MIND
A COMPUTER PROGRAM?

Can a machine think? Can a machine have conscious thoughts in exactly the same sense that you and I have? If by "machine" one means a physical system capable of performing certain functions (and what else can one mean?), then humans are machines of a special biological kind, and humans can think, and so of course machines can think. And, for all we know, it might be possible to produce a thinking machine out of different materials altogether—say, out of silicon chips or vacuum tubes. Maybe it will turn out to be impossible, but we certainly do not know that yet.

In recent decades, however, the question of whether a machine can think has been given a different interpretation entirely. The question that has been posed in its place is, Could a machine think just by virtue of implementing a computer program? Is the program by itself constitutive of thinking? This is a completely different question because it is not about the physical, causal properties of actual or possible physical systems but rather about the abstract, computational properties of formal computer programs that can be implemented in any sort of substance at all, provided only that the substance is able to carry the program.

A fair number of researchers in artificial intelligence (AI) believe the answer to the second question is yes; that is, they believe that by designing the right programs with the right inputs and outputs, they are literally creating minds. They believe furthermore that they have a scientific test for determining success or failure: the Turing test devised by Alan M. Turing, the founding father of artificial intelligence. The Turing test, as currently understood, is simply this: if a computer can perform in such a way that an expert cannot distinguish its performance from that of a human who has a certain cognitive ability—say, the ability to do addition or to understand Chinese—then the computer also has that ability. So the goal is to design programs that will simulate human cognition in such a way as to pass the Turing test. What is more, such a program would not merely be a model of the mind; it would literally be a mind, in the same sense that a human mind is a mind.

From John R. Searle, "Is the Brain's Mind a Computer Program?" *Scientific American* (January 1990). Copyright © 1990 by Scientific American, Inc. Reprinted by permission.

By no means does every worker in artificial intelligence accept so extreme a view. A more cautious approach is to think of computer models as being useful in studying the mind in the same way that they are useful in studying the weather, economics or molecular biology. To distinguish these two approaches, I call the first strong AI and the second weak AI. It is important to see just how bold an approach strong AI is. Strong AI claims that thinking is merely the manipulation of formal symbols, and that is exactly what the computer does: manipulate formal symbols. This view is often summarized by saying, "The mind is to the brain as the program is to the hardware."

* * *

Strong AI is unusual among theories of the mind in at least two respects: it can be stated clearly, and it admits of a simple and decisive refutation. The refutation is one that any person can try for himself or herself. Here is how it goes. Consider a language you don't understand. In my case, I do not understand Chinese. To me Chinese writing looks like so many meaningless squiggles. Now suppose I am placed in a room containing baskets full of Chinese symbols. Suppose also that I am given a rule book in English for matching Chinese symbols with other Chinese symbols. The rules identify the symbols entirely by their shapes and do not require that I understand any of them. The rules might say such things as, "Take a squiggle-squiggle sign from basket number one and put it next to a squoggle-squoggle sign from basket number two."

Imagine that people outside the room who understand Chinese hand in small bunches of symbols and that in response I manipulate the symbols according to the rule book and hand back more small bunches of symbols. Now, the rule book is the "computer program." The people who wrote it are "programmers, and I am the "computer." The baskets full of symbols are the "data base," the small bunches that are handed in to me are "questions" and the bunches I then hand out are "answers."

Now suppose that the rule book is written in such a way that my "answers" to the "questions" are indistinguishable from those of a native Chinese speaker. For example, the people outside might hand me some symbols that unknown to me mean, "What's your favorite color?" and I might after going through the rules give back symbols that, also unknown to me, mean, "My favorite is blue, but I also like green a lot." I satisfy the Turing test for understanding Chinese. All the same, I am totally ignorant of Chinese. And there is no way I could come to understand Chinese in the system as described, since there is no way that I can learn the meanings of any of the symbols. Like a computer, I manipulate symbols, but I attach no meaning to the symbols.

The point of the thought experiment is this: if I do not understand Chinese solely on the basis of running a computer program for understanding Chinese, then neither does any other digital computer solely on that basis. Digital computers merely manipulate formal symbols according to rules in the program.

What goes for Chinese goes for other forms of cognition as well. Just manipulating the symbols is not by itself enough to guarantee cognition, perception, understanding, thinking and so forth. And since computers, qua computers, are symbol-manipulating devices, merely running the computer program is not enough to guarantee cognition.

This simple argument is decisive against the claims of strong AI. The first premise of the argument simply states the formal character of a computer program. Programs are defined in terms of symbol manipulations, and the symbols are purely formal, or "syntactic." The formal character of the program, by the way, is what makes computers so powerful. The same program can be run on an indefinite variety of hardwares, and one hardware system can run an indefinite range of computer programs. Let me abbreviate this "axiom" as

Axiom 1. Computer programs are formal (syntactic).

This point is so crucial that it is worth explaining in more detail. A digital computer processes information by first encoding it in the symbolism that the computer uses and then manipulating the symbols through a set of precisely stated rules. These rules constitute the program. For example, in Turing's early theory of computers, the symbols were simply 0's and 1's, and the rules of the program said such things as, "Print a 0 on the tape, move one square to the left and erase a 1." The astonishing thing about computers is that any information that can be stated in a language can be encoded in such a system, and any information-processing task that can be solved by explicit rules can be programmed.

* * *

Two further points are important. First, symbols and programs are purely abstract notions: they have no essential physical properties to define them and can be implemented in any physical medium whatsoever. The 0's and 1's, qua symbols, have no essential physical properties and a fortiori have no physical, causal properties. I emphasize this point because it is tempting to identify computers with some specific technology—say, silicon chips—and to think that the issues are about the physics of silicon chips or to think that syntax identifies some physical phenomenon that might have as yet unknown causal powers, in the way that actual physical phenomena such as electromagnetic radiation or hydrogen atoms have physical, causal properties. The second point is that symbols are manipulated without reference to any meanings. The symbols of the program can stand for anything the programmer or user wants. In this sense the program has syntax but no semantics.

The next axiom is just a reminder of the obvious fact that thoughts, perceptions, understandings and so forth have a mental content. By virtue of their content they can be about objects and states of affairs in the world. If the content involves language, there will be syntax in addition to semantics, but linguistic understanding requires at least a semantic framework. If, for example, I am thinking about the last presidential election, certain words will go through my mind, but the words are about the election only because I attach specific meanings to these words, in accordance with my knowledge of English. In this respect they are unlike Chinese symbols for me. Let me abbreviate this axiom as

Axiom 2. Human minds have mental contents (semantics).

Now let me add the point that the Chinese room demonstrated. Having the symbols by themselves—just having the syntax—is not sufficient for having the semantics. Merely manipulating symbols is not enough to guarantee knowledge of what they mean. I shall abbreviate this as

Axiom 3. Syntax by itself is neither constitutive of nor sufficient for semantics.

At one level this principle is true by definition. One might, of course, define the terms syntax and semantics differently. The point is that there is a distinction between formal elements, which have no intrinsic meaning or content, and those phenomena that have intrinsic content. From these premises it follows that

Conclusion 1. Programs are neither constitutive of nor sufficient for minds.

And that is just another way of saying that strong AI is false.

It is important to see what is proved and not proved by this argument.

First, I have not tried to prove that "a computer cannot think." Since anything that can be simulated computationally can be described as a computer, and since our brains can at some levels be simulated, it follows trivially that our brains are computers and they can certainly think. But from the fact that a system can be simulated by symbol manipulation and the fact that it is thinking, it does not follow that thinking is equivalent to formal symbol manipulation.

Second, I have not tried to show that only biologically based systems like our brains can think. Right now those are the only systems we know for a fact can think, but we might find other systems in the universe that can produce conscious thoughts, and we might even come to be able to create thinking systems artificially. I regard this issue as up for grabs.

Third, strong AI's thesis is not that, for all we know, computers with the right programs might be thinking, that they might have some as yet undetected psychological properties; rather it is that they must be thinking because that is all there is to thinking.

Fourth, I have tried to refute strong AI so defined. I have tried to demonstrate that the program by itself is not constitutive of thinking because the program is purely a matter of formal symbol manipulation—and we know independently that symbol manipulations by themselves are not sufficient to guarantee the presence of meanings. That is the principle on which the Chinese room argument works.

I emphasize these points here partly because it seems to me the Churchlands [see "Could a Machine Think?" by Paul M. Churchland and Patricia Smith Churchland, *Scientific American* (January 1990), page 321] have not quite understood the issues. They think that strong AI is claiming that computers might turn out to think and that I am denying this possibility on commonsense grounds. But that is not the claim of strong AI, and my argument against it has nothing to do with common sense.

I will have more to say about their objections later. Meanwhile I should point out that, contrary to what the Churchlands suggest, the Chinese room argument also refutes any strong-AI claims made for the new parallel technologies that are inspired by and modeled on neural networks. Unlike the traditional von Neumann computer, which proceeds in a step-by-step fashion, these systems have many computational elements that operate in parallel and interact with one another according to rules inspired by neurobiology. Although the results are still modest, these "parallel distributed processing, or connectionist," models raise useful questions about how complex, parallel network systems like those in brains might actually function in the production of intelligent behavior.

The parallel, "brainlike" character of the processing, however, is irrelevant to the purely computational aspects of the process. Any function that can be computed on a parallel machine can also be computed on a serial machine. Indeed, because parallel machines are still rare, connectionist programs are usually run on traditional serial machines. Parallel processing, then, does not afford a way around the Chinese room argument.

What is more, the connectionist system is subject even on its own terms to a variant of the objection presented by the original Chinese room argument. Imagine that instead of a Chinese room, I have a Chinese gym: a hall containing many monolingual, English-speaking men. These men would carry out the same operations as the nodes and synapses in a connectionist architecture as described by the Churchlands, and the outcome would be the same as having one man manipulate symbols according to a rule book. No one in the gym speaks a word of Chinese, and there is no way for the system as a whole to learn the meanings of any Chinese words. Yet with appropriate adjustments, the system could give the correct answers to Chinese questions.

There are, as I suggested earlier, interesting properties of connectionist nets that enable them to simulate brain processes more accurately than traditional serial architecture does. But the advantages of parallel architecture for weak AI are quite irrelevant to the issues between the Chinese room argument and strong AI.

The Churchlands miss this point when they say that a big enough Chinese gym might have higher-level mental features that emerge from the size and complexity of the system, just as whole brains have mental features that are not had by individual neurons. That is, of course, a possibility, but it has nothing to do with computation. Computationally, serial and parallel systems are equivalent: any computation that can be done in parallel can be done in serial. If the man in the Chinese room is computationally equivalent to both, then if he does not understand Chinese solely by virtue of doing the computations, neither do they. The Churchlands are correct in saying that the original Chinese room argument was designed with traditional AI in mind but wrong in thinking that connectionism is immune to the argument. It applies to any computational system. You can't get semantically loaded thought contents from formal computations alone, whether they are done in serial or in parallel; that is why the Chinese room argument refutes strong AI in any form.

* * *

Many people who are impressed by this argument are nonetheless puzzled about the differences between people and computers. If humans are, at least in a trivial sense, computers, and if humans have a semantics, then why couldn't we give semantics to other computers? Why couldn't we program a Vax or a Cray so that it too would have thoughts and feelings? Or why couldn't some new computer technology overcome the gulf between form and content, between syntax and semantics? What, in fact, are the differences between animal brains and computer systems that enable the Chinese room argument to work against computers but not against brains?

The most obvious difference is that the processes that define something as a computer—computational processes —are completely independent of any reference to a specific type of hardware implementation. One could in principle make a computer out of old beer cans strung together with wires and powered by windmills.

But when it comes to brains, although science is largely ignorant of how brains function to produce mental states, one is struck by the extreme specificity of the anatomy and the physiology. Where some understanding exists of how brain processes produce mental phenomena— for example, pain, thirst, vision, smell —it is clear that specific neurobiological processes are involved. Thirst, at least of certain kinds, is caused by certain types of neuron firings in the hypothalamus, which in turn are caused by the action of a specific peptide, angiotensin II. The causation is from the "bottom up" in the sense that lower-level neuronal processes cause higher-level mental phenomena. Indeed, as far as we know, every "mental" event, ranging from feelings of thirst to thoughts of mathematical theorems and memories of childhood, is caused by specific neurons firing in specific neural architectures.

But why should this specificity matter? After all, neuron firings could be simulated on computers that had a completely different physics and chemistry from that of the brain. The answer is that the brain does not merely instantiate a formal pattern or program (it does that, too), but it also *causes* mental events by virtue of specific neurobiological processes. Brains are specific biological organs, and their spe-

cific biochemical properties enable them to cause consciousness and other sorts of mental phenomena. Computer simulations of brain processes provide models of the formal aspects of these processes. But the simulation should not be confused with duplication. The computational model of mental processes is no more real than the computational model of any other natural phenomenon.

One can imagine a computer simulation of the action of peptides in the hypothalamus that is accurate down to the last synapse. But equally one can imagine a computer simulation of the oxidation of hydrocarbons in a car engine or the action of digestive processes in a stomach when it is digesting pizza. And the simulation is no more the real thing in the case of the brain than it is in the case of the car or the stomach. Barring miracles, you could not run your car by doing a computer simulation of the oxidation of gasoline, and you could not digest pizza by running the program that simulates such digestion. It seems obvious that a simulation of cognition will similarly not produce the effects of the neurobiology of cognition.

All mental phenomena, then, are caused by neurophysiological processes in the brain. Hence,

Axiom 4. Brains cause minds.

In conjunction with my earlier derivation, I immediately derive, trivially,

Conclusion 2. Any other system capable of causing minds would have to have causal powers (at least) equivalent to those of brains.

This is like saying that if an electrical engine is to be able to run a car as fast as a gas engine, it must have (at least) an equivalent power output. This conclusion says nothing about the mechanisms. As a matter of fact, cognition is a biological phenomenon: mental states and processes are caused by brain processes. This does not imply that only a biological system could think, but it does imply that any alternative system, whether made of silicon, beer cans or whatever, would have to have the relevant causal capacities equivalent to those of brains. So now I can derive

> Conclusion 3. Any artifact that produced mental phenomena, any artificial brain, would have to be able to duplicate the specific causal powers of brains, and it could not do that just by running a formal program.

Furthermore, I can derive an important conclusion about human brains:

> Conclusion 4. The way that human brains actually produce mental phenomena cannot be solely by virtue of running a computer program.

* * *

I first presented the Chinese room parable in the pages of *Behavioral and Brain Sciences* in 1980, where it appeared, as is the practice of the journal, along with peer commentary, in this case, 26 commentaries. Frankly, I think the point it makes is rather obvious, but to my surprise the publication was followed by a further flood of objections that—more surprisingly—continues to the present day. The Chinese room argument clearly touched some sensitive nerve.

The thesis of strong AI is that any system whatsoever—whether it is made of beer cans, silicon chips or toilet paper—not only might have thoughts and feelings but *must* have thoughts and feelings, provided only that it implements the right program, with the right inputs and outputs. Now, that is a profoundly antibiological view, and one would think that people in AI would be glad to abandon it. Many of them, especially the younger generation, agree with me, but I am amazed at the number and vehemence of the defenders. Here are some of the common objections.

a. In the Chinese room you really do understand Chinese, even though you don't know it. It is, after all, possible to understand something without knowing that one understands it.

b. You don't understand Chinese, but there is an (unconscious) subsystem in you that does. It is, after all, possible to have unconscious mental states, and there is no reason why your understanding of Chinese should not be wholly unconscious.

c. You don't understand Chinese, but the whole room does. You are like a single neuron in the brain, and just as such a single neuron by itself cannot understand but only contributes to the understanding of the whole system, you don't understand, but the whole system does.

d. Semantics doesn't exist anyway; there is only syntax. It is a kind of prescientific illusion to suppose that there exist in the brain some mysterious "mental contents," "thought processes" or "semantics." All that exists in the brain is the same sort of syntactic symbol manipulation that goes on in computers. Nothing more.

e. You are not really running the computer program—you only think you are. Once you have a conscious agent going through the steps of the program. It ceases to be a case of implementing a program at all.

f. Computers would have semantics and not just syntax if their inputs and outputs were put in appropriate causal relation to the rest of the world. Imagine that we put the computer into a robot, attached television cameras to the robot's head, installed transducers connecting the television messages to the computer and had the computer output operate the robot's arms and legs. Then the whole system would have a semantics.

g. If the program simulated the operation of the brain of a Chinese speaker, then it would understand Chinese. Suppose that we simulated the brain of a Chinese person at the level of neurons. Then surely such a system would understand Chinese as well as any Chinese person's brain.

And so on.

All of these arguments share a common feature: they are all inadequate because they fail to come to grips with the actual Chinese room argument. That argument rests on the distinction between the formal symbol manipulation that is done by the computer and the mental contents biologically produced by the brain, a distinction I have abbreviated—I hope not misleadingly—as the distinction between syntax and semantics. I will not repeat my answers to all of these objections, but it will help to clarify the issues if I explain the weaknesses of the most widely held objection, argument c—what I call the systems reply. (The brain simulator reply, argument g, is another popular one, but I have already addressed that one in the previous section.)

* * *

The systems reply asserts that of course *you* don't understand Chinese but the whole system—you, the room, the rule book, the bushel baskets full of symbols —does. When I first heard this explanation, I asked one of its proponents, "Do you mean the room understands Chinese?" His answer was yes. It is a daring move, but aside from its implausibility, it will not work on purely logical grounds. The point of the original argument was that symbol shuffling by itself does not give any access to the meanings of the symbols. But this is as much true of the whole room as it is of the person inside. One can see this point by extending the thought experiment. Imagine that I memorize the contents of the baskets and the rule book, and I do all the calculations in my head. You can even imagine that I work out in the open. There is nothing in the "system" that is not in me, and since I don't understand Chinese, neither does the system.

The Churchlands in their companion piece produce a variant of the systems reply by imagining an amusing analogy. Suppose that someone said that light could not be electromagnetic because if you shake a bar magnet in a dark room, the system still will not give off visible light. Now, the Churchlands ask, is not the Chinese room argument just like that? Does it not merely say that if you shake Chinese symbols in a semantically dark room, they will not give off the light of Chinese understanding? But just as later investigation showed that light was entirely constituted by electromagnetic radiation, could not later investigation also show that semantics are entirely constituted of syntax? Is this not a question for further scientific investigation?

Arguments from analogy are notoriously weak, because before one can make the argument work, one has to establish that the two cases are truly analogous. And here I think they are not. The account of light in terms of electromagnetic radiation is a causal story right down to the ground. It is a causal account of the physics of electromagnetic radiation. But the analogy with formal symbols fails because formal symbols have no physical, causal powers. The only power that symbols have, qua symbols, is the power to cause the next step in the program when the machine is running. And there is no question of waiting on further research to reveal the physical, causal properties of 0's and 1's. The only relevant properties of 0's and 1's are abstract computational properties, and they are already well known.

The Churchlands complain that I am "begging the question" when I say that uninterpreted formal symbols are not identical to mental contents. Well, I certainly did not spend much time arguing for it, because I take it as a logical truth. As with any logical truth, one can quickly see that it is true, because one gets inconsistencies if one tries to imagine the converse. So let us try it. Suppose that in the Chinese room some undetectable Chinese thinking really is going on. What exactly is supposed to make the manipulation of the syntactic elements into specifically Chinese thought contents? Well, after all, I am assuming that the programmers were Chinese speakers, programming the system to process Chinese information.

Fine. But now imagine that as I am sitting in the Chinese room shuffling the Chinese symbols, I get bored with just shuffling the—to me—meaningless symbols. So, suppose that I decide to interpret the symbols as standing for moves in a chess game. Which semantics is the system giving off now? Is it giving off a Chinese semantics or a chess semantics, or both simultaneously? Suppose there is a third person looking in through the window, and she decides that the symbol manipulations can all be interpreted as stock-market predictions. And so on. There is no limit to the number of semantic interpretations that can be assigned to the symbols because, to repeat, the symbols are purely formal. They have no intrinsic semantics.

Is there any way to rescue the Churchlands' analogy from incoherence? I said above that formal symbols do not have causal properties. But of course the program will always be implemented in some hardware or another, and the hardware will have specific physical, causal powers. And any real computer will give off various phenomena. My computers, for example, give off heat, and they make a humming noise and sometimes crunching sounds. So is there some logically compelling reason why they could not also give off consciousness? No. Scientifically, the idea is out of the question, but it is not something the Chinese room argument is supposed to refute, and it is not something that an adherent of strong AI would wish to defend, because any such giving off would have to derive from the physical features of the implementing medium. But the basic premise of strong AI is that the physical features of the implementing medium are totally irrelevant. What matters are programs, and programs are purely formal.

The Churchlands' analogy between syntax and electromagnetism, then, is confronted with a dilemma: either the syntax is construed purely formally in terms of its abstract mathematical properties, or it is not. If it is, then the analogy breaks down, because syntax so construed has no physical powers and hence no physical, causal powers. If, on the other hand, one is supposed to think in terms of the physics of the implementing medium, then there is indeed an analogy, but it is not one that is relevant to strong AI.

* * *

Because the points I have been making are rather obvious—syntax is not the same as semantics, brain processes cause mental phenomena—the question arises, How did we get into this mess? How could anyone have supposed that a computer simulation of a mental process must be the real thing? After all, the whole point of models is that they contain only certain features of the modeled domain and leave out the rest. No one expects to get wet in a pool filled with Ping-Pong-ball models of water molecules. So why would anyone think a computer model of thought processes would actually think?

Part of the answer is that people have inherited a residue of behaviorist psychological theories of the past generation. The Turing test enshrines the temptation to think that if something behaves as if it had certain mental processes, then it must actually have those mental processes. And this is part of the behaviorists' mistaken assumption that in order to be scientific, psychology must confine its study to externally observable behavior. Paradoxically, this residual behaviorism is tied to a residual dualism. Nobody thinks that a computer simulation of digestion would actually digest anything, but where cognition is concerned, people are willing to believe in such a miracle because they fail to recognize that the mind is just as much a biological phenomenon as digestion. The mind, they suppose, is something formal and abstract, not a part of the wet and slimy stuff in our heads. The polemical literature in AI usually contains attacks on something the authors call dualism, but what they fail to see is that they themselves display dualism in a strong form, for unless one accepts the idea that the mind is completely independent of the brain or of any other physically specific system, one could not possibly hope to create minds just by designing programs.

Historically, scientific developments in the West that have treated humans as just a part of the ordinary physical, biological order have often been opposed by various rearguard actions. Copernicus and Galileo were opposed because they denied that the earth was the center of the universe; Darwin was opposed because he claimed that humans had descended from the lower animals. It is best to see strong AI as one of the last gasps of this antiscientific tradition, for it denies that there is anything essentially physical and biological about the human mind. The mind according to strong AI is independent of the brain. It is a computer program and as such has no essential connection to any specific hardware.

Many people who have doubts about the psychological significance of AI think that computers might be able to understand Chinese and think about numbers but cannot do the crucially human things, namely—and then follows their favorite human specialty—falling in love, having a sense of humor, feeling the angst of postindustrial society under late capitalism, or whatever. But workers in AI complain—correctly—that this is a case of moving the goalposts. As soon as an AI simulation succeeds, it ceases to be of psychological importance. In this debate both sides fail to see the distinction between simulation and duplication. As far as simulation is concerned, there is no difficulty in programming my computer so that it prints out, "I love you, Suzy"; "Ha ha"; or "I am suffering the angst of postindustrial society under late capitalism." The important point is that simulation is not the same as duplication, and that fact holds as much import for thinking about arithmetic as it does for feeling angst. The point is not that the computer gets only to the 40-yard line and not all the way to the goal line. The computer doesn't even get started. It is not playing that game.

POSTSCRIPT

Will It Be Possible to Build a Computer That Can Think?

Moravec develops his ideas at much greater length in two books: *Mind Children* (Harvard University Press, 1988) and *Mind Age* (Bantam Books, forthcoming). In the first book, he focuses on the development of motor and sensory apparatus for robots, forecasts the transfer of human minds into immensely capable machines, and speculates on the replacement of biological intelligence by machine intelligence. He also discusses some of the ideas behind the growing field of "artificial life." Steven Levy, in *Artificial Life* (Pantheon, 1992), expands on this last topic.

Currently being developed is a combination of electroencephalography (EEG) and magnetic resonance imaging (MRI), two technologies that allow exceedingly detailed recording and analysis of brain activity. Future extensions of the technique could conceivably permit the recording of a human mind, just as Moravec projects.

In discussing *Mind Age*, Moravec says, "Technical civilization, and the human minds that support it, are the first feeble stirrings of an entirely new form of existence.... The next big milestone along this road is the development of artificial minds that avoid or exceed many of the limitations of our haphazardly built biological brains." The book takes Moravec's speculations much further into the future, culminating in a time when humans will exist as streamlined minds residing in a world simulated within computers and when the very definition of "reality" must be changed to encompass the new conditions of human life. For another interesting discussion along the same lines, see Frederick Pohl and Hans Moravec, "Souls in Silicon," *Omni* (November 1993).

Not everyone is willing to go as far as Moravec. Searle's essay presented here was paired in the January 1990 issue of *Scientific American* with Paul M. Churchland and Patricia Smith Churchland's "Could a Machine Think?" According to the article, the authors "reject the Turing test as a sufficient condition for conscious intelligence [because it is] very important... that the right sorts of things be going on inside the artificial machine." Unlike Searle, however, true "artificial intelligence, in a nonbiological but massively parallel machine, remains a compelling and discernible prospect" for the Churchlands.

Searle is by no means alone in objecting to the idea of the mind as a computer program (also known as "strong AI"). Roger Penrose, a renowned physicist and mathematician at the University of Oxford in England, attacks the idea of strong AI vigorously and at length in *The Emperor's New Mind:*

Concerning Computers, Minds, and the Laws of Physics (Penguin Books, 1991) and concludes, "Is it not 'obvious' that mere computation cannot evoke pleasure or pain; that it cannot perceive poetry or the beauty of an evening sky or the magic of sounds; that it cannot hope or love or despair; that it cannot have a genuine autonomous purpose?... Perhaps when computations become extraordinarily complicated they can begin to take on the more poetic or subjective qualities that we associate with the term 'mind.' Yet it is hard to avoid an uncomfortable feeling that there must always be something missing from such a picture."

It is clear from the incomplete manuscript of *Mind Age* that Moravec intends to directly respond to Penrose in considerable detail, defending his claim that a machine could be as conscious of its actions and self as humans are. Students who wish to dig deeper into the debate over whether or not machines can think should consult this book.

PART 4

Risky Business

Many people worry that technology is often accompanied by unexpected—and unfortunate—side effects. Whether a technology is old or new and whether its side effects are old or new, the worry rarely fades away. This concern raises the question of whether society should accept a particular technology at a price—in lives or health or environmental degradation—or reject it.

Such questions arise in many areas. This section deals with only four: genetic engineering, electric power, food irradiation, and the final eradication of smallpox.

■ Should Attempts at Genetic Engineering to Cure Diseases Be Continued?

■ Are Electromagnetic Fields Dangerous to Your Health?

■ Are Irradiated Foods Safe to Eat?

■ Should Smallpox Be Completely Eradicated?

ISSUE 13

Should Attempts at Genetic Engineering to Cure Diseases Be Continued?

YES: Mark A. Findeis, from "Genes to the Rescue," *Technology Review* (April 1994)

NO: Andrew Kimbrell, from *The Human Body Shop: The Engineering and Marketing of Life* (HarperSanFrancisco, 1993)

ISSUE SUMMARY

YES: Mark A. Findeis, a group leader at OsteoArthritis Sciences in Cambridge, Massachusetts, describes several methods of correcting genetic disorders that are now under development and argues that although genetic therapy cannot be a panacea, it does hold great promise for battling diseases.

NO: Andrew Kimbrell, the policy director of the Foundation on Economic Trends in Washington, D.C., argues that the development of genetic engineering is so marked by scandal, ambition, and moral blindness that society should be deeply suspicious of its purported benefits.

In the early 1970s, scientists first discovered that it was technically possible to move genes—biological material that determines a living organism's physical makeup—from one organism to another and thus (in principle) to give bacteria, plants, and animals new features and to correct genetic defects of the sort that cause many diseases, such as cystic fibrosis. Most researchers in molecular genetics were excited by the prospects that suddenly seemed within their grasp. However, a few researchers—as well as many people outside the field—were disturbed by the idea; they thought that genetic mix-and-match games might spawn new diseases, weeds, and pests. Some people even argued that genetic engineering should be banned at the outset, before unforeseeable horrors were unleashed.

Researchers in support of genetic experimentation responded by declaring a moratorium on their own work until suitable safeguards could be devised. Once those safeguards were in place in the form of government regulations, work resumed. Before long, it became clear that the hazards of transplanting genes among plants and animals were less than had been feared, although the benefits were going to take years of hard work to achieve. James D. Watson and John Tooze document the early years of this research in *The DNA Story: A Documentary History of Gene Cloning* (W. H. Freeman, 1981). For a shorter, more recent review of the story, see Bernard D. Davis, "Genetic Engineering: The Making of Monsters?" *The Public Interest* (Winter 1993).

By 1989, the technology had developed tremendously: researchers could obtain patents for mice with artificially added genes ("transgenic" mice); firefly genes had been added to tobacco plants to make them glow (faintly) in the dark; and growth hormone produced by genetically engineered bacteria was being used to grow low-fat pork and to increase milk production by cows. While these developments were being made, a storm of protest was gathering strength. Critics argued a number of points against genetic engineering: it was unnatural, and it violated the rights of both plants and animals to their "species integrity"; expensive, high-tech, tinkered animals gave a competitive advantage to big agricultural corporations and drove small farmers out of business; and putting human genes into animals, plants, or bacteria was downright offensive. See Betsy Hanson and Dorothy Nelkin, "Public Responses to Genetic Engineering," *Society* (November/December 1989).

By 1990, the first proposals to add genes to *human* cells in order to restore normal function were being made (see Inder M. Verma, "Gene Therapy," *Scientific American*, November 1990). Not long after, the first gene therapy attempts were approved by the National Institutes of Health (NIH), despite many people's objections that altering a human being's genes meant violating that person's nature and identity at the deepest possible level.

To prevent producing genetic changes that would be passed on to future generations, researchers have been restricted to modifying only somatic (body) cells, not germ cells (sperm and eggs). Here, an individual's rights come into play. That is, therapy that changes somatic cells affects only the patient, who can give consent for the change. Therapy that changes germ cells, which carry the genes that determine one's children's makeup, affects all the patient's descendants, who cannot give consent.

People have also objected that the engineering of human beings will lead inevitably to a new form of *eugenics*, which refers to the science of improving the genetic makeup of the human species. In the past, the concept has been used to justify sterilizing genetic "defectives" (such as criminals and people with mental retardation) and exterminating undesirable groups (such as Jews during the Holocaust).

As time passes and genetic engineering becomes more advanced, the voices of optimism grow stronger. In the following selections, Mark A. Findeis, who has been an instructor at Harvard Medical School and has done research in the medical use of genetic engineering, describes techniques of genetic therapy now being developed for "fighting diseases at their source" and argues that the therapy will "eventually offer safe, effective, and affordable treatments."

Andrew Kimbrell, the policy director of the Foundation on Economic Trends, takes a very skeptical, alarmist view of genetic engineering and finds that its history is so marked by scandal, ambition, and moral blindness that it sets an exceedingly disturbing precedent for the future.

YES

Mark A. Findeis

GENES TO THE RESCUE

People with cystic fibrosis, one of the most common lethal hereditary diseases, usually die early in adulthood unless they undergo a lung transplant. During the last year several laboratories in the United States and Britain have begun experiments to treat the disease, which afflicts 30,000 Americans, by transferring into patients' airways copies of a critical gene that they lack. The theory is that, if the gene can enter the cells lining the lungs, that should allow the cells to produce the critical protein that cystic fibrosis patients cannot make themselves.

In a recent report on such a gene-therapy effort, Michael J. Welsh, a professor of internal medicine at the University of Iowa College of Medicine and an investigator at the Howard Hughes Medical institute, has shown that cystic fibrosis patients have been able to produce—albeit in minute quantities—the critical protein. Although Welsh's research was designed to examine the safety of his particular technique rather than to alleviate patients' medical problems, it has nevertheless raised hopes that cystic fibrosis could someday be treated by gene therapy.

Research on gene therapy has grown dramatically in just a few years. The National Institutes of Health's Recombinant DNA Advisory Committee, which reviews federally funded therapeutic gene-transfer experiments, has approved more than 40 such protocols on humans since the first trial in 1990. At the time, W. French Anderson, then chief of the molecular hematology branch at the National Heart, Lung, and Blood Institute; R. Michael Blaese, deputy chief of the metabolism branch at the National Cancer Institute (NCI); and Kenneth W. Culver, then a senior clinical investigator in NCI's metabolism branch, treated a girl with severe combined immunodeficiency disease, which ordinarily results in childhood death from overwhelming infection. The immune systems of that patient and another girl who periodically receives gene therapy for the disease have subsequently improved so much that they can now attend public school.

There is even some commercial activity. At least 18 companies have become directly involved in gene-therapy research and development. But almost all of the human trials have involved only single or a few individuals at a time, and most researchers have not yet published results. Despite widespread news reports, in fact, few results from human trials are yet available. Much of the work is still trying to establish the safety of experimental protocols.

Still, given positive results in animal models, many researchers believe that gene transfer potentially could be used someday to combat perhaps dozens of serious human diseases caused by genetic mutations, including sickle-cell anemia, emphysema, hemophilia, and a malady marked by extremely high levels of cholesterol. For some diseases, gene therapy might provide the first effective treatment. For those genetic diseases that can already be treated, gene therapy could be better than what is now the top-of-the-line technique: providing patients with essential proteins, such as insulin for diabetics. Such treatment isn't always ideal. Because of the cost of purified clotting factor, for example, hemophiliacs usually take that protein only after bleeding begins, risking damage to joints by the delay.

Inserting genes that stimulate the production of immune cells might also help fight cancer. Although the number of patients involved in anticancer gene-therapy trials is small, well over half of today's gene-transfer experiments on humans are devoted to combatting cancers. Researchers are also trying to develop gene therapies for hepatitis and other liver diseases, AIDS, and diseases of the cardiovascular and central nervous systems.

THE MOST COMMON
GENE-THERAPY TECHNIQUE

The first clinical gene-therapy trials—and the majority of those now under way—

depend on a viral "vector," a viruslike particle into which researchers have placed a therapeutic gene. Clinicians introduce the vector to cells that have been removed from a patient and are growing and dividing in culture, and the vector transfers the therapeutic gene into the cells' chromosomes (large pieces of DNA into which the cells' genes are organized). Researchers later return these "transfected" cells to the body, and the molecular machinery inside the cells that reads chromosomal information begins making the needed protein. In principle, the therapeutic gene can remain in the patient's chromosomes as long as the cells stay alive in the body.

The virus employed in these "ex-vivo" experiments is a mouse retrovirus. Researchers use retroviruses because, after entering cells, those take advantage of processes that occur during cell division to introduce viral genetic material permanently into the cells' chromosomes. In this way, a therapeutic gene is reproduced with the chromosomes when the cell divides.

The ex-vivo viral-vector strategy raises some safety concerns, although the vectors do not contain all of a retrovirus's genes and therefore should not be able to reproduce and cause a viral infection. Safe vectors are technically difficult to produce; scientists have to be careful that a parent virus able to cause disease does not contaminate batches of modified vector. The possibility of developing cancerous cells is another worry with retroviruses. In the process of being integrated into a patient's chromosomes, a new gene may interfere with a normal one, since retroviruses insert their genes into chromosomes indiscriminately. While the chances are low, if a region of a chromosome that regulates cell growth was affected, the patient's cells might conceivably become cancerous and one disease might be cured at the expense of causing another. Researchers may need more than a decade to see if the few viral genes employed cause cellular changes other than the production of a therapeutic protein.

The costs associated with ex-vivo gene therapy could also prove formidable in some cases. In a common approach to gene therapy for long-term treatment of familial diseases, for example, doctors harvest the patient's born-marrow cells and treat them with a retroviral vector. (Such cells, unlike most in the body, are rapidly dividing and, since that is a necessary condition for retroviruses to insert genetic material, are useful candidates for retroviral vectors.) This procedure, similar to that used for a bone-marrow transplant, might cost up to $150,000. In some cases the surgery might have to be repeated (and costs commensurately increased), since the research so far—which is still quite limited—indicates that retroviral gene transfer sometimes modifies only 10 percent of treated cells, and more than that may be required. Also, protein production may stop entirely after several weeks, for as yet unknown reasons.

To raise and maintain the levels of protein manufacture, researchers are trying to manipulate particular DNA sequences that lie adjacent to therapeutic genes. Through a series of steps, these sequences —called promoters and enhancers— boost protein production. Work involving these sequences remains experimental at this point.

NEWER GENE-THERAPY TECHNIQUES

Some researchers are devising different approaches to gene therapy, although most of these have not yet made it to the clinical-trial stage. An approach employing another viral vector—one derived from adenovirus, which causes the common cold—is what Welsh's team at the University of Iowa, as well as researchers at the University of Pennsylvania and the National Institutes of Health, have been using, or expect to use, to transfer the therapeutic gene into cystic fibrosis patients. Adenovirus is attractive partly because it can insert its genes into non-dividing cells, which make up most of the body. This could eliminate the expense of conducting surgery along the lines needed to remove bone marrow. (For the experimental cystic fibrosis therapy, clinicians have simply dripped or sprayed modified adenovirus into a patient's lungs. The vector then inserts the critical gene into lung cells.) Moreover, cellular chromosomes do not incorporate adenovirus genes, lowering concerns that those genes could lead to unrestrained cell growth and cancer.

Still, researchers have a long way to go before they fully understand the value of this gene-therapy approach. The treatment would have to be administered repeatedly, since the airway cells targeted by adenovirus have lifetimes of only a month or so. And scientists have not yet tested adenovirus-derived vectors to know whether the needed gene prompts patients to reduce therapeutic amounts of protein, although researchers expect about 10 percent of the airway cells to be transfected. It is also not clear whether a certain amount of adenoviral vectors will have side effects. Last year one of three cystic fibrosis patients being treated with an adenoviral vector at the National Institutes of Health experienced fever, lung inflammation, and reduced levels of oxygen in the blood. The affected patient, who was receiving a higher dose of modified virus than her cohorts, recovered from the problems after researchers stopped the experiment. They decided that they would use lower doses in future work.

Another technique that has recently been tried is much simpler than the ex-vivo method: several researchers have directly injected naked genes into body cells and observed their expression as different proteins. But the research suggests that the genes work their way only into cells adjacent to the injection site. Probably too many injections would be required to have a therapeutic effect.

Still, this approach should prove useful for another medical goal: vaccinations, in which the aim is to develop an immune response. In general, a small amount of protein production elicits this reaction. Therefore, the vaccination of animals, including humans, requires only a limited number of injections. Moreover, vaccinating with genes rather than inactivated pathogens or pathogen-derived proteins (the present methods) may be superior since the genes can maintain a low level of protein production for a prolonged period. This could yield an improved immune response, at lower cost.

Meanwhile, an injection approach that shows more promise for treating diseases entails the use of proteins that bind to "receptors" on cell surfaces. Following injection of a complex consisting of such proteins and a plasmid—a circular bit of DNA produced in bacteria—into which a therapeutic gene has been inserted, receptors carry the DNA inside the cells. George Wu, associate professor of gastroenterology at the University of Connecticut Health Center, has pioneered this research by mixing plasmids including therapeutic genes with proteins that bind to a receptor located on liver cells. For instance, in 1992 with James Wilson, than an associate professor of internal medicine and biological chemistry at the University of Michigan, Wu transferred to rabbits a complex involving a gene whose corresponding protein lowers circulating levels of low-density lipoprotein, or "bad cholesterol." The protein works by absorbing the cholesterol in the liver, where it is metabolized. A single transfer of the gene lowered the animals' bad cholesterol levels for a week. TargeTech, my former employer, is now developing Wu's technique commercially.

Wu's approach is appealing partly because the complex of proteins, plasmid, and therapeutic gene is easier to produce than retroviral vectors. The bacteria that produce the plasmid are relatively simple to grow in large quantities through fermentation, and blood plasma from donors can be the source of at least one of the proteins that can be used. Also, tests have indicated that the receptor absorbs as much as 80 percent of the DNA-protein complex from circulating blood within five minutes. Therefore the blood, which has enzymes that break down genes, has little time to degrade the therapeutic genes because this is where many genes are "expressed" into proteins. Delivering a gene through retroviral therapy to the liver is not a good idea because liver cells don't normally divide, and they can be difficult to grow in culture before being returned to a patient.

But introducing genes to cells through receptors has limitations. For reasons that aren't yet completely clear, the resulting protein production can be minimal and usually lasts only several days to a week. Both Wu and Max Birnstiel, director of the Research Institute of Molecular Pathology in Vienna, Austria, have tried remedial techniques in animals. One approach has been to add to the complexes inactivated viruses or viral surface proteins.

Unlike viral vectors, these viral components do not carry the therapeutic gene. Rather, their job is simply to help in opening the cell membrane. The researchers' hunch that this would allow the gene to pass more easily into the cell and hence make it available for greater levels of expression appears correct: various reports suggest that the level of protein production can be raised many times. Scientists have also prolonged gene expression for at least three months in rats using a chemical compound that stimulates liver metabolism.

One of the most immediately promising gene-therapy approaches has been developed by Robert Debs, associate research physician, and coworkers at the Cancer Research Institute of the University of California at San Francisco, who have sprayed an aerosol into the lungs of mice. The aerosol attaches the gene that produces the protein for counteracting cystic fibrosis to a positively charged lipid mixture—a fatty material similar to others used in drug delivery. The material brings the gene to the surface of a cell by electrostatically binding to its outer membranes. Then, as the positively charged lipids mix with other lipids in the membrane, the gene can enter the cell. After a single 90-minute inhalation, Debs could still see gene expression above normal background levels in most of the airway cells 60 days later.

There is so far no clear indication of a downside to Debs's approach, although the procedure has yet to be tried in humans. While the lipid mixture is relatively expensive to use in the small amounts needed for research, if it were produced on a larger scale its cost would probably be low compared with the price tag for introducing therapeutic genes by means such as viral vectors. In large quantities, the positively charged lipids are toxic, but since very low amounts would be needed the approach should be safe. At this point, MEGABIOS Corp. of San Francisco is developing Debs's technique further.

Yet one more approach related to gene therapy is on the horizon today. Called "antisense," this method attempts the opposite of what the other techniques do: it aims to turn *off* genes that code for the production of harmful proteins. For example, Robert D. Rosenberg, a professor of biology at MIT, is testing a technique to stop the manufacture of a protein that normally helps promote the development of cells responsible for narrowing coronary arteries months after balloon angioplasty....

Antisense researchers use analogs of DNA sequences or short pieces of DNA called oligonucleotides as drugs to target a gene sequence. The compounds, which are complementary to key sections of a gene, bind to it, thereby interfering with its expression. Another technique is to use ribozymes, sequences of the genetic material RNA that cleave the nucleic acids found in genes. Ribozymes can be engineered to bind to specific nucleic-acid sequences, cutting them and ruining their ability to instruct for the synthesis of proteins.

But it's difficult to deliver enough antisense agents to the particular cells where they need to act because they often decompose quickly in the body. In general, therefore, the agents need to be administered in quantities high enough that they may be toxic. Targeting techniques may deliver the compounds more effectively to specific areas. To inhibit hepatitis B infection in the liver, for example, TargeTech has injected woodchucks with a complex containing an antiviral oligonucleotide and a protein that binds to liver cell receptors. (Woodchucks develop a form of hepatitis B similar to the human form and are therefore used as a model for the disease.) Researchers have found that the approach, which was supposed to stop a gene in hepatitis B virus that coopts the liver to make copies of the virus, successfully lowered the level of virus in the woodchucks for several days. Preclinical testing continues.

LIMITS AND HOPES

At least some of these techniques should eventually offer safe, effective, and affordable treatments, but gene therapy is not likely to prove useful against all genetic diseases. Some, such as hypertension, gout, and diabetes, would appear difficult to treat because they involve multiple genes. And some diseases pose problems because the genes require regulation and therefore patients need varying amounts of a protein at different times. The amount of insulin required by diabetics, for example, depends on exercise, food intake, and other factors. Treating such diseases could require transferring not only the therapeutic gene but also the genes regulating it. Diseases of the central nervous system, such as Huntington's chorea and Alzheimer's, could also be difficult to treat, since doing so would require delivering genes to the brain—not a simple matter.

Even for diseases that seem like prime gene-therapy candidates, other therapeutic strategies may be the better choice in many cases. Patients with high cholesterol levels are often well served by available drugs and treatments, for example. Transplants of organs and bone marrow are also increasingly successful in treating diseases such as leukemia, as the techniques for that work are refined and improved immunosuppressive drugs reduce the risk of rejection. Despite the potential glamour of gene therapy, then, physicians will have to compare the safety, effectiveness, cost, and convenience of administration among different treatments.

Still, while at least 10 years will elapse before those comparisons become clear, gene therapy could eventually become a truly important medical tool. The situation may prove analogous to the use of penicillin and related compounds decades after the initial discoveries of antibiotics. While those substances have turned out to have limits and must be used correctly, they are indeed wonder drugs for treating most bacterial infections. Similarly, gene therapy may offer much hope in fighting diseases at their source.

NO

Andrew Kimbrell

ENGINEERING OURSELVES

In an age of protests, this was the first of its kind. It was early March 1977, and hundreds of demonstrators had flocked to the futuristic, domed auditorium of the National Academy of Sciences (NAS). The protesters chanted slogans such as "We will not be cloned," and they carried signs bearing warnings, including "Don't Tread on My Genes."

The object of the protest was a three-day symposium being held under the auspices of the NAS. The forum was intended to bring together scientists, government officials, and business leaders to discuss the future prospects of genetically altering life-forms, including humans. The chairman of the meeting, Dr. David Hamburg, president of the NAS Institute for Medicine, undoubtedly had anticipated that this would be the usual scientific conference, a collegial discussion of current scientific and legislative issues that had been cropping up as a result of advances in genetic manipulation. It was not to be.

The demonstrators, led by activist Jeremy Rifkin, crowded the auditorium with their signs and dominated the session with their chants and shouted questions to the symposium's panels. They relentlessly prodded the scientists and bureaucrats, urging them to confront the moral and ethical implications of engineering the genetic code of life. They also repeatedly demanded that speakers disclose who was financing their research. (The forum was supported in part by funds from a variety of drug manufacturers.) Finally, under a barrage of questions about the eugenic [breed- or race-improving] and discriminatory potential of biotechnology, the chairman had no choice but to offer the podium to Rifkin and others to air their concerns.

Speaking up with the protesters were many prominent scientists. At a press conference prior to the demonstration, Nobel Prize winner George Wald called the use of genetic engineering "the biggest break in nature that has occurred in human history." Renowned biochemist Dr. Erwin Chargoff warned against the use of genetic research to attempt to control the evolution of humans and other life-forms.

The activists and scientists who voiced their concerns that day were part of a growing chorus of those who feared the engineering of life. As early as

1967, Marshall Nirenberg, the Nobelist who first described the "language" of the genetic code, had delivered a stern lecture about engineering human beings, along with a remarkably prescient prophecy:

> My guess is that cells will be programmed with synthetic messages within 25 years.... The point that deserves special emphasis is that man may be able to program his own cells long before he will be able to assess adequately the long-term consequences of such alterations, long before he will be able to formulate goals, and long before he can resolve the ethical and moral problems which will be raised.

The fears of the early gene engineering critics focused on proposals to engineer the human germline—to permanently alter the genetic makeup of an individual that is passed on to succeeding generations. Many scientists were predicting that, by manipulating the genes in sperm, eggs, or embryos, future physicians would be able to excise "bad" genes from the human gene pool. Critics envisioned a future human body shop industry in eliminating the genes responsible for sickle-cell anemia or cystic fibrosis by mass engineering of these "problem" genes from the sex cells (the sperm and ova) of individuals. Future genetic engineers could also add foreign genes to a patient's genome, genes from other humans or even different species. These genes might protect an individual from various diseases, or confer desired qualities like better looks or brains. Ultimately, they believed that as scientists learned more about the relationship of genes to disease and other human traits, there would be an inevitable push to treat life-forms as so many machines whose working parts, genes, could be engineered or replaced if they were "defective."

Moreover, it was clear that if the genetic engineering of human beings should come, and most believed it would, there would be a quantum leap in both negative and positive eugenics. No longer would it be necessary to attempt to carefully control generations of breeding to create "good" characteristics, or to resort to sterilization, abortion, or genocide in order to remove abnormal or undesirable traits. Individuals could be altered through genetic surgery that would repair or replace bad genes and add good ones. Nobel Prize winner Jean Rostand's early visions of the eugenic potential of gene engineering went even further: "It would be no more than a game for the 'man farming biologist' to change the subject's sex, the colour of his eyes, the general proportions of body and limbs and perhaps the facial features." Many agreed with scientists such as Wald and Chargoff that the genetic alteration of people could eventually change the course of evolution. In 1972, ethicist Dr. Leon Kass wrote, "The new technologies for human engineering may well be 'the transition to a wholly new path of evolution.' They may therefore mark the end of *human* life as we and all other humans know it."

For over two decades, scientists, activists, ethicists, and the media have engaged in the debate over the medical and moral questions surrounding the germline genetic engineering of human beings. Editorials have appeared with headlines questioning "Whether to Make Perfect Humans" and how to arrive at "The Rules for Reshaping Life." Many critics have continued to argue against the entire enterprise of "the remaking of man." They question the wisdom of having scientists decide which part of the human genome should be eliminated and which enhanced. And if not scientists, who, they ask, will determine which human genes are bad and which good? They warn that even supposedly "bad" genes may bring extraordinary benefits to humanity. Recently, it was discovered that cystic fibrosis genes appear to provide individuals with protection from melanoma, an increasingly common form of skin cancer. Research conducted in the 1980s determined that sickle-cell anemia genes appear to help provide individuals with immunity to malaria. Excising such genes from the human gene pool in the effort to eliminate human disease could backfire with potentially catastrophic results.

There is also the question of how and when society will ensure that the powerful technology of germline gene engineering will be limited to the treatment of serious human diseases.... [G]enetic screening of embryos is already being used for eugenic purposes, including sex selection; and genetically engineered drugs are being used for cosmetic purposes in a way that helps foster certain forms of discrimination. Who will ensure that germline therapy is not abused in the same discriminatory and eugenic way? Will those with under normal height or I.Q. become key targets of the future entrepreneurs of germline therapy? Other novel legal questions arise from the prospect of germline therapy, issues similar to those being asked in reference to advances in prenatal genetic screening. Do children have the right to an unmanipulated germline? Or, conversely, do they have a right to the best germline that genetic surgery can offer and money can buy?

As the debate around germline gene therapy continues, another form of human genetic engineering has already begun. This form of genetic manipulation does not involve sex cells, but rather those cells that do not partake in reproduction. These cells are called *somatic cells*. Engineering these cells is both easier and far less controversial than attempting to manipulate germ cells. Altering somatic cells triggers far less concern about eugenics, in that the cells being repaired or added affect only the single individual being engineered. They do not affect the inheritance of genetic traits. Early uses of somatic cell engineering include providing individuals with healthy or repaired genes that might replace those that are faulty and causing disease.

Though somatic cell gene therapy does not affect the genetic inheritance of future generations, there are still fears. Will individuals with "poor" genetic readouts —those predisposed to a variety of disorders or abnormal traits—be under pressure by parents, education providers, insurance companies, and employers to undergo gene therapy to remove their "bad" genes? Will the therapy be used "cosmetically" to add or eliminate nondisease traits, such as growth, skin color, or intelligence? Will victims of discrimination be pressured by societal prejudice to alter in themselves those traits society views as negative?

The early concerns about germline and somatic cell genetic engineering relied primarily on future projections of the potential abuse of the technology. However, two early cases involving misuse of gene therapy contributed significantly to the controversy that marked the early years of experimentation on the genetic manipulation of humans. The first scandal involving the nascent technology happened over two decades ago.

[In the next section of the original source, which is not reprinted here, Kimbrell discusses two instances of early gene therapy experimentation, one in 1970 and one in 1980, that were considered unethical because of the scientists' seeming lack of regard for the treated patients. The first case, which involved Dr. Stanfield Rogers, led to the first proposed legislation on genetic engineering and eventually provoked the National Institutes of Health (NIH) to produce guidelines regulating the use of human gene engineering. The later case, which involved Dr. Martin Cline of the University of California, also contributed to a promulgation of legislative and regulatory action on human gene engineering, including the establishment of a White House commission led by ethicist Alexander Morgan Capron and of the Biomedical Ethics Review Board to explore the ethical implications of human gene technology.—Ed.]

Throughout the 1980s, the criticisms of gene therapy continued. In 1983, Jeremy Rifkin organized a religious and scientific coalition against the use of genetic engineering on humans. The coalition and its signed statement opposing germline engineering were front-page stories around the United States. Unlike Capron's commission, the coalition's resolution on germline therapy was unambiguous: "Resolved, the efforts to engineer specific genetic traits into the germline of the human species should not be attempted." Its logic on prohibiting heritable gene alterations was also straightforward: "No individual, group of individuals, or institutions can legitimately claim the right or authority to make such decision on behalf of the rest of the species alive today or for future generations." The resolution, which was presented to Congress, was signed by a remarkable variety of religious leaders, including mainstream Jewish, Catholic, and Protestant religious organizations, as well as by many prominent scientists.

Six years later, an important and detailed religious statement on biotechnology was issued by the World Council of Churches (WCC). It contained a strong policy statement calling on all churches to support a "ban on experiments involving the genetic engineering of the human germline." The WCC was also deeply concerned about somatic cell gene experiments. The report called upon member churches to urge "strict control on experiments involving genetically engineered somatic cells, drawing attention to the potential misuse of . . . [this technique] against those held to be 'defective.'" The timing of the WCC statement could not have been more pertinent, for 1989 was to be the year that the age of human genetic engineering officially began.

PLAYING GOD?

On January 30, 1989, almost twelve years after the first demonstration on human genetic engineering, another such protest took place. The protesters came to a meeting of the National Institutes of Health Recombinant DNA Advisory Committee (RAC). Since publishing its guidelines in 1976, RAC had met dozens of times to discuss and approve experiments in genetic engineering. The advisory committee, composed mainly of scientists, held meetings that were usually staid affairs replete with lengthy discussion of arcane data and procedures.

This RAC meeting was like no other. There, demanding to be heard by the NIH scientists and genetic engineers, were fifteen of the nation's most prominent leaders in disability rights, many themselves suffering from disabilities. Additionally, several biotechnology activists were present to demand accountability of the scientists on the RAC. Many of the scientists appeared visibly uncomfortable at the prospect of discussing human gene engineering with people concerned about a new age of eugenics—and all under the unaccustomed glare of TV cameras. Those present knew that they were at a historic moment in the genetic engineering revolution, for this RAC meeting had as an agenda item discussion of approval for the world's first legally sanctioned genetic engineering experiment on humans.

The experiment involved genetic engineering but was not intended to be a cure. Researchers wished to insert novel genetic "markers" into certain immune cells taken from the bodies of terminally ill cancer patients, and then transfuse those cells back into the patients. With the help of the markers, they hoped to track which cells were working effectively and which were not. The procedure was to be carried out by the NIH's prime genetic engineering team of Drs. French Anderson, Steven A. Rosenberg, and Michael Blaese.

Minutes after RAC chairman Dr. Gerard J. McGarrity called the meeting to order, critics began to express deep concern that the NIH had begun the historic process of approving human gene engineering protocols while still doing nothing to put in place a review process on the ethical and legal implications of human genetic alteration. Jeremy Rifkin announced that his Foundation on Economic Trends had filed suit that morning, calling on a federal court to halt the experiment until the NIH committed itself to allowing the public a greater voice in decisions on gene therapy. Rifkin also noted that the lawsuit was based on the fact that the historic experiment was approved by a secret mail ballot, the first in RAC's history. He repeated the concerns he and other demonstrators had expressed over a decade before: "Genetic engineering raises unparalleled ethical and social questions for the human race. They cannot be ignored by the NIH. If we are not careful we will find ourselves in a world where the disabled, minorities, and workers will be genetically engineered." Another protesting voice at the meeting was Evan Kemp, then Commissioner of the Equal Opportunity Commission (EEOC), and himself disabled:

> The terror and risk that genetic engineering holds for those of us with disabilities are well grounded in recent events.... Our society seem to have an aversion to those who are physically and mentally different. Genetic engineering could lead to the elimination of the rich diversity in our peoples. It is a real and frightening threat.

Those present asked the RAC to set up an outside review board for human genetic engineering experiments that would include experts in the rights of minorities, workers, and the disabled. They insisted that the RAC scientists, though astute on advances in genetics, were no experts in the public policy implications of their work. "This group cannot play God when it comes to deciding what genes should be engineered in and out of individual patients," Rifkin said during heated arguments with members of the committee. "What will be the criteria for good or bad genes? Who will decide what genes, and which people, will be engineered?" he continued. "The people in this room are just not qualified to raise these monumental social issues. You're just not going to be able to maintain that control of power within a small group. We need to broaden this group." A few members of the RAC board became belligerent, denying, sometimes angrily, the suggestion that they lacked the expertise to oversee the larger social and political implications of their work. Others simply ignored the proposal. When the vote came, the RAC board unanimously (twenty in favor, three abstentions) turned down the proposal to set up a public policy review committee.

The RAC critics lost the NIH vote, but they won the battle in court. On May 6, the NIH settled the law case filed against the NIH, agreeing to immediately make changes in the RAC guidelines that would forbid mail or secret ballots and would also provide more review for gene therapy experiments. The legal settlement cleared the way for the first legally sanctioned gene engineering experiment on humans. The gene "marker" experiment took place a few days later, on May 22, 1989.

CLAIMING IMMUNITY

The second gene experiment on humans was performed just over a year after the first. It was the first official attempt to use somatic cell human gene engineering as a therapy for disease. On September 14, 1990, a four-year-old girl from Cleveland with the immune disorder popularly known as the "bubble boy syndrome" was injected with a billion cells into which a new gene had been inserted. The girl was born without the gene that controls successful functioning of certain immune cells called T lymphocytes. The rare condition (it affects only about twenty children worldwide), known as adenosine deaminase (ADA) deficiency, leaves victims helpless in the face of disease and infection. Many children suffering from ADA deficiency have been kept alive by isolating them in a germ-free capsule, as was "David," the famous "Boy in the Bubble" at Baylor College of Medicine in Houston, Texas.

Dr. French Anderson and a team at NIH intravenously infused the child with blood cells containing the missing ADA gene in hope that it would help her recover normal functioning of her immune system. On the surface the medical procedure looked little different from a normal blood transfusion. The procedure, which took place in the Pediatric Intensive Care Unit of the Clinical Center of NIH, in Bethesda, Maryland, lasted twenty-eight minutes. One hour later the young patient was wandering around the hospital playroom, eating M&Ms.

The young girl who had become the first human gene therapy patient to be legally engineered with human genes became something of a celebrity, as did Dr. Anderson. The media reported the historic occasion in glowing terms. Soon reporters were writing about "Dr. Anderson's Gene Machine." After some initial reports of success, it was not uncommon to hear that genetic engineering had cured the "bubble boy syndrome." A second patient began gene treatment in January 1991. It was hard to imagine a more altruistic beginning for a technological development that so many had feared as the beginning of a new eugenic movement.

The experiment had its dark side, however, including some unfortunate parallels with Rogers's scandalous experiments on children in the early 1970s. A careful examination revealed that Anderson's procedure may have been more hype than cure. The "bubble boy syndrome" cases were now a misnomer:

None of the handful of existent cases required the bubble to protect the immunologically impaired children from disease. Since the mid-1980s, these children were being adequately treated with a new drug therapy. Anderson, however, had started his research into ADA before the drug therapy was available. Many felt that he continued on with his protocol more out of stubbornness and ambition than medical necessity. Months before the experiment took place, members of the Human Genome Subcommittee had openly questioned Anderson on the rationale for subjecting children to the risks of gene therapy when they were already being treated successfully. So concerned were the RAC members about the effectiveness of Anderson's therapy that they restricted Anderson and his team to working only with patients who were already receiving the drug therapy. This in turn led to the question of how Anderson could accurately assess the results of his experiment. One scientist noted that it would be a little like attempting to assess the results of aspirin on a patient who was being treated with antibiotics.

Whether or not Anderson is using his patients as gene therapy guinea pigs, his experiments appear to violate the general bioethical rule that the expected benefits to an individual from an experimental therapy should equal or exceed the potential harm. The experiment's protocol was clear. The procedure did not offer children suffering from the genetic disorder a cure, but merely a supplemental therapy. The beneficial results of the experiment are at best marginal. A cure awaits improvements in bone marrow transplantation.

By contrast, the dangers to children from Anderson's experiment could be quite real. Anderson and others involved in inserting genes into patients use animal retroviruses to carry those genes. The retrovirus used in all early gene therapy experiments, including the ADA experiment, is one called murine leukemia virus (MuLV). It is a retrovirus obtained from mice. Anderson engineers the ADA gene into the retrovirus and then injects the gene package into a patient. Once inside the patient, the retrovirus invades cells and drops off the genes. Genetic engineers like Anderson attempt to render these carrier retroviruses harmless, but there are still concerns that these viruses could cause cancer or other serious disease in patients. Except in the case of Anderson's ADA experiments, MuLV had only been approved for use in terminally ill patients in whom the retrovirus could do little additional harm. Yet Anderson used this suspect retrovirus on children who were living relatively normal lives with potentially long life spans ahead of them.

In December 1991, less than a year after Anderson began genetically engineering his second patient, an unsettling report was made public. A researcher, Arthur Nienhaus, described his discovery that the MuLV virus had caused cancer in primate. The researcher suspects that the cancer may have been caused by a contaminant that leaked into the virus during production. Anderson and others were quick to note that they used a different system to produce their MuLV, one less prone to contamination. However, the discovery bolsters the view that much more needs to be learned before MuLV is widely used as a gene therapy tool.

In a rare demonstration of scientific breaking of ranks, several fellow genetic engineers openly expressed their displeasure with the Anderson experiment. One gene therapy expert called the Anderson procedures "absolutely crazy." Dr. Arthur Bank, professor of medicine and human genetics at Columbia University, charged that gene therapy researchers at NIH were driven by ambition and not by good science. "The main impetus [for the ADA experiment] is the need for French Anderson to be the first to do gene therapy in man.... This may turn out to be bad news for all of us," Bank told a genetics conference within a week after the experiment had started. Dr. Stuart Orkin, professor of pediatric medicine at Harvard Medical School, noted, "A large number of scientists believe the experiment is not well founded scientifically.... I'm quite surprised that there hasn't been more of an outcry against the experiment by scientists who are completely objective." Dr. Richard Mulligan, a pioneer in gene therapy work and a member of the RAC board—the only one who voted against the experiment—was more direct. "If I had a daughter, no way I'd let her get near these guys if she had that defect."

Anderson has more than his experiments to defend. Critics of the approvals of the first gene therapy experiments also point out that over a five-year period, Anderson has almost singlehandedly pioneered delivering federally funded human gene engineering research to a private company with which he is a collaborator. In 1987, Anderson did what many viewed as "scientifically unthinkable" when he joined forces with venture capitalist Wallace Steinberg to help build a human gene engineering company, Genetics Therapy, Inc. (GTI), a company one observer has called the "ultimate body shop."

Steinberg had long headed the venture capital arm of Johnson & Johnson and was looking for a new market challenge in what promised to be the cutting-edge industry of the future—human genetic engineering. Traditionally, government scientists have regarded joining forces with private investors as unseemly if not unethical. Anderson's relationship to human gene engineering entrepreneurs has cast a shadow over both the science and the procedures that led to the approval of the first of several human gene therapy experiments. Concerns about conflict of interest were heightened in late 1990 when GTI hired former NIH/RAC chairman Gerard McGarrity. McGarrity had been a leading supporter of GTI's and Anderson's gene therapy experiments, and as chairman of RAC had helped shepherd the therapy proposals through the NIH approval process. In 1991, GTI's numerous maneuvers paid off: Sandoz Pharma, Ltd., one of the world's major multinational companies, bought $10 million of GTI stock and agreed to provide $13.5 million over the subsequent three years in project funding. GTI ended 1991 with cash and marketable securities of $20.8 million.

Human gene engineering is progressing quickly. Currently, over a dozen somatic cell gene engineering experiments are ongoing on three continents. Numerous other gene engineering protocols are being developed for approval in the near future. Large-scale use of gene engineering to cure disease or cosmetically change individuals is still several years away; nevertheless, the scandal, ambition, and moral blindness that have characterized the early history of human genetic engineering set a profoundly disturbing precedent for the future.

Moreover, many of the protections against abuses in the use of gene technology put in place in the 1980s are fast disappearing. The Congressional Biomedical Ethics Board, established in 1985, was disbanded in 1990. Additionally, in 1991 Dr. Anderson and others successfully urged the disbanding of the RAC Human Gene Therapy Subcommittee. Finally, in the face of a massive influx of profit-seeking and potential conflicts of interest, the viability of RAC as a responsible regulatory agency of human gene engineering is in considerable doubt.

In the future we will be genetically engineering ourselves in numerous ways—applications of biotechnology with which our society is ill prepared to deal. As researchers successfully locate genes responsible for height, weight, and I.Q., there are still no restrictions that would prevent an industry from altering these traits through somatic gene therapy. Further, researchers are now more determined than ever to begin the first germline gene engineering experiments on humans. There is general consensus that such research will become a reality over the next decade. We have no national or international mechanisms that will prevent germline engineering from permanently altering our human genome, no restrictions on the unlimited genetic alteration of sperm and eggs, or the engineering of embryos. Despite continuing controversy, publicity, and massive public funding of gene technology research, the questions demonstrators shouted at scientists over fifteen years ago have still not been answered.

POSTSCRIPT

Should Attempts at Genetic Engineering to Cure Diseases Be Continued?

As Findeis makes clear, advances in gene therapy are constantly being made. For example, in October 1993 researchers reported that giving dogs afflicted with hemophilia (poor blood-clotting ability) a copy of the gene for the blood-clotting agent that they lacked improved the ability of their blood to clot. In March 1994 a similar approach repaired mice with an autoimmune condition similar to the human disease lupus erythematosus. In April 1994 researchers announced that a woman with familial hypercholesterolemia (a rare genetic disorder that is marked by very high levels of blood cholesterol and early death from heart attack) was given the proper version of her defective gene, and it reduced her cholesterol levels by 20 percent.

For some detailed discussions of how researchers are transferring genes into human cells, see Richard C. Mulligan, "The Basic Science of Gene Therapy," *Science* (May 14, 1993); Fred Levine and Theodore Friedmann, "Gene Therapy," *American Journal of Diseases of Children* (November 1993); and Mario R. Capecchi, "Targeted Gene Replacement," *Scientific American* (March 1994).

Despite the many tests of gene therapy now under way and despite many reports of successful therapies, many people and policymakers remain worried. In Germany, tough regulations have made genetic engineering research of any kind almost impossible to carry out. In England, a cancer research project was shut down in February 1994 because of fears that common cold viruses, which were being engineered to carry cancer genes, might escape and cause a cancer plague. The actual risk of that happening was almost zero because the viruses had been manufactured without the ability to reproduce in cells, but government regulators halted the project anyway.

Many ethical issues concerning genetic engineering are being widely discussed. See the editorial entitled "The Genetic Revolution: Despite Perfection of Elegant Techniques, Ethical Answers Still Elusive" in the November 1993 issue of the *Journal of the American Medical Association*. Also see Norman Fost's "Genetic Diagnosis and Treatment: Ethical Considerations," *American Journal of Diseases of Children* (November 1993).

In February 1994, scientists from several disciplines met at Rice University to discuss issues of public policy and ethics raised by genetic engineering. See Pamela S. Zurer, "Scientists Confront Ethical Challenges Posed by Progress in Biotechnology," *Chemical and Engineering News* (March 14, 1994).

ISSUE 14

Are Electromagnetic Fields Dangerous to Your Health?

YES: Paul Brodeur, from *The Great Powerline Coverup: How the Utilities and the Government Are Trying to Hide the Cancer Hazard Posed by Electromagnetic Fields* (Little, Brown, 1993)

NO: Thomas S. Tenforde, from Statement Before the Subcommittee on Energy and Power, Committee on Energy and Commerce, U.S. House of Representatives (April 1, 1993)

ISSUE SUMMARY

YES: Writer Paul Brodeur argues that there is an increased risk of developing cancer from being exposed to electromagnetic fields given off by electric power lines and that the risk is significant enough to warrant immediate measures to reduce exposures to the fields.

NO: Scientist Thomas S. Tenforde argues that the evidence indicating adverse health effects from electromagnetic fields is very weak. The chief effect, he asserts, is upon public anxiety, which is enough to warrant further research but not enough to require implementing measures aimed at reducing exposures.

Electromagnetic fields (EMFs) are emitted by any device that uses electricity. They weaken rapidly as one gets further from the source, but they can be remarkably strong close to the source. Users of electric blankets, before the blankets were redesigned to minimize EMFs, were among those who were most exposed to EMFs. People who use computers regularly are another highly exposed population. And, since EMF strength depends also on how much electricity is flowing through the source, so are people who live near power lines, especially high-tension, long-distance transmission lines.

Early research shows the difficulties of nailing down any possible side effects of EMF exposure. In 1979 researchers at the University of Colorado Health Center in Denver reported that, in a study of 344 childhood cancer deaths, children whose homes were exposed to higher EMF levels were two to three times more likely to die of leukemia or lymphoma. At the time, however, no one could suggest any mechanism by which EMFs could cause cancer, especially since the body generates its own EMFs of strength similar to those produced in the body by high-tension lines. Some other studies found similar links between EMF exposure and cancer; some did not.

y has been the curse of research in this area. Speaking on the effects of extremely low frequency (ELF) EMFs on cells in .ory (which was performed in an effort to find mechanisms by MFs might cause cancer), Larry Cress of the U.S. Food and Drug stration's Center for Devices and Radiological Health said, "Many iers have been able to reproduce their effects most, but not all, of the and we don't see a dose response, as with some radiation, such as x-ray. ne laboratory may see an *increase* in something in a cell when the field is turned on, while another laboratory sees a corresponding *decrease* when the field is turned on" (Dixie Farley, "The ELF in Your Electric Blanket [and Other Appliances]," *FDA Consumer*, December 1992).

In 1992 the Committee on Interagency Radiation Research and Policy Coordination, an arm of the White House's Office of Science and Technology Policy, released *Health Effects of Low Frequency Electric and Magnetic Fields*, a report that concluded, "There is no convincing [published] evidence... to support the contention that exposures to extremely low frequency electric and magnetic fields generated by sources such as household appliances, video terminals, and local powerlines are demonstrable health hazards."

However, at about the same time, Swedish researchers announced that a study of leukemic children showed an association between their disease and the distances of their homes from power lines. The researchers also reported finding that the risk of leukemia increases in adults with exposure to EMFs in the workplace. Critics have objected that the correlations in such studies are weak—that they could easily be due to nothing more than coincidence or that they might reflect exposure to something other than EMFs whose levels nevertheless fluctuate in step with EMF levels (perhaps herbicides used to control the growth of vegetation under power lines or vapors given off by electrical insulation).

Yet, the associations are there for scientists, as well as for journalists such as Paul Brodeur, to consider. In July 1990 Brodeur published a long article in *The New Yorker* in which he describes clusters of cancer cases that seemed to be linked to EMFs from power lines and reviews both the evidence and the responses of public utility representatives. In a later article, reprinted here, Brodeur summarizes his earlier report, adds further cases, and urges immediate measures to reduce what he feels are dangerous EMF exposures.

Thomas S. Tenforde, an EMF researcher at the Battelle Pacific Northwest Laboratories, reviews the evidence on links between EMFs and cancer for the Subcommittee on Energy and Power of the House of Representatives' Committee on Energy and Commerce. He argues that the evidence of risk to public health from EMF exposure is weak but suggestive enough to justify further research. Until more is known, however, measures to reduce exposure to electromagnetic fields are not justified.

YES

Paul Brodeur

THE GREAT POWERLINE COVERUP

In my Annals of Radiation about the health hazard posed by the sixty-hertz magnetic fields that are given off by high-current and high-voltage power lines (July 9, 1990) I cited evidence suggesting that a cancer cluster had occurred among residents of Meadow Street in Guilford, Connecticut. During the past twenty years, seven tumors—two malignant brain tumors, two cases of meningioma (a rare and generally nonmalignant tumor of the brain), a malignant eye tumor, an ovarian tumor, and a tumor of the tibia—have been recorded among children and adults living on that street, which is only two hundred and fifty yards long and has only nine houses on it. Because all seven tumors developed in people who were living or had lived for significant periods of time in five of six adjacent houses situated near an electric-power substation and next to some main distribution power lines carrying high current from the substation, I suggested that the cancer among the residents of Meadow Street was associated with chronic exposure to the magnetic fields that are given off by such wires. To support that contention, I cited the fact that during the past decade some two dozen epidemiological studies had been conducted and published in the medical literature of the United States and other parts of the world showing that children and workers exposed to power-line magnetic fields were developing cancer—chiefly leukemia, lymphoma, melanoma, brain tumors, and other central-nervous-system cancers—at rates significantly higher than those observed in unexposed people, and the fact that between 1985 and 1989 no fewer than twelve studies had shown more brain tumors than were to be expected among people exposed to electric and magnetic fields at home or at work.

At a public meeting held in the Guilford Public Library on August 20th, David R. Brown, chief of the Connecticut Department of Health Services' Division of Environmental Epidemiology and Occupational Health, and Sandy Geschwind, an epidemiologist with the division, declared that there was no cancer cluster on Meadow Street. To support their contention, they distributed a document entitled "Guilford Cancer Cluster Preliminary Investigation," claiming that "there was not a cluster of the same kind of tumors on Meadow Street," and that from 1968 through 1988 "Guilford as a whole did not experience a higher than expected number of brain cancer or meningioma cases." The document stated, further, that "mapping of these brain tumor and meningioma cases showed that they did not cluster in a particular area but were scattered throughout the town."

At the meeting, Geschwind gave a presentation in which she said that one of the brain cancers on Meadow Street was not a primary tumor but an esophageal cancer that had metastasized. She also said that the malignant eye tumor in question was a melanoma—a type of cancer that she claimed had never been associated with exposure to electromagnetic fields—and she assured her listeners that meningioma had never been associated with exposure to such fields. Toward the end of her presentation, Geschwind displayed a map showing the location of ten meningiomas and nineteen other brain and central-nervous-system tumors listed by the Connecticut Tumor Registry as having occurred in Guilford between 1968 and 1988, and told the hundred or so members of her audience—they included a dozen newspaper and television reporters—that the map proved that there was "absolutely no clustering" in Guilford and that the state investigation showed "no cancer cluster on Meadow Street."

However, the fact that Guilford as a whole—the town now has a population of twenty thousand five hundred, living in seventy-three hundred dwellings— did not experience a higher than expected number of meningiomas and other brain and nervous-system tumors during those twenty-one years does not address the situation on Meadow Street. Second, while there is no reason to doubt Geschwind's assertion that one of the two brain cancers among Meadow Street residents was

not a primary tumor, eye melanoma— the one in question was a malignant tumor involving the optic nerve, an extension of the brain—has been found to be "notably high for electrical and electronics workers," who are known to be exposed to strong magnetic fields. The finding appeared in a highly regarded study entitled "Epidemiology of Eye Cancer in Adults in England and Wales, 1962–1977," which was conducted by Dr. A. J. Swerdlow, a physician at the Department of Community Medicine of the University of Glasgow, in Scotland. Swerdlow reported his findings in 1983, in Volume 118, No. 2, of the *American Journal of Epidemiology*, which is published by the Johns Hopkins University School of Hygiene and Public Health, in Baltimore. Moreover, melanoma of the skin is one of three types of cancer listed by scientists of the Environmental Protection Agency in a recent draft report, "An Evaluation of the Potential Carcinogenicity of Electromagnetic Fields," as being prevalent among workers in electrical and electronic occupations, and thus associated with exposure to magnetic fields.

The conclusion of Brown and Geschwind that there is no cancer cluster among people who have lived on Meadow Street seems disingenuous, to say the least. As Geschwind noted, the Connecticut Tumor Registry recorded ten cases of meningioma and nineteen other primary tumors of the brain and central nervous system among Guilford residents between 1968 and 1988—a span in which the average population of the town was seventeen thousand five hundred. Thus the meningioma rate in Guilford is consistent with the Connecticut statewide incidence, of 2.6 cases per hundred thousand people per year—I was in error when I gave it in my article as one case per hundred thousand—and the incidence of other brain and central-nervous-system tumors in Guilford is also close to the number that would normally be expected. The fact that three of the twenty-nine primary brain and central-nervous-system tumors that occurred in Guilford during those twenty-one years developed among a handful of people who lived in four of five adjacent houses on Meadow Street that are situated near a substation and very close to a pair of high-current distribution lines, called feeders, together with the fact that a malignant eye tumor, involving a tract of brain tissue, occurred in a woman who had lived in a sixth adjacent dwelling, next to a third feeder line, surely suggests that there is a cancer cluster of some significance on Meadow Street.

Finally, and somewhat ironically, further evidence of cancer clustering associated with exposure to power-line magnetic fields can be found in the very map that Geschwind displayed in an effort to persuade the people of Guilford that no cancer cluster existed there. Among those listening to her presentation was Robert Hemstock, a Guilford resident, who, in January of this year, first sounded the alarm about a cluster on Meadow Street. When Geschwind held up the map, Hemstock noticed that three of the twenty-nine cancers on it appeared to have occurred along the route of a feeder line that carried high current from the Meadow Street substation to other towns during the nineteen-sixties, seventies, and early eighties, when the substation was being operated by its owner, the Connecticut Light & Power Company, as a bulk-supply station for large-load areas in Madison and Clinton —neighboring towns with a total population of about twenty thousand dur-

ing that period. He also noticed that an unusually large proportion of the other brain tumors on the map appeared to have occurred among people living along the routes of other primary distribution lines emanating from the substation.

After the meeting, Hemstock shared his observation with Don Michak, a reporter for the Manchester Enfield *Journal Inquirer*, who on August 23rd asked the Department of Health Services for a copy of the map. As it happened, Brown had displayed the map the day before at a Rotary Club meeting in Guilford, and told the Rotarians that he saw no need for the department to make any further inquiry into the incidence of cancer on Meadow Street. However, Health Services officials refused to release the map to Michak, on the ground that to do so might violate the confidentiality of cancer victims by revealing their addresses. The *Journal Inquirer* reported this development in an article by Michak on September 6th, and on September 10th it published an editorial pointing out that if the withheld map showed that the distribution of cancer cases in Guilford corresponded to the Meadow Street substation and to a power line running north from it "the public's concern might be overwhelming not only in Guilford but throughout Connecticut and even nationally." The editorial went on to question Health Services' rationale for secrecy, declaring that the map "is just a matter of dots superimposed on a map of Guilford; it apparently doesn't include names and addresses," and that "anyone seeking to use the map to find people who have or had cancer would have to knock on doors in the area of the dots on the map and ask such people to identify themselves." After observing that "the health department undermined its own rationale by displaying the map at the public hearing in Guilford in the first place," the editorial concluded by stating that if the department failed to make the map available "the public will have to assume that the department wants to protect something else more than it wants to protect public health."

In September, a reporter for the New Haven *Register* obtained a copy of the map from an assistant to the Guilford health officer. (The assistant later said that she had given it out by mistake.) The *Register* reporter also went to the Connecticut Light & Power Company's office in Madison and obtained a company map of the routes of existing high-current and high-voltage distribution lines in Guilford. On October 3rd, the *Register* published its own map—one combining the locations of the brain tumors and other central-nervous-system tumors with the routes of Connecticut Light & Power's distribution lines. It clearly showed that Hemstock's observation was correct—that an inordinately high number of the meningiomas and other brain and central-nervous-system tumors that had occurred in Guilford over the twenty-one-year period between 1968 and 1988 had developed in people living close to primary distribution wires.

This correlation notwithstanding, Brown and Geschwind denied that the map furnished any evidence of a link between the occurrence of such tumors and proximity to power lines in Guilford. "You can't use the map to show that kind of association," Geschwind told the *Register*. She added that such tumors could be found on streets near main distribution power lines because those streets were densely populated, and heavily populated areas would have proportionally higher cancer rates.

To the contrary, anyone who knows the addresses of the twenty-nine brain-and-other-central-nervous-system-tumor victims in Guilford, and follows the routes of the feeder lines and primary distribution wires leading from the Meadow Street substation, will find not only that there is a strong correlation between the occurrence of these tumors and living close to high-current or high-voltage wires but also that most of the tumors have not occurred in areas of notably dense population. The feeder that carried high current from the substation to Madison and Clinton was abandoned a few years ago; it ran across Meadow Street from the substation and proceeded east for about a mile and a half, to a point near the junction of Stone House Lane, South Union Street, and Sawpit Road. (Up to that point, the poles and the wires of the line remain in place, but they have been removed from the rest of the route—across an uninhabited salt marsh and the East River, which is the eastern boundary of Guilford, to a substation on Garnet Park Road, in Madison.) This feeder line ran for a mile and a half through Guilford, and it passed close —within a hundred and fifty feet or so —to only twelve houses. One of the ten meningiomas and two of the nineteen other brain and central-nervous-system tumors listed by the Tumor Registry as having occurred in Guilford between 1968 and 1988 afflicted people living in three of those twelve dwellings. All three are situated within about forty feet of the high-current wires. Moreover, a former Meadow Street resident who developed eye cancer at the age of forty-four, and has since died of it, lived for fourteen years in one of the twelve houses close to the abandoned feeder line. It is at 56 Meadow, and is situated only about thirty feet from the wires....

All told, seven of the ten meningiomas and ten of the nineteen other brain and central-nervous-system tumors—that is, seventeen of the total of twenty-nine—have afflicted people living near high-current or high-voltage power lines in Guilford. The total combined length of the lines is about forty-five miles, and along this distance some seven hundred and twenty-two out of a total of eight hundred and six houses are situated within a hundred and fifty feet of the wires. It seems obvious that in a town of seventy-three hundred dwellings the occurrence of this proportion of meningiomas and other brain and central-nervous-system tumors in residents of just over eight hundred dwellings strung out along some forty-five miles of roadway cannot be ascribed to heavy population—as the Connecticut Department of Health Services has done. It also seems obvious that people living in houses close to high-current wires and high-voltage transmission lines in Guilford are especially susceptible to developing meningiomas and other brain tumors. Particularly disturbing in this regard is the fact that in March of 1989—too late to be counted among the twenty-nine tumors listed by the Registry on the map that the Connecticut Department of Health Services displayed to reassure the townspeople of Guilford—a seventeen-year-old girl living in a house close to one of the high-current feeder lines was found to be suffering from an astrocytoma, the same type of malignant brain tumor that has afflicted a seventeen-year-old girl living near the same line on Meadow Street.

Instead of continuing to extend the presumption of benignity to power-line magnetic fields, the Connecticut Department of Health Services could require its Division of Environmental Epidemiology and Occupational Health to conduct a thorough study of the apparent strong association between the occurrence of meningiomas and other brain and central-nervous-system tumors, on the one hand, and, on the other, chronic exposure to the magnetic fields given off by high-current and high-voltage power lines in Guilford. Moreover, since Connecticut is one of the few states that have collected data on the occurrence of such tumors over a significant period, the department has a unique opportunity to perform an important service for public health nationwide by conducting a detailed investigation of the seventeen hundred and three meningiomas and the four thousand one hundred and two other brain and central-nervous-system tumors that have been diagnosed among Connecticut residents over the twenty-one years between 1968 and 1988, in order to determine whether, as is clearly the case in Guilford, a disproportionately high percentage of them have developed in people living close to wires giving off strong magnetic fields. If such an association should prevail throughout the state, meningioma and other brain tumors would have to be considered marker diseases for exposure to power-line magnetic fields.

* * *

Later in my article I described a cluster of seven brain cancers that had been reported to have occurred over the past fifteen or twenty years among the residents of Trading Ford and Dukeville—two small communities near Salisbury, in Rowan County, North Carolina—who had either worked at a nearby power-generating plant, owned by the Duke Power Company, or lived in a company village, Dukeville, that was situated close to the plant and adjacent to a large substation and some high-voltage transmission lines giving off strong magnetic fields. I suggested that officials of the North Carolina Department of Environment, Health, and Natural Resources' environmental-epidemiology section were remiss in not having investigated this brain-cancer cluster during the eight and a half months since it was reported in the Salisbury *Post* on July 12 and 18, 1989, especially since one of the officials, Dr. Peter D. Morris, had made a point of stating that such a cluster might be significant if all the cancer victims had worked in the same plant twenty years earlier. I also suggested that the health experience of the three hundred or so people who lived in the company village or worked at the plant, or did both, should be thoroughly investigated, because, in addition to the seven of those people who had died of brain cancer, four others, who simply lived near the plant or the high-voltage transmission lines radiating from it, had died of the disease, and because a preliminary inquiry revealed that there had also been at least eight deaths from leukemia, lymphoma, and other cancers among these people.

In a recent letter to the editor of *The New Yorker* three officials of the environmental-epidemiology section stated that they had evaluated the seven cases of brain cancer, in order to "determine whether or not they should be included in our study of brain cancer in Rowan County from 1980 through 1989," and had found that "two of the seven cases had metastatic brain cancer, a different type of tumor originating in another part of the body and later spreading to the brain." They went on to say that four of the remaining cases were excluded from their study because the di-

agnoses of two of them were made prior to 1979, an unconfirmed diagnosis of another was made prior to 1979, and one of the victims lived outside Rowan County at the time of diagnosis.

In the final report of their study, which is entitled "Rowan County Brain Cancer Investigation," the North Carolina health officials state that Rowan County did not have a significantly greater incidence of malignant brain cancer between 1980 and 1989 than each of the five surrounding counties. During a press conference at the Rowan County Health Department on October 25th, Dr. Morris told the Salisbury *Post* that brain cancer in the Trading Ford–Dukeville area during the ten-year period "was not studied as a separate cluster."

The rationale of the North Carolina health officials is as faulty as that of their counterparts in Connecticut, because they not only have failed to address the brain-cancer situation in Trading Ford and Dukeville in its entirety but also have submerged the small part they did address in the larger study of Rowan County. In order to understand how flawed their investigation has been, one must remember that the power plant, which was built in 1926, was partly shut down during the nineteen-fifties and sixties, and the eighty-six houses in Dukeville, which were built between 1926 and 1945, were moved elsewhere in 1955. Thus, in addition to the one case of primary brain cancer among Trading Ford and Dukeville residents that the North Carolina officials included in their study, and the four cases of brain cancer that they saw fit to exclude, other people who were exposed to the electric and magnetic fields from the plant, its substation, and its high-voltage transmission lines by virtue of working at the plant or living in the company village during the nineteen-thirties, forties, and fifties may well have developed the disease and died of it before 1979. By deciding not to include brain cancers diagnosed among residents of the Trading Ford–Dukeville area before 1979, the North Carolina health officials decided not to investigate the health experience of people who worked at or lived near the Duke Power Company plant—a decision that makes about as much epidemiological sense as a decision to study the incidence of gray hair in a given population after excluding all those persons in the study group who became gray more than ten years earlier.

* * *

Still later in my article I wrote that cancer among the student population of the Montecito Union School—an elementary school with four hundred pupils in Montecito, California—was "at least a hundred times what might have been expected." This was an error. The incidence of cancer at the school is considerably less than that, though far greater than it should be. Between 1981 and 1988, six cases of cancer are known to have occurred among children who attended the Montecito Union School: two children developed leukemia; three children developed lymphoma; and one child developed testicular cancer. As I wrote in my article, cancer is a rare event in children, occurring annually in about one of ten thousand children per year under the age of fifteen. However, as several readers have pointed out, the child-years at risk should be calculated at eight times four hundred students per year; that comes to thirty-two hundred child-years at risk. Six cases of cancer out of thirty-two hundred child-years

translates to 18.75 cases per ten thousand children per year. According to the National Cancer Institute's Surveillance, Epidemiology and End Results (SEER) data, the all-sites cancer rate for white children of both sexes, aged five to nine, between 1983 and 1987 in the San Francisco–Oakland area (the closest metropolitan area to Santa Barbara for which SEER data exist) was 11.9 cases per hundred thousand children per year. Thus the cancer rate over those eight years at the Montecito Union School—18.75 cases per ten thousand—is more than fifteen times the expected rate.

In their assessment of this cancer cluster officials of California's Department of Health Services' environmental-epidemiology-and-toxicology branch have maintained that magnetic-field levels at the school—which is situated within forty feet of a sixty-six-thousand-volt feeder line originating at an adjacent substation—were not unusually high, and that there was no evidence that they posed a health hazard. The fact is, however, that magnetic-field levels measured at the school's kindergarten patio by Enertech, an engineering consulting firm in the Bay Area, were between four and six milligauss; that is, approximately twice the levels that have been associated with a doubling of the expected rate of childhood cancer in three epidemiological studies cited by staff scientists of the Environmental Protection Agency as providing the strongest evidence that there may be a causal relationship between certain forms of childhood cancer —chiefly leukemia, nervous-system cancer, and lymphoma—and exposure to power-line magnetic fields. (Incidentally, on February 26th of this year I measured the magnetic fields at the kindergarten patio of the Montecito Union School, and found them to be about the same as those reported by Enertech.) It is also a fact that the magnetic-field levels at the kindergarten patio are at least equal to, and, for the most part, greater than, the exposure levels of forty-five hundred New York Telephone Company cable splicers, in whom cancer of all types—particularly leukemia—has been found to be higher than expected.

California health officials decided not to include the case of testicular cancer, which occurred in a second-grader, in their assessment of the cancer hazard at the Montecito Union School, and that decision seems arbitrary, in the light of the fact that cancer of all types was elevated in the childhood-cancer studies cited by the E.P.A. and also in the study of the telephone-cable splicers. It seems all the more arbitrary in the light of SEER data that estimate the chances of a seven- or eight-year-old child's developing testicular cancer to be nearly zero in one hundred thousand children per year. Also disturbing is the fact that since the publication of my article a teacher's aide with several years' experience in the kindergarten of the Montecito Union School has developed a brain tumor. This occurrence, together with the fact that four cases of leukemia have been reported among children who attended the Montecito Union School in the late nineteen-fifties, should encourage the California officials to conduct a full-scale investigation of the health experience of all the children who have attended this school during the past thirty-five years, just as the cancer clusters that have been found among the residents of Guilford and Dukeville should occasion in-depth investigations of the health experience of all the people who have lived near high-voltage and high-current power lines in those communities over a similarly appropriate period.

While these studies are in progress, interim preventive measures should be undertaken to reduce the magnetic-field exposure of children in hundreds of schools and day-care centers across the nation which have been built perilously close to high-voltage and high-current power lines. That can be accomplished by rerouting such lines, or burying them in a manner that will prevent hazardous magnetic-field emissions. Needless to say, such measures should be supported by the parents of schoolchildren, by members of parent-teacher associations, and by officials of school districts, of city and state health departments, and of the federal Environmental Protection Agency.

NO

Thomas S. Tenforde

ELECTRIC AND MAGNETIC FIELDS

I am pleased to have been invited to speak to the Subcommittee on Energy and Power on the subject of the biological interactions and possible health effects of power-frequency electric and magnetic fields. The issue of whether an elevation in cancer risk is associated with exposure to these fields has sparked considerable scientific debate and public controversy. Both the social and economic implications of this association, if in fact it proves to be real, could be significant. Unfortunately, the information available at this time is not adequate to make an informed judgment as to whether there is indeed a public health problem. Epidemiological studies have provided limited evidence of a slight elevation in cancer risk among individuals who are the most highly exposed to power-infrequency fields, and laboratory research has yielded some intriguing insights on how these weak environmental fields could possibly alter the functions of living tissues. Nevertheless, we are faced with the puzzling fact that epidemiological studies have, in general, not directly linked exposure to power-frequency electrical and magnetic fields per se to an elevation in cancer risk, but instead, have provided only some limited evidence for an association based on surrogate measures of exposure such as residential power line configurations and employment in electrical trades. The confusion on this issue is confounded by the lack of strong laboratory evidence for plausible biological mechanisms through which power-frequency fields could facilitate the development of cancer or other health problems. Without a clear knowledge of a causal mechanism, it is not possible to judge whether epidemiological reports of an apparent association between power-frequency fields and health risks are credible.

[My] primary objectives ... will be to review the current state of knowledge on this subject, and to urge that increased Federal funding be provided for several key areas of investigation: (1) epidemiological studies that are more comprehensive in scope than those conducted to date; (2) the development and application of improved dosimetry techniques to characterize human exposures in the home and workplace; and (3) an expanded effort in laboratory research to elucidate whether mechanisms exist through which exposure to power-frequency electric and magnetic fields could produce adverse health

From U.S. House of Representatives. Committee on Energy and Commerce. Subcommittee on Energy and Power. *Electric and Magnetic Fields*. Hearing, April 1, 1993. Washington, DC: Government Printing Office, 1993. (Y 4. En 2/3: 103–9.)

effects. The level of public concern has grown to a point where the issue of health effects from exposure to common sources of power-frequency fields must be resolved in a timely manner. Without a significantly greater federally-sponsored research program than now exists, it is certain that there will be a further escalation in public concern over this troublesome issue, accompanied by a growth in the level of public resistance to the installation of new transmission and distribution lines needed to meet a continually increasing demand for electric power.

The electric and magnetic fields that will be discussed are those with frequencies of 50 or 60 Hz (Hertz, or cycles per second), which are used for electric power transmission, distribution, and consumer end uses throughout the world. Because 60 Hz is the primary frequency at which power is transmitted and distributed in the United States, the terms power-frequency and 60 Hz will be used interchangeably in this testimony.

Power-frequency fields have a very long wavelength in materials with the composition of living tissue, and they have energies that are far below the level that could break chemical bonds in biological molecules (by a factor of approximately 10^{12}). Because of their low energy, these fields interact with body tissues in a very different manner than various types of ionizing radiation (e.g., X-rays or gamma rays), which disrupt the chemical bonds of biomolecules such as DNA (deoxyribonucleic acid) and proteins. Another important aspect of exposure of the body to power-frequency fields is that the rate of energy deposition in tissue is far below a level that could produce significant heating effects. In this sense power-frequency fields are quite

different from microwaves, which can produce substantial tissue damage by thermal mechanisms. As a consequence of their extremely weak interactions with the body and their inability to break chemical bonds or heat tissue, we would not expect power-frequency fields to cause irreversible damage to the genetic information encoded by DNA and by DNA-protein complexes (known as chromatin) that are present in each living cell and control its functional and growth properties. As discussed in a later section, this expectation has been confirmed through laboratory research with cells and animal tissues.

Although power-frequency fields do not break chemical bonds, there are several other less severe mechanisms through which they can potentially alter the functional properties of living tissues at the molecular and cellular levels. Some of the types of interactions that have been examined as potential mechanisms of biological effects are the following: (1) Induced electric fields and currents in tissue. In accord with fundamental physical laws, both the electric and magnetic components of a power-frequency electromagnetic wave, which oscillate in space and time at right angles to each other, induce electric fields and currents in body tissues. . . . (2) Direct magnetic field effects. The magnetic field component of a 60-Hz wave exerts oscillating forces on magnetic particles such as the magnetite found in tissues of many species of animals, including the human brain. However, the strength of the field required to produce significant oscillations of mineral deposits such as magnetite are predicted from simple physical theory to be on the order of several gauss, which is a high level relative to most human exposure situations. (3) Resonance interactions. It has been proposed that fields with power frequencies could act in consort with the earth's static magnetic field (which does not vary with time and ranges from 0.3 to 0.7 gauss depending upon geographical location) to produce resonant motions of ions and larger structures within biological tissues. Although some experimental studies have been cited as supporting the existence of such effects, there are strong theoretical reasons to believe that they do not occur, as well as a number of negative findings in careful laboratory research.

The range of environmental electric and magnetic fields to which humans are exposed varies quite widely, depending upon the nature of the source, the proximity of an individual to the source, and the presence of objects that shield an individual from the field. The highest level of exposure to power frequency electric fields is associated with high-voltage power transmission lines and the generators and busbars present in electrical substations, near which fields in air as high as 10,000 to 15,000 volts per meter can be encountered. In the home or workplace, or near power distribution lines, field levels greater than 1,000 volts per meter are seldom found. At locations away from appliances and machinery, the levels of 60-Hz electric fields in residences, work environments, and public places are typically in the range of 5 to 50 volts per meter. The contribution of electric fields from nearby power lines to the total 60-Hz electric field measured inside homes and other buildings is usually negligible because of the shielding provided by walls, trees, and other structures.

The highest levels of power-frequency magnetic fields are found near the surfaces of various types of appliances (e.g., hair dryers, electric razors, massage units, electric can openers) and machine tools (e.g., electric saws and drills). The 60-Hz magnetic fields near these devices can reach levels of 10 gauss or more, which is about 20 times the strength of the static magnectic field generated by the earth. At locations away from appliances and machinery, typical values of 60-Hz magnetic fields found in the home and in most workplaces are in the range of 1 to 3 milligauss (more than one hundred times less than the magnitude of the static geomagnetic field). In certain electrical occupations, the average exposure level to 60-Hz magnetic fields can be somewhat higher, typically on the order of 10 milligauss. The 60-Hz magnetic fields near power lines range from a few milligauss for distribution lines carrying low currents to about 300 milligauss under 765-kilovolt transmission lines with a load current of 2 kiloamperes. Unlike the electric component of a 60-Hz field, the magnetic component is poorly shielded by trees, building walls, and many other nonferrous structures. Several studies have demonstrated that 60-Hz magnetic fields from power distribution lines can contribute to the total magnetic field level measured within a home.

In summary, the typical levels of 60-Hz fields in air to which humans are exposed on a routine basis range from about 5 to 50 volts per meter for the electric field component and 1 to 10 milligauss for the magnetic field component. These weak environmental fields induce electric signals in tissue that range from about 1 to 10 microvolts per meter, which is much lower by several orders of magnitude than the fields produced by electrically active tissues such as the heart, brain and muscles. However, it must be borne in mind that much stronger electric fields can be induced in the body during short-term exposures to the 60-Hz fields that emanate from high-voltage equipment, various machine tools, and several types of common household appliances. Brief transient exposures to fields with high amplitudes can also occur during the process of switching equipment and appliances on and off. The biological consequences of intermittent and transient exposures to relatively strong 60-Hz fields is not clear from laboratory research conducted to date, and deserves more intensive study both in terms of characterizing human exposures to such fields and determining whether these exposures have potentially adverse health consequences.

Several types of health effects have been reported to result from exposure to 60-Hz fields in residential and occupational settings, including an increased risk of miscarriage, birth defects, depression, and an elevated risk of cancer. Evidence for the first three of these health effects is relatively weak by virtue of the small number of studies conducted and the contradictory results obtained by different groups of investigators. By far the greatest public attention and concern has been focused on the issue of an increased cancer risk in children exposed to slightly elevated 60-Hz magnetic fields in homes near high-current power distribution lines, and in workers employed in various trades classified as electrical occupations.

Since 1979 there have been a dozen publications and reports that have examined whether an association exists between childhood and adult cancer risk and the configuration of neighborhood power lines or the proximity of residences to these power lines. Although there is little convincing evidence for an elevation in cancer risk among adults, five separate case-control studies have indicated that a statistically significant increase in childhood leukemia (by approximately a factor of 2) may be associated with residing near high-current power lines. Some evidence for an increased risk of nervous tissue tumors in children has also been presented. However, several of these epidemiological studies directly measured 60-Hz fields in homes and found only a weak, statistically insignificant, association between the measured fields and an elevated risk of childhood cancer.

In the last 10 years more than three dozen epidemiological studies have been conducted to determine whether a link exists between working in electrical occupations and an elevated risk of cancer. The majority of these studies have indicated that occupational exposure to 60-Hz fields may be associated with an elevated cancer risk, primarily leukemia, nervous tissue tumors and male breast cancer. Again, however, there is little evidence to directly relate the strength of the average fields to which these workers are exposed and their risk of cancer.

On the basis of studies conducted to date, there is only suggestive evidence of an association between exposure to 60-Hz fields and cancer risk, with the most strongly correlated variables being power line configuration and job title rather than actual strength of the fields in residential or occupational settings. Several alternative explanations could be given for these results: (1) power-frequency fields per se may not be causally linked to cancer risk; (2) surrogate measures of exposure such as power line configurations and job titles may be better predictors of historical exposures to 60-Hz fields than are present day field measurements carried out over a short time interval (minutes to days); (3) surrogate measures of exposure may actually be serving as indicators of exposure to cancer-causing agents such as chemicals in the home or workplace, and 60-Hz fields themselves may not be the biologically active factors; and (4) measurements of average 60-Hz fields conducted to date may not have captured the relevant aspects of exposure to electric and magnetic fields (for example, high-amplitude transient exposures to fields from power tools or personal appliances have generally not been recorded). The uncertainty in the interpretation of epidemiological results obtained to date is further increased by a number of deficiencies in the way these studies were conducted, including (1) a failure to control adequately for confounding variables (such as exposure to hazardous chemicals, etc.) In many of the studies, (2) the use of poor study designs and data collection methods that could have introduced selection bias among the case and control subjects, and (3) weak statistical methods of data analysis were used in a number of studies, which could have resulted in false positive outcomes.

Although the majority of published results to date indicate the existence of a small elevation in cancer risk among the most highly exposed individuals, there is not a convincing body of evidence linking this risk to 60-Hz electric and magnetic fields per se. However, there is a compelling need to perform a more detailed characterization of human exposures to these fields, especially transient exposures to strong fields from electrical devices. Equally important is the need to perform large-scale epidemiological studies that avoid biases in the method of data collection and that control for the influence of confounding factors such as exposure to cancer-causing chemicals in the home or workplace.

Research over the past several decades, and particularly since the mid-1970's, has provided extensive information on biological responses to power-frequency electric and magnetic fields. Although the majority of these studies have failed to find significant adverse effects, several phenomena have been observed at relatively high levels of exposure typical of fields associated with power transmission lines and certain types of appliances and machinery. Among the responses to 60-Hz fields observed in animal experiments have been small, and generally reversible, changes in the functional properties of electrically active tissues. For example, acute effects on the visual system, alterations in brain electrical activity, and small changes in heart rate have been reported in studies on laboratory animals and human subjects under carefully controlled exposure conditions. Changes in hormone biosynthesis patterns, especially melatonin production by the pineal gland, have also been reported to occur in response to both electric and magnetic fields. All of these effects are associated with relatively high levels of exposure, close to the highest levels to which humans are generally exposed, and exhibit complete reversibility following termination of the exposure. The health implications of small effects of power-frequency fields on electrically active tissues or hormone systems are not clear from studies conducted to date, although changes in hormone balance can produce secondary effects that would facilitate the development of cancer (e.g., suppression of the immune system and increases in the levels of hormones that stimulate the proliferation of cancer cells).

A large number of studies have also demonstrated effects of power-frequency fields on cell growth and functional properties, including the synthesis of macromolecules such as DNA and proteins and the uptake into cells of biologically important ions such as calcium. Nearly all of these studies have been conducted with isolated cells and tissue preparations grown in tissue culture (in vitro), although there is evidence for the stimulation of cell growth in vivo as a basis for the successful clinical treatment of bone fractures using electromagnetic fields. Estimates of the strength of power-frequency electric fields required to produce effects on cellular metabolism, growth, and functional properties have varied widely depending upon the types of cells and tissues used for the study and the biological end points that were examined. However, there is a growing body of evidence that power-frequency fields exceeding approximately 1 to 100 millivolts per meter in the solution that bathes in vitro cell and tissue preparations can produce effects on ion balance and the biosynthesis of macromolecules. Fields of this strength are higher by a factor of at least 100 than those induced in body tissues as a result of exposure to typical environmental 60-Hz fields present in air. However, they are within the range of tissue electric fields induced by the highest levels of human exposures to fields from transmission lines and various types of machinery and appliances.

The biological basis for effects of power-frequency fields on the functional and growth properties of cells is an active area of research that has led to some useful insights over the past several years. Evidence is mounting that power-frequency fields can influence various properties of the membrane that forms the outer surface of a living cell and controls its interactions with chemical and electrical signals present in the extracellular fluid. A number of laboratory studies indicate that extracellular 60-Hz signals can influence calcium ion binding to cell surfaces and transport across cell membranes. In addition, extracellular 60-Hz signals have been demonstrated in several studies to alter the functional properties of specialized chemical receptors that reside in the cell membrane and bind substances such as hormones that regulate cellular metabolism and growth. Such changes in membrane properties produced by extracellular 60-Hz fields would be expected to provide chemical signals that are transmitted into the interior of a cell and influence its metabolic and growth states. Evidence for effects of this nature have been provided by a number of laboratory studies....

An important aspect of laboratory research on the biological effects of 60-Hz fields is the application of information gained from these studies to the prediction of possible human health effects. As discussed earlier, the extremely low energy of a 60-Hz environmental field is well below the level that could structurally damage DNA and chromatin through the breakage of chemical bonds. We would therefore not expect these fields to directly cause genetic mutations that can lead to health problems such as birth defects and cancer. This expectation has been confirmed in a large number of laboratory studies in which it has been demonstrated that high-intensity 60-Hz fields do not alter the structure of DNA or chromosomes, nor do they initiate cancer in laboratory animals. It has been proposed, however, that the effects of 60-Hz fields on biosynthesis and cell growth... could promote the development of tumors once they are initiated by spontaneous mutations or cancer-causing agents such as ionizing radiation or toxic chemicals that damage DNA and produce genetic mutations. This "tumor promotion" hypothesis for the possible action of 60-Hz fields has gained some support from at least two lines of evidence: (1) Several of the membrane interactions of power-frequency fields and the resultant changes in ion balance and metabolism in cells are similar to effects produced by chemicals such as phorbol esters that are known to promote tumor development. (2) Two recent laboratory studies with rodents have indicated that exposure to power-frequency magnetic fields may accelerate cancer development from pre-initiated cells in a manner similar to chemical tumor promoters. Both of these studies used high field levels (2 and 20 gauss) that are in the upper range of field levels to which humans are exposed, and no effort has yet been made to determine the minimum field level that produces a tumor-promoting effect. It should also be noted that in one of these studies an accelerated growth of skin tumors in mice was observed only when exposure to a 60-Hz field was accompanied by the simultaneous application of a chemical cancer promoter, which is a complex and poorly understood biological phenomenon referred to as "tumor co-promotion."

Although the results of several laboratory studies are consistent with the hypothesis that environmental 60-Hz fields could increase cancer risk through a tumor-promoting or co-promoting effect, the data are much too preliminary to form a strong basis for this hypothesis. A great deal of additional research must be carried out in an effort to replicate and to extend the initial results of animal cancer studies. In addition, further research is needed to elucidate the molecular mechanisms through which power-frequency fields could influence the functional and growth properties of cells and organized tissues. Until the state of knowledge of how these fields affect biological systems has advanced well beyond what we know today, it must remain an open question as to whether biologically plausible mechanisms exist to explain a causal role for environmental electric and magnetic fields in the development of cancer or other health disorders.

A sufficiently large body of suggestive information has been obtained in both epidemiological studies and laboratory research to merit an expanded scientific program funded by both Federal and private sector sources to clarify the issue of whether exposure to environmental levels of power-frequency fields increases the risk of cancer or other health problems. Despite the weak evidence obtained to date, public concern over the possible health effects of fields from power lines and other common sources has grown to the point where significant economic impacts are becoming evident. These impacts result from (1) cancellation and delays in the installation of cost-effective power transmission lines; (2) costly efforts to minimize exposures to 60-Hz fields through the rerouting, reconfiguration, or burying of power lines and the installation of shielding materials in buildings, tools and appliances, office machines, and other equipment; (3) the decline in value of properties near high-voltage power lines; and (4) the costs of litigation related to the siting of power lines and claims of adverse health effects from exposure to fields emitted by power lines and various devices.

Social impacts are also becoming evident through an increasing tendency among members of the public to avoid or minimize their exposures to 60-Hz fields from power lines, household appliances, and other devices. Manufacturers have attempted to keep pace with this trend by implementing design changes in business machines (e.g., video display units) and household items (e.g., electric blankets) that reduce the user's exposure to 60-Hz fields. There is clearly not enough information at present to ascertain whether behavioral changes or technical innovations that mitigate exposure to 60-Hz fields are necessary. Only an expanded research program that advances our understanding of the biological interactions and possible human health effects of power-frequency electric and magnetic fields can provide the information we need to make rational judgments in the areas of public policy and individual behavior.

POSTSCRIPT

Are Electromagnetic Fields Dangerous to Your Health?

Around the same time that Brodeur published *The Great Power-Line Cover-Up,* from which his selection was adapted, a group of Danish researchers reported in the *British Medical Journal* that, of the children they studied, those with the highest exposures to EMFs (they lived 25–50 meters from the most powerful power lines) showed a slightly greater risk of developing all cancers. Critics objected that this association emerged only when the data were searched for correlations, a practice statisticians object to on the grounds that chance alone will always provide some positive correlations. Proper scientific practice requires specifying what one seeks—the hypothesis being tested—in advance.

In the same journal, a group of Finnish researchers reported a study covering 135,000 children in which "no statistically significant increases... in leukemia, lymphoma, and overall cancer in children at any exposure level were found."

Do EMFs pose a genuine hazard? If they do, the threat is not yet clear beyond a doubt (otherwise there would be no controversy). Unfortunately, society cannot always wait for certainty. Gordon L. Hester, in "Electric and Magnetic Fields: Managing an Uncertain Risk," *Environment* (January/February 1992), notes that just the possibility of a health hazard from EMFs is sufficient to justify further research into the problem. The guiding principle, says Hester, is " 'prudent avoidance,' which was originally intended to mean that people should avoid fields 'when this can be done with modest amounts of money and trouble.' " H. Keith Florig, in "Containing the Costs of the EMF Problem," *Science* (July 24, 1992), makes a similar point in his discussion of the expenses that utilities, manufacturers, and others are incurring to reduce EMF exposures in the absence of solid evidence that there is a hazard but in the presence of public concern and lawsuits.

These calls for further research were met when, in 1993, Congress asked the National Institute of Environmental Health Sciences (NIEHS) and the Department of Energy (DOE) to study EMF risks. It will be some time before much can come of this legislative request, but many research projects have been under way for years, and their results have been coming in regularly. Even as the NIEHS and DOE were beginning to plan their EMF risk study, some researchers were reporting at a meeting of the American Geophysical Union that magnetic fields could affect brain activity, thus perhaps showing that the body does respond to EMFs from electrical apparatus.

In April 1994 a group of French and Canadian researchers reported in the *American Journal of Epidemiology* the results of a study of 4,151 cancer cases among more than 220,000 employees of electrical utilities in France and Canada. News reports emphasized the researchers' statement that one kind of cancer, acute nonlymphoid leukemia, was significantly more common and seemed to be associated with increasing exposure to magnetic (but not electric) fields. However, it is worth noting that the researchers themselves said that they had not *proven* that EMFs cause cancer and, indeed, that they were unable to confirm the results of the Swedish studies mentioned in the introduction to this issue.

University of North Carolina epidemiologist David Savitz called the Canada-France study "one of the best if not the best study of this issue ever done," but he also said that "the results are not definitive or conclusive." He had hoped that research he had under way would provide more satisfying answers. See "Canada-France EMF Study Inconclusive," *Science* (April 8, 1994). However, the results of Savitz's research, which appear in the *Journal of the National Cancer Institute* (June 15, 1994), indicate that a link between EMFs and breast cancer is, in Savitz's own words, "tenuous" and "awfully tentative."

So far, the jury remains out. Researchers may never provide a definitive verdict on EMF risks. The question is, then, What should society do in the face of weak, uncertain, and even contradictory data? Can society afford to conclude that there is no hazard? Or must people redesign equipment and relocate power lines and homes with little justification but their fear that there *might* be a real hazard?

ISSUE 15

Are Irradiated Foods Safe to Eat?

YES: Andrzej E. Olszyna-Marzys, from "Radioactivity and Food Preservation," *Bulletin of the Pan American Health Organization* (vol. 25, 1991)

NO: Donald B. Louria, from "Zapping the Food Supply," *The Bulletin of the Atomic Scientists* (September 1990)

ISSUE SUMMARY

YES: Andrzej E. Olszyna-Marzys, who works in a food and drug control laboratory, argues that sterilizing food by means of ionizing radiation has clear economic advantages and health benefits and that no hazards associated with the process have been demonstrated.

NO: Donald B. Louria, a consultant in infectious diseases, argues that the studies used to judge the safety of food irradiation are flawed, that the process destroys nutrients, and that irradiated food may prove to increase the consumer's risk of developing cancer.

Wilhelm von Roentgen discovered X rays in 1895, and 10 years later, the first patents were issued for the use of ionizing radiation (such as X rays) for destroying bacteria in food. Some 35 years later, during World War II, Massachusetts Institute of Technology researchers showed that ground beef could be preserved by exposing it to X rays. Further research followed in the late 1940s and 1950s, when government agencies that were concerned with nuclear technology sought to demonstrate how atomic energy could be used to promote human welfare, not just to destroy humanity (the prevailing image of nuclear technology at that time was of the atomic bomb). But in 1958 the U.S. Food and Drug Administration (FDA) decided that radiation sources intended for use in food processing were "food additives," so it required safety tests before irradiated food could be marketed.

During the 1960s, FDA regulations approved the use of radiation for a variety of foods—to preserve canned bacon, to kill insects in stored wheat and flour, and to inhibit potato sprouting, for example. However, when the army asked the FDA in 1968 to approve irradiating canned ham to retard spoilage in tropical areas, then–FDA commissioner James L. Goddard raised questions about the safety of the process, noting that laboratory animals fed irradiated meat had developed cancers and cataracts and had shown slower reproduction. Shortly after, the FDA rescinded earlier approvals of food irradiation.

Commercial interest in food irradiation stopped dead until 1980, when an FDA report based on new research said that the only possible hazard of irradiated food lay in "radiolytic products," or chemicals that form when radiation strikes chemicals that are normally present in food. The army researchers who performed the study found only six chemicals present in irradiated foods that were not present in nonirradiated foods. Furthermore, they found the chemicals only in foods that were exposed to very high doses (50 kilograys) of radiation. (A gray is a measure of absorbed radiation equal to 100 rads. A kilogray is equal to 100,000 rads.) The FDA report concluded that food irradiated at low doses (1 kilogray) was safe enough that it did not need to be tested extensively on laboratory animals.

In 1986 the FDA issued regulations permitting the irradiation of fruits, vegetables, and pork at doses of under 1 kilogray and of dried spices and herbs at doses of up to 30 kilograys and requiring that irradiated foods be appropriately labeled. In 1990 the FDA approved the irradiation of poultry at doses of up to 3 kilograys. The poultry industry welcomed this approval, for it had suffered bad publicity over bacterial contamination of its products. More recently, incidents of food contamination have similarly occurred at some fast-food outlets.

One might expect that any technological development that promised to put an end to problems like contaminated fast food, such as food irradiation, would be welcomed with open arms. However, only the food-processing industry seems to think that food irradiation is a good idea. Large portions of the general public have protested so effectively that many food manufacturers and marketers have refused to have anything to do with food irradiation; at least, in the words of Quaker Oats public relations director Ron Bottrell, "until consumer confidence in the process reaches a level where we feel more comfortable with it."

Should the public accept food irradiation as a valuable adjunct to traditional methods of food preservation? In the selections that follow, Andrzej E. Olszyna-Marzys of the Pan American Health Organization's Unified Laboratory of Food and Drug Control in Guatemala argues that the food irradiation process has many advantages and that no hazards have been demonstrated. The technique, says Olszyna-Marzys, is not the answer to all food preservation problems, but it has clear advantages over traditional methods and should be seriously considered in some cases. Donald B. Louria, chairman of the preventive medicine department at the New Jersey Medical School in Newark, New Jersey, argues that the studies used to judge the safety of food irradiation are untrustworthy and that the process appears to destroy the vitamin content of foods. He also warns that a growing food irradiation industry would create new environmental and security problems.

YES

Andrzej E. Olszyna-Marzys

RADIOACTIVITY AND FOOD PRESERVATION

INTRODUCTION

There are two completely different aspects of radioactivity as it relates to food:

1. *Preservation* through ionizing radiation, a beneficial utilization of radioactivity, and
2. *Contamination*, through exposure to radioisotopes from natural, artificial, or accidental sources, and measures used to protect food against such contamination.

The two subjects are quite different and should be discussed separately. This helps to avoid confusion about possible toxicologic effects.

However, it is necessary to note that such confusion does exist in the minds of consumers. Their resistance to accepting irradiated food has been, above all, a product of the emotions derived from the fact that many individuals consider anything associated with nuclear energy to carry with it danger of radioactivity. Furthermore, the terminology used to describe irradiation of foods is frequently confused with that employed to describe radioactive contamination, leading some consumers to believe falsely that they themselves could be exposed to radioactivity by eating irradiated foods, and also to fear that introduction of a new nuclear technology could raise the chances for accidents causing environmental contamination.

In the health field, radioactive isotopes are used daily for diagnosis and treatment, and medical and sanitary products are sterilized by radiation. Indeed, most of the facilities where food is now irradiated were originally constructed for irradiation of medical products. Like medical products, foods treated with radiation under prescribed conditions do not become radioactive.

Several methods are used for irradiating food. Their purposes, advantages, limitations, and control, the types of foods that can benefit from these methods, and any possible toxic side-effects they might have are discussed below.

From Andrzej E. Olszyna-Marzys, "Radioactivity and Food Preservation," *Bulletin of the Pan American Health Organization*, vol. 25 (1991), pp. 27–40. Copyright © 1991 by The Pan American Health Organization, Washington, DC. Reprinted by permission. Notes omitted.

FOOD IRRADIATION

Irradiation is a physical method of food processing comparable to methods such as heating or freezing. It consists of exposing food for a limited time to radiation that destroys microorganisms, insects, or vital processes such as germination.

Ionizing radiation's value for food preservation lies in its capacity to kill microorganisms that are pathogenic or cause adverse food changes and deterioration, to destroy insects, and to hinder germination of vegetable products, such as cereals, potatoes, or onions, while in the process causing little or no change in the food's temperature.

Furthermore, for this and other reasons, radiation has certain distinct advantages over conventional food-processing methods:

1. The food can be treated after being packaged and/or frozen.
2. Irradiation permits preservation and more extensive distribution of foods in a state of freshness or near-freshness.
3. Perishable foods can be kept longer without perceptible loss of quality.
4. Once a plant is installed, irradiation's low cost and energy requirements compare favorably with conventional food processing methods.

Irradiation of foods that lend themselves to this type of treatment has two principal benefits, one related to health and the other to economics:

1. By destroying certain human pathogens transmitted by foods (such as the almost inevitable *Salmonella* found in chickens), it makes food safer.
2. By prolonging foods' useful shelf life, killing pests such as insects, and

hindering plant germination, it slows the deterioration of foods, thereby increasing their availability.

Irradiated foods can be particularly useful for certain population groups, including:

1. People at high risk of contracting infectious diseases, such as hospital inpatients, residents of homes for the elderly, children in kindergartens, and (especially) patients with incompetent immune systems, and
2. People for whom weight and space are important, such as members of the armed forces, astronauts, air travelers, and campers.

Food irradiation also has certain limitations, one of the most important being the high initial cost of irradiation facilities —unless existing installations for irradiation of medical products are available for adaptation to food irradiation.

Types of Ionizing Radiation

In general, the following types of ionizing radiation are distinguished: nuclear particles—neutrons, protons (hydrogen nuclei), and alpha particles (helium nuclei); electrons (cathode and beta rays); and electromagnetic radiation (x-rays and gamma rays). Neutrons generate radioactivity in the materials that absorb them, while protons and alpha particles have too little penetrating power to be of practical importance in food preservation. This leaves x-rays, gamma rays, and electrons as types of radiation usable in food preservation.

Usable x-rays and electrons are produced by appropriate machines, whereas usable beta and gamma rays are emitted by the radionuclides cobalt 60 (^{60}Co) and cesium 137 (^{137}Cs). Cobalt 60 is manufactured specifically for use in radiotherapy, sterilization of medical products, and irradiation of foods. Cesium 137 is one of the fission products contained in spent nuclear fuel rods; it must be extracted in reprocessing plants before being employed as a source of useful radiation. At present, almost all gamma-ray facilities in the world use ^{60}Co rather than ^{137}Cs.

From the point of view of safety, it is important to regulate the level of energy applied in order not to induce radioactivity in irradiated food. For purposes of measuring emitted radiation, the international unit used is the electron-volt (eV), 1 eV being the energy acquired by an electron in moving through a potential of one volt, or 1.602×10^{-12} ergs. In practice, the unit used is the mega-electron volt (MeV), equal to one million electron-volts.

In addition, the effective dose of radiation absorbed must be considered. Originally, the measure of absorption employed for this purpose was the rad (*radiation absorbed dose*), 1 rad equaling an absorbed energy of 10^{-5} joules (100 ergs) per gram of irradiated material. The practical unit is the megarad (Mrad), equal to one million rads. However, the term used by the Systeme International (SI) is the gray (Gy), 1 gray equaling 1 joule per kilogram or 100 rads, with 10 kilograys (kGy) equaling 1 Mrad.

The isotopes commonly used in food irradiation (^{60}Co and ^{137}Cs) emit radiation with a maximum energy of 1.33 MeV. Since this is insufficient to induce radioactivity in foods, control of this variable in practice is only important in the case of instrument-generated radiation.

Wholesomeness of Irradiated Foods

The requirements necessary to ensure the wholesomeness of irradiated foods were discussed by the Joint Food and Agriculture Organization (FAO), the International Atomic Energy Agency (IAEA), and the World Health Organization (WHO) Expert Committee on Irradiated Foods in Rome in 1964. These deliberations indicated that x-rays were one acceptable type of radiation produced by instruments. An unedited report presented to WHO by the International Project on Food Irradiation in 1979 also showed that instrument sources of electrons operating below 16 MeV induced only radioactivity of a negligible and very short-lived nature.

On the basis of these two reports, at its last meeting in Geneva in 1980 the committee recommended including sources of x-rays and electrons on the list of acceptable sources of radiation. It also endorsed a statement contained in a report of the Joint FAO/IAEA Advisory Group on the International Acceptance of Irradiated Foods to the effect that radiation permitted for irradiation of foods should have a maximum energy level of 10 MeV if comprised of electrons and of 5 MeV if comprised of gamma or x-rays.

While irradiation with electrons (at energies up to 10 MeV) or gamma and x-rays (at energies up to 5 MeV) does not induce radioactivity, the need for toxicologic evaluation of irradiated foods is justified by the fact that irradiation can cause chemical changes ("secondary reactions") liberating potentially toxic products, and may also prompt undesirable organoleptic changes (of color, taste, and physical properties). The aforementioned Joint Committee meeting in Rome in 1964 adopted the view that such possibly liberated radiolytic products should be treated as food additives. It therefore concluded that the safety of irradiated foods should be confirmed by following procedures similar to those generally used to confirm the safety of food additives and by considering the foods one by one.

The nature of the chemical compounds induced by radiation depends primarily on the chemical composition of the irradiated foods. The concentration of these compounds generally increases with the radiation dose but can be modified in the course of the irradiation by factors such as temperature, the presence or absence of air, and water content.

The energy absorbed by the irradiated food is much less than that absorbed through heating. Therefore, it is not surprising to find that the chemical changes produced by irradiation are quantitatively much less than those produced by heating. For example, an absorbed dose of 10 kGy (1 Mrad) corresponds to an increase in temperature of only 2.4°C in a food that has the heat capacity of water. This amounts to about 3% of the energy needed to heat water from 20°C to 100°C.

The Joint FAO/IAEA/WHO Expert Committee meeting in 1976 concluded that the radiolytic products detected in a great variety of foods and food constituents that had been studied did not appear to represent any toxicologic hazards at the concentrations detected. The same committee also agreed that in dealing with a dose of less than 10 kGy (1 Mrad), the data could be extrapolated from one article in a given food class to related articles, and that if certain radiation chemistry and toxicology studies were pursued, it would be possible to apply purely chemical criteria in evaluating the wholesomeness of irradiated foods.

On the basis of these findings and new information, at its last meeting in 1980 the Joint Committee was able to formulate a recommendation on the acceptability of foods irradiated up to an average dose of 10 kGy. The following considerations led to this recommendation:

1. None of the toxicologic studies performed on a large number of different foods demonstrated the existence of adverse effects as a result of irradiation.
2. It was found that the radiolytic products of the principal components of irradiated foods were identical among themselves and were also identical with the products encountered in foods conserved by other preservative methods.
3. Feeding irradiated foods to laboratory animals, cattle, and immunologically incompetent patients did not result in any adverse effects.

In addition, the committee considered another initially feared possibility, that of microbiologic consequences of food irradiation, specifically addressing concern about possible microbial development of resistance to radiation, increased pathogenicity, and induction of mutations endangering human health. All of these matters were duly investigated.

The committee found no risk of inducing major microbial resistance to radiation except under special laboratory conditions. Nor was any case found in which food irradiation applied under proper operating conditions increased the pathogenicity of bacteria, yeasts, or viruses, or induced health-threatening mutations that were different from those produced by other food-preservation methods.

In sum, the committee concluded that irradiation of any food item with a total average dose of 10 kGy posed no special nutritional or microbiologic problems and presented no toxicologic risks; therefore, further toxicologic testing of foods so treated was not necessary. Nevertheless, the committee insisted on the need to analyze carefully any significant *change* [chemical transformation, e.g., oxidation] related to each particular irradiated food and to its effect in the diet.

Based on these findings and recommendations, up to the date of writing of this article some 32 countries had given limited or unconditional approval for consumption of more than 40 irradiated food products. In general, these foods are treated in multipurpose industrial installations that were initially constructed for radiosterilization of medical, pharmaceutical, and biological products —a technique that preceded commercial food irradiation by some 20–25 years. A total of 140 installations around the world are dedicated, at least in part, to these commercial applications.

Under the auspices of FAO, IAEA, and WHO, an International Consultative Group of Food Irradiation was established on May 9, 1984, to assist member states in evaluating and applying food irradiation technologies. The group's principal objectives are to evaluate the global evolution of food irradiation and to provide international agencies and their member states with a central point for consultation about application of this process.

At present, 26 governments, half of which are governments of developing countries, belong to the group and contribute to its activities. Between 1984 and 1989 the group met five times. In addition, on December 12–16, 1988, an international conference on the acceptance, control, and trade of irradiated foods was held in Geneva under sponsorship of the group's three parent organizations, the United Nations Conference on Trade and Development (UNCTAD), the International Trade Center, and the General Agreement on Tariffs and Trade (GATT).

It should also be noted that the FAO/WHO Codex Alimentarius Commission has issued a Codex General Standard for Irradiated Foods and Recommended International Code of Practice for the Operation of Radiation Facilities Used for the Treatment of Foods.

At this stage types of food irradiation offering the greatest health benefits would appear to be treatment of refrigerated or frozen poultry to destroy *Salmonella* and *Campylobacter*, treatment of pork to inactivate *Trichinella* larvae, and decontamination of spices and other food ingredients. Treatment of frogs' legs and frozen shrimp destined for export also has considerable potential for reducing public-health risks.

In conclusion, compared to traditional food treatment methods, irradiation has certain concrete advantages. However, the technique offers no panacea for the whole broad spectrum of existing food preservation problems, and so it should be seriously considered only in those specific circumstances where it offers clear advantages over the other methods.

NO

Donald B. Louria

ZAPPING THE FOOD SUPPLY

New arguments are boiling up over an old idea—irradiating food with ionizing radiation to kill microorganisms and prolong shelf life. The idea of exposing food to gamma radiation is over 30 years old, and in 1963 the Food and Drug Administration (FDA) began to permit the irradiation of wheat. Over the years, a few more foodstuffs such as spices and tea were added to the FDA's list of candidates for irradiation. But in 1984 the FDA started to approve irradiation of a much broader list of products which now includes meat, poultry, and fresh fruits and vegetables. Simultaneously the FDA has increased the levels of radiation that may be used. The FDA's recent willingness to allow most of the food supply to be irradiated—and at high doses—has triggered an acrimonious debate.

The amount of radiation involved is substantial. The FDA has approved a 3,000,000 rad dosage for treating spices, 300,000 rad for pork, and 100,000 rad for fresh fruits and vegetables. These intensities are millions of times greater than that of an ordinary chest X-ray (which is typically about 20 millirad). The announced goal of promoters of food irradiation is to obtain general approval for the use of up to one million rad.

Irradiation does not make food radioactive, nor has alleged radioactivity been at issue in the debate. But there is concern that foods processed by irradiation may contain radiolytic products that could have toxic effects.

The source of radiation is either cobalt 60 or cesium 137. The prospect of increased transportation and handling of cobalt and cesium—dangerous substances—has caused negative publicity. Some irradiation proponents say food processors could theoretically use as-yet-undeveloped linear acceleration techniques instead. But if food irradiation becomes commonplace any time soon, cesium or cobalt will be used.

* * *

The major objective of irradiation is to destroy microorganisms that cause food to spoil. For example, irradiating chicken should reduce the outbreaks of salmonella that are probably caused by careless or unhygienic methods in production and processing. Irradiating pork might reduce the already

From Donald B. Louria, "Zapping the Food Supply," *The Bulletin of the Atomic Scientists,* vol. 46, no. 7 (September 1990). Copyright © 1990 by The Educational Foundation for Nuclear Science, 6042 South Kimbark, Chicago, IL 60637, USA. Reprinted by permission. Notes omitted. A one-year subscription is $30.

limited risk of trichinosis, and irradiating turkey would diminish the number of episodes of diarrhea that result from eating undercooked meat. William McGivney, an advocate of the technology, asserts that "irradiation offers a means to decontaminate, disinfect and retard the spoilage of the food supply." Most opponents counter that adequate cooking and hygienic preparation will accomplish the same goal.

Promoters of irradiation emphasize that the shelf life of various foods will be increased. But these proponents have not produced any projections of the actual economic, or other, benefits of longer shelf life, especially in a developed country that has an abundant food supply. It may be easier to imagine that less developed countries might benefit if the shelf life of foodstuffs could be prolonged. But advocates have made no estimates of the extent to which better preservation would reduce world hunger, or of the cost of widespread food irradiation in less developed countries.

Irradiation is expected to reduce the need to use toxic chemicals as postharvest fumigants, but some evidence indicates that irradiated foods are more, not less, subject to infection with certain fungi.

* * *

At dispute in the controversy over food irradiation are the quality of the FDA's safety assessment, the loss of nutritional value that irradiated foods undergo, the risk of environmental contamination posed by irradiation facilities, and the possible cancer-causing nature of irradiated foods. An additional dispute revolves around the motives of the Energy Department, which has promoted irradiation and is the potential supplier of ce-

sium 137, a waste byproduct of nuclear reactors.

Safety. The FDA judged safety based on five of 441 available toxicity studies. Of the available literature, claimed the FDA, only these five animal studies were "properly conducted, fully adequate by 1980 toxicological standards and able to stand alone in support of safety."

But when these studies were reviewed at the Department of Preventive Medicine and Community Health of the New Jersey Medical School, two were found to be methodologically flawed, either by poor statistical analyses or because negative data were disregarded. One of the two also suggested that irradiated food could have adverse effects on older animals. In a third FDA-cited study, animals fed a diet of irradiated food experienced weight loss and miscarriage, almost certainly due to irradiation-induced vitamin E dietary deficiency. This study, which used foods that had been subjected to large doses of radiation, indicated that irradiated food suffered nutritional loss.

These three studies do not document the safety of food irradiation, and why the FDA relied on them is mystifying. The two other studies cited by FDA appear to be sound, but these studies investigated the effects of diets consisting of foods irradiated at doses below the current FDA-approved general level of 100,000 rad. Therefore they cannot be used to justify irradiation of foods at the levels currently approved by the FDA. Now, as the FDA considers adopting 300,000 rad as the general dosage level, the agency has not requested new studies, but is relying on some of the older studies it failed to include as methodologically sound.

Ethical and methodological barriers make it nearly impossible to study the effects of a diet of irradiated foods in human subjects. One small, controversial study carried out in India in the mid-1970s looked at the effects of feeding irradiated and unirradiated foods to 15 children with severe protein and total-calorie malnutrition. Five children were fed unirradiated wheat, five freshly irradiated wheat, and five ate irradiated wheat that had been stored for a minimum of three months. Children who had eaten freshly irradiated wheat had unusually high rates of chromosomal abnormalities in their blood.... No such changes occurred in the group that ate irradiated wheat that had been stored. Although some animal studies have supported the results of this study, it has provoked an acerbic debate. Clearly, the study has major flaws: the size of the sample is too small, subjects were not properly randomized, and statistical methods are unclear.

A more recent study of 70 subjects was conducted in China. In contrast to the severely malnourished subjects in the Indian study, all the Chinese subjects were healthy young men and women. The experimental group ate irradiated foods that had been stored for an extended period of time. (Also, the group's diet was essentially wheat-free.) Both groups—those receiving irradiated foods and the control group—showed some increases in chromosomal abnormalities during the test period. Those given irradiated foods appeared to have a slightly increased rate of abnormalities. While neither of these studies are conclusive, they should not be dismissed. If the malnourished are particularly vulnerable to the dangers of an irradiated diet, hundreds of millions of malnourished people could be at risk.

More studies on chromosomal abnormalities are necessary, but there are ethical as well as methodological problems in designing and conducting them.

Nutrition. There is impressive evidence that irradiated foods lose vitamin content, particularly vitamins A, C, E, and some of the B complex. The amount of vitamin loss varies from one type of food to another, but in general there is a direct relationship between the amount of irradiation and the extent of nutritional value lost. Data on foods irradiated with 100,000 rad cannot be relied on to predict vitamin losses in foods irradiated with 300,000 or 1,000,000 rad. Some studies indicate that cooking irradiated foods causes an additional, inordinate loss of nutrients. In addition, little is known about the nutritional effects of freezing and thawing food that has been irradiated.

Those who favor irradiation do not deny the loss of vitamin content, but often assert that these nutritional losses will not harm people who eat a generally nutritious and balanced diet. Others suggest that irradiated foods should be fortified with vitamins, or that the public should be urged to take vitamin supplements. In less developed countries, reducing the food supply's nutritional value would seem to raise a major ethical question. Asking the world's 800 million malnourished and 2 billion undernourished to make a possible trade-off between longer shelf life and less nutrition seems harsh, particularly before more complete information on the nutritional value of irradiated foods is available.

Environmental issues. Opponents of food irradiation have raised four interrelated environmental issues: the dangers of transporting radioactive isotopes to hundreds of treatment facilities, the environmental practices of those facilities, the danger of worker exposure in environments where irradiation chambers are frequently opened to allow foodstuffs to pass in and out rapidly, and potential security problems at irradiation plants.

If all the poultry in the United States were to be irradiated, hundreds of new irradiation plants would be needed. There are about forty plants of a size suitable for food irradiation already in operation. Most of these plants are used primarily to irradiate disposable medical equipment. In New Jersey, which has the highest concentration of these facilities, plant safety records are not encouraging. Virtually every New Jersey plant has a record of environmental contamination, worker overexposure, and regulatory failings.

A serious accident occurred at a Decatur, Georgia, cesium irradiator in June 1988. That facility was shut down after a cesium leak exposed 10 workers to radiation and contaminated medical supplies and consumer products. Cleanup costs at the Decatur plant have climbed to more than $15 million, and no conclusions have been reached about the cause of the accident.

Unlike major nuclear facilities, irradiation plants will be relatively small and are unlikely to be well protected. Opponents fear these plants will be particularly vulnerable to sabotage or terrorist attack and express similar concerns about the safety and security of large numbers of shipments of highly radioactive materials. If food irradiation becomes commonplace, hundreds of irradiation plants will need to have their inventories of cesium 137 or cobalt 60 replenished on a regular basis.

The cancer threat. The irradiation process produces unique radiolytic products whose chemical and toxic properties have not been characterized. In-vitro tests in the laboratory suggest that some of these products may cause mutations, and these tests have led critics of irradiation to contend that some irradiated foods may prove carcinogenic. But there are no substantial data from epidemiological studies on either animals or humans to support that contention. Unless the chemical properties of all the radiolytic products are identified, and animal studies using amplified doses are conducted, there is no way to prove that a cancer risk exists and, if so, whether it would fall within acceptable limits. Adequate evidence for prudent decisions on the cancer risk of food irradiation will not be available for some time.

The Energy Department connection. The Energy Department, through its Byproducts Utilization Program, tries to develop commercial uses for radioactive waste products. Creating a commercial demand for cesium, which is a waste product of both weapons production and civilian nuclear power, has been one of its expressed goals since the early 1980s. Energy Department memoranda indicate that the department's plan included pricing cesium so low that it would drive Canadian cobalt out of the market.

Some critics charge that the Energy Department has been even more devious. They claim that the department was less interested in disposing of cesium than it was in overturning the ban on reprocessing civilian nuclear fuel. These critics claim that the department calculated that widespread food irradiation would eventually deplete the available supplies of cesium 137. At that point, the irradiation industry would begin to lobby for the reprocessing of spent fuel, and the department could use the industry to overcome the political and economic obstacles to reprocessing nuclear fuel. Once reprocessing was permitted, the Energy Department could separate the plutonium in spent fuel, which it could then use in weapons.

* * *

There is no reason to adopt every new technology that is suggested. Ideally, food irradiation should be made to compete on a commercial basis with other technologies. If it had no disadvantages or dangers, the marketplace alone would decide its fate. Most food processors now think that irradiation is costly and less effective than other methods of preservation, and consumers are resistant to the idea of radiation-treated foods. But the adoption of food irradiation technologies raises questions of public health. Many local authorities have opted for alternative technologies. In Florida, the Citrus Commission/Department of Agriculture has chosen to use two other processes—fly-free zones and cold treatment. Hawaiian officials rejected federal funds offered to build an irradiation facility for processing papaya; instead, the papaya processor will use non-chemical treatments such as dry and steam heat or double hot water dips. Some biotechnological researchers are confident that recombinant DNA technologies will eventually create pest-resistant fruits and vegetables with extraordinarily long shelf lives.

If food irradiation is adopted prematurely, research on its health effects will be hampered. Widespread use of the technology will make it impossible to detect any but the most obvious of adverse effects, because it will be impossible to define a control population for purposes of study. This problem will be further complicated if irradiation levels are increased to 1 million rad.

Labeling is currently required to notify the consumer when whole foods have been irradiated. The label includes written notice and the international irradiation symbol, the "radura"—a stylized flower which has caused some confusion because of its close resemblance to the Environmental Protection Agency's logo. Prepared or packaged foods, foods prepared for restaurant or school cafeteria use, and foods which merely contain some irradiated ingredients are exempt from labeling.

While the FDA has approved wholesale food irradiation, other regulators are less eager. More than a dozen state legislatures, concerned about the environmental and health risks of irradiated food, have restricted its sale and distribution. Maine has banned both irradiation facilities and all irradiated food except spices. New York and New Jersey recently enacted two-year moratoriums on the sale or distribution of irradiated foods, and New Jersey has prohibited the "manufacture" of such food items. Other states contemplating restrictive legislation include Massachusetts, Pennsylvania, Minnesota, Oregon, and Alaska. Bills have been introduced in Congress to place a two-year moratorium on irradiated foods while the National Academy of Sciences reviews the health, environment, and worker safety issues. Great Britain has banned irradiated food, although legislation has been introduced into Parliament to overturn the ban. West Germany, Australia, Denmark, Sweden, and New Zealand have all banned or severely limited the implementation of food irradiation.

POSTSCRIPT

Are Irradiated Foods Safe to Eat?

Shortly after the Food and Drug Administration (FDA) approved the use of food irradiation for poultry, Jacques Leslie, in "Food Irradiation," *The Atlantic Monthly* (September 1990), wrote, "Most opposition...starts from the assumption that radiation, frequently a lethal agent, cannot possibly affect food in safe ways.... [T]he dispute thus chiefly pits experts who support food irradiation against laymen who oppose it. Instead of grappling with the details of scientific inquiry, the coalition of anti-nuclear activists, organic-food advocates, and holistic-health practitioners who compose the organized opposition to food irradiation habitually make startling but invariably hollow claims of conspiracy.... Of the hundreds of scientists in this country who have done extensive research on the wholesomeness of food irradiation, only a few have publicly expressed opposition to it, and the several other scientists who are actively against food irradiation are not experienced in the field.... [T]he preponderance of evidence refutes the opposition's claims." The article is well worth reading for its detailed refutations of several objections to food irradiation, including some mentioned by Louria. See also Richard L. Worsnop, "Food Irradiation," *CQ Researcher* (June 12, 1992).

Refutations have had little effect on those who oppose food irradiation, whose activities are covered in Larry Katzenstein, "Good Food You Can't Get," *American Health* (December 1992). Also see James Mason, "Food Irradiation: Let's Move Ahead," *American Family Physician* (April 1993), in which the author says that the opposition, "citing discredited research, [had] voiced unfounded fears often enough to make some consumers think twice." This fear is maintained, Mason notes, despite the fact that two years earlier Fritz Kaferstein, head of the United Nations World Health Organization, said that food irradiation "is a perfectly sound food preservation technology badly needed in a world where food-borne disease is on the increase," that the process had been endorsed by the FDA and numerous scientific groups and institutes, and that 36 nations had approved its use. For a review of the international regulatory status of food irradiation, see Donald D. Derr, "International Regulatory Status and Harmonization of Food Irradiation," *Journal of Food Protection* (October 1993).

The opposition was as vocal as ever in February 1994, when the U.S. Department of Agriculture (USDA) sought approval for the irradiation of red meat, and again in April 1994, when a New Jersey firm, Isomedix Inc., announced plans to ask the FDA for approval to irradiate beef. In both cases, the hazards of undercooked fast-food hamburgers—which in 1993 killed three children in the Pacific Northwest—were cited. Critics were also heard in March 1994, when the Maine legislature—which in 1987 had made it illegal to produce or sell irradiated food in the state—considered a bill that would have added Maine to the current list of 48 states that permit food irradiation. The USDA and Isomedix cases are still not settled; the Maine bill died in committee.

Is the issue of food irradiation one of public safety or of public anxiety? Most risk analysts say that it does not matter, at least from the point of view of those who are responsible for processes or products that provoke public concern. No matter how safe irradiated food may be, no one will build irradiation facilities, process irradiated food, or stock irradiated food in stores if the public refuses to buy the product. Those who try will go out of business. It is the public's *perception* of risk that matters and must be dealt with by educating the public, modifying the process or product, or turning to alternatives that are perceived as safe.

ISSUE 16

Should Smallpox Be Completely Eradicated?

YES: Brian W. J. Mahy et al., from "The Remaining Stocks of Smallpox Virus Should Be Destroyed," *Science* (November 19, 1993)

NO: Wolfgang K. Joklik et al., from "Why the Smallpox Virus Stocks Should Not Be Destroyed," *Science* (November 19, 1993)

ISSUE SUMMARY

YES: Virus researcher Brian W. J. Mahy and his colleagues argue that since smallpox is no longer a threat to human beings, there is no reason to keep potentially dangerous samples of the deadly disease alive in the laboratory.

NO: Professor of microbiology Wolfgang K. Joklik and his colleagues argue that there is no substitute for studying the intact smallpox virus to understand how it and other viruses work and that, therefore, the samples should be preserved.

The earliest known case of smallpox was that of the Egyptian pharaoh Ramses V, who died around 1156 B.C. Between then and the middle of the twentieth century, smallpox raged across Europe, Asia, and Africa in periodic epidemics that killed as many as 30 percent of those infected. In Europe in the 1700s, it killed 200,000–600,000 people per year. In populations that had never before been exposed to the virus (such as Native Americans before the arrival of the colonists), the death rate from an initial epidemic of smallpox went as high as 50 percent.

Fortunately, those who survive smallpox infection do not get it again. In fact, those who have been infected with related viruses, such as the cowpox (vaccinia) virus, do not get smallpox. These two observations have been the key to stopping the disease. In 1796 English physician Edward Jenner deliberately infected (vaccinated) people with cowpox in order to immunize them against smallpox. The process did not work perfectly, but it greatly reduced the death toll of the next outbreak of smallpox, and improvements were not long in coming.

One of the distinguishing features of smallpox is that, in order to survive, it requires a population of vulnerable hosts. That is, it must be passed from person to person indefinitely. If the chain of transmission is broken, the virus dies out. An effort launched by the World Health Organization (WHO) in 1950 to exterminate smallpox was based on this feature. The approach hinged on identifying new cases of the disease, isolating victims to keep them from passing the virus on, and then vaccinating everyone in the vicinity of the victims to ensure that there were no potential hosts.

Progress was rapid after 1967, when the WHO mounted a massive 10-year program to finally eliminate the disease, and 1975 saw the last natural case of variola major, in Bangladesh. (Variola major is the deadlier of the two forms of smallpox; the other, variola minor, has a death rate of around 1 percent). In "The Eradication of Smallpox," *Scientific American* (October 1976), Donald A. Henderson announced that the complete eradication of the disease was imminent. The last natural case of variola minor was in 1977, in Somalia. The last "unnatural" cases of smallpox occurred in 1978, in England, where a laboratory accident at Birmingham University infected two people, one of whom died.

In 1980 the WHO declared that smallpox was extinct ("The Global Eradication of Smallpox: Final Report of the Global Commission for the Certification of Smallpox Eradication," *History of International Public Health,* no. 4, 1980). The only traces of smallpox known to remain were samples of the virus that were stored in various laboratory freezers around the world. Most of these samples were soon destroyed or shipped to either the Centers for Disease Control in Atlanta, Georgia, or the Institute for Viral Preparations in Moscow, Russia.

The question of what to do with the remaining samples has been debated since 1981. Should they be destroyed to prevent accidental release or theft and deliberate release by terrorists? Or should they be kept and studied in case there is ever an outbreak from some unsuspected source, such as an animal reservoir, an infected corpse unearthed by erosion or anthropologists, a stored tissue sample from some long-dead patient, or even a nation's secret stocks of virus kept for use as biological weapons?

In the following selections, Brian W. J. Mahy, director of the Division of Viral and Rickettsial Diseases, National Center for Infectious Diseases of the Centers for Disease Control and Prevention, and his colleagues argue that any remaining samples of the smallpox virus should be destroyed because of its hazards and because any reemergence of the virus can be handled by stored vaccine. Wolfgang K. Joklik, a microbiologist at Duke University Medical Center, and his colleagues argue that the remaining smallpox virus samples should be preserved chiefly because of their value in research. Any hazards, they maintain, are either controllable or highly unlikely.

YES

Brian W. J. Mahy et al.

THE REMAINING STOCKS OF SMALLPOX VIRUS SHOULD BE DESTROYED

Smallpox (variola) was a human infectious disease that was endemic through-out much of the world for more than 2000 years (1). Case-fatality rates were frequently 20 to 40 percent in nonimmune populations, and over the centuries smallpox killed more people of all ages, classes, and races than any other infectious disease. In the late 18th century Jenner first showed that material from a cowpox lesion could protect against smallpox, and this finding led eventually to vaccination with vaccinia virus, resulting in eradication of the disease from the United States by 1950 (1).

The global eradication of smallpox formally began as a resolution of the Twentieth World Health Assembly in 1967, when more than 40 countries still had endemic smallpox, and ended successfully with the last natural case in Somalia in 1977 (1, 2). By that time vaccination of the general public had already been discontinued in parts of the world, and since 1985, all routine vaccination has ceased. In 1978, a photographer working at the University of Birmingham, United Kingdom, became infected with a strain of smallpox virus that was being studied in a supposedly secure laboratory some distance from the room in which she worked (3). Her death, together with the suicide of the head of the smallpox laboratory, sharply emphasized the dangers of continued laboratory investigation of viable smallpox virus during the post-eradication era.

In December 1979 the Global Commission for the Certification of Smallpox Eradication recommended that any remaining stocks of viable smallpox virus should be destroyed or transferred to one of four designated reference laboratories in the United States, United Kingdom, South Africa, and Russia. This idea was endorsed by the World Health Assembly in May 1980. However, by the end of 1983, all variola virus stocks in South Africa were destroyed and the stocks in the United Kingdom were transferred to the Centers for Disease Control (CDC), so that all smallpox virus was at the CDC in Atlanta or the Research Institute for Viral Preparations in Moscow. CDC maintains a repository of approximately 450 smallpox virus samples that originated worldwide, which includes collections from many different countries that

From Brian W. J. Mahy, Jeffrey W. Almond, Kenneth I. Berns, Robert M. Chanock, Dmitry K. Lvov, Ralf F. Pettersson, Hermann G. Schatzmayr, and Frank Fenner, "The Remaining Stocks of Smallpox Virus Should Be Destroyed," *Science*, vol. 262 (November 19, 1993), pp. 1223–1224. Copyright © 1993 by The American Association for the Advancement of Science. Reprinted by permission.

were transferred from the U.S. Army, the American Type Culture Collection, the National Health Institute of Japan, the National Health Institute of the Netherlands, and the Microbiological Research Establishment of the United Kingdom. The Russian collection contains some 150 smallpox virus samples from Brazil, Botswana, the Congo, Ethiopia, India, Indonesia, Pakistan, Tanzania, and the former Soviet Union.

With the development of DNA restriction endonucleases and cloning techniques during the 1970s, different orthopoxviruses were found to have characteristic DNA restriction patterns that could be used to distinguish smallpox from other potential human infections, such as vaccinia, monkeypox, and cowpox (4–6). Appropriate DNA restriction fragments representing the smallpox virus genome were cloned in bacterial plasmids, providing further specific reference reagents for the resolution of any future diagnostic problem involving suspected smallpox infections (7). Since 1983 such clones have been kept in a few laboratories in the United Kingdom, United States, the former Soviet Union, and South Africa, but because the cloned DNAs potentially could be used to create a smallpox-like virus by recombination with vaccinia or monkeypox viruses, in 1990 the World Health Organization (WHO) requested registration of all clones of smallpox virus DNA and restricted their use and distribution (7).

Because the smallpox virus DNA clones obviated the need for infectious virus for reference purposes, the WHO Ad Hoc Committee on Orthopoxvirus Infections resolved in 1986 that the remaining virus stocks in Atlanta and Moscow should be destroyed if no serious objections were received from the international health community. In addition, the committee recommended that smallpox vaccination to protect military personnel against the disease should be terminated (8).

Although smallpox was officially declared to have been eradicated in 1980, vaccination continued until recently for certain military personnel in a few nations. The continued existence of smallpox virus stocks in Russia and the United States was thought to represent a potential military hazard from any terrorist group that succeeded in gaining access to the virus. Recent political uncertainty in several parts of the world, including the former Soviet Union and its satellite countries, has reemphasized this danger. Destruction of the remaining smallpox virus stocks would eliminate this potential weapon, consistent with the aims of the International Biological and Toxic Weapons Convention of 1972.

Of course we cannot guarantee that somewhere in the world there is not another potential source of smallpox virus. For example, the corpse of a person who died of smallpox and was preserved in the Arctic permafrost, or a vial unknowingly retained in a laboratory, might still contain infectious virus. It is also possible that vials containing smallpox virus have been deliberately retained out of a misplaced suspicion of the motives of the U.S. and Russian governments. As long as work continues with infectious virus in Atlanta and Moscow, this may be seen to legitimize the holding of such stocks, and even continued work on smallpox, especially in the eyes of countries that may be engaged in the development of biological weapons. Destruction of the official WHO stocks would send the clearest possible signal to all countries that any work with live smallpox virus will from now on be regarded as criminal activity punishable by national and international authorities, and that the mere possession of such virus is illegal.

In an address to the World Health Assembly in May 1990, the then Secretary for Health and Human Services, Dr. Louis Sullivan, stated that technological advances now made it possible to sequence the entire smallpox virus genome within 3 years (7). He went on to say that after the completion of this project, the United States would destroy all remaining smallpox virus stocks held at the CDC. He invited the Soviet Union to consider the same course of action. In December 1990 the WHO Ad Hoc Committee on Orthopoxvirus Infections endorsed proposals from the United States and the Soviet Union to sequence the smallpox virus genome, and unanimously agreed that all remaining smallpox virus stocks should be destroyed by 31 December 1993, provided that sufficient sequence information is available, and serious scientific objections have not been raised (7).

Since 1991, molecular biologists in the United States and in Russia have completely sequenced the genomes of two strains of variola major virus (Bangladesh 1975 and India 1967), and by the end of 1993 a third sequence is likely to be available, from a variola minor virus strain (Garcia 1966). (Variola minor strains, associated with case-fatality rates of less than 1 percent, are mild varieties of smallpox.) The complete nucleotide sequence of variola virus DNA (9, 10) provides a valuable archival record. Although there is close sequence similarity to vaccinia virus DNA (11) over most of the central core region, the terminal regions display divergent sequences that probably encode proteins involved in the restricted

human host range and virulence that distinguish smallpox from vaccinia (10). In the unlikely event that a smallpox-like virus were ever to reemerge in the future, the nucleotide sequence information now available could be used in confirming its identity. Adequate stocks of vaccinia virus (smallpox vaccine) will always be maintained at CDC to prevent transmission of a possible smallpox infection should such an event occur at any time in the future.

Destruction of the remaining stocks of smallpox virus would represent the first deliberate elimination of a biological species from this planet. Whether humanity has the right to exterminate a "living" species is controversial, and since 1991, when the proposal to destroy smallpox virus was brought to the attention of American microbiologists (7), strongly held views have been expressed both for and against the proposal. However, after debating this issue, the American Type Culture Collection through its Board of Directors, the American Society for Microbiology through its Council, and the International Union of Microbiological Societies through its Executive Board have all agreed that the remaining stocks of variola virus should be destroyed by 31 December 1993.

During an open debate held on 11 August 1993 at the IXth International Congress of Virology in Glasgow, Scotland, a number of other arguments were raised against virus destruction. It was suggested that publication of the complete nucleotide sequence might allow a future scientist to recreate virulent smallpox virus, and therefore that destruction of existing virus stocks is pointless. This argument is not compelling. Even though smallpox virus DNA (186,102 base pairs) might be synthesized in the future on the basis of the published sequence, the DNA would not be infectious. Co-infection of cells with smallpox DNA together with a related poxvirus, such as vaccinia virus, might yield a virulent virus, but how would this be assessed? Humans are the only natural hosts of smallpox virus. It would never be morally defensible to confirm the infectivity and virulence of a newly created smallpox recombinant virus by deliberate human infection.

A second proposal in favor of retaining the virus was that further research on smallpox virus with new or as yet undeveloped techniques might shed light on mechanisms of smallpox pathogenesis and yield information of benefit to mankind. But where would these experiments be carried out? There are now millions of unvaccinated persons worldwide who might suffer terrible consequences if the virulent virus were to escape from the laboratory as happened in Birmingham in 1978 (3). CDC has a biosafety level 4, maximum containment laboratory that has recently been used to grow smallpox virus for DNA sequencing purposes, but an equivalent facility does not exist in Moscow. The CDC laboratory is now fully engaged with work on new, highly dangerous viral pathogens such as Lassa virus, Ebola virus, and the new hantavirus pulmonary syndrome, for which no vaccines exist (12). If indeed further studies on poxvirus pathogenesis are needed, they should be carried out with a good animal model, such as ectromelia virus (mouse pox) or the Utrecht strain of rabbitpox in mice. There is no justification for retaining smallpox virus to study the pathogenesis of generalized poxvirus infections; the activity of particular genes that are peculiar to smallpox virus can be studied by use of cloned smallpox

virus DNA, although the use of such clones and plasmids is now regulated by WHO (6), and should continue to be so regulated. Recombinant plasmids that contain smallpox virus DNA sequences are registered with WHO and may only be provided to requesting scientists after informing WHO and on the strict understanding that they must not be distributed to third parties or used in laboratories handling other orthopoxviruses.

Other infectious pathogens will be globally eradicated in the future. Immediate targets of WHO campaigns are dracunculiasis (guinea-worm disease) by 1995 (13) and poliomyelitis by 2000 (14). The guinea-worm is a parasite that cannot be stored frozen and would require infection of human subject volunteers if it were to be preserved. Yet we know little concerning the pathogenesis of dracunculiasis. In less than 10 years it is likely that all neurovirulent poliovirus stocks will be held in a few secure institutions, such as CDC. Should we continue to work on such infectious agents when so many new and reemerging infectious diseases make demands on our limited resources? We think not. And when viewed against the regrettable but wholesale extinction of species that results from human interventions in natural ecosystems, concern about the preservation of smallpox virus seems misplaced.

REFERENCES

1. F. Fenner et al., Smallpox and its Eradication (WHO, Geneva, 1988).

2. I. Arita, Nature 279, 293(1979).

3. "Report of the Investigation into the cause of the 1978 Birmingham smallpox occurrence" (Her Majesty's Stationery Office, London, 1980).

4. J. J. Esposito, J. F. Obijeski, J. H. Nakano, *Virology* **89**, 53 (1978).

5. M. Mackett and L. C. Archard, *J. Gen. Virol.* **45**, 683 (1979).

6. J. J. Esposito and J. C. Knight, *Virology* **143**, 230 (1985).

7. B. W. J. Mahy, J. J. Esposito, J. C. Venter, *ASM News* **57**, 577 (1991).

8. Weekly Epidemiological Record **61**, 289 (1986).

9. S. N. Shchelkunov *et al.*, in *Concepts of Virology from Ivanovsky to the Present*, B. W. J. Mahy and D. K. Lvov, Eds. (Harwood Academic, New York, 1993), p. 93.

10. R. F. Massung *et al.*, *Nature*, in press.

11. S. J. Goebel *et al.*, *Virology* **179**, 247 (1990).

12. J. M. Hughes, C. J. Peters, M. L. Cohen, B. W. J. Mahy, *Science*, in press.

13. D. R. Hopkins, *Epidemiol. Rev.* **5**, 208 (1983), in *The Cambridge World History of Human Disease*, K. F. Kipple, Ed. (Cambridge Univ. Press, New York, 1993), p. 687.

14. C. A. de Quadros *et al.*, *Ann. Rev. Publ. Health* **13**, 239 (1992); World Health Assembly, "Global eradication of poliomyelitis by the year 2000," Resolution WHA41.28, Geneva, 1988.

NO

Wolfgang K. Joklik et al.

WHY THE SMALLPOX VIRUS STOCKS
SHOULD NOT BE DESTROYED

Unlimited by climate and ever present, smallpox virus (also known as varida virus) was one of the most devastating scourges of humanity. In 18th-century Europe it regularly killed 200,000 to 600,000 people every year, with case mortalities ranging from 10 to 30%; in nonimmune populations such as the Amerindians of Mexico and Peru in the 16th century and of North America in the 18th century, case mortalities often exceeded 50 percent. Fortunately, the fact that smallpox virus has only one host, humans, made eradication of the disease possible. In 1967, when the number of smallpox cases world-wide approached 10 million, the World Health Organization (WHO) initiated a smallpox eradication campaign that was based on vaccination of large populations and on rigorous follow-up and treatment of case contacts. This campaign was spectacularly successful; the last case of smallpox occurred in October 1977 and in October 1979 the world was declared free of smallpox (1).

Almost immediately thereafter the possibility of destroying all existing stocks of smallpox virus began to be discussed. In 1981 WHO recommended that this be done with the exception of the stocks in the Centers for Disease Control (CDC) in Atlanta and the Institute for Viral Preparations in Moscow. To clear the way for the subsequent destruction of these stocks (2), work was initiated in these two laboratories, under P4 safety/isolation conditions, to clone and sequence the genomes of selected smallpox virus isolates (variola major strains Bangladesh 1975 and India 1967 and variola minor strain Garcia 1966) (3). At least two smallpox virus strains have now been sequenced completely; their sequences have been discussed extensively at several meetings and are about to be published.

The WHO recommendation to destroy all smallpox virus stocks in Atlanta and Moscow was not widely discussed in the scientific community. However, it was debated this summer in a workshop held during the IXth International Congress of Virology in Glasgow, Scotland. The main arguments for destruction are (i) to prevent the accidental release of the virus from its two isolation facilities; (ii) to prevent terrorists from acquiring the virus as an agent of

From Wolfgang K. Joklik, Bernard Moss, Bernard N. Fields, David H. L. Bishop, and Lev S. Sandakhchiev, "Why the Smallpox Virus Stocks Should Not Be Destroyed," *Science*, vol. 262 (November 19, 1993), pp. 1225–1226. Copyright © 1993 by The American Association for the Advancement of Science. Reprinted by permission.

biological warfare; and (iii) to eliminate this, the most devastating of all human pathogens. Elimination of the virus is, according to this line of reasoning, acceptable because its genome has been cloned into plasmids and has been sequenced. However, the arguments are not persuasive. The danger of accidental smallpox virus release from the two isolation laboratories is surely minimal. Although three smallpox deaths resulted from accidental laboratory infections in the 1970s (4), these tragedies occurred because simple but essential administrative precautions were ignored, which could not occur in P4 isolation facilities. As for the use of smallpox virus as a military or terrorist weapon, this is also a most unlikely scenario because smallpox virus can be readily controlled by public health measures including rigorous case contact evaluations and vaccination. In addition, many far more readily accessible and effective potential biological weapons exist. It is naïve to imagine that the destruction of smallpox virus would contribute substantially to reducing the terrorist armamentarium.

The third argument relates to the emotional, sociological, and political desirability of eliminating this frightening scourge of humanity. However, the destruction of smallpox virus in its two established locations provides only an illusory increment of safety because at least three additional potential sources of smallpox virus still exist. First, there are the cadavers of smallpox patients preserved in permafrost. Such cadavers, which could easily become exposed, have been shown to contain smallpox virus antigens and are being tested for the presence of infectious smallpox virus (5). Second, it is possible that smallpox virus–containing specimens collected during the smallpox eradication campaign still exist, unrecognized and unidentified, in laboratories in various parts of the world. Third, monkeypox virus causes a disease in humans that resembles smallpox (6). The two viruses are similar but monkeypox virus has a much wider host range; its primary natural hosts are monkeys and squirrels. The major difference between monkeypox virus and smallpox virus is that monkeypox virus is transmitted poorly in humans; there is no recorded case of more than four successive horizontal human-to-human transmissions. Four hundred and four cases of human monkeypox virus infections (of which 33 were fatal) were recorded during the period 1970 to 1986, mostly in Zaire.

With the recent example of the emergence of human immunodeficiency virus (HIV) as a human pathogen vividly before us, there is ample room for concern that monkeypox virus could evolve into a threat. Even more to the point, the recent publication of the genomic sequences of at least two smallpox virus strains and the existence of plasmids containing all segments of the smallpox virus genome have made it possible to insert specific smallpox virus genes into the monkeypox virus genome by homologous recombination. There is the distinct possibility that replacement of a single monkeypox virus gene with the corresponding smallpox virus gene could result in a virus with all the virulence characteristics for humans of smallpox virus itself.

In summary, the destruction of the smallpox virus isolates in the high-security laboratories in Atlanta and Moscow does not remove the threat of smallpox from the world.

By contrast, retaining the smallpox virus stocks in Atlanta and Moscow and studying in detail their molecular pathogenesis would be of enormous benefit to humanity. For this purpose the complete virus is required; mere knowledge of the smallpox virus genome sequence, and availability of smallpox genes cloned into plasmids, will not suffice. The reason is that we are only just beginning to understand how viruses cause disease at the biochemical and molecular level. Viral pathogenesis is an extremely complex process that involves not only the interaction of structural components of the virus with those of the host cell, but also, especially in the case of poxviruses in general and smallpox virus in particular, proteins that mimic or interfere with host immune and regulatory functions. Among such virus-encoded proteins identified thus far in poxviruses are the following: cytokines and lymphokines resembling epidermal growth factor and transforming growth factor (7); proteins similar to the receptors for interleukin-1β, interferon-γ, and tumor necrosis factor (8); cytokine and lymphokine response modifiers (9); proteins involved in the regulation of complement (10); and proteins that bind to interleukin-1 or have zinc finger motifs (11). All of these proteins are expressed in a precisely regulated temporal sequence in precisely regulated amounts. The combined effects of these proteins cannot be gauged merely by guessing at motifs in strange sequences that may or may not be operative, and if operative, may or may not be produced from cloned fragments at levels corresponding to the situation in vivo. Furthermore, clones representing individual or small groups of smallpox virus genes will not suffice because their coding regions would very likely be separated from the control elements that regulate their expression, such as enhancers and promoters, as well as genes that en-

code transcription factors and repressors for them.

The realization that poxvirus genomes encode all these hitherto undreamt of proteins that function to counteract host defense mechanisms is less than 10 years old (12). Should we now destroy this extraordinary paradigm of host-virus interactions before we have discovered which human defense mechanisms smallpox virus has evolved to evade? Lacking such knowledge we would certainly be in a poor position to cope with a poxvirus that may evolve to fill the biological niche once occupied by smallpox virus. To answer such questions, research with active smallpox virus, both in vitro and in vivo, is needed. Who is to say that knowledge of the mode of action of some smallpox virus–encoded factor or factors may not point the way to solving the problem of HIV pathogenesis?

The following additional observations are relevant in this regard. First, smallpox virus is uniquely adapted to the human organism. Its study should therefore provide information concerning viral mechanisms for evading the human immune system in particular and human defense mechanisms in general, that may be exploitable for drug development. Comparing the mechanisms that operate during smallpox virus infection with those that operate in infections with monkeypox virus and cowpox virus may also provide valuable insights. Further, both smallpox virus genomes that have been sequenced are derived from isolates that were passaged in eggs, a procedure that may select variants that lack genes found in natural smallpox virus isolates. It is essential that isolates that have not been passaged be sequenced, as well as additional isolates possessing differing degrees of virulence, so as to identify the nature and interplay of the gene products responsible for such differences.

Second, no animal model for infection by smallpox virus is available. However, techniques have recently been developed for studying viruses outside their normal host species. For example, poliovirus normally infects primates and humans. Transgenic mice have been generated that contain the poliovirus receptor and can be infected by poliovirus; thus, it has become possible to study this virus in mice. The future will almost certainly provide a broad range of opportunities for studying how smallpox virus causes disease in experimental animals.

Third, one of the most serious current threats to human health is posed by reemerging infectious agents—agents that were once thought to be controlled, but have reappeared, often in the form of variants. They are causing disease not only where they were once endemic, but also where they had never been encountered before. For all the reasons discussed above, smallpox virus is a prime candidate for becoming such a reemerging infectious agent. Clearly, intensified efforts to understand the mechanisms by which it causes disease, and how such mechanisms could be countered, are required.

In summary, we should be much more alarmed by the thought of smallpox virus being destroyed than by smallpox virus being studied responsibly and expertly in one or two laboratories. The intact smallpox virus is infinitely more valuable than knowledge of the sequence of its nearly 200,000 base pairs; in intact form it provides an unrivalled opportunity for broadening our base for understanding not only smallpox, but also other virus-caused diseases. There is no question that the cost involved in guaranteeing the safe preservation of smallpox virus

is negligible compared with the cost that would be incurred if the opportunity for gaining insight into the mechanisms of viral pathogenesis that would result from studying it were lost irretrievably. For all these reasons it would be most inadvisable to abort research into the mechanisms of smallpox pathogenesis at this time. Rather, such research should be supported vigorously, and decisions concerning the destruction of smallpox virus should be deferred for at least 10 years.

REFERENCES

1. The Global Eradication of Smallpox: Final report of the global commission for the certification of smallpox eradication (*History of International Public Health*, No. 4, WHO, Geneva, 1980).

2. Report of the fourth meeting of the Committee on Orthopoxvirus Infections (WHO, Geneva, 1986).

3. B. W. J. Mahy, J. J. Esposito, J. C. Venter, *ASM News* 57, 577(1991).

4. "Report of the Committee of inquiry into the smallpox outbreak in London in March and April 1973" (Her Majesty's Stationery Office, London, 1974); "Report of the Investigation into the cause of the 1978 Birmingham Smallpox Occurrence" (Her Majesty's Stationery Office, London, 1980).

5. L. S. Sandakhchiev, unpublished data.

6. F. Fenner, in *Emerging Viruses*, S. S. Morse, Ed. (Oxford Univ. Press, New York, 1993), pp. 176–183; Z. Jezek and F. Fenner, *Human Monkeypox*, vol. 17 of *Monographs in Virology* (Karger, Basel, Switzerland, 1988).

7. J. P. Brown, D. R. Twardzik, H. Marquardt, G. J. Todaro, *Nature* 313, 491(1985); D. R. Twardzik, J. P. Brown, J. E. Ranchalis, G. J. Todaro, B. Moss, *Proc. Natl. Acad. Sci. U.S.A.* 82, 5300 (1985).

8. A. Alcami and G. L. Smith, *Cell* 71, 153 (1992); C. Upton, K. Mossman, G.

McFadden, *Science* **258**, 1369 (1992); C. Upton, J. L. Macen, M. Schreiber, G. McFadden, *Virology* **184**, 370 (1991).

9. D. J. Pickup, B. S. Ink, W. Hu, C. A. Ray, W. K. Joklik, *Proc. Natl. Acad. Sci. U.S.A.* **83**, 7698 (1986); G. J. Palumbo, D. J. Pickup, T. N. Fredrickson, L. J. McIntyre, R. M. Buller, *Virology* **171**, 262 (1989); C. A. Ray *et al.*, *Cell* **69**, 597 (1992).

10. G. J. Kotwal and B. Moss, *Nature* **335**, 176 (1988); G. J. Kotwal, S. N. Isaacs, R. McKenzie, M. M. Frank, B. Moss, *Science* **250**, 827 (1990).

11. M. K. Spriggs *et al.*, *Cell* **71**, 145 (1992); T. G. Senkevich, E. V. Koonin, R. M. L. Buller, *Virology*, in press.

12. P. C. Turner and R. W. Moyer, *Curr. Topics Microbiol. Immunol.* **163**, 125 (1990); R. M. Buller and G. J. Palumbo, *Microbiol. Rev.* **55**, 80 (1991).

POSTSCRIPT

Should Smallpox Be Completely Eradicated?

In the months after the essays presented here first appeared, several responses from *Science* readers appeared as letters to the editor in various issues. David Baltimore of Rockefeller University, for example, said that Mahy et al. had convinced him: eradicate the virus. William J. Turner, emeritus professor of psychiatry at the State University of New York, Stony Brook, wrote that he agreed. Patrick Hess of the National Health Laboratories in Louisville, Kentucky, suggested that the virus should be kept in storage "until future scientists deem what further research may be necessary."

As Mahy et al. note in their essay, in 1990 a WHO committee agreed that by December 31, 1993—provided the smallpox virus's genetic "recipe" was all on file by then—all remaining stocks of the virus should be destroyed. The debate over whether or not this was the appropriate thing to do peaked in the months just before the deadline; the essays reprinted here effectively represent the two sides.

By November 1993 the WHO was reconsidering the 1990 decision to destroy the virus stocks on the grounds that the debate had raised "solid arguments for and against the destruction of the virus," according to senior WHO virologist Yuri Ghendon. He also noted that "a report based on the opinions of the committee members will be prepared for the General Assembly of the WHO," which was to make its decision by May 1994 (see *American Scientist*, November–December 1993). If the verdict were still to eradicate the virus, then the remaining stocks could be destroyed at any time thereafter. Parker A. Small, Jr., of the Department of Immunology and Medical Microbiology at the University of Florida, Gainesville, in a letter to the editor (*Science*, February 18, 1994), wrote that he thinks it would be appropriate for the virus to be destroyed on May 14, 1996, which will be the 200th anniversary of Edward Jenner's first smallpox vaccination experiment.

By the end of December 1993, the destruction of the virus stocks was on hold. According to the front page of the December 25, 1993, *New York Times*, a January meeting was planned for the WHO's Geneva headquarters to "review the progress made in genetically mapping the virus and determine whether other things still should be done." Since the last remaining smallpox virus was stored safely in freezers in Atlanta, Georgia, and Moscow, Russia, Walter R. Dowdle, acting director of the Centers for Disease Control and Prevention, said, "Everybody's feeling is, what's the hurry, give it a little more time and let's talk further about this." He noted that similar debates were going on in Russia. The *Times* assured its readers that if the smallpox virus *is* eventually destroyed, they need not fear the reappearance of the disease from some hidden source. There is vaccine in storage, and—since the vaccine is made from the vaccinia (cowpox) virus, not variola (smallpox)—more could be prepared at any time.

In June 1994 the *New York Times* reported that the WHO had given the virus a reprieve for at least another year in order to let WHO officials consider more fully claims that the virus remains valuable to biomedical researchers. The point is worth stressing that we are here considering the deliberate extermination of a species. Does it really matter that smallpox is a deadly disease, not a cute, fuzzy animal or a pretty, green plant? Should smallpox be protected as other endangered species are protected? Students who wish to dig deeper into the issue might well compare the debate over the extinction of the smallpox virus with the debate over reintroducing wolves into parts of the United States where farmers and ranchers long ago exterminated them. The debate over biodiversity—that is, the advantages of having a variety of species of plants and animals in an environment—is also worth examining, for it includes the argument that species are valuable for whatever unknown future benefits they may hold. See, for instance, chapter 8, entitled "Biodiversity," in *World Resources 1994–95: A Guide to the Global Environment* (Oxford University Press, 1994).

PART 5

Ethics

Society's standards of right and wrong have been hammered out over thousands of years of trial, error, and (sometimes violent) debate. Accordingly, when science and technology offer society new choices to make and new things to do, debates are renewed over whether or not these choices and actions are ethically acceptable.

Today there is vigorous debate on such topics as the use of fetal tissue in medical research and treatment as well as some of the practices of science itself. This section explores some ethical issues regarding these subjects, starting with a discussion on the use of animals in research and including a debate on human experimentation.

■ Is the Use of Animals in Research Justified?

■ Is It Ethical to Use Humans as "Experimental Animals"?

■ Should Fetal Tissue Be Used to Heal Adults?

ISSUE 17

Is the Use of Animals in Research Justified?

YES: Jerod M. Loeb et al., from "Human vs. Animal Rights: In Defense of Animal Research," *Journal of the American Medical Association* (November 17, 1989)

NO: Steven Zak, from "Ethics and Animals," *The Atlantic Monthly* (March 1989)

ISSUE SUMMARY

YES: Physiologist Jerod M. Loeb and his colleagues at the American Medical Association argue that the use of animals for probing the nature of physiology and for testing medical drugs and procedures is so essential to human welfare that the concept of "animal rights" must not be permitted to interfere.

NO: Research attorney Steven Zak argues that current animal protection laws do not adequately protect animals used in medical and other research and that, for society to be virtuous, it must recognize the rights of animals not to be sacrificed for human needs.

Modern biologists and physicians know a great deal about how the human body works. Some of that knowledge has been gained by studying human cadavers and tissue samples acquired during surgery and through "experiments of nature" (strokes, for example, have taught a great deal about what the various parts of the brain do; extensive injuries from car accidents and wars have also been edifying). Some knowledge of human biology has also been gained from experiments on humans, such as when brain surgery patients agree to let their surgeons stimulate different parts of their brains electrically while the brains are exposed or when cancer patients agree to try experimental treatments.

The key word here is *agree*. Today it is widely accepted that people have the right to consent or not to consent to whatever is done to them in the name of research or treatment. In fact, society has determined that research done on humans without their free and informed consent is a form of scientific misconduct. However, this standard does not apply to animals, experimentation on which has produced the most knowledge of the human body.

Although animals have been used in research for at least the last 2,000 years, during most of that time, physicians who thought they had a workable treatment for some illness commonly tried it on their patients before they had any idea whether or not it worked or was even safe. Many patients, of course, died during these untested treatments. In the mid-nineteenth century, the French physiologist Claude Bernard argued that it was sensible to try such treatments first on animals to avoid some human suffering and death. No one then questioned whether or not human lives were more valuable than animal lives.

Today millions of animals are used in research. Geneticists generally study fruit flies, roundworms, and zebra fish. Physiologists study mammals, mostly mice and rats but also rabbits, cats, dogs, pigs, sheep, goats, monkeys, and chimpanzees. Experimental animals are often kept in confined quarters, cut open, infected with disease organisms, fed unhealthy diets, and injected with assorted chemicals. Sometimes the animals suffer. Sometimes the animals die. And sometimes they are healed, albeit often of diseases or injuries induced by the researchers in the first place.

Not surprisingly, some observers have reacted with extreme sympathy and have called for better treatment of animals used in research. This "animal welfare" movement has, in turn, spawned the more extreme "animal rights" movement, which asserts that animals—especially mammals—have rights as important and as deserving of regard as those of humans. In its most extreme form, this movement insists that animals are persons in every moral sense. Thus, to kill an animal, whether for research, food, or fur, is the moral equivalent of murder.

This attitude has led to important reforms in the treatment of animals and to the development of several alternatives to using animals (see Alan M. Goldberg and John M. Frazier, "Alternatives to Animals in Toxicity Testing," *Scientific American*, August 1989). However, it has also led to hysterical objections to in-class animal dissections, terrorist attacks on laboratories, the destruction of research records, and the theft of research materials (including animals). In 1989 an undersecretary of the Department of Health and Human Services, in attacking the animal rights movement, said, "We must not permit a handful of extremists to deprive millions of the life-sustaining and life-enhancing fruits of biomedical research."

The American Medical Association takes a very similar tack in a report analyzing the animal research controversy. Jerod M. Loeb and his colleagues summarize that report in the following selection. They maintain that using animals to discover the nature of physiology and whether or not medical drugs and procedures are safe and effective is essential to human welfare. Morality demands that researchers treat animals humanely and use alternatives when possible but not that animal research be stopped.

In opposition, Steven Zak, who has written numerous articles on animals with regard to ethics and the law, argues that morality requires society to recognize the right of animals not to be made to suffer at all for the benefit of humans. Therefore, researchers should always find alternative modes of research.

YES

Jerod M. Loeb et al.

HUMAN VS. ANIMAL RIGHTS: IN DEFENSE OF ANIMAL RESEARCH

Research with animals is a highly controversial topic in our society. Animal rights groups that intend to stop all experimentation with animals are in the vanguard of this controversy. Their methods range from educational efforts directed in large measure to the young and uninformed, to promotion of restrictive legislation, filing lawsuits, and violence that includes raids on laboratories and death threats to investigators. Their rhetoric is emotionally charged and their information is frequently distorted and pejorative. Their tactics vary but have a single objective—to stop scientific research with animals.

The resources of the animal rights groups are extensive, in part because less militant organizations of animal activists, including some humane societies, have been infiltrated or taken over by animal rights groups to gain access to their fiscal and physical holdings. Through bizarre tactics, extravagant claims, and gruesome myths, animal rights groups have captured the attention of the media and a sizable segment of the public. Nevertheless, people invariably support the use of animals in research when they understand both sides of the issue and the contributions of animal research to relief of human suffering. However, all too often they do not understand both sides because information about the need for animal research is not presented. When this need is explained, the presentation often reveals an arrogance of the scientific community and an unwillingness to be accountable to public opinion.

The use of animals in research is fundamentally an ethical question: is it more ethical to ban all research with animals or to use a limited number of animals in research under humane conditions when no alternatives exist to achieve medical advances that reduce substantial human suffering and misery?...

ANIMALS IN SCIENTIFIC RESEARCH

Animals have been used in research for more than 2000 years. In the third century BC, the natural philosopher Erisistratus of Alexandria used animals

From Jerod M. Loeb, William R. Hendee, Steven J. Smith, and M. Roy Schwarz, "Human vs. Animal Rights: In Defense of Animal Research," *Journal of the American Medical Association*, vol. 262, no. 19 (November 17, 1989), pp. 2716–2720. Copyright © 1989 by The American Medical Association. Reprinted by permission.

to study bodily function. In all likelihood, Aristotle performed vivisection on animals. The Roman physician Galen used apes and pigs to prove his theory that veins carry blood rather than air. In succeeding centuries, animals were employed to confirm theories about physiology developed through observation. Advances in knowledge from these experiments include demonstration of the circulation of blood by Harvey in 1622, documentation of the effects of anesthesia on the body in 1846, and elucidation of the relationship between bacteria and disease in 1878.[1] In his book *An Introduction to the Study of Experimental Medicine* published in 1865, Bernard[2] described the importance of animal research to advances in knowledge about the human body and justified the continued use of animals for this purpose.

In this century, many medical advances have been achieved through research with animals.[3] Infectious diseases such as pertussis, rubella, measles, and poliomyelitis have been brought under control with vaccines developed in animals. The development of immunization techniques against today's infectious diseases, including human immunodeficiency virus disease, depends entirely on experiments in animals. Antibiotics that control infection are always tested in animals before use in humans. Physiological disorders such as diabetes and epilepsy are treatable today through knowledge and products gained by animal research. Surgical procedures such as coronary artery bypass grafts, cerebrospinal fluid shunts, and retinal reattachments have evolved from experiments with animals. Transplantation procedures for persons with failed liver, heart, lung, and kidney function are products of animal research.

Animals have been essential to the evolution of modern medicine and the conquest of many illnesses. However, many medical challenges remain to be solved. Cancer, heart disease, cerebrovascular disease, dementia, depression, arthritis, and a variety of inherited disorders are yet to be understood and controlled. Until they are, human pain and suffering will endure, and society will continue to expend its emotional and fiscal resources in efforts to alleviate or at least reduce them.

Animal research has not only benefited humans. Procedures and products developed through this process have also helped animals.[4,5] Vaccines against rabies, distemper, and parvovirus in dogs are a spin-off of animal research, as are immunization techniques against cholera in hogs, encephalitis in horses, and brucellosis in cattle. Drugs to combat heartworm, intestinal parasites, and mastitis were developed in animals used for experimental purposes. Surgical procedures developed in animals help animals as well as humans.

Research with animals has yielded immeasurable benefits to both humans and animals. However, this research raises fundamental philosophical issues concerning the rights of humans to use animals to benefit humans and other animals. If these rights are granted (and many people are loath to do so), additional questions arise concerning the way that research should be performed, the accountability of researchers to public sentiment, the nature of an ethical code for animal research, and who should compose and approve the code. Today, some animal activists are asking whether humans have the right to exercise dominion over animals for any purpose, including research. Others suggest that because humans have dominion over other forms of life, they are obligated to protect and preserve animals and ensure that they are not exploited. Still others agree that animals can be used to help people, but only under circumstances that are so structured as to be unattainable by most researchers. These attitudes may all differ, but their consequences are similar. They all threaten to diminish or stop animal research.

CHALLENGE TO ANIMAL RESEARCH

Challenges to the use of animals to benefit humans are not new—their origins can be traced back several centuries. With respect to animal research, opposition has been vocal in Europe for more than 400 years and in the United States for at least 100 years.[6]

Most of the current arguments against research with animals have historic precedents that must be grasped to understand the current debate. These precedents originated in the controversy between Cartesian and utilitarian philosophers that extended from the 16th to the 18th centuries.

The Cartesian-utilitarian debate was opened by the French philosopher Descartes, who defended the use of animals in experiments by insisting the animals respond to stimuli in only one way —"according to the arrangement of their organs."[7] He stated that animals lack the ability to reason and think and are, therefore, similar to a machine. Humans, on the other hand, can think, talk, and respond to stimuli in various ways. These differences, Descartes argued, make animals inferior to humans and justify their use as a machine, including as experimental subjects. He proposed that animals learn only by experience, whereas

humans learn by "teaching-learning." Humans do not always have to experience something to know that it is true.

Descartes' arguments were countered by the utilitarian philosopher Bentham of England. "The question," said Bentham, "is not can they reason? nor can they talk? but can they suffer?"[8] In utilitarian terms, humans and animals are linked by their common ability to suffer and their common right not to suffer and die at the hands of others. This utilitarian thesis has rippled through various groups opposed to research with animals for more than a century.

In the 1970s, the antivivisectionist movement was influenced by three books that clarified the issues and introduced the rationale for increased militancy against animal research. In 1971, the anthology *Animals, Men and Morals*, by Godlovitch et al,[9] raised the concept of animal rights and analyzed the relationships between humans and animals. Four years later, *Victims of Science*, by Ryder,[10] introduced the concept of "speciesism" as equivalent to fascism. Also in 1975, Singer[11] published *Animal Liberation: A New Ethic for Our Treatment of Animals*. This book is generally considered the progenitor of the modern animal rights movement. Invoking Ryder's concept of speciesism, Singer deplored the historic attitude of humans toward nonhumans as a "form of prejudice no less objectionable than racism or sexism." He urged that the liberation of animals should become the next great cause after civil rights and the women's movement.

Singer's book not only was a philosophical treatise; it also was a call to action. It provided an intellectual foundation and a moral focus for the animal rights movement. These features attracted many who were indifferent to the emotional appeal based on a love of animals that had characterized antivivisectionist efforts for the past century. Singer's book swelled the ranks of the antivivisectionist movement and transformed it into a movement for animal rights. It also has been used to justify illegal activities intended to impede animal research and instill fear and intimidation in those engaged in it.

ANIMAL RIGHTS ACTIVISM

The animal rights movement is supported financially by a wide spectrum of individuals, most of whom are well-meaning persons who care about animals and wish to see them treated humanely. Many of these supporters do not appreciate the diverse philosophies and activities of different groups of animal activists, and they have not explored differences between animal welfare and animal rights in any depth. They believe that their financial contributions pay for animal shelters and efforts to find homes for stray animals. They do not realize that their contributions also support illegal activities that have been classified as terrorist actions by the US Federal Bureau of Investigation and the New Scotland Yard. Many of these illegal activities are conducted by a clandestine group called the Animal Liberation Front. Other groups alledged to be engaged in illegal activities include Earth First, Last Chance for Animals, People for the Ethical Treatment of Animals, Band of Mercy, and True Friends.

In the United States, illegal activities conducted by these groups since July 1988 include the following (F. Trull, personal communication):

- break-in, theft, and arson at the University of Arizona in Tucson, with more than 1000 animals stolen and arson damage of $250,000;
- break-in and theft at Duke University in Durham, NC;
- break-in and theft at the Veterans Administration Medical Center in Tucson (Arizona);
- bomb threat to the director of the lab animal facility, Stanford (Calif) University;
- attempted bombing, US Surgical Corporation, Norwalk, Conn;
- vandalism, University of California, Santa Cruz; and
- break-in and theft, Loma Linda (Calif) University.

Illegal actions have been pursued with even greater vigor in the United Kingdom.

Recent examples related to medical research in the United Kingdom include the following (M. Macleod, personal communication):

- home and car damage of two investigators at a Wellcome research facility;
- home and car damage of three investigators at St George's Hospital, Tooting;
- bomb planted and warning given to director of construction firm building laboratory for Glaxo Corporation;
- five incendiary devices that caused $50,000 damage to company that supplied portable offices to Glaxo Corporation during laboratory construction;
- property damage at Bromley High School, where animals are used in dissection classes; and
- mailing of hundreds of incendiary devices, including one to Prime Minister Margaret Thatcher.

Other countries that experienced similar terrorist activities include Italy, Japan, New Zealand, Sweden, Holland, Belgium, Canada, and West Germany. Some officials believe that these activities are part of an international conspiracy operating under the rubric of animal rights but dedicated to general anarchy. They also feel that support for these efforts is derived principally from thousands of well-meaning but naive individuals who contribute to organizations that plead the cause of animal welfare but actually serve as fronts for terrorist activities.

DEFENSE OF ANIMAL RESEARCH

The issue of animal research is fundamentally an issue of the dominion of humans over animals. This issue is rooted in the Judeo-Christian religion of western culture, including the ancient tradition of animal sacrifice described in the Old Testament and the practice of using animals as surrogates for suffering humans described in the New Testament. The sacredness of human life is a central theme of biblical morality, and the dominion of humans over other forms of life is a natural consequence of this theme.[12] The issue of dominion is not, however, unique to animal research. It is applicable to every situation where animals are subservient to humans. It applies to the use of animals for food and clothing; the application of animals as beasts of burden and transportation; the holding of animals in captivity such as in zoos and as household pets; the use of animals as entertainment, such as in sea parks and circuses; the exploitation of animals in sports that employ animals, including hunting, racing, and animal shows; and the eradication of pests such as rats and mice from homes and farms. Even provision of food and shelter to animals reflects an attitude of dominion of humans over animals. A person who truly does not believe in human dominance over animals would be forced to oppose all of these practices, including keeping animals as household pets or in any form of physical or psychological captivity. Such a posture would defy tradition evolved over the entire course of human existence.

Some animal advocates do not take issue with the right of humans to exercise dominion over animals. They agree that animals are inferior to humans because they do not possess attributes such as a moral sense and concepts of past and future. However, they also claim that it is precisely because of these differences that humans are obligated to protect animals and not exploit them for the selfish betterment of humans.[13] In their view, animals are like infants and the mentally incompetent, who must be nurtured and protected from exploitation. This view shifts the issues of dominion from one of rights claimed by animals to one of responsibilities exercised by humans.

Neither of these philosophical positions addresses the issue of animal research from the perspective of the immorality of not using animals in research. From this perspective, depriving humans (and animals) of advances in medicine that result from research with animals is inhumane and fundamentally unethical. Spokespersons for this perspective suggest that patients with dementia, stroke, disabling injuries, heart disease, and cancer deserve relief from suffering and that depriving them of hope and relief by eliminating animal research is an immoral and unconscionable act. Defenders of animal research claim that animals sometimes must be sacrificed in the development of methods to relieve pain and suffering of humans (and animals) and to affect treatments and cures of a variety of human maladies.

The immeasurable benefits of animal research to humans are undeniable. One example is the development of a vaccine for poliomyelitis, with the result that the number of cases of poliomyelitis in the United States alone declined from 58,000 in 1952 to 4 in 1984. Benefits of this vaccine worldwide are even more impressive.

Every year, hundreds of thousands of humans are spared the braces, wheelchairs, and iron lungs required for the victims of poliomyelitis who survive this infectious disease. The research that led to a poliomyelitis vaccine required the sacrifice of hundreds of primates. Without this sacrifice, development of the vaccine would have been impossible, and in all likelihood the poliomyelitis epidemic would have continued unabated. Depriving humanity of this medical advance is unthinkable to almost all persons. Other diseases that are curable or treatable today as a result of animal research include diphtheria, scarlet fever, tuberculosis, diabetes, and appendicitis.[3] Human suffering would be much more stark today if these diseases, and many others as well, had not been amendable to treatment and cure through advances obtained by animal research.

ISSUES IN ANIMAL RESEARCH

Animal rights groups have several stock arguments against animal research. Some of these issues are described and refuted herein.

The Clinical Value of Basic Research

Persons opposed to research with animals often claim that basic biomedi-cal research has no clinical value and therefore does not justify the use of animals. However, basic research is the foundation for most medical advances and consequently for progress in clinical medicine. Without basic research, including that with animals, chemotherapeutic advances against cancer (including childhood leukemia and breast malignancy), beta-blockers for cardiac patients, and electrolyte infusions for patients with dysfunctional metabolism would never have been achieved.

Duplication of Experiments

Opponents of animal research frequently claim that experiments are needlessly duplicated. However, the duplication of results is an essential part of the confirmation process in science. The generalization of results from one laboratory to another prevents anomalous results in one laboratory from being interpreted as scientific truth. The cost of research animals, the need to publish the results of experiments, and the desire to conduct meaningful research all function to reduce the likelihood of unnecessary experiments. Furthermore, the intense competition of research funds and the peer review process lessen the probability of obtaining funds for unnecessary research. Most scientists are unlikely to waste valuable time and resources conducting unnecessary experiments when opportunities for performing important research are so plentiful.

The Number of Animals Used in Research

Animal rights groups claim that as many as 150 million animals are used in research each year, most of them needlessly. However, the US Office of Technology Assessment has estimated that only 17 to 22 million animals were involved in experimental studies in 1983, including 12.2 to 15.2 million rats and mice bred especially for research. Also used were 2.5 to 4 million fish, 100,000 to 500,000 amphibians, 100,000 to 500,000 birds, 500,000 to 550,000 rabbits, 500,000 guinea pigs, 450,000 hamsters, 182,000 to 195,000 dogs, 55,000 to 60,000 cats, and 54,000 to 59,000 primates.[14]

Animal activists claim that research with animals is institutionalized and that investigators do not consider ways to reduce the number of animals involved in research. In contrast, evidence suggests that the number of research animals is decreasing each year, according to surveys by the National Research Council of the National Academy of Sciences.[15] In 1978, for example, the Council estimated that the total of 20 million research animals was 50% less than the number for 1968.

The number of animals used in research is limited by the cost of animals (especially in the present period of limited funds for research), the availability and expense of facilities to house them, and by the compassion of investigators to use no more animals than needed to perform meaningful research. It also is controlled by institutional animal-use committees that are empowered to monitor animal experimentation to ensure that experimental design is appropriate and animals are treated humanely and compassionately. These committees also are obligated to ensure that animals are properly housed and cared for. The performance of these committees is evaluated by various federal and voluntary agencies, including the American Association of Laboratory Animal Care.

The Use of Primates in Research

Animal activists often make a special plea on behalf of nonhuman primates, and many of the sit-ins, demonstrations, and break-ins have been directed at primate research centers. Efforts to justify these activities invoke the premise that primates are much like humans because they exhibit suffering and other emotions.

Keeping primates in cages and isolating them from others of their kind is considered by activists as cruel and destructive of their "psychological well-being." However, the opinion that animals that resemble humans most closely and deserve the most protection and care reflects an attitude of speciesism (i.e., a hierarchical scheme of relative importance) that most activists purportedly abhor. This logical fallacy in the drive for special protection of primates apparently escapes most of its adherents.

Some scientific experiments require primates exactly because they simulate human physiology so closely. Primates are susceptible to many of the same diseases as humans and have similar immune systems. They also possess intellectual, cognitive, and social skills above those of other animals. These characteristics make primates invaluable in research related to language, perception, and visual and spatial skills.[14] Although primates constitute only 0.5% of all animals used in research, their contributions have been essential to the continued acquisition of knowledge in the biological and behavioral sciences.[15]

Do Animals Suffer Needless Pain and Abuse?

Animal activists frequently assert that research with animals causes severe pain and that many research animals are abused either deliberately or through indifference. Actually, experiments today involve pain only when relief from pain would interfere with the purpose of the experiments. In any experiment in which an animal might experience pain, federal law requires that a veterinarian must be consulted in planning the experiment, and anesthesia, tranquilizers, and analgesics must be used except when they would compromise the results of the experiment.[16]

In 1984, the Department of Agriculture reported that 61% of research animals were not subjected to painful procedures, and another 31% received anesthesia or pain-relieving drugs. The remaining 8% did experience pain, often because improved understanding and treatment of pain, including chronic pain, were the purpose of the experiment.[14] Chronic pain is a challenging health problem that costs the United States about $50 billion a year in direct medical expenses, lost productivity, and income.[15]

Alternatives to the Use of Animals

One of the most frequent objections to animal research is the claim that alternative research models obviate the need for research with animals. The concept of alternatives was first raised in 1959 by Russell and Burch[17] in their book, *The Principles of Humane Experimental Technique*. These authors exhorted scientists to reduce the pain of experimental animals, decrease the number of animals used in research, and replace animals with nonanimal models whenever possible.

However, more often than not, alternatives to research animals are not available. In certain research investigations, cell, tissue, and organ cultures and computer models can be used as adjuncts to experiments with animals, and occasion-ally as substitutes for animals, at least in preliminary phases of the investigations. However, in many experimental situations, culture techniques and computer models are wholly inadequate because they do not encompass the physiological complexity of the whole animal. Examples where animals are essential to research include development of a vaccine against human immunodeficiency virus, refinement of organ transplantation techniques, investigation of mechanical devices as replacements for and adjuncts to physiological organs, identification of target-specific pharmaceuticals for cancer diagnosis and treatment, restoration of infarcted myocardium in patients with cardiac disease, evolution of new diagnostic imaging technologies, improvement of methods to relieve mental stress and anxiety, and evaluation of approaches to define and treat chronic pain. These challenges can only be addressed by research with animals as an essential step in the evolution of knowledge that leads to solutions. Humans are the only alternatives to animals for this step. When faced with this alternative, most people prefer the use of animals as the research model.

COMMENT

Love of animals and concern for their welfare are admirable characteristics that distinguish humans from other species of animals. Most humans, scientists as well as laypersons, share these attributes. However, when the concern for animals impedes the development of methods to improve the welfare of humans through amelioration and elimination of pain and suffering, a fundamental choice must be made. This choice is present today in the conflict between animal rights activism and scientific research. The American Medical Association made this choice more than a century ago and continues to stand squarely in defense of the use of animals for scientific research. In this position, the Association is supported by opinion polls that reveal strong endorsement of the American public for the use of animals in research and testing.[18] ...

The American Medical Association believes that research involving animals is absolutely essential to maintaining and improving the health of people in America and worldwide.[6] Animal research is required to develop solutions to human tragedies such as human immunodeficiency virus disease, cancer, heart disease, dementia, stroke, and congenital and developmental abnormalities. The American Medical Association recognizes the moral obligation of investigators to use alternatives to animals whenever possible, and to conduct their research with animals as humanely as possible. However, it is convinced that depriving humans of medical advances by preventing research with animals is philosophically and morally a fundamentally indefensible position. Consequently, the American Medical Association is committed to the preservation of animal research and to the conduct of this research under the most humane conditions possible.[19,20]

REFERENCES

1. Rowan AN, Rollin BE. Animal research—for and against: a philosophical, social, and historical perspective. *Perspect Biol Med.* 1983; 27:1–17.

2. Bernard C; Green HC, trans. *An Introduction to the Study of Experimental Medicine.*

New York, NY: Dover Publications Inc; 1957.

3. Council on Scientific Affairs. Animals in research. *JAMA*, 1989; 261:3602–3606.

4. Leader RW, Stark D. The importance of animals in biomedical research. *Perspect Biol Med.* 1987; 30:470–485.

5. Kransney JA. Some thoughts on the value of life. *Buffalo Physician*, 1984; 18:6–13.

6. Smith SJ, Evans RM, Sullivan-Fowler M, Hendee WR. Use of animals in biomedical research: historical role of the American Medical Association and the American physician. *Arch Intern Med.* 1988; 148:1849–1853.

7. Descartes R. *'Principles of Philosophy,' Descartes: Philosophical Writings.* Anscombe E. Geach PT, eds. London, England: Nelson & Sons; 1969.

8. Bentham J. *Introduction to the Principles of Morals and Legislation.* London, England: Athlone Press; 1970.

9. Godlovitch S, Godlovitch, Harris J. *Animals, Men and Morals.* New York, NY: Taplinger Publishing Co Inc; 1971.

10. Ryder R. *Victims of Science.* London, England: Davis-Poynter; 1975.

11. Singer P. *Animal Liberation: A New Ethic for Our Treatment of Animals.* New York, NY: Random House Inc; 1975.

12. Morowitz HJ, Jesus, Moses, Aristotle and laboratory animals. *Hosp Pract.* 1988; 23:23–25.

13. Cohen C. The case for the use of animals in biomedical research. *N Engl J Med.* 1986; 315: 865–870.

14. *Alternatives to Animal Use in Research, Testing, and Education.* Washington, DC: Office of Technology Assessment; 1986. Publication OTA-BA-273.

15. Committee on the Use of Laboratory Animals in Biomedical and Behavioral Research. *Use of Laboratory Animals in Biomedical and Behavioral Research.* Washington, DC: National Academy Press; 1988.

16. *Biomedical Investigator's Handbook.* Washington, DC: Foundation for Biomedical Research; 1987.

17. Russell WMS, Burch RL. *The Principles of Humane Experimental Technique.* Springfield, Ill: Charles C Thomas Publisher; 1959.

18. Harvey LK, Shubat SC. *AMA Survey of Physician and Public Opinion on Health Care Issues.* Chicago, Ill: American Medical Association; 1989.

19. Smith SJ, Hendee WR. Animals in research. *JAMA* 1988; 259:2007–2008.

20. Smith SJ, Loeb JM, Evans RM, Hendee WR. Animals in research and testing; who pays the price for medical progress? *Arch Ophthalmol.* 1988; 106:1184–1187.

NO

Steven Zak

ETHICS AND ANIMALS

In December of 1986 members of an "animal-liberation" group called True Friends broke into the Sema, Inc., laboratories in Rockville, Maryland, and took four baby chimpanzees from among the facility's 600 primates. The four animals, part of a group of thirty being used in hepatitis research, had been housed individually in "isolettes"—small stainless-steel chambers with sealed glass doors. A videotape produced by True Friends shows other primates that remained behind. Some sit behind glass on wire floors, staring blankly. One rocks endlessly, banging violently against the side of his cage. Another lies dead on his cage's floor.

The "liberation" action attracted widespread media attention to Sema, which is a contractor for the National Institutes of Health [NIH], the federal agency that funds most of the animal research in this country. Subsequently the NIH conducted an investigation into conditions at the lab and concluded that the use of isolettes is justified to prevent the spread of disease among infected animals. For members of True Friends and other animal-rights groups, however, such a scientific justification is irrelevant to what they see as a moral wrong; these activists remain frustrated over conditions at the laboratory. This conflict between the NIH and animal-rights groups mirrors the tension between animal researchers and animal-rights advocates generally. The researchers' position is that their use of animals is necessary to advance human health care and that liberation actions waste precious resources and impede the progress of science and medicine. The animal-rights advocates' position is that animal research is an ethical travesty that justifies extraordinary, and even illegal, measures.

The Sema action is part of a series that numbers some six dozen to date and that began, in 1979, with a raid on the New York University Medical Center, in which members of a group known as the Animal Liberation Front (ALF) took a cat and two guinea pigs. The trend toward civil disobedience is growing. For example, last April members of animal-rights groups demonstrated at research institutions across the country (and in other countries, including Great Britain and Japan), sometimes blocking entrances to them by forming human chains. In the United States more than 130 activists were arrested, for offenses ranging from blocking a doorway and trespassing to burglary.

To judge by everything from talk-show programs to booming membership enrollment in animal-rights groups (U.S. membership in all groups is estimated at 10 million), the American public is increasingly receptive to the animal-rights position. Even some researchers admit that raids by groups like True Friends and the ALF have exposed egregious conditions in particular labs and have been the catalyst for needed reforms in the law. But many members of animal-rights groups feel that the recent reforms do not go nearly far enough. Through dramatic animal-liberation actions and similar tactics, they hope to force what they fear is a complacent public to confront a difficult philosophical issue: whether animals, who are known to have feelings and psychological lives, ought to be treated as mere instruments of science and other human endeavors....

Animal-rights activists feel acute frustration over a number of issues, including hunting and trapping, the destruction of animals' natural habits, and the raising of animals for food. But for now the ALF considers animal research the most powerful symbol of human dominion over and exploitation of animals, and it devotes most of its energies to that issue. The public has been ambivalent, sometimes cheering the ALF on, at other times denouncing the group as "hooligans." However one chooses to characterize the ALF, it and other groups like it hold an uncompromising "rights view" of ethics toward animals. The rights view distinguishes the animal-protection movement of today from that of the past and is the source of the movement's radicalism.

"THEY ALL HAVE A RIGHT TO LIVE"

Early animal-protection advocates and groups... seldom talked about rights. They condemned cruelty—that is, acts that produce or reveal bad character. In early-nineteenth-century England campaigners against the popular sport of bull-baiting argued that it "fostered every bad and barbarous principle of our nature." Modern activists have abandoned the argument that cruelty is demeaning to human character ("virtue thought") in favor of the idea that the lives of animals have intrinsic value ("rights thought"). Rights thought doesn't necessarily preclude the consideration of virtue, but it mandates that the measure of virtue be the foreseeable consequences to others of one's acts.

"Michele" is thirty-five and works in a bank in the East. She has participated in many of the major ALF actions in the United States. One of the missions involved freeing rats, and she is scornful of the idea that rats aren't worth the effort. "These animals feel pain just like dogs, but abusing them doesn't arouse constituents' ire, so they don't get the same consideration. They all have a right to live their lives. Cuteness should not be a factor."

While most people would agree that animals should not be tortured, there is no consensus about animals' right to live (or, more precisely, their right not to be killed). Even if one can argue, as the British cleric Humphrey Primatt did in 1776, that "pain is pain, whether it be inflicted on man or on beast," it is more difficult to argue that the life of, say, a dog is qualitatively the same as that of a human being. To this, many animal-rights activists would say that every morally relevant characteristic that is lacking in all animals (rationality might be one, according to some ways of defining that term) is also lacking in some "marginal" human beings, such as infants, or the senile, or the severely retarded. Therefore, the activists argue, if marginal human beings have the right to live, it is arbitrary to hold that animals do not. Opponents of this point of view often focus on the differences between animals and "normal" human beings, asserting, for instance, that unlike most human adults, animals do not live by moral rules and therefore are not part of the human "moral community."

The credibility of the animal-rights viewpoint, however, need not stand or fall with the "marginal human beings" argument. Lives don't have to be qualitatively the same to be worthy of equal respect. One's perception that another life has value comes as much from an appreciation of its uniqueness as from the recognition that it has characteristics that are shared by one's own life. (Who would compare the life of a whale to that of a marginal human being?) One can imagine that the lives of various kinds of animals differ radically, even as a result of having dissimilar bodies and environments—that being an octopus feels different from being an orangutan or an oriole. The orangutan cannot be redescribed as the octopus minus, or plus, this or that mental characteristic; conceptually, nothing could be added to or taken from the octopus that would make it the equivalent of the oriole. Likewise, animals are not simply rudimentary human beings, God's false steps, made before He finally got it right with us.

Recognizing differences, however, puts one on tentative moral ground. It is easy to argue that likes ought to be treated alike. Differences bring problems: How do we think about things that are unlike? Against what do we measure and evaluate them? What combinations of likeness and difference lead to what sorts of moral consideration? Such problems may seem unmanageable, and yet in a human context we routinely face ones similar in kind if not quite in degree: our ethics must account for dissimilarities between men and women, citizens and aliens, the autonomous and the helpless, the fully developed and the merely potential, such as children or fetuses. We never solve these problems with finality, but we confront them....

Both advocates and opponents of animal rights also invoke utilitarianism in support of their points of view. Utilitarianism holds that an act or practice is measured by adding up the good and the bad consequences—classically, pleasure and pain—and seeing which come out ahead. There are those who would exclude animals from moral consideration on the grounds that the benefits of exploiting them outweigh the harm. Ironically, though, it was utilitarianism, first formulated by Jeremy Bentham in the eighteenth century, that brought animals squarely into the realm of moral consideration. If an act or practice has good and bad consequences for animals, then these must be entered into the moral arithmetic. And the calculation must be genuinely disinterested. One may not baldly assert that one's own interests count for more. Animal researchers may truly believe that they are impartially weighing all interests when they conclude that human interests overwhelm those of animals. But a skeptical reader will seldom be persuaded that they are in fact doing so....

Even true utilitarianism is incomplete, though, without taking account of rights. For example, suppose a small group of aboriginal tribespeople were captured and bred for experiments that would benefit millions of other people by, say, resulting in more crash-worthy cars. Would the use of such people be morally acceptable? Surely it would not, and that point illustrates an important function of rights thought: to put limits on what can be done to individuals, even for the good of the many. Rights thought dictates that we cannot kill one rights-holder to save another—or even more than one other—whether or not the life of the former is "different" from that of the latter.

Those who seek to justify the exploitation of animals often claim that it comes down to a choice: kill an animal or allow a human being to die. But this claim is misleading, because a choice so posed has already been made. The very act of considering the taking of life X to save life Y reduces X to the status of a mere instrument. Consider the problem in a purely human context. Imagine that if Joe doesn't get a new kidney he will die. Sam, the only known potential donor with a properly matching kidney, himself has only one kidney and has not consented to give it—and his life—up for Joe. Is there really a choice? If the only way to save Joe is to kill Sam, then we would be unable to do so—and no one would say that we chose Sam over Joe. Such a choice would never even be contemplated.

In another kind of situation there *is* a choice. Imagine that Joe and Sam both need a kidney to survive, but we have only one in our kidney bank. It may be that we should give the kidney to Joe, a member of our community, rather than to Sam, who lives in some distant country (though this is far from clear—maybe flipping a coin would be more fair). Sam (or the loser of the coin flip) could not complain that his rights had been violated, because moral claims to some resource—positive claims—must always be dependent on the availability of that resource. But the right not to be treated as if one were a mere resource or instrument—negative, defensive claims —is most fundamentally what it means to say that one has rights. And this is what members of the ALF have in mind when they declare that animals, like human beings, have rights.

Where, one might wonder, should the line be drawn? Must we treat dragonflies the same as dolphins? Surely not. Distinctions must be made, though to judge definitively which animals must be ruled out as holders of rights may be impossible even in principle. In legal or moral discourse we are virtually never able to draw clear lines. This does not mean that drawing a line anywhere, arbitrarily, is as good as drawing one anywhere else.

The line-drawing metaphor, though, implies classifying entities in a binary way: as either above the line, and so entitled to moral consideration, or not. Binary thinking misses nuances of our moral intuition. Entities without rights may still deserve moral consideration on other grounds: one may think that a dragonfly doesn't quite qualify for rights yet believe that it would be wrong to crush one without good reason. And not all entities with rights need be treated in precisely the same way. This is apparent when one compares animals over whom we have assumed custody with wild animals. The former, I think, have rights to our affirmative aid, while the latter have such rights only in certain circumstances. Similar distinctions can be made among human beings, and also between human beings and particular animals. For example, I recently spent $1,000 on medical care for my dog, and I think he had a right to that care, but I have never given such an amount to a needy person on the street. Rights thought, then, implies neither that moral consideration ought to be extended only to the holders of rights nor that all rights-holders must be treated with a rigid equality. It implies only that rights-holders should never be treated as if they, or their kind, didn't matter.

ANIMALS, REFRIGERATORS, AND CAN OPENERS

The question of man's relationship with animals goes back at least to Aristotle, who granted that animals have certain senses—hunger, thirst, a sense of touch —but who held that they lack rationality and therefore as "the lower sort [they] are by nature slaves, and... should be under the rule of a master." Seven centuries later Saint Augustine added the authority of the Church, arguing that "Christ himself [teaches] that to refrain from the killing of animals...is the height of superstition, for there are no common rights between us and the beasts...." Early in the seventeenth century René Descartes argued that, lacking language, animals cannot have thoughts or souls and thus are machines.

One may be inclined to dismiss such beliefs as archaic oddities, but even today some people act as if animals were unfeeling things. I worked in a research lab for several summers during college, and I remember that it was a natural tendency to lose all empathy with one's animal subjects. My supervisor seemed actually to delight in swinging rats around by their tails and flinging them against a concrete wall as a way of stunning the animals before killing them. Rats and rabbits, to those who injected, weighed, and dissected them, were little different from cultures in a petri dish: they were just things to manipulate and observe. Feelings of what may have been moral revulsion were taken for squeamishness, and for most of my lab mates those feelings subsided with time.

The first animal-welfare law in the United States, passed in New York State in 1828, emphasized the protection of animals useful in agriculture. It also promoted human virtue with a ban on "maliciously and cruelly" beating or torturing horses, sheep, or cattle. Today courts still tend to focus on human character, ruling against human beings only for perpetrating the most shocking and senseless abuse of animals....

Most states leave the regulation of medical research to Washington. In 1966 Congress passed the Laboratory Animal Welfare Act, whose stated purpose was not only to provide humane care for animals but also to protect the owners of dogs and cats from theft by proscribing the use of stolen animals. (Note the vocabulary of property law; animals have long been legally classified as property.) Congress then passed the Animal Welfare Act [AWA] of 1970, which expanded the provisions of the 1966 act to include more species of animals and to regulate more people who handle animals. The AWA was further amended in 1976 and in 1985.

The current version of the AWA mandates that research institutions meet certain minimum requirements for the handling and the housing of animals, and requires the "appropriate" use of pain-killers. But the act does not regulate research or experimentation itself, and allows researchers to withhold anesthetics or tranquilizers "when scientifically necessary." Further, while the act purports to regulate dealers who buy animals at auctions and other markets to sell to laboratories, it does little to protect those animals....

The 1985 amendments to the AWA were an attempt to improve the treatment of animals in laboratories, to improve enforcement, to encourage the consideration of alternative research methods that use fewer or no animals, and to minimize duplication in experiments. One notable change is that for the first time, research institutions using primates must keep them in environments conducive to their psychological well-being; however, some animal-rights activists have expressed skepticism, since the social and psychological needs of primates are complex, and the primary concern of researchers is not the interests of their animal subjects. Last September [1988] a symposium on the psychological well-being of captive primates was held at Harvard University. Some participants contended that we lack data on the needs of the thirty to forty species of primates now used in laboratories. Others suggested that the benefits of companionship and social life are obvious.

The U.S. Department of Agriculture is responsible for promulgating regulations under the AWA and enforcing the law. Under current USDA regulations the cages of primates need only have floor space equal to three times the area occupied by the animal "when standing on four feet"—in the words of the USDA, which has apparently forgotten that primates have hands. The 1985 amendments required the USDA to publish final revised regulations, including regulations on the well-being of primates, by December of 1986. At this writing the department has yet to comply, and some activists charge that the NIH and the Office of Management and Budget have delayed the publication of the new regulations and attempted to undermine them.

One may believe that virtue thought —which underlies current law—and rights thought should protect animals equally. After all, wouldn't a virtuous person or society respect the interests of animals? But virtue thought allows the law to disregard these interests, because virtue can be measured by at least two yardsticks: by the foreseeable effects of an act on the interests of an animal or by the social utility of the act. The latter standard was applied in a 1983 case in Maryland in which a researcher appealed his conviction for cruelty to animals after he had performed experiments that resulted in monkeys' mutilating their hands. Overturning the conviction, the Maryland Court of Appeals wrote that "there are certain normal human activities to which the infliction of pain to an animal is purely incidental"—thus the actor is not a sadist—and that the state legislature had intended for these activities to be exempt from the law protecting animals.

The law, of course, is not monolithic. Some judges have expressed great sympathy for animals. On the whole, though, the law doesn't recognize animal rights. Under the Uniform Commercial Code, for instance, animals—along with refrigerators and can openers—constitute "goods."

ALTERNATIVES TO US-VERSUS-THEM

Estimates of the number of animals used each year in laboratories in the United States range from 17 million to 100 million: 200,000 dogs, 50,000 cats, 60,000 primates, 1.5 million guinea pigs, hamsters, and rabbits, 200,000 wild animals, thousands of farm animals and birds, and millions of rats and mice. The conditions in general—lack of exercise, isolation from other animals, lengthy confinement in tiny cages—are stressful. Many experiments are painful or produce fear, anxiety, or depression. For instance, in 1987 researchers at the Armed Forces Radiobiology Research Institute reported that nine monkeys were subjected to whole-body irradiation; as a result, within two hours six of the monkeys were vomiting and hypersalivating. In a proposed experiment at the University of Washington pregnant monkeys, kept in isolation, will be infected with the simian AIDS virus; their offspring, infected or not, will be separated from the mothers at birth.

Not all animals in laboratories, of course, are subjects of medical research. In the United States each year some 10 million animals are used in testing products and for other commercial purposes. For instance, the United States Surgical Corporation, in Norwalk, Connecticut, uses hundreds of dogs each year to train salesmen in the use of the company's surgical staple gun. In 1981 and 1982 a group called Friends of Animals brought two lawsuits against United States Surgical to halt these practices. The company successfully argued in court that Friends of Animals lacked "standing" to sue, since no member of the organization had been injured by the practice; after some further legal maneuvering by Friends of Animals

both suits were dropped. Last November [1988] a New York City animal-rights advocate was arrested as she planted a bomb outside United States Surgical's headquarters.

In 1987, according to the USDA, 130,373 animals were subjected to pain or distress unrelieved by drugs for "the purpose of research or testing." This figure, which represents nearly seven percent of the 1,969,123 animals reported to the USDA that year as having been "used in experimentation," ignores members of species not protected by the AWA (cold-blooded animals, mice, rats, birds, and farm animals). Moreover, there is reason to believe that the USDA's figures are low. For example, according to the USDA, no primates were subjected to distress in the state of Maryland, the home of Sema, in any year from 1980 to 1987, the last year for which data are available.

Steps seemingly favorable to animals have been taken in recent years. In addition to the passage of the 1985 amendments to the AWA, the Public Health Service [PHS], which includes the NIH, has revised its "Policy on Humane Care and Use of Laboratory Animals," and new legislation has given legal force to much of this policy. Under the revised policy, institutions receiving NIH or other PHS funds for animal research must have an "institutional animal care and use committee" consisting of at least five members, including one nonscientist and one person not affiliated with the institution.

Many activists are pessimistic about these changes, however. They argue that the NIH has suspended funds at noncompliant research institutions only in response to political pressure, and assert that the suspensions are intended as a token gesture, to help the NIH regain lost credibility. They note that Sema, which continues to keep primates in isolation cages (as regulations permit), is an NIH contractor whose principal investigators are NIH employees. As to the makeup of the animal-care committees, animal-rights advocates say that researchers control who is appointed to them. In the words of one activist, "The brethren get to choose."

However one interprets these changes, much remains the same. For example, the AWA authorizes the USDA to confiscate animals from laboratories not in compliance with regulations, but only if the animal "is no longer required... to carry out the research, test or experiment"; the PHS policy mandates pain relief "unless the procedure is justified for scientific reasons." Fundamentally, the underlying attitude that animals may appropriately be used and discarded persists.

If the law is ever to reflect the idea that animals have rights, more-drastic steps—such as extending the protection of the Constitution to animals—must be taken. Constitutional protection for animals is not an outlandish proposition. The late U.S. Supreme Court Justice William O. Douglas wrote once, in a dissenting opinion, that the day should come when "all of the forms of life... will stand before the court—the pileated woodpecker as well as the coyote and bear, the lemmings as well as the trout in the streams."

Suppose, just suppose, that the AWA were replaced by an animal-rights act, which would prohibit the use by human beings of any animals to their detriment. What would be the effect on medical research, education, and product testing? Microorganisms; tissue, organ, and cell cultures; physical and chemical systems that mimic biological functions; computer programs and mathematical models that simulate biological interactions; epidemiologic data bases; and clinical studies have all been used to reduce the number of animals used in experiments, demonstrations, and tests. A 1988 study by the National Research Council, while finding that researchers lack the means to replace all animals in labs, did conclude that current and prospective alternative techniques could reduce the number of animals—particularly mammals—used in research.

Perhaps the report would have been more optimistic if scientists were as zealous about conducting research to find alternatives as they are about animal research. But we should not be misled by discussions of alternatives into thinking that the issue is merely empirical. It is broader than just whether subject A and procedure X can be replaced by surrogates B and Y. We could undergo a shift in world view: instead of imagining that we have a divine mandate to dominate and make use of everything else in the universe, we could have a sense of belonging to the world and of kinship with the other creatures in it. The us-versus-them thinking that weighs animal suffering against human gain could give way to an appreciation that "us" includes "them." That's an alternative too.

Some researchers may insist that scientists should not be constrained in their quest for knowledge, but this is a romantic notion of scientific freedom that never was and should not be. Science is always constrained, by economic and social priorities and by ethics. Sometimes, paradoxically, it is also freed by these constraints, because a barrier in one direction forces it to cut another path, in an area that might have remained unexplored.

Barriers against the exploitation of animals ought to be erected in the law, because law not only enforces morality but defines it. Until the law protects the interests of animals, the animal-rights movement will by definition be radical. And whether or not one approves of breaking the law to remedy its shortcomings, one can expect such activities to continue. "I believe that you should do for others as you would have done for you," one member of the ALF says. "If you were being used in painful experiments, you'd want someone to come to your rescue."

POSTSCRIPT

Is the Use of Animals in Research Justified?

Scientists tend to believe that they are involved in the pursuit of truth. Therefore, all questions are worth asking, and all research methods are worth using, as long as they lead to the answers sought.

Some groups object to the asking of certain questions (such as, "Are there differences in intelligence between races?" or "Is there a genetic basis for violence?"), perhaps out of fear that the answers will not suit their political agendas. As for methods, much debate about the lethal experiments that were conducted on nonconsenting human subjects by the Nazis during World War II, as well as the ensuing trials of the Nazi physicians in Nuremburg, Germany, has established a consensus that no scientist can treat people the way the Nazis did. Informed consent is essential, and research on humans must aim to benefit those same humans.

As these ideas have gained currency, some people have tried to extend them to say that, just as scientists cannot do whatever they wish to humans, they cannot do whatever they wish to animals. Harriet Ritvo, in "Toward a More Peaceable Kingdom," *Technology Review* (April 1992), says that the animal rights movement "challenges the ideology of science itself... forcing experimenters to recognize that they are not necessarily carrying out an independent exercise in the pursuit of truth—that their enterprise, in its intellectual as well as its social and financial dimensions, is circumscribed and defined by the culture of which it is an integral part." The result is a continuing debate, driven by the periodic discovery of researchers who seem quite callous (at least to the layperson's eye) in their treatment of animals (see Kathy Snow Guillermo, *Monkey Business: The Disturbing Case That Launched the Animal Rights Movement*, National Press, 1993) and by the assumption that animal rights advocates just do not understand nature (see Richard Conniff, "Fuzzy-Wuzzy Thinking About Animal Rights," *Audubon*, November 1990).

For a good overview of the subject, see Marc Leepson, "Animal Rights," *CQ Researcher* (May 24, 1991). Also, several pertinent books include: Michael P. T. Leahy, *Against Liberation: Putting Animals in Perspective* (Routledge, 1992); Lorenz Otto Lutherer and Margaret Sheffield Simon, *Targeted: The Anatomy of an Animal Rights Attack* (University of Oklahoma Press, 1992); F. Barbara Orlans, *In the Name of Science: Issues in Responsible Animal Experimentation* (Oxford University Press, 1993); Peter Singer, *Animal Liberation*, rev. ed. (Avon Books, 1990); and Rod Strand and Patti Strand, *The Hijacking of the Humane Movement* (Doral, 1993).

ISSUE 18

Is It Ethical to Use Humans as "Experimental Animals"?

YES: Charles C. Mann, from "Radiation: Balancing the Record," *Science* (January 28, 1994)

NO: Arjun Makhijani, from "Energy Enters Guilty Plea," *The Bulletin of the Atomic Scientists* (March/April 1994)

ISSUE SUMMARY

YES: Science writer Charles C. Mann makes the point that, under certain conditions, experiments done on human beings—even those involving radiation—can be ethically sound.

NO: Arjun Makhijani, president of the Institute for Energy and Environmental Research in Takoma Park, Maryland, argues that, because the subjects of the radiation experiments were exposed to great risks without their knowledge, the experiments were grossly unethical.

Biological and medical experimentation on human beings has a bad reputation. This is partly because of what came to light after World War II: Under the Nazi regime, German researchers had, in the name of science, used prisoners to study amputation, healing, infection, and hypothermia. Many of the subjects died during the experiments. The researchers, however, did not ask their subjects for consent, nor did they supply painkillers or try to put the pieces back together afterward. To them, human prisoners were as disposable as lab rats.

The reputation of psychological experimentation also suffered when—in an effort to learn how people could follow authority, even if it meant committing atrocities against another individual (such as the Nazi acts during the Holocaust)—social psychologist Stanley Milgram devised an experiment in which subjects were told that they were to be the teachers in an experiment on the effects of punishment on memory. The subject's job was to give the learner electric shocks of increasing intensity each time the learner made an error. However, the "learner" was an actor who purposely gave wrong answers, and the shocks were not real, but the subjects did not know that. Although some of the subjects balked partway through the experiment, an appalling number continued to increase the strength of the shocks until the "learner" was in obvious agony. Critics of Milgram's research (and research like it) have objected that the essential role that deception plays in such research means that true informed consent is not possible. Critics also object to the psychological harm that such experiments may cause to subjects by showing them things about themselves that they would rather not know (such as a capacity for cruelty).

American medical researchers have also done some apparently very cruel experiments on human subjects. Consider, for instance, the Tuskegee syphilis project. In 1932 researchers began to study 400 black men from Tuskegee, Alabama, who were infected with syphilis, as well as 200 uninfected black men as the control group. The purpose of the study was to learn exactly how the disease progressed from infection to the subject's death (whether of syphilis or of other causes, including old age), and, in fact, the project has provided large amounts of information now found in medical textbooks.

However, when antibiotics—which can cure syphilis very quickly—became available in the 1940s, the experimenters denied them to their subjects. Studying syphilis was evidently more important to the researchers than saving the lives of the subjects, and it remained so until the media revealed the project in 1972. Public outcry soon resulted in the project's termination and, in 1974, in the National Research Act, which calls for institutional review boards to approve all federally funded research on human beings.

The existence of the National Research Act implies that human experimentation can be done under suitable circumstances. Those circumstances require informed consent and concern for the subjects' welfare, among other things. In the following selections, Charles C. Mann argues that, although these conditions were missing or insufficient in some of the radiation experiments that were performed on humans in the United States beginning after World War II, many of the experiments paid due attention to informed consent and were carefully designed to expose subjects to little or no harm. Indeed, in some of the studies the subjects were the experimenters themselves. Arjun Makhijani argues that he objects to the radiation experiments in large part because they involved military interests—implicitly if not explicitly—and therefore could not possibly be directed toward anyone's welfare. He emphasizes the secrecy with which the research was conducted as well as the vulnerability of many of the chosen subjects, such as prisoners and terminally ill patients.

YES

Charles C. Mann

RADIATION: BALANCING THE RECORD

On November 15, 1993, the *Albuquerque Journal* published the first of three horrifyingly detailed articles about Manhattan Project scientists injecting plutonium into human beings. Three weeks later, Department of Energy Secretary Hazel O'Leary told a press conference that she was "appalled, shocked, and saddened" by the report. The head of the agency—notorious in the past for secrecy—vowed to "open the archives," triggering a media firestorm....

Is it conceivable that just after the Second World War—when Nazi doctors tortured concentration camp inmates in the name of science—U.S. researchers treated unknowing patients with similar disregard? Or, as some researchers have claimed in defense, did the experiments have a historic context and scientific value that provides justification for these seemingly inhumane actions?

Press reports have overwhelmingly favored the former, cynical, explanation. The *Albuquerque Journal* described a single incident in which 18 terminal patients were injected with plutonium. Then newspapers such as *The Boston Globe* and *The Portland Oregonian* dug up research that involved feeding radioactive milk to retarded children and zapping the testicles of prisoners with high-energy radiation. Other journalists added to the impression of widespread abuse with their belated discovery of a 1986 congressional report detailing cases in which "nuclear guinea pigs" tested radioactive compounds such as tritium and technetium.

But an inquiry by *Science* shows that reality is, as usual, more complex than this sensational picture. For instance, at least five of the 31 experiments in the congressional report were apparently performed by researchers on themselves—hardly unknowing human guinea pigs. At least nine others cited in that document (known as the Markey Report, after Edward Markey (D-MA), head of the subcommittee that produced it) involved the use of minute, harmless quantities of radioactive isotopes to follow biochemical reactions within the body. "The trouble with the reporting today is that it doesn't make any distinctions," complains Sanford Miller, dean of the Graduate School of Biomedical Sciences at the University of Texas Health Science Center in San Antonio. "It's all radiation with a capital R. But there's various

From Charles C. Mann, "Radiation: Balancing the Record," *Science*, vol. 263 (January 28, 1994), pp. 470–473. Copyright © 1994 by The American Association for the Advancement of Science. Reprinted by permission.

radiations—it's not a single golem rising out of the grave. And how people have thought about it over time is a lot more complicated than the newspapers make out."

That doesn't mean all of this research was valid—or even defensible. All evaluations are provisional, because some of the researchers are dead and complete explanations for their behavior are hard to come by, and records and accusations are still coming in. But at this point, it appears that the radiation experiments in the United States can be broadly classified in three groups. In one, researchers knowingly inflicted potential harm on patients, using methods that are difficult to justify even by the standards of the past. By contrast, a second, larger group of investigations involved perfectly good work by any standards, with appropriate safeguards taken. And a third group of studies falls between these extremes: The experiments provided useful information but had ethical flaws.

Doing possible damage. Most of the media attention has been paid to the injections of plutonium that took place between April 1945 and July 1947—a period that began a few months before Hiroshima and ended at the time of the Nuremberg trials. The nation then faced a serious public health problem, recalls J. Newell Stannard, a health physicist at the University of California, San Diego, and author of the 2000-page study *Radioactivity and Health: A History.* "Thousands of workers at the Manhattan Project had been potentially exposed to plutonium," he says. "Physicians were able to monitor how much [plutonium] the workers excreted, but they didn't know how much they had taken in, because the exposures were accidental."

Since it already seemed clear that many more workers would be exposed to radioactivity over time, plant safety officials were frantic for information about the effects of plutonium. But nobody even knew whether it was quickly excreted, limiting its potential for danger, or retained in the body, where it could keep irradiating tissue for years. A few studies had been done with rats, mice, rabbits, and dogs. But the data were contradictory, partly because species metabolize plutonium differently. So radiologist Stafford Warren and the other members of the Manhattan Project Health Group came up with the plan of introducing known quantities of plutonium into the bodies of terminally ill volunteers. Their already-short life expectancies would both duck the question of long-term harm and allow any remaining plutonium in their bodies to be measured at an autopsy. Warren's team chose 18 men and women, all terminal patients, from San Francisco, Chicago, and Rochester.

Today, any research like this must obtain human subjects' "informed consent." Such consent means that the subjects of the experiment appreciate the known —and suspected—risks of participation and voluntarily agree to participate even after knowing those risks. At the time of Warren's plan, the term "informed consent" was not yet widely used, but the principle had been established in court cases during the 1930s, and other researchers did follow it. The idea was explicitly codified during the prosecution of the Nazi doctors, which began in December 1946.

For plutonium, though, informed consent was out of the question—because the military wouldn't hear of it. General Leslie Groves, director of the Manhattan

Project, was "paranoid about security," says Stannard. "Plutonium couldn't even be named—it had to be called 'product.' All [Warren and the other doctors] could tell them was that they were going to get a product in a small dose."

Even taking the rigid constraints imposed by the military into account, there is little to suggest that the subjects were thoughtfully chosen—a necessity if one has a small number, says Richard Griesemer, deputy director of the National Institute of Environmental Health Sciences (NIEHS). According to the *Albuquerque Tribune*, at least six had been wrongly diagnosed and were not about to die; two more were suffering from conditions disrupting the metabolic pathways the investigators were examining. Many injectees were apparently lost to follow-up. Only five are known to have been autopsied, one of the express purposes of the research.

According to toxicologists such as James Huff, a senior scientist in the environmental carcinogenesis program at NIEHS, researchers usually minimize possible toxic effects by administering slowly increasing doses to subjects. This did not occur.... The second dose was the lowest given; the third, administered less than a month later, was the third highest.

"The experiment did not have a rigid protocol established by some central authority," says biophysicist Patricia Durbin from Lawrence Berkeley Laboratory, who worked with the plutonium data for decades. Nonetheless, she says, the study was invaluable. "It is the *only* human data where the actual quantity inside the body is known and the time it was acquired is known." And Kenneth L. Mossman, president of the Health Physics Society, told Congress on 18 January that data from this "ex-

tremely important" study "serves as the principal database for current plutonium standards."

But even if the results stand up, many scientists say, the ethics do not. "People didn't know a lot of the things we know now," says Huff. "Toxicology didn't really exist as a field. Still, they knew that you shouldn't give people things that might harm them in the long term and try to get around it by saying they would die soon, anyway."

Two other sets of experiments raise similar concerns. Between 1963 and 1971, Carl G. Heller of the University of Oregon and the Pacific Northwest Research Foundation exposed the testicles of 67 prisoners at Oregon State Prison to ionizing radiation. One of Heller's protégés, C. Alvin Paulsen of the University of Washington, irradiated the testicles of 64 inmates at Washington State Prison between 1963 and 1980.

The reason for the testicular work was a 1962 accident at the Hanford Nuclear Reservation, in Richland, Washington, which exposed three workers to high doses of gamma radiation. Hanford officials asked Paulsen, a reproductive physiologist, to inform the men about their prospects for fatherhood. Little was known, it turned out. This was alarming to contemplate in an era that envisioned the rapid spread of nuclear power.

"We didn't have the knowledge for effective safety standards," Paulsen says. "I decided it was important to have certain information, such as the ED-50 —the effective dose that would impair sperm production in 50% of men." Some animal research had been done, but, as in other areas of radiation research, the behavior of animal and human reproductive systems often differs. The best way to learn more, Paulsen reasoned,

ETHICS IN RADIOACTIVITY EXPERIMENTS

In some of the radiation studies cited in newspapers and in a congressional report, known as the Markey Report, subjects did not freely consent to the experiments. In other studies it is doubtful whether informed consent was obtained. But in some of the studies informed consent was truly given. Here are examples from each category.

Possible Infliction of Harm or No Informed Consent

1945–47 Injecting 18 supposedly terminal patients with high doses of plutonium to learn whether the body absorbed it.

1946–47 6 hospital patients injected with uranium salts to determine the dose that produced renal injury.

1963–71 67 prison inmates had testicles exposed to x-rays to measure radiation damage to production of sperm.

1963–70 Another 64 prison inmates had testicles exposed to x-rays to relate radiation damage to sperm production.

Questionable Consent (6 other studies cited in Markey report)

1946 17 retarded teenagers at the Fernald School in Waltham, Massachusetts, ate meals with trace amounts of radioactive iron to learn about iron absorption in body.

1954–56 32 retarded teenagers at the Fernald School drank milk with trace amounts of radioactive calcium to learn whether oatmeal impeded its absorption by the body.

1953–57 Injecting 11 comatose brain cancer patients with uranium to learn whether it is absorbed by brain tumors.

Informed Consent (17 other studies cited in Markey Report)

1951 14 researchers at Hanford Nuclear Reservation voluntarily exposed patches of their skin to gaseous tritium.

1945 10 researchers and workers at Clinton Laboratory, in Oak Ridge, Tennessee, voluntarily exposed patches of their skin to radioactive phosphorus.

1965 Trace doses of radioactive technetium given to 8 healthy volunteers to determine its utility as medical diagnostic tool.

1963 54 hospital patients volunteered to take trace amounts of radioactive lanthanum in effort to measure effects on large intestine.

was to expose men to single blasts of radiation and measure the reaction, gradually increasing the amount with each group of subjects to construct a dose-response curve. "And that," he says, "brought up the issue of what type of population should be exposed."

Experimentation with prisoners was not unusual at the time—Heller, Paulsen's mentor, had been using them for years. "You had a wonderfully controlled population that was highly cooperative," dryly observes Wil Nelp, chairman of the department of nuclear medicine at the University of Washington. "They couldn't go anywhere, so follow-up was easy." Inmates often were housed in special state-hospital wards and fed fancy diets. Researchers sometimes filed notices of cooperation in their records. These were hard things for prisoners to turn down. "It was a good deal for them," Nelp says. "Probably too good of a deal."

Paulsen obtained permission for his study from the university, the state, and the prison. He then asked for volunteers among the inmates, asking them to promise to have vasectomies afterward. Before starting, Paulsen says, he privately interviewed each volunteer "and gave him every opportunity to say yea or nay." Then he gave all the participants (except a control group) between 7.5 to 400 roentgens, a high dose. Heller began a similar program a month later, with still higher doses: 8 to 600 roentgens.

Despite the chance to "say yea or nay," questions soon arose about the nature of the prisoners' consent. In 1966, the late anesthesiologist Henry Beecher published two landmark articles in the *New England Journal of Medicine* arguing, among other things, that patients' consent to a procedure that will harm them indicates some coercion, since people

who are free to choose won't usually allow themselves to be hurt. Further extension of this reasoning implies that prisoners cannot give informed consent at all, since their circumstances make them particularly prone to such coercion. The articles provoked enormous controversy, and, concerned about the combination of radiation and prisoners, the University of Washington halted Paulsen's work in 1969, rejecting his pleas to continue with additional measurements. Heller had a stroke in 1972, ending his efforts before anyone else could.

Yet the ethical flaws did not obviate its scientific interest. A 1974 paper based on Heller's prisoner work has been cited 135 times, according to the Institute for Scientific Information, a rate that places it in the top 1% of all the papers they track. And Paulsen says, "My colleagues were interested in what I was doing. I was not off by myself."

Valid research. In sharp contrast to these experiments, much of the other work attacked in the Markey Report seems entirely blameless. Five 1950s-era experiments, for example, involved volunteers bathing patches of their skin in tritium, a radioactive form of hydrogen gas. One subject was exposed over his entire body. These people, the report charges, "thus became nuclear calibration devices." True. But the saving grace, which the report doesn't mention, is that in at least five of these studies the calibration devices apparently were the experimenters themselves.

At the time, atmospheric nuclear tests were creating lots of tritium, and scientists like Harry A. Kornberg of Hanford wanted to find out whether people could absorb tritium from water and air. After exposing rats, the team learned that living systems could, in fact, absorb tritium. But, again, the key question was whether the rat data could be applied to people.

The only way to find out was to perform tests on human beings. According to Chester W. DeLong, a team member who is now retired in Virginia, the volunteers were other researchers at the Hanford health lab. Kornberg insisted on doing the whole-body immersion himself. "He said, 'Well, I'm past child-bearing stage and I can tolerate it,'" recalls DeLong. "And I don't want anybody else exposed this way.'" And the work paid off, showing that people absorbed tritium four times faster than rats.

These results became mostly irrelevant, however, after the atmospheric test ban treaty was signed in 1963. But such self-experimentation was and is considered acceptable, and even heroic, according to *Who Goes First?*, Lawrence Altman's 1987 book on the subject. As for the "guinea pig" characterization in the Markey Report, DeLong says, "They never bothered to call and ask me about the work."

Four other experiments involving radioactive tracers that are mentioned in the Markey Report seem to be equally acceptable ethically. In those experiments, researchers introduced tiny amounts of short-lived radioactive isotopes into human subjects. The radioactivity allows the tracers to be followed through the body. Afterward, they decay into harmless substances. In some media reports, this has been described as feeding people radioactivity. True enough—but the technique has been used for 60 years with no apparent ill effect.

In one example from 1965, the University of Washington's Nelp and two colleagues from the Pacific Northwest Laboratory, then a nonprofit organization based in Richland, Washington, injected technetium-95 or -96 into eight students and housewives in Seattle. Because technetium has a half-life of just a few hours, doctors hoped they would be able to inject it into patients, use its radiation to take a kind of internal x-ray, and then have it decay quickly into a harmless substance.

"I said that the first thing we ought to do was find out the ABCs of how technetium behaved in the body," Nelp says. He found eight volunteers—students and housewives—by word of mouth. After he explained the procedure to them, the volunteers signed consent forms. They stayed in or visited hospitals for up to 2 months while researchers collected samples of their blood, tears, perspiration, urine, and feces.

Partly as a result of this work, which revealed that the body quickly excretes technetium, it is now widely used in nuclear medicine. Doctors attach it to phosphate compounds and inject the ensemble into patients and wait for the body to incorporate the phosphates into bone, along with the technetium. "Afterward, you take a total body survey," Nelp explains. "You can see every bone in the body with much less radiation than if you took a series of x-rays."

So why was Nelp's research singled out in the Markey Report? Apparently because the dose given to the volunteers—20 to 60 microcuries—was up to six times higher than what the report described as the "occupational maximum permissible body burden" for these isotopes. But a "body burden" refers to the long-term buildup of a substance within the body, not a one-time shot, as in Nelp's experiment. And "you can't translate a one-time exposure for a volunteer into a standard designed for workers who might be breathing in something 8 hours a day, five days a week," says Lauriston S. Taylor, former head of the National Council on Radiation Protection and Measurements, the independent advisory panel that has recommended U.S. radiation safety standards since 1930. The difference, in other words, is the difference between a heart patient's one-time binge on six hamburgers and a diet of one greasy hamburger a day, which is more harmful.

Much of the research now being denounced in the media was tracer research, Taylor says. "It's not generally appreciated, apparently, that the magnitude of the dose from these tracer tests is just awfully small."

The gray area.   In between the reprehensible and the praiseworthy are studies that appear to have been designed to ensure no harm came to people, but fell short on informed consent. Particularly worrisome is research on disabled or unconscious people—a red flag to medical ethicists today. Perhaps the best-known cases occurred in 1954 and 1956, when scientists affiliated with the Massachusetts Institute of Technology (MIT) Radioactivity Center fed radio-tagged milk to 36 mentally-retarded children at the Fernald School in Waltham, Massachusetts. The purpose was to answer a then-current puzzle: whether children who eat oat cereals, which are rich in compounds that bind to calcium, are thereby flushing calcium through their systems before their bones can use it to grow.

Like Nelp, the MIT researchers used a radioactive tracer—in this case, calcium-32. The idea was to "label" children's milk with this isotope and find out whether eating oat cereal would affect

the amount that stayed in the body. This involved feeding children a uniform diet and collecting all their urine and feces for some time—a complicated prospect. Team leader Robert Harris had decided that such experiments would best succeed if the subjects were in a confined location and under medical supervision. The Fernald children met those criteria. The experiment suggested that oatmeal did indeed flush calcium from the system, but at a slow rate that would only affect children with very low-calcium diets.

Only "a tiny, tiny amount" of radioactive calcium was used, says Constantine Maletskos, a member of the team. According to MIT Radiation Protection Officer director Francis Masse, the dose was 4 to 11 millirems above background. (Typical background levels are about 300 millirems.) By comparison, a typical treatment for hyperthyroidism involves hitting the thyroid with a drink that delivers about 10 million millirems. "They would have had more if they had flown to Denver for a while," Maletskos says, where they would have been exposed to that high-altitude city's greater number of cosmic rays.

Although the doses of radiation were small, the consent for the experiment would not have met today's standards. "In those days doctors were the kings of their facilities," says Maletskos. "They were in charge of their patients. [The Fernald supervisors] told us they had consent, and it would never have occurred to us to question them." Maletskos says he was horrified to learn on 26 December in a story from *The Boston Globe* that the consent forms sent to the parents by the school had neglected to mention "radioactivity." The school merely asked parents about participating in nutritional experiments. But even if the forms had mentioned radioactivity, there are doubts consent could ever be properly obtained from retarded subjects or their parents. Indeed, today the whole issue of informed consent by the mentally impaired is regarded as so blurred that experimenters believe they should not be used as a study population.

Similar questions of consent dog some of the cases mentioned in the Markey Report. An example is the injection of radioactive uranium-235 into at least 11 comatose, terminal cancer patients between 1953 and 1957 by William Sweet of Massachusetts General Hospital, in Boston, and his associates. The procedures were done as part of the development of what is called "neutron-capture therapy." Neutron-capture therapy takes advantage of the fact that tumors absorb more of certain isotopes than healthy tissues do. After placing those isotopes in the body, doctors bombard the patients with neutrons, which split the isotopes, releasing radiation that kills surrounding cancer cells.

In the 1950s, this idea was little more than plausible-sounding speculation. No one knew which isotope would best be absorbed by tumors. Sweet decided to find out. After obtaining permission for the injections from the patients' families, he carried out the study. The results were disappointing. Uranium, it seemed, was not absorbed in sufficient quantities by the tumor to make the therapy practical; in current attempts at neutron-capture therapy, boron is used.

Even at the time this work could have aroused qualms. In 1953, the year Sweet began his experiments, the British Medical Council campaigned against the use of comatose subjects in research. And as far back as 1948, the Federation of American Societies of Experimental Biology expressed concern that experimenting on the "hopelessly incurable" would "corrupt" the doctor-patient relationship, because it could make their rapid deaths desirable if an autopsy was needed. Nowadays, research with no potential for direct benefit to the terminally ill subject is generally avoided.

Yet these matters of consent and safety frequently fall into gray areas, as researchers acknowledge. People with AIDS, for instance, clamor to be experimented on with medications whose effects are so poorly understood that neither physician nor patient can give consent truly informed by knowledge of risks and benefits. "Who knows what people will think of that in the future?" Stannard says. "We should be humble and wonder what we now are doing that will horrify our descendants." Unlike radioactive decay rates, the rate of change in morality standards has never been accurately measured.

NO

Arjun Makhijani

ENERGY ENTERS GUILTY PLEA

"We were shrouded and clouded in an atmosphere of secrecy. And I would take it a step further—I would call it repression."

—Energy Secretary Hazel O'Leary,
press conference, December 7, 1993

The shaft of light Hazel O'Leary has shone into the darkness of the nuclear establishment's human experiments has revealed a reality as awesome as the first secret, blinding flash of the atomic explosion in the New Mexico desert on July 16, 1945. It was a stunning admission. For the first time, the head of the nuclear weapons establishment was admitting that government agencies had conducted secret, dangerous, and assuredly immoral experiments on the American people. "The only thing I could think of was Nazi Germany," O'Leary later told *Newsweek*. Similar thoughts undoubtedly crossed the minds of millions who wondered how the citizens of a country with democratic checks and balances could have been used as unwitting guinea pigs.

It was the beginning of an historic month. Until last December, the Energy Department had steadfastly resisted pleas for recognition, treatment, and compensation from those who had suffered radiation exposure as workers, as members of the armed forces who attended nuclear tests in the atmosphere, or those who had lived downwind from weapons testing and production sites. Before any fresh lawsuits were filed, O'Leary said: "For people who were wronged, it would seem that some compensation is appropriate. Let the Congress and the American people determine the level that would be appropriate."

After the press conference, the Energy Department set up a "hotline" to hear from people who might have information about the experiments or who felt they might have been exposed to radiation in an experiment. Very quickly the number of operators required to staff the hotline rose to more than 30, with calls running as high as 700 per hour. O'Leary also declassified other information on December 7, including data on plutonium production and

From Arjun Makhijani, "Energy Enters Guilty Plea," *The Bulletin of the Atomic Scientists*, vol. 50, no. 2 (March/April 1994). Copyright © 1994 by The Educational Foundation for Nuclear Science, 6042 South Kimbark, Chicago, IL 60637, USA. Reprinted by permission. References omitted. A one-year subscription is $30.

information about 204 previously secret underground nuclear weapons tests. And that, she said, was just the beginning.

It was soon apparent that other agencies, including the Defense Department, the National Aeronautics and Space Administration, the Department of Veterans Affairs, and the Central Intelligence Agency had been involved in human radiation experiments. As a result, a White House interagency task force was formed. A task force of independent health professionals is also being formed.

Also in December, the General Accounting Office revealed for the first time that from 1948 to 1952 the Defense Department deliberately released radionuclides into the air to gather data as part of an effort to evaluate the feasibility of radiation weapons. Such weapons, which would have created temporarily high radiation fields designed to kill or to debilitate enemy soldiers, were never deployed....

The experiments on human subjects have attracted intense media interest. They have been called "an enormous scandal for science and government, greater than Watergate." The stately, well-funded ship of nuclear weapons production now finds itself in unexpectedly stormy seas.

Five decades into the nuclear era, the people of the United States finally seem ready to reassess what Robert Alvarez, a long-time critic of the atomic establishment and now an aide to Secretary O'Leary, has called "America's romance with the atom."

A TENSE ROMANCE

The romance began with Hiroshima and Nagasaki. Americans were horrified, as was the rest of the world, by the effects of atomic bombs on human life and habitation. Yet the vast majority of U.S. citizens also associated the bombings with victory over Japan.

It had been widely supposed, and with good reason, that the invasion of Japan, scheduled for November 1945, would be a brutal affair. Millions of soldiers and their families and friends came to believe that the atomic bomb had saved their lives or those of their loved ones. Their belief was reinforced by U.S. and British leaders' repeated exaggerations of the number of American and Allied lives that were supposed to have been saved.

These exaggerations were accompanied by seductive tales of the technological wonders that nuclear energy would produce—it was to be used in everything from scuba-diving suits to airplanes and would produce atomic electricity that would one day be "too cheap to meter," in Lewis Strauss's memorable phrase.

The promise of civilian applications and a strong distrust of putting world-destroying weapons in the hands of the military alone resulted in the creation of a civilian agency, the Atomic Energy Commission (AEC), to oversee both civilian and military nuclear programs.

The AEC was given unprecedented power. It owned the nuclear weapons plants, chose the contractors, created the regulations that the contractors followed, and was both judge and jury for deciding when its regulations were violated and what the punishment should be.

The Joint Committee on Atomic Energy was established to provide congressional oversight. But it was not very watchful on health and environmental matters. The AEC became a world unto itself, a quasi-government and private corporation in one. It preempted local and state laws, and it could ignore any federal law but the Atomic Energy Act.

As an economic enterprise, the AEC quickly became larger than most countries. By the mid-1950s, the AEC was responsible for almost 4 percent of U.S. industrial production; it consumed 5 percent of all the electricity generated in the United States; and its construction budget amounted to 3.4 percent of all U.S. construction. The total work force involved in bomb production and testing (including contractor employees and construction workers) was about 140,000. The work force included some of the most highly trained scientists in the country.

THE COLD WAR

Winston Churchill formally declared the Cold War in his 1946 "Iron Curtain" speech at Fulton, Missouri, with President Harry Truman at his side. In the early 1950s, the extreme secrecy that characterized the Manhattan Project turned to McCarthyite paranoia. Critics of any type were regarded with suspicion or worse.

Shielded from the light of public scrutiny, the AEC's power went unchecked. The agency systematically deceived those the weapons were supposed to protect, subverted democracy, and regarded as expendable anyone who got in its path.

W. Henson Moore, the deputy secretary of energy during the Bush administration—when the environmental mismanagement of the weapons complex brought the nuclear enterprise under greater public scrutiny—characterized the complex's culture bluntly: Nuclear weapons production was, he said, "a secret operation not subject to laws.... No one was to know what was going on."

The AEC's attitude was: "This is our business, it's national security, everybody else butt out."

The managers of the nuclear weapons complex arrogated to themselves the right of deciding questions of life and death and right and wrong, not only for the United States, but for the world. In April 1960, *California Engineer* told its readers that nuclear tests in the atmosphere, conducted to develop an arsenal for fighting "brush fire wars" such as the Korean War, had increased "your babies' chances of having a major birth defect by one part in 5,000 approximately. Percentage-wise, this is insignificant. When applied to the population of the world, it means that nuclear testing so far has produced about an additional 6,000 babies born with major birth defects. Whether you choose to look at 'one part in 5,000' or '6,000 babies,' you must weigh this acknowledged risk with the demonstrated need of the United States for a nuclear arsenal."

Many of those who experimented on human subjects and their present-day defenders claim that not enough was known about radiation to know that harm might be caused to the experimental subjects. These claims are disingenuous, as the publication of the risk of genetic defects in a 1960 engineering magazine demonstrates.

The level of radiation regarded as safe has fallen, but the dangers of radiation exposure were well known at the time of the experiments. For instance, the amounts of plutonium injected into human subjects in experiments conducted by Los Alamos and the University of Rochester School of Medicine and Dentistry during 1945–47 ranged from 0.095 to 5.9 microcuries, which were about 2.4–14.7 times the "tolerance dose" of 0.04 microcuries set for workers in 1944 in the Manhattan Project; the average dose was 0.35 microcuries, or almost nine times the tolerance dose, according to Patricia Durbin of the Lawrence Berkeley Laboratory. She stated in testimony that the standard tolerance dose was established at a level at which "no clinically detectable biological damage would result" during an exposed worker's entire life. The standard was based mainly on animal studies and on analysis of the deaths of radium dial painters in the early part of this century. In other words, doses greatly in excess of those thought not to produce damage were given to all the plutonium-injection experimental subjects.

It is true that low levels of external radiation were considered less dangerous than they are today. Still, radiation standards for workers were 5 rem per year in the late 1950s, the same as they are today, but much of the human experimentation continued into the early 1970s. Allowable limits for civilians were a tenth of this worker limit and are still lower today.

California Engineer could confidently discuss worldwide rates of genetic damage in 1960, even though fallout worldwide was estimated at only a few millirem per year, far lower than the doses given during most of the experiments. And the danger of low levels of radiation from fallout downwind from a nuclear test was recognized from the start. After studying the widespread fallout produced by the first nuclear weapons test in New Mexico on July 16, 1945, Col. Stafford L. Warren, chief of radiological safety, recommended that no tests be conducted within 150 miles of human habitation.

By 1947, the military was considering the potential effect of spreading fallout on enemy territory, which, it was thought, could be a major weapon....

At the same time that the nuclear establishment was evaluating fallout as a weapon, it was waging a campaign to convince the American public that fallout from nuclear tests in Nevada was harmless. One document deemed it "a matter of reeducation" to get Americans to "accept the possibility of an atomic explosion within a matter of a hundred or so miles of their homes." Major William Sturges, who participated in discussions of the safety of atmospheric tests in 1950, noted, "It appeared that the idea of making the public feel at home with neutrons trotting around is the most important angle to get across."

The nuclear establishment's insistence on immunity from legal liability also casts doubt on its claims of ignorance about potential dangers. From the first, the fear of liability so haunted the U.S. nuclear weapons establishment that commercial contractors demanded and got complete immunity from liability, even for gross negligence or violation of contract. The government's response in the mid-1980s to a lawsuit filed by Pat Broudy, a widow of one of the veterans of atmospheric testing in the 1950s, is also instructive. She claimed that the government should have informed the veterans about the dangers of radiation as more was learned in the 1960s. In its rejoinder, the government asserted that it already knew the dangers of radiation in the mid-1940s and early 1950s. It also asserted sovereign immunity—arguing that national security concerns gave it the right to expose servicemen to danger and excused it from informing them.

Legal liability was also a concern with regard to human experiments. For instance, Dr. Charles Edington, who approved the irradiation of the testicles of inmates in Washington and Oregon prisons from 1963 to 1971, wrote: "All of our mammalian work has been carried out to get a better idea of radiation effects on germ cells and spermatogenesis, etc., with the hope of extrapolating the results to man. This proposal is a direct attack on our problem. I'm for support at the requested level as long as we are not liable. I wonder about the possible carcinogenic effects of such treatments."

Finally, although the researchers and their defenders say that the experimental doses were too low to cause harm, many of the experiments were in fact designed to harm, including those that involved the irradiation of the testicles of prisoners. Irradiation levels ranged up to 600 rads, a level known to be dangerous even during the Manhattan Project. In 1946 and 1947, uranium salts were injected into subjects at the University of Rochester at levels that were known to injure the kidneys. It is noteworthy that in almost every case, the experimenters chose vulnerable people rather than themselves or their peers as subjects.

WHY?

There were at least five purposes behind the exposure of human subjects to radiation. First, the United States wanted to develop instruments for spying on the Soviet nuclear complex. The deliberate releases of radioactivity from Hanford such as the "Green Run," which sought to mimic the presumed signature of Russian plutonium production, belong in this category. But how relevant these experiments were to tracking developments in the Soviet Union or Soviet production practices remains to be established.

A second purpose was to aid in developing radiation weapons. In this type of experiment, large quantities of radioactivity were released in order to measure its spread and to estimate, through extrapolation, its potential to produce illness, injury, and death among enemy soldiers. These tests included releases of radioisotopes such as lanthanum 140 and tantalum 182 over the Oak Ridge and Los Alamos areas in the 1940s and 1950s.

At the time of the Manhattan Project, Joseph G. Hamilton, an assistant professor of medicine at the University of California's Radiation Laboratory, proposed contaminating water supplies with radioactive isotopes in order to poison large numbers of people.

In 1950, Hamilton proposed an experiment in which healthy human volunteers would inhale near-lethal doses of radioactive aerosols. He seems not to have found either approval or volunteers, but he continued to pursue the matter, recommending in 1952 that the radiological warfare program "continue to develop as rapidly as possible. (Yet, it was Hamilton who said in 1950 in a secret memo that the human experiments could be construed as having "a little of the Buchenwald touch.") In any event, the people who were exposed to radiation from the weapon-related tests that were carried out were apparently not of scientific interest to researchers, and no follow-up studies were conducted in most cases.

A third purpose underlying the exposure of humans to radiation was to study how long and how well soldiers could continue to function on the "nuclear battlefield." In a broad sense, all the members of the armed forces who participated in military exercises during and after atmospheric tests were a part of this experiment.

But there were also more specific experiments. The object of "Human Experiment Number 133," for instance, was to discover how well pilots who flew through a radioactive mushroom cloud 20–45 minutes after an atomic detonation would function. Tests on charity patients at the University of Cincinnati who were exposed to high levels of radiation also belong in this category. Some terminally ill participants may have benefited, but whether the treatment they received was comparable to or better than other available therapies needs independent evaluation. The radiation exposures in these experiments were high.

NASA was also interested in some experiments—those that involved the irradiation of the testicles of prisoners, and the high-level irradiation of patients at Oak Ridge and at the University of Cincinnati. The space agency wanted to know how radiation, including levels that might be produced by bursts of solar radiation, might affect astronauts.

A fourth type of experiment was to determine the effects of external beta radiation on workers, as, for instance, when phosphorous 32 was placed on subjects' skins.

Finally, a number of experiments were done to study how the human body metabolized radioactive materials. These tests included the feeding of radioactive iron to pregnant women by Vanderbilt University; the injection or ingestion by older people of radium and thorium, a study carried out by the Massachusetts Institute of Technology; and plutonium injection experiments carried out by the University of Rochester School of Dentistry and Medicine and the Los Alamos National Laboratory and run by the University of California.

The subjects of the last two types of experiments were followed for some time. But in many or most cases, follow-up was designed to further the above goals of the experimentation, not to evaluate the health of the subjects.

Some experiments were joint AEC-NASA activities. Any particular experiment might have had more than one purpose. The true goals of individual experiments will not be clear until all the relevant documents have been made public....

The subject of human experiments remained peripheral in the 1980s. Markey's 1986 appeal* to Energy Secretary John S. Herrington to find the victims and treat and compensate them went unheeded. Now Secretary O'Leary, in an act of historic leadership, has explicitly and unequivocally rejected the department's past behavior. She is calling for treatment and compensation of the victims. The rest of the Clinton administration, including the Justice Department, appears to be following her lead, though perhaps not yet with the same dedication.

Energy and the Clinton administration have several options. Stepping back from full disclosure of the human experiments is not one of them. It is too late for that. But the human tests could be treated as a narrow matter—resolved by releasing a few documents and finding, treating, and compensating a few hundred or a few thousand victims. This would let an historic opportunity slip by.

*[This refers to the House Subcommittee on Energy Conservation and Power's 1986 report detailing experiments involving humans and radioactive compounds. The committee was headed by Edward J. Markey (D-Massachusetts).—Ed.]

The public has a right to know more about the effects of nuclear weapons production and testing on atomic veterans, downwinders, and workers who were exposed to radiation and other dangers.

This is an ethical matter and more. The quality of the Energy Department's and its contractors' scientific work is also in question. They have an abysmal record when it comes to researching health and environmental issues. In some instances, data has been fabricated. In other cases, mathematical deficiencies have been exposed. But neither Energy nor its contractors have tried to attack the underlying problems that have led to inferior work.

The Clinton administration should use this occasion to begin a much-needed national debate on science, ethics, environmental protection and clean-up, and nuclear weapons. There are at least six areas that should be examined:

• The poor quality of scientific research on health and environmental issues, including exposures of workers, military personnel, and off-site populations.
• The ethics of using science and technology to produce weapons of mass destruction.
• The ethics of building, testing, threatening to use, and actually using nuclear weapons.
• The effects on universities and other research institutions of working on secret military contracts.
• The conflict between scientific inquiry and technological innovation and the risks they may impose on population and the environment. The discussion should include the dimensions of risk and the question of who bears the burden of proof—those conducting and financing the experiments, or those upon whom the risk is imposed.
• The potential conflict between the interests of scientists and their funding agencies on the one hand and those of their subjects. In most of these cases, the health of the subjects was not of interest to the researchers—or to their colleagues in radiology, radiobiology, and health physics who knew about these experiments and used their results. The conflict between the needs and desires of scientists and the welfare of their human subjects is usually hidden. But it is dramatically transparent in this case.

It would be fitting for the Energy Department to advocate a wide-ranging inquiry into these issues. Secretary O'Leary has already taken the unusual step of asking ethicists to assist her department in evaluating the human experiments, releasing the information, and doing justice to the victims.

Without an open and thorough examination of the record, the revelation that the government conducted secret experiments on its own people has the potential to increase distrust of government more than anything since Watergate or the war in Vietnam. Public cynicism will extend to research institutions that are now held in relatively high esteem. But the fresh winds of truth from Hazel O'Leary's office could help to reverse the long decline of confidence in the government and in democratic processes. A vigorous debate also has the potential for the first global evaluation, free from the blinders of the Cold War, on using and threatening to use nuclear weapons.

As we approach 1995, the fiftieth anniversary of the first nuclear explosions, the world needs to plot a course that will lead to effective nuclear non-proliferation and disarmament in the foreseeable future. It cannot come too soon. The dangers of nuclear proliferation and of political and military disintegration in Russia —with its tens of thousands of nuclear weapons and large quantities of radioactive materials—become more apparent everyday. Does the United States have the will to rise to the occasion?

POSTSCRIPT

Is It Ethical to Use Humans as "Experimental Animals"?

The issue of human experimentation arises most often in medical research, in which drugs and surgical procedures are tested for efficacy and safety generally by giving them to one group of patients while denying them to another (the control group). Today, when an experimental treatment shows strong signs of being more effective than a control treatment, it is immediately offered to the control group. If the treatment shows signs of causing more harm than no treatment at all, the experiment is halted. That is, concern for the patient's well-being is recognized as a primary concern in medical research.

Informed consent is also a primary concern, as evidenced by the debate about the radiation experiments. Among the studies mentioned by Mann are two in which students at a school for the retarded in Waltham, Massachusetts, were fed small (tracer) amounts of radioactive material to study nutrient absorption. Using tracers in such a way was (and is) an accepted technique. Mann questions the research not because tracers were used but because consent forms given to the students' parents did not mention radiation and because the current view is that neither people with mental retardation nor their parents can give "proper" consent.

In April 1994 the *Boston Globe* reported that a draft report by the Massachusetts Task Force on Human Subject Research declared that consent for these experiments was even more flawed than Mann indicates, for the researchers had openly discussed using pressure (such as promises of privileges) to make reluctant students participate in the experiments. The report addressed a total of eight studies of 289 retarded students at the Waltham school and at another school in Wrentham. One Wrentham study sought antidotes to radioactive fallout and involved subjects as young as one year old. The Task Force's draft report said that these experiments were unacceptable even by the standards of the time; the amounts of radioactive material had to be regarded as hazardous because some (but not all) scientists believe even small amounts can increase the risk of cancer, and the subjects' fundamental human rights were violated according to standards defined by the 1947 Nuremberg Code, which was formulated in reaction to the Nazi atrocities. The report concluded that the subjects of these experiments must "be compensated for any and all damage incurred as a result of such research," and it recommended further research to learn what damage may have resulted from the experiments.

Measures such as the National Research Act have not stopped human experimentation, but they have made such work more difficult. It is therefore worth noting that there are alternative ways of studying processes that hold the potential to damage human health. One is "experiments of nature," where "nature" includes human accident and neglect as well as war. In connection with radiation, intense studies of the survivors of the Hiroshima and Nagasaki atomic bombings that have been pursued since the end of World War II are good examples of modern experiments of nature.

The end of the cold war and the collapse of the Iron Curtain have revealed to the world that the Soviet Union and East Germany ignored precautions against exposing uranium miners and processors to radioactive material but kept careful records of worker exposures and any health effects. Now available to researchers is an archive of data on some 450,000 workers, which German science writer Patricia Kahn called "the world's biggest data collection on low-level radiation and health—and potentially one of the most valuable for studying the associated cancer risks." See "A Grisly Archive of Key Cancer Data," *Science* (January 22, 1993). Other data collections covering Soviet nuclear accidents are also now becoming available. As researchers analyze these data, they will surely learn a great deal that they could not learn in other ways (the necessary experiments would never be permitted by institutional review boards).

For more details on the Nazi experiments, see A. Mitscherlich and F. Mielke, *Doctors of Infamy* (Henry Schuman, 1949), and Arthur L. Caplan, ed., *When Medicine Went Mad: Bioethics and the Holocaust* (Humana Press, 1992). For an analysis of Stanley Milgram's obedience experiments, see his *Obedience to Authority: An Experimental View* (Harper & Row, 1974). And for more on the ethics of experimentation on human beings, see Caplan's "When Evil Intrudes," *Hastings Center Report* (November–December 1992) and Bernard Barber's "The Ethics of Experimentation With Human Subjects," *Scientific American* (February 1976).

ISSUE 19

Should Fetal Tissue Be Used to Heal Adults?

YES: Council on Scientific Affairs and Council on Ethical and Judicial Affairs, from "Medical Applications of Fetal Tissue Transplantation," *Journal of the American Medical Association* (January 26, 1990)

NO: James Tunstead Burtchaell, from "University Policy on Experimental Use of Aborted Fetal Tissue," *IRB: A Review of Human Subjects Research* (July/August 1988)

ISSUE SUMMARY

YES: The American Medical Association's Council on Scientific Affairs and Council on Ethical and Judicial Affairs argue that using fetal tissue to treat adult illnesses is ethical, provided appropriate precautions are taken, and that related research should be funded by the federal government.

NO: Theologian James Tunstead Burtchaell asserts that research with aborted fetal tissue is unethical because informed consent cannot be obtained from a fetus and because the researcher cannot be morally separated from the abortion itself.

Physicians have long wished to be able to replace their patients' missing or defective parts, just as an auto mechanic can replace a brake pad, a spark plug, or a carburetor. The earliest attempts to replace a person's "parts" included performing transfusions with sheep's blood, which seemed like a good idea at the time (after all, blood is blood, isn't it?) but failed dismally (the patients died). In time, researchers learned that biological parts have subtleties that machine parts do not—they are labeled by their chemistry as belonging to one individual of one species, and the body rejects those parts that have the wrong labels. Individuals who share the same genes (such as identical twins) also share the same labels, so the first successful human organ transplants were between identical twins. Later, researchers discovered drugs that suppress the immune system and prevent the rejection of parts with different labels. Today, many body parts are transplanted almost routinely.

Yet, not all body parts are equivalent. A heart is a heart; it pumps blood. A piece of brain tissue, however, is not like heart tissue; it must be able to grow and establish connections with other parts of the brain in order to function. And adult brain tissue does not do this well. Fetal tissue does because it is still relatively unformed and is not yet locked into a single function within the body. The cells of fetal tissue are still able to multiply, assume special functions (differentiate), and stimulate the growth of neighboring cells. In a transplant, they are also less likely to provoke the recipient's immune system to reject them.

Fetal brain tissue, bone marrow, pancreatic tissue, and liver tissue all have similar advantages. Some physician researchers have considered transplanting these tissues into patients who could not otherwise be helped, such as the 500,000 Americans with Parkinson's disease, a progressive disease that causes deterioration of the brain and that is marked by progressively worsening tremors and other movement difficulties. Drugs are of limited value for this disorder and have serious side effects. However, researchers have theorized that if the damaged portion of the brain could somehow be replaced or if the brain's production of the chemical dopamine (which functions as a neurotransmitter in the brain) could be supplemented by the active fetal tissue, patients could at least be helped.

Whether or not fetal transplants will work is almost beside the point because as soon as the *possibility* of using fetal tissue in this way arose, many people asked, "Where does the fetal tissue come from?" Since the answer was necessarily "abortions," many people reacted strongly against the transplants. They felt that if fetal tissue proved useful for saving people's lives, then abortion might become widespread: women who would otherwise not choose to have abortions might change their minds because of the potential benefits; doctors might encourage women to abort their fetuses for the sake of other patients; and women might get pregnant deliberately in order to provide fetal tissue to treat a friend's or loved one's illness or even to sell.

In the mid-1970s, soon after abortion was legalized in the United States, the National Institutes of Health (NIH) established a moratorium on (a suspension of) federal funding of research using human fetuses, either alive or dead. Legislation soon changed the moratorium to a ban, with the only exception being research intended to aid the fetus. In 1988 an NIH panel declared that the government should fund research on fetal tissue transplantation, and in 1992 Congress voted to end the ban. However, then-president George Bush vetoed the legislation because he felt that it might encourage abortion.

Despite the ban on federal funding of fetal tissue transplantation research, the work has continued with private funding in the United States and with public funding in other countries. In the selections that follow, the American Medical Association's Council on Scientific Affairs and Council on Ethical and Judicial Affairs summarize much of the work that had been done by 1990, stress its potential value, and argue that using fetal tissue to treat adult illnesses is ethical with appropriate precautions. James Tunstead Burtchaell objects to fetal transplantation research on the grounds that informed consent cannot be adequately obtained, and he argues that the association of the researcher with the destruction of the fetus raises further moral questions.

YES

Council on Scientific Affairs and
Council on Ethical and
Judicial Affairs

MEDICAL APPLICATIONS OF FETAL TISSUE TRANSPLANTATION

The prospect of therapeutically effective fetal tissue transplants for disorders such as diabetes and Parkinson's disease has raised new questions in the ethical discussion on fetal research. These questions are distinct from those addressed in the 1970s that focused on invasive procedures performed by some researchers on living, viable fetuses. They are also separate from the questions that were raised by the development of new techniques for prenatal diagnosis, such as fetoscopy and chorionic villus sampling. Although the use of transplanted tissue from a fetus after spontaneous or induced abortion appears to be analogous to the use of cadaver tissue and organs, the moral issue for many is the possibility that the decision to have an abortion will become coupled with the decision to donate fetal tissue for transplantation procedures.

The utilization of human fetal tissue for transplantations is, for the most part, based on research data derived from experimental animal models. At this time, the number of such transplantations performed has been relatively small, but the various applications are promising avenues of clinical investigation for certain disorders. The purpose of this report is to (1) review the data on fetal tissue transplantation in animals and in specific clinical disorders, (2) review the legal and ethical issues involved in fetal tissue transplantation, and (3) provide ethical guidelines for the use of fetal tissue for transplantation.

FETAL TISSUE TRANSPLANTATION

Human fetal tissue research has led to the development of a number of important research and medical advances. Embryonic human tissues have been the source of scientifically valuable cell lines in culture that have been important research models for studying cell-to-cell interactions and gene expression.

From Council on Scientific Affairs and Council on Ethical and Judicial Affairs, "Medical Applications of Fetal Tissue Transplantation," *Journal of the American Medical Association*, vol. 263, no. 4 (January 26, 1990), pp. 565–569. Copyright © 1990 by The American Medical Association. Reprinted by permission. References omitted.

The research and development of the polio vaccine was accomplished with the use of human fetal kidney cells. Currently, human fetal cells are being used to study the mechanism of viral infections and to diagnose viral infections and inherited diseases.

Fetal cells have four basic properties that make them clinically useful for grafting or transplantation applications: (1) the ability to grow and proliferate, (2) the ability to undergo cell and tissue differentiation (intrinsic plasticity), (3) the ability to produce growth factors, and (4) reduced antigenicity compared with adult tissue (although this property does not always apply).

The plasticity of transplanted fetal tissue has been demonstrated in numerous animal studies. Embryonic wing tissue from a chicken retains the functional capacity to differentiate into a leg when transplanted into the appropriate limb bud region of the developing chick. In animal experiments in which the recipient is a fully differentiated adult, intracerebral implants of fetal neurons can establish extensive synaptic connection and under certain conditions can become partially integrated into the circuitry of adjacent neural tissue. The ability of fetal cells to grow and proliferate in vivo [in the living body] following transplantation increases the success rate of functional engraftment....

Fetal cells have the additional ability to produce trophic substances that not only can increase their own ability to survive and grow but also can promote regeneration of nearby damaged tissue. Angiogenic factors from fetal tissue can promote blood vessel formation, and nerve growth factors released by fetal neuroblasts can assist in neural tissue regeneration.

A theoretically important factor in successful fetal tissue engraftment is the ability of the transplanted cells to escape the immune surveillance of the host, but this is not true for all fetal tissues....

Human fetal tissue transplantations have been attempted in a number of human disorders, including Parkinson's disease, diabetes, severe combined immunodeficiency, DiGeorge's syndrome, aplastic anemia, leukemia, thalassemia, Fabry's disease, and Gaucher's disease. With the immunodeficiency disorders, restoration of immune function and long-term patient survival have been achieved. The following sections review the major research areas for the clinical application of human fetal transplants.

Immunodeficiency Disorders

... Since graft-vs-host disease (GvHD) is a major barrier to the transplantation of allogeneic hematopoietic [blood-forming] cells and since immunocompetent T cells present in transplanted bone marrow are associated with GvHD, the fetal liver has been considered a possible alternative source of hematopoietic tissue. Animal experiments have shown that transplanted fetal liver cells are capable of restoring hematopoiesis and immunity in lethally irradiated rodents. Even when the fetal tissue donor and recipient are mismatched for histocompatibility [HLA] antigens, the resulting GvHD was mild and delayed compared with what occurred following bone marrow transplantations (BMTs)....

Clinically, fetal liver transplantations have been attempted in patients with SCID [severe combined immunodeficiency]. This relatively heterogeneous condition often leads to death from opportunistic infections before the age of 1 year. Bone marrow transplantation has resulted in long-term survival in patients with SCID; the success rate is as high as 80% when the HLA type of the donor is identical to that of the recipient....

Fetal liver transplantation represents a third approach to immune reconstitution in SCID, but it currently is of less clinical significance.... Sustained engraftment of lymphoid progenitor cells from fetal liver has been achieved in a number of patients. Complete immunologic reconstitution, including normal T-cell function, has been demonstrated despite HLA mismatch between donor and recipient cells. Fetal liver grafts may be optimal when used in conjunction with fetal thymus tissue from the same donor, but this has not been established conclusively. Clinical experience indicates that the optimal age of the fetal liver for transplantation is 8 to 13 weeks; the risk of GvHD is higher in livers older than 20 weeks. The relative efficacy of fetal liver compared with HLA haploidentical T-cell–depleted BMT has not been studied....

Hematologic Disorders

More than 100 patients with aplastic anemia have undergone treatment with fetal liver transplants. However, because these patients still have functioning immune systems that react against HLA-mismatched fetal liver tissues, transplantation cannot be successful in most instances; engraftment has been low (3%), as documented by cytogenetic analysis. Therefore, the true efficacy of fetal liver transplantation for aplastic anemia cannot be evaluated until transplantations have been attempted following immunosuppressive therapy.

Fetal liver transplantations have been attempted in 39 patients with acute myelogenous leukemia. In treating acute myelogenous leukemia, human fetal liver transplantations could result in successful engraftment, with reconstitution of hematopoietic function and/or expedited recovery of the patient's own hematologic system. However, transplant failure is common. Antigenic barriers appear to be too great for successful engraftment without prior immunosuppression with drugs and radiation. As with aplastic anemia, human fetal liver transplantation for acute myelogenous leukemia has not been conducted under immunosuppressive conditions that would permit evaluation of engraftment success. Part of the problem in determining the efficacy of fetal liver cells in accelerating hematopoietic tissue recovery is the dependency of this procedure on the initial effectiveness of chemotherapy against acute myelogenous leukemia. Because of the variable response to chemotherapy, further evaluation of any additional improvement resulting from the fetal liver infusion will require controlled clinical trials.

Diabetes

The potential to cure experimentally induced diabetes mellitus in animals through the syngeneic [genetically identical] transplantation of fetal pancreatic tissue has been documented. That human fetal pancreatic tissue transplantations could cure patients has been proposed as a result of these preclinical studies. However, the application of fetal cell transplantations to diabetes is complicated by inadequate engraftment success in immunosuppressed recipients as well as insufficient quantities of viable fetal tissue and storage arrangements for such tissue.

Transplantation of cultured fetal pancreas cells has been tried in more than 100 insulin-dependent patients. So far there have been no successful grafts as judged by complete long-term withdrawal of insulin therapy, but there has been one report of survival of transplanted fetal pancreas tissue for 13 weeks. Reduced insulin requirements ... also have been reported, but the effects have been transient. Although the current attempts have been relatively unsuccessful, the human fetal pancreas does exhibit the necessary plasticity and proliferative properties outlined earlier....

With ... encouraging results in animal studies together with advances in the cryopreservation of the fetal pancreas tissue, research on fetal cell transplantation for diabetes is worth pursuing....

Other Metabolic and Genetic Disorders
Fetal liver transplantations have been tried in a small number of patients with thalassemia, Fabry's disease, and Gaucher's disease. Treatment by this approach is preliminary, but some beneficial clinical results have been reported. Fetal tissue transplantation experiments for these and other inherited disorders have been suggested as forerunners to the use of genetically engineered cells.

Parkinson's Disease
Fetal nerve-cell grafts have been carried out successfully in animal models of neurodegenerative disease. The technique of neural grafting was initially used in neurobiology to study nerve-cell development and regeneration, primarily in invertebrate models. The consistent transplant-induced improvements in motor, sensory, cognitive, and endocrine functions in animal models prompted the rationale that similar transplantations of human fetal neurons could improve the clinical symptoms of neurologic disorders such as Parkinson's disease. New approaches to the treatment of this disorder are critical, since the response to cur-

rently available drug therapy is reduced as the disease state progresses....

[Work on primates] suggests that fetal neural grafts will be an effective treatment of Parkinson's disease in human patients. Fetal implants for Parkinson's disease have been performed in the People's Republic of China, Mexico, Sweden, Canada, Great Britain, Cuba, and the United States. Little information is available on the outcome of the Chinese and Cuban transplantations. In the Mexican trial, the two patients receiving human fetal nerve cell transplants appeared to improve progressively following surgery; however, no reliable signs of symptom alleviation could be demonstrated. Similarly, the degree of long-term improvement in motor function in the American, Canadian, English, and Swedish transplant patients has not yet been ascertained.

The inconclusive results of the clinical trials together with the complexities of human fetal neural grafting suggest that caution must be exercised in promoting these types of transplantations.

FUTURE DIRECTIONS

[Some] alternatives to the use of human fetal tissue are available [or are being researched, including] ... genetically engineer[ed] cell lines capable of both proliferating and producing a specific neurotransmitter.

Many of these manipulative procedures, particularly the development of genetically engineered cells, will not be accomplished in the near future. In the meantime, human fetal tissue transplantation research may eventually lead to some beneficial therapeutic approaches to patients with Parkinson's disease and those suffering from other disorders. For example, the continued efforts to purify specific fetal cell populations may improve the application of fetal cell transplantation for immunodeficient disorders and diabetes. The results of future transplantation studies will be needed to further assess this procedure.

LEGAL AND ETHICAL IMPLICATIONS

The transplantation of human fetal neural or pancreatic tissue and, to a lesser extent, fetal lymphoid cells is subject to federal regulations protecting human subjects (ie, recipients of the procedure). Approval of the transplantation protocol requires review and approval by an institutional review board to ensure that the risks to the patient are minimized. The acquisition of tissue from an aborted fetus is not governed by federal regulations. Instead, federal regulations leave the disposition of fetal remains to state and local regulation....

The acquisition and use of tissue obtained from dead fetuses is governed by the Uniform Anatomical Gift Act, which has been adopted by all states and the District of Columbia. The Uniform Anatomical Gift Act provides the primary legal standard for fetal tissue use, permitting fetal tissue to be donated for research purposes with the consent of either parent and if there is no objection from the other parent.

Several states have restrictive statutes governing the donation of fetal tissue for research. Massachusetts and Michigan have laws that prohibit abortion if it is conditional on the use of the fetal tissue for research. Arizona law specifically prohibits the postmortem use of fetal remains for "any medical experimentation" if the tissue is derived from an induced abortion. Other states (eg, Ohio, Oklahoma, and Indiana) have statutes that restrict research on abortion fetal remains.

The demand for fetal tissue transplantation for neural or pancreatic cell engraftments may be expected to increase if further clinical studies conclusively show that these procedures provide long-term reversal of neural or endocrine deficits. The ethical issues that fetal cell transplantation has raised are distinct from ethical points addressed during the previous discussions of fetal tissue research.

Prominent among the currently identified ethical concerns is the potential for fetal transplantations to influence a woman's decision to have an abortion. These concerns are based at least in part on the possibility that some women may wish to become pregnant for the sole purpose of aborting the fetus and either donating the tissue to a relative or selling the tissue for financial gain. Others suggest that a woman who is ambivalent about a decision to have an abortion might be swayed by arguments about the good that could be achieved if she opts to terminate the pregnancy. These concerns demand the prohibition of (1) the donation of fetal tissue to designated recipients, (2) the sale of such tissue, and (3) the request for consent to use the tissue for transplantation before a final decision regarding abortion has been made.

The abortion process may also be influenced inappropriately by the physician. Consequently, measures must be taken to ensure that decisions to donate fetal tissue for transplantation do not affect either the techniques used to induce the abortion or the timing of the procedure itself with respect to the gestational age of the fetus. Also, to avoid conflicts of interest, physicians and other health care personnel involved in performing abortions should not receive any direct benefit from the use of tissues derived from the aborted fetus for research or transplantation. The retrieval and preservation of usable tissue cannot become the primary focus of abortion. Therefore, members of the transplantation team should not influence or participate in the abortion process.

There is potential commercial gain for those involved in the retrieval, storage, testing, preparation, and delivery of fetal tissues. Providing fetal tissue by nonprofit mechanisms designed to cover costs only would reduce the possibility of direct or indirect influence on a woman to acquire her consent for donation of the aborted fetal remains.

In summary, the use of fetal tissues for transplantation purposes is ethically permissible when (1) the guidelines of the Council on Ethical and Judicial Affairs on clinical investigation and organ transplantation are followed as they pertain to the recipient of the fetal tissue transplant, (2) fetal tissue is not provided in exchange for financial renumeration above what is necessary to cover reasonable expenses, (3) the recipient of the tissue is not designated by the donor, (4) a final decision regarding abortion is made before discussion of the transplantation use of fetal tissue is initiated, (5) decisions regarding the technique used to induce abortion as well as the timing of the abortion in relation to the gestational age of the fetus are based on concern for the safety of the pregnant woman, (6) health care personnel involved in the termination of a particular pregnancy do not participate in or receive any benefit from the transplantation of tissue from the abortus of the same pregnancy, and (7) informed consent on behalf of both donor and the recipient is obtained in accordance with applicable law.

CONCLUSION

At this time, fetal neural grafting is a promising area of clinical investigation that should receive federal funding. The current transplantation experiments may be viewed as the initial step in determining the effectiveness of this approach for the treatment of Parkinson's disease, other neurodegenerative conditions, and diabetes. Parkinson's disease remains the most attractive disorder for this procedure because of the relatively localized region of deficit compared with the more widespread degeneration observed in such neurologic disorders as Alzheimer's disease.

The donation of fetal tissue for transplantation from spontaneous or induced abortions is governed legally by the Uniform Anatomical Gift Act. A number of states prohibit experiments on fetal remains from elected abortions, but such statutes may not apply if fetal cell transplantation becomes routine (ie, nonresearch in nature). The principal ethical concern in the use of human fetal tissue transplants is the degree to which the decision to have an abortion can be separated from the decision to donate the postmortem tissue. Safeguards to reduce any motivation, reason, or incentive by the woman to have an abortion can be developed to allow the benefits of this procedure to be made available to those who are in need of improved therapies.

NO

James Tunstead Burtchaell

UNIVERSITY POLICY ON EXPERIMENTAL USE OF ABORTED FETAL TISSUE

In December 1987 the University of Notre Dame's IRB [internal review board] concluded several years' deliberation and decided that research should not be permitted on fetal materials derived from elective abortion. This article sets forth most of the course of reasoning that led to the decision.

Human tissue has become an effective medium for medical therapy. Examples are the transfusion of blood and its derivatives; the transplanting of organs such as kidneys, eye parts, hearts and lungs; and immunization by pathogens, antigens, or antibodies. New therapies are now being proposed through the implantation of fetal tissues, which appear to have especially potent regenerative effects upon neural and endocrine systems. The therapeutic use of tissue from human bodies aroused a series of ethical concerns. May one put parts of someone's body to alien use? Need consent be obtained and, if so, from whom and under what conditions? May human tissue be bought or sold? The recent proposal to use fetal tissue—typically obtained from aborted subjects—puts a new spin on those questions.

The issue raised here, however, concerns the use of human fetal tissue for experimentation, not for therapy.

There are distinct advantages in the laboratory use of fetal remains. This is notably so, for instance, in studying neural tissue. In comparison with tissues obtained from mature bodies, those of the unborn or very young adapt more readily to *in vitro* environments, proliferate more abundantly, are less differentiated and therefore more versatile for experimental uses. In a word, they perform much more naturally and normally and responsively *in vitro*.

Are there countervailing moral realities that would dissuade or interdict the use of human fetal tissue for experiment? One considers with repugnance the prospect of women hired to conceive and nurture offspring intended for abortion and marketing as a prime supply of tissue for research and therapy. But the basic moral issue is, in its substance, not all that new. One must decide at the outset not to exploit any human individuals to obtain prospective benefits for others. The scientific result from such exploitation might be good

From James Tunstead Burtchaell, "University Policy on Experimental Use of Aborted Fetal Tissue," *IRB: A Review of Human Subjects Research* (July/August 1988). Copyright © 1988 by The Hastings Center. Reprinted by permission.

but the undertaking could not be. That principle has always been at the heart of the need to protect the human subjects of research.

INFORMED CONSENT

The first consideration is that of informed consent. Who can grant consent for experimental use of electively aborted fetal remains? One might propose that the mother can do so, because the tissue is from her body. The flaw in this claim is that the tissue is from within her body but it is the body of another, with distinct genotype, blood, gender, etc. Thus she cannot assign rights to its use in her own name. She would have to be acting as the parent/protector of her offspring.

In that role she could give consent, as mother, at the time she signs the consent form for the surgery. But there is a growing conviction that when a parent resolves to destroy her unborn fetus she has abdicated her office and duty as the guardian of her offspring, and thereby forfeits her tutelary powers. She abandons her parental capacity to authorize research on that offspring and on his or her remains.

An alternative might be that the right to dispose of the remains devolves upon the abortionist, as the physician in possession. But there is no ground for claiming that medical professionals incur rights over the bodies or the corpses of their patients. Still less is that so when death has resulted from nontherapeutic intervention by the practitioner, most especially when the victim has not consented to that activity.

The prerogative of the father to release the remains of his aborted offspring for medical research is rarely considered, yet in comparable instances of significant parental guardianship neither parent is considered to act rightfully when he or she avoids consultation or consensus with the other parent. Fathers are by design almost never involved in consent procedures prior to abortion. The absence of their consent, unless the right to give it could credibly be assumed to have been waived, would further encumber any others' claim to dispose of the remains.

When the natural protectors of the immature have either deserted or abused or absented themselves from their wards, guardianship usually devolves upon the State as *parens patriae*. But if the State agrees—as some have suggested—to consign to research the remains of only those fetuses who have perished under the ultimate abuse, that inevitably places the State in a position of patronage toward their destruction. The State would, like the aborting mother, also be implicitly derelict in its protective powers.

Thus no guardian emerges whose consent would rightfully suffice to release the remains of the deceased fetus for research.

Yet how prohibitive is that? Physicians and surgeons since Vesalius have sought cadavers to study anatomy. Their first obstacle was the conviction that the human body, live or dead, was inviolable. Their way round that resistance was to appeal to free consent (of the decedent or a guardian). But since, until recently, their usual supply had to be the corpses of derelicts, what really counted was the absence of anyone to object, more than the presence of anyone to consent. Thus consent has been interpreted as removing an obstacle, not as a positive and necessary warrant. But there may be more at stake here than this suggests.

Ours is an ancient obligation to treat human remains—body and property—

with deference. The body may be mere corpse and the estate mere chattels, but our treatment of them—insofar as they are identifiable with the person who left them behind—takes on the color of our relationship to that person. How we treat human remains is both a function and a cause of our bond with human persons. No one who remembers Mussolini's body hanging by the heels from a Milan lamppost could doubt it. The partisans were dishonoring his person, and enacting defiance against any future tyrant. Creon's insistence that Polyneice's corpse lie exposed, and Antigone's determination to bury her brother at peril of her own life, are both quite personal actions: toward the dead youth, and toward all whose spirits crave rest. John Kennedy's funeral and the disposal of Adolph Eichmann's remains both illustrate how our treatment of bodies is, in a powerful way, our definitive treatment of those they embodied.

If we honor a person while she is living we have no choice but to honor her body after death. To confiscate it discredits all ostensible dignity we accorded that person *in vivo* and orients us to treat still other persons with contempt. If my property is the extension of my person, then my body is my surrogate. Especially if one has had an ambiguous association with someone's death, to appropriate the dead person's remains for one's own purposes dissolves all ambiguity. When we requisition someone's body we are treating that person—not just that person's corpse—as of negligible dignity, or none.

There is nothing inherently unethical in experimentation upon the remains of humans who are victims of homicide, provided that consent is given, as is normally required, by the surviving guardian or next-of-kin. But the very agents of someone's death would surely be disqualified to act on the behalf or in the stead of the victim—disqualified as a man who has killed his wife is morally disqualified from acting as her executor. And in the case of a human abortus, it is the very guardians of the unborn who have collaborated in his or her destruction.

MORAL COMPLICITY

There is an additional ethical question, quite beyond the absence of rightful consent. The researcher would become a party, after the fact, to the destruction of the unborn.

The notion of complicity in mischief has been blurred and perhaps trivialized by its reduction in the popular mind to a legality. It is a much larger reality than that. It is the awesome moral fact that often we fancy ourselves as bystanders to injustice and injury—distressed and regretful bystanders, to be sure—when actually we are confederates in the very affliction we ostensibly deplore.

One can discern four types of moral complicity in evil: active collaboration in the deed; indirect association that implies approval; failure to prevent the evil when possible; and shielding the perpetrator from penalty.

The classic cooperator in evil is the driver of the getaway car. Without ever entering the bank, he or she is an active and causative member of the team. Every member of that team is the coauthor, *in solido*, of all the harm any one of them inflicts.

One way of disavowing the moral burden of complicity is the claim that "If I hadn't done it, they would simply have gotten someone else to do it." If we don't sell arms to General Stroessner to subdue the Paraguayans he will buy them from the Belgians or the Czechs. Medical personnel are asked to perform civil executions because with or without their participation the prisoners would meet the same doom. This proves to be only a rationalization, however, for the arms merchants soon lose an ethical restraint in purveying their merchandise of death, and the medics who kill are deformed in a way their recusant colleagues are not. There is, after all, a stark moral difference between beholding outrage and staffing it. It is not an indifferent matter whether I or another is the cooperator, since the cooperator is the one stunted personally and morally by his involvement.

There is a second mode of moral complicity, by association, when one is not actually joining in the work itself but somehow enters into a supportive alliance. The difference here between a neutral (or even an opponent) and an ally derives from the way in which one does or does not hold oneself apart from the enterprise and its purposes.

One may be an adverse observer, as when one consorts with an organized crime ring as a journalist or a researcher or a covert agent of law enforcement. This by itself would not necessarily make the observer a party to immoral activity. In a different mode, one might be associated with immoral activity in order to serve its victims, as when a chaplain or a physician agrees to serve the inmates of a genocidal concentration camp. Even in this close association, one can refrain from being party to the operation, for instance, by specifically refusing to be a staff member. The International Red Cross, in its services to war prisoners, must cooperate with belligerents but hold itself aloof from any partnership that would convert it into a partisan or a confederate.

As one enters into closer association, however, one eventually becomes party to the activity. Suppose that a sociologist struck an agreement with a child pornography operation in order to study the effects of such employment on the children. Or suppose an economist secured admission to the workings of a red-lining real estate operation in order to study the racial discrimination at work there. These researchers would undertake their studies, not with the informed consent of persons at risk, but with the informed consent of the victimizers. This would have the effect of drawing them into a sort of acquiescent partnership.

It is the sort of association which implies and engenders approbation that creates moral complicity. This situation is detectable when the associate's ability to condemn the activity atrophies.

There is no measurable way to determine such complicity. One must use sense and judgment, and one's assessments will be arguable. But they will be real. Imagine a pharmaceutical experiment carried out on an unsuspecting group of women in a Third World country: an experiment which leads to the death of several dozen subjects. If tissue from their cadavers were available from the experimenters for further research, it would seem that those who used the specimens could not avoid being complicit, albeit after the fact, with those who had destroyed those women. If the primary research, however, had led to the production of a new and powerfully therapeutic medication, a physician who prescribed that drug, even though sadly aware of its malicious origins, could reasonably be considered not to have entered into confederacy with the offense.

This is a distinction arrived at by analogy, not by measurement. The moral realities it detects are no less objective.

A third sort of complicity arises from culpable negligence. When parents are derelict in supervising their children they become responsible for their children's vandalism. When an employer turns a blind eye upon careless safety compliance by workers, she is morally complicit in the injuries that result. Anyone with supervisory responsibility who defaults in that duty becomes morally engaged precisely by that inactivity. One is morally complicit, not only by involvement in another's actions but also by shirking an obligatory involvement.

To go still further, it is possible to be morally complicit in another's wrongful behavior by actions that purport to curb the ill effects of the behavior but actually legitimate it or even stimulate its continuance. The single-minded policy of many public agencies in this country to curb adolescent pregnancy simply by proffering contraceptives and abortions to teenagers has had a misplaced effect. By addressing only the consequences (pregnancy) and not the activity (inappropriate sex), the program tacitly approves of what its sponsors deplore, and in the eyes of the sexually active teenagers it seems not only to acquiesce in their promiscuity but even to facilitate it. Thus the puzzling research finding that the incidence of teenage sexual activity and pregnancy and abortion has resolutely increased in direct proportion to the benevolent availability of contraceptives. Any venture that prescinds from the ethical aspect of someone's behavior, to alleviate only its consequences, may become naively complicit in it.

One can discern, then, four modes of moral complicity: direct and active participation, association that fails to disentangle itself, dereliction of the duty to supervise, and protective assistance. The common reality which is steadily present throughout these different ways of sharing moral intentionality is approbation. However one aligns oneself with another's act, by collaboration or working alongside or looking the other way or shielding from after-effects; whether by being active or by being passive; whether it furthers another's undertaking or merely endorses it: the complicity puts one person in the same moral stance that another person has assumed by direct action.

Naturally, all of these forms of association with harm vary in degree. There is a difference between the driver of the getaway car and the mother who prepares breakfast on the day of the crime with the faint intuition that mischief is afoot. It must be a human estimate how close and operative complicity actually is.

There is difficulty for some in identifying complicity after the fact. One cannot cause a deed that is already done. But this is to misconstrue the two elements in complicity. I am an accomplice in evil, first, insofar as I produce the harmful or immoral event, and second, insofar as my association with the evil causes me to be corrupted alongside the principal agent. Actually the chief effect of evil behavior is not the harm it inflicts on another but the moral disintegration and compromise it incurs in myself. This latter, more intrinsic element of complicity is present even when actual causative harm is not.

Experimentation upon fetal tissue derived from elective abortion places the scientist in moral complicity with the abortionist. The mode would be the second described above. The researcher is a confederate by resorting to the abortionist as a ready supplier of tissue from un-born humans who have been purposely destroyed.

Scholars anxious to perform research on such subjects often plead that their involvement offers them no financial ad-vantage, plays no causative role in the harmful activity because it would have occurred with or without their presence, and at least allows them to extract some beneficial result from an otherwise regrettable enterprise. The gist of this plea is that conspiracy in harm requires causative responsibility. But this argument from moral nonchalance, as we have stated, does not disengage one from complicity. A partnership whereby one achieves direct benefit from another person's injurious behavior, after the fact, can place the former in silent but unmistakable alliance with what the latter is doing.

When this argument is employed to justify medical experimentation on the re-mains of those who have suffered injury or death at the hands of others, there is a special irony. For the obligation in the Helsinki Declaration to obtain informed consent from the subjects of research was one of the chief outcomes of the Medical Trials for war crimes after World War II. The physicians who experimented upon the Nazi victims argued that they played absolutely no part in the decisions to im-prison, torment, and exterminate those subjects. That would have happened with or without their participation. The re-sponse of the witnessing world was that their professional presence offered en-dorsement and legitimacy to the victimiz-ers, and established them as accomplices in the exploitation of the helpless. No benefit, it was asserted, could morally be derived for medical therapy if it were ex-torted from the innocent and helpless an-guish of the afflicted. The doctors had en-tered fully into collusion with the SS by accepting their victims as experimental subjects. One need not cause a wrongful act to be party to it; it is enough to have abetted it.

There are then two sturdy ethical objections to experimentation upon the remains of fetuses aborted electively: absence of informed consent by anyone who could rightfully act on behalf of the unborn; and complicity in the elective destruction of the unborn by the researchers themselves.

ALTERNATIVE SOURCES FOR RESEARCH MATERIAL: CELL LINES

There are other possible sources of fetal materials for research. There is no moral objection to using the remains of unborn or newborn children who have perished from spontaneous abortion or trauma. The same would be true when surgery to save a pregnant mother's life has unavoidably aborted or destroyed her child. The parents would retain the right to release the body of the child for study. The drawbacks here are scientific, not ethical. Spontaneous abortion is often associated with genetic abnormalities that would compromise the physical remains as material for research, as would also be the case with many neo-natal deaths.

A second drawback arises from the dif-ficulty in approaching emotionally trau-matized parents to ask them to release portions of the bodies of their stillborn or deceased newborn children for research. While these are real obstacles, however, they make the acquisition of fetal or newborn tissue difficult, not impossible. There are enough fetal deaths with no ge-netic abnormality to yield considerable research material if there is a concerted effort to solicit it. And the emotional difficulty of asking parental consent in the wake of a wrenching loss is no more difficult than that faced by surgical teams doing heart transplants, who typically obtain the organs from young motorcyclists just killed in road accidents.

There is another possible source: cell lines cultured from fetal tissue. Some kinds of human tissue can be cultured *in vitro* and induced to reproduce and metabolize and proliferate. Though there is great variation among the kinds of tissue and their respective susceptibilities to cultivation, when it is possible it can produce stable, controlled and plentiful tissue that can last through as many as 50 cycles of replication. In a few cases a tissue culture will undergo "transformation" and become a quasi-permanent "cell line."

The proposal has been made to secure a modest amount of primary tissue from electively aborted abortuses (usually in their second-trimester) and culture that tissue to produce stable cell lines available for research. Is this any different ethically from using fresh aborted remains?

MORAL DISTANCE

There is a significant difference, one might suggest. A moral distance intervenes between the abortion that yielded the original tissue and the cultured cells that are many generations descended from that original flesh. But this is an assumption we must examine.

Let a parallel illustration serve to illustrate. If I defraud your mother of her life's savings and then launder the money by converting the dollars into pesos, there is no acceptable moral claim that those pesos need not be returned since they are not what was stolen. There is a moral identity between the money before and after the exchange. And if I use those pesos to buy a house for my own mother who is unaware of its source, the house would still revert by ethical right to your mother. My mother would incur the duty to restore it to your mother when she learned the truth. And if she refused, she would then become my partner in the fraud. No claim of moral distance through transaction would protect her.

But the legal and moral rule of prescription holds that wrongfully obtained property, if held long enough, should eventually be considered a rightful possession by the one who holds it. Thus a piece of land which B obtained from A by fraud a century or so earlier should now be left in quiet title to the innocent heirs of B and not subject to claim by the aggrieved descendants of A. In criminal law the statute of limitations serves a similar purpose: the people agree not to prosecute anyone for a crime committed so long ago that its reality has really faded from present human relations.

It would appear that the reality of moral distance which would enable an injustice or an injury to fade away is merely a matter of time. This purifying moral distance, however, is not absolute. It has exceptions. Prescription is usually not recognized, even after centuries have passed, if the beneficiaries were aware that their possession was wrongfully obtained, or if the aggrieved parties have in the intervening period been pressing their claim for justice. And certain crimes of greater enormity are exempted from most statutes of limitations. In fact the willingness to allow moral claims of justice to expire seems based entirely on society's need, for the common peace, to have limits put on the investigation and possible upheaval of present circumstances.

Stipulate that a laboratory—one of the National Institutes of Health, for instance—were to culture and make available on a nonprofit basis certain cell lines derived years previously from aborted tissue. The technicians at the NIH had no participation in the events that yielded the primary tissue. Even less would the experimenter/user be associated with those events. Could it not be said that the tissue has been purged of the stigma of complicity in the original destruction? Can bygones be ethical bygones in this case?

The question is whether the generation of cells cultured *in vitro* creates a significant enough moral distance to neutralize the original lack of informed consent and complicity in abortion. There are grounds to propose that it might not.

Moral association in the activities of others allows of a more and a less, and therefore it can be attenuated to the point of insignificance. For instance, would it amount to a protest against war to picket or boycott a corporation because it manufactured cluster bombs with a fragmentation effect calculated to destroy civilian populations? If we grant that it would, then compare that to an identical demonstration against a corporation which produces soap, on the grounds that the nation's troops at war bathed with that soap. Surely the latter demonstration would carry with it very little moral credibility by comparison with the former.

If it were known that an abundant supply of cadavers of persons in relative youth and sound health were available internationally for medical research, that would surely present to medical schools a better learning medium than the cadavers of aged people or derelicts that they receive now through donation arrangements. But suppose that those bodies were all black, and all from South Africa. Then would medical school deans think it ethically neutral to avail themselves of this supply source?

Perhaps the most widely known human tissue supply in modern research is the "HeLa" cell-line derived from the body of Henrietta Lacks (generally known pseudonymously as Helen Lane), an American woman who died of cancer in 1951. That tissue has been cultured and manipulated in virtually all major teaching laboratories in this country. But suppose that it were the "EsDa" cell-line instead, derived from the body of a Polish woman named Esther Dawidowicz who died of typhus in 1944... in Auschwitz. It is very doubtful that scientists would have considered themselves as free to retain and use that material, for a nonchalance about it would make a moral statement: a statement of neutrality about the Holocaust.

There are indeed limits to the persistence of moral taint. It can attenuate. But when, in human experience, its source is particularly odious, a casual willingness to ignore it would still constitute complicity even when separated by the passage of time. If an attentive world failed to see the moral taint of the Bitberg war cemetery bleached out after four quiet decades, or that of President Kurt Waldheim's wartime involvements neutralized after four decades of energetic public service to the world, can we believe that the casual experimental usage of abortion-derived tissue could fail to embody a moral indifference toward an intentional victimization whose death toll in this country alone now stands at nearly four times that of the genocide which provoked the first explicit moral norms about research on human subjects? It would be a nonchalance imbued with moral apathy.

In any case, the claim that moral distance has obliterated or attenuated all significant association of researchers with the original destruction may at least be argued when the offense has been publicly repudiated and terminated. The claim is hardly credible if the exploitation is still ongoing and enjoys a measure of public indifference which scientific collaboration could only legitimate.

It would seem that the moral reality of abortion resonates about as clearly and distinctly along the cell-line as it does in primary tissue taken directly from abortuses. Indeed, the readiness of researchers to accept such material must exercise a considerable moral influence in awarding to the abortion industry the quiet and complicit acquiescence of the scientific profession.

This article concludes with the proposition that, in terms of both primary tissue and of cultured cells and cell lines, it is difficult but not impossible to obtain human fetal materials, fresh or cultured, that derive from unintentional death instead of intentional destruction, and that are made available by informed consent. This alternative renders moot the question of whether one need or ought, out of the urgent potentialities of research, resort to using aborted tissue. But even were that option to be considered, it ought be rejected as unethical, for lack of informed consent and because it would place the researchers in complicity with the abortion.

POSTSCRIPT

Should Fetal Tissue Be Used to Heal Adults?

Warren Kearney, Dorothy E. Vawter, and Karen G. Gervais, in "Fetal Tissue Research and the Misread Compromise," *Hastings Center Report* (September–October 1991), discuss the bill to restore federal funding for human fetal tissue research and conclude that even though it would require women who donate fetal tissue to certify that they are not having their abortions with the intent to donate, that requirement could not possibly be more than a symbolic gesture. That symbol was too tenuous for conservative Republicans, and the bill was vetoed. The ban on federal funding for fetal tissue research remained in place until 1993, when President Bill Clinton ended it.

The Clinton administration also abolished a fetal tissue bank that was established by former president George Bush in May 1992. The goal of the tissue bank was to store fetal tissue obtained from spontaneous abortions (miscarriages) and ectopic pregnancies (in which the embryo implants itself somewhere other than in the uterus) and to make that tissue available for research and medical treatment. Unfortunately, tissue from these sources proved to be unobtainable in useful quantities, and the tissue bank was canceled in 1993. See C. B. Cohen and A. R. Jonsen, "The Future of the Fetal Tissue Bank," *Science* (December 10, 1993).

In January 1994 the NIH awarded a research grant to Curt Freed of the University of Colorado Health Sciences Center to study the use of fetal tissue in treating Parkinson's disease. According to Jon Cohen, in "New Fight Over Fetal Tissue Grafts," *Science* (February 4, 1994), Freed's $4.5 million study of 40 patients would be "the largest, most ambitious study of implants to date." However, some researchers in the field are objecting that the study is too narrow in concept and that it involves some questionable procedures.

In April 1994 researchers working on a procedure that would benefit a much larger population of people reported that they had successfully implanted fetal heart cells into a mouse's heart. They hope to be able to develop this procedure to the point where the added cells can strengthen the mouse's heartbeat and then to use fetal heart cells to repair the damage done to humans by heart attacks. If they are successful, human fetal tissue will become a lifesaver for millions of people, and objections to research and treatment will likely be difficult to sustain.

For other views on this issue, see Emanuel D. Thorne, "Tissue Transplants: The Dilemma of the Body's Growing Value," *The Public Interest* (Winter 1990), and Stephen G. Post, "Fetal Tissue Transplant: The Right to Question Progress," *America* (January 12, 1991).

CONTRIBUTORS TO THIS VOLUME

EDITOR

THOMAS A. EASTON is an associate professor in the Department of Science at Thomas College in Waterville, Maine, where he has been teaching since 1983. He received a B.A. in biology from Colby College in 1966 and a Ph.D. in theoretical biology from the University of Chicago in 1971, and he has also held academic appointments at Bangor Community College and the University of Maine. He is a prolific writer, and his articles on scientific and futuristic issues have appeared in the scholarly journals *Experimental Neurology* and *American Scientist* as well as in such popular magazines as *Astronomy, Consumer Reports,* and *Robotics Age.* His other publications include *Bioscope,* 2d ed. (Scott Foresman, 1984), coauthored with Carl E. Rischer, and *Careers in Science* (National Textbook, 1989). Dr. Easton is also a well-known writer and critic of science fiction.

STAFF

Mimi Egan   Publisher
Brenda S. Filley   Production Manager
Libra Ann Cusack   Typesetting Supervisor
Juliana Arbo   Typesetter
Lara Johnson   Graphics
Diane Barker   Editorial Assistant
David Brackley   Copy Editor
David Dean   Administrative Editor
Richard Tietjen   Systems Manager

AUTHORS

SY ALPERT is a fellow of and an executive scientist at the Electric Power Research Institute in Palo Alto, California, which was founded in 1972 to conduct a broad economically and environmentally acceptable program of research and development in technologies for producing and utilizing electric power. An expert in energy technology, he has directed the development of new energy systems and has experience in developing new technology for the chemical and petroleum industries. He is currently performing exploratory research in biological systems and mitigation strategies for global climate change.

DOUG BEASON is the director of research at the U.S. Air Force Academy in Colorado Springs, Colorado. He was a member of the Synthesis Group for the Bush administration's White House Science Office, which was formulated to find the best way to travel to Mars, and he has also served on the White House staff for the Clinton administration.

WILFRED BECKERMAN is a fellow of Balliol College at Oxford University in Oxford, England, where he has been teaching since 1975. He has also been a professor of economy at the University of London and the chair of the Department of Political Economy at the University College in London. He is the coauthor, with Stephen Clark, of *Poverty and Social Security in Britain Since 1961* (Oxford University Press, 1982). He received a Ph.D. from Trinity College at Cambridge University in 1950.

PAUL BRODEUR is an author and a staff writer for *The New Yorker* magazine. He has published books on asbestos, ozone depletion, and the electromagnetic field–cancer link, including *Currents of Death: Power Lines, Computer Terminals, and the Attempt to Cover Up Their Threat to Your Health* (Simon & Schuster, 1989) and *The Great Powerline Coverup: How the Utilities and the Government Are Trying to Hide the Cancer Hazard Posed by Electromagnetic Fields* (Little, Brown, 1993).

WALLACE S. BROECKER is a professor of geology in the Lamont-Doherty Geological Observatory at Columbia University in New York City.

JAMES TUNSTEAD BURTCHAELL is a former professor of theology at the University of Notre Dame in Notre Dame, Indiana, where he served as the chair of the University Committee for the Protection of Human Subjects in Research. He is currently a priest at Our Lady of Princeton Church in Princeton, New Jersey. His publications include *Rachel Weeping, and Other Essays on Abortion* (Andrews & McMeel, 1982) and *The Giving and Taking of Life: Essays Ethical* (University of Notre Dame Press, 1989).

DONALD E. BUZZELLI is the deputy assistant inspector general for oversight at the National Science Foundation in Washington, D.C.

DAVID CALLAHAN is a writer on and an analyst of national security and foreign policy matters.

CENTER FOR MEDIA EDUCATION, the president of which is Kathryn C. Montgomery, is a nonprofit organization in Washington, D.C., founded in 1991 to promote the democratic potential of the electronic media. Its two current projects are the Campaign for Kids' TV, which aims to improve the quality of children's television, and the Future of Media Project, which is dedicated to fostering a public interest vision for the new media and information superhighway of the twenty-first century.

PURNELL CHOPPIN is the president of the Howard Hughes Medical Institute in Bethesda, Maryland, a private health research organization dedicated to funding basic medical research.

WENDY CLELAND-HAMNETT is the acting deputy assistant administrator for policy, planning, and evaluation at the U.S. Environmental Protection Agency in Washington, D.C.

MARY H. COOPER is a staff writer for the Congressional Quarterly's CQ Researcher, a weekly magazine providing in-depth analysis of current issues. She is the author of The Business of Drugs (Congressional Quarterly, 1988).

LAURA CORNWELL is a policy analyst for the Regulatory Innovations Staff of the U.S. Environmental Protection Agency in Washington, D.C. She is also a graduate research assistant in the International Institute for Ecological Economics at the University of Maryland in College Park, Maryland.

ROBERT COSTANZA is the director of the International Institute for Ecological Economics at the University of Maryland in College Park, Maryland, and a professor at the University of Maryland's Center for Environmental and Estuarine Studies in Solomons, Maryland. He is a cofounder and the president of the International Society for Ecological Economics, and his research focuses on the interface between ecological and economic systems.

COUNCIL ON ETHICAL AND JUDICIAL AFFAIRS, established in 1990 by the American Medical Association, includes as members Russell H. Patterson, Jr. (chairman), John A. Barrasso, Oscar W. Clarke, Nancy W. Dickey, John Glasson, Douglas D. Lind (resident representative), Richard J. MacMurray (vice chairman), Michael A. Puzak, Robert Wolski (medical student representative), and David Orentlicher (secretary).

COUNCIL ON SCIENTIFIC AFFAIRS, established in 1990 by the American Medical Association, includes as members William C. Scott (chairman), Scott L. Bernstein (medical student representative), Yank D. Coble, Jr., A. Bradley Eisenbrey (resident representative), E. Harvey Estes, Jr., Mitchell S. Karlan, William R. Kennedy, Patricia J. Numann, Joseph H. Skom, Richard M. Steinhilber, Jack P. Strong, Henry N. Wagner, William R. Hendee (secretary), and William T. McGivney (assistant secretary).

DOROTHY E. DENNING is the chair of the Department of Computer Science at Georgetown University in Washington, D.C. She is the author of Cryptography and Data Security (Addison-Wesley, 1982).

FRANK DRAKE is a professor of astronomy and astrophysics at the University of California, Santa Cruz, where he has also served as dean of natural sciences. He is the president of the SETI Institute and a former president of the Astronomical Society of the Pacific, which is one of the world's leading astronomical organizations.

K. O. EMERY is an author of geology books, including Geology of the Atlantic Ocean (Springer-Verlag, 1984), coauthored with Elazar Uchupi. He was the Henry Bigelow Oceanography Chair at the Woods Hole Oceanographic Institution in Woods Hole, Massachusetts, from 1962 to his retirement in 1979, and he has also worked as a marine geologist for the U.S. Navy. He received an M.A. and a Ph.D. in marine geology from the University of Illinois, and he has also held an academic appointment at the University of Southern California.

MARK A. FINDEIS is a group leader at OsteoArthritis Sciences in Cambridge, Massachusetts. He has also been an instructor at Harvard Medical School and a postdoctoral fellow of the Bioorganic Chemistry and Biochemistry Laboratory at Rockefeller University.

CHRISTOPHER FLAVIN is the vice president for research at the Worldwatch Institute, a private nonprofit research organization devoted to the analysis of global environmental issues. His research and writing focus on solutions to global environmental problems, particularly sustainable development and strategies to slow climate change, and he has written extensively on the implications of new energy technologies and new approaches to energy policy.

MIKE GODWIN is a staff counsel for the Electronic Frontier Foundation in Cambridge, Massachusetts, which was founded in 1990 to promote the creation of legal and structural frameworks to help ease the assimilation of new technologies into society for the benefit of the public and industry.

JAMES P. HOGAN is a writer of science fiction novels. Before moving to the United States in 1977, he was a systems-design engineer.

WOLFGANG K. JOKLIK is the James B. Duke Professor of Microbiology in the Department of Microbiology and Immunology at the Duke University Medical Center in Durham, North Carolina. He has also held academic appointments at the Australian National University and the Albert Einstein College of Medicine. He is the editor in chief of *Microbiological Reviews*, and he is the author or coauthor of more than 250 scientific papers on molecular virology.

ANDREW KIMBRELL is the policy director of the Foundation on Economic Trends in Washington, D.C., which was founded in 1977 to disseminate information through lectures and the distribution of educational materials on issues such as the environment, religion, genetics, and engineering in order to effect social change.

NICHOLAS LENSSEN is a senior researcher with the Worldwatch Institute, a nonprofit research organization devoted to the analysis of global resource and environmental issues. His research and writing focus on energy policy, alternative energy sources, nuclear power, radioactive waste, and global climate change, and he has testified before the U.S. Congress and the European Parliament on energy issues. His publications include *Power Surge: Guide to the Coming Energy Revolution* (W. W. Norton, 1994).

JEROD M. LOEB is the assistant vice president for science and technology at the American Medical Association in Chicago, Illinois, and an adjunct professor of physiology at Northwestern University Medical School in Evanston, Illinois. He is also a cardiovascular physiologist, and he has published widely in areas related to the heart, the use of animals in biomedical research, science education, and science policy.

DONALD B. LOURIA is the chair of the Department of Preventive Medicine and Community Health at the New Jersey Medical School in Newark, New Jersey. He received a B.S. from Harvard University in 1949 and an M.D. from Harvard Medical School in 1953. He is the author of more than 300 articles and 6 books, including *Your Healthy Body, Your Healthy Life* (Master Media, 1992).

BRIAN W. J. MAHY is the director of the Division of Viral and Rickettsial Diseases for the National Center for Infectious Diseases division of the Centers for Disease Control and Prevention in Atlanta, Georgia. He received a Ph.D. from the University of Southampton and an Sc.D. (by publications) from the University of Cambridge. His research interests focus on the molecular biology of viruses and the prevention and control of viral infections.

ARJUN MAKHIJANI is the president of the Institute for Energy and Environmental Research in Takoma Park, Maryland. He holds a Ph.D. in electrical engineering from the University of California, Berkeley. He has produced studies on nuclear fuel cycle–related issues—including weapons production, testing, and nuclear waste—for over a decade, and he is the principal author of the first study ever done on energy conservation potential in the U.S. economy.

JESSE MALKIN writes about economic issues for *Investor's Business Daily*. He is a Rhodes scholar, and he holds B.A. degrees from Oxford University and Oberlin College.

MICHAEL J. MANDEL is an economics writer for *Business Week*.

CHARLES C. MANN is a science writer who resides in Amherst, Massachusetts.

BARBARA A. MIKULSKI, senator (D) from Maryland (1987–present; term ends 1999), is the chair of the Appropriations Subcommittee on Veterans Affairs, Housing and Urban Development, and Independent Agencies, and of the Labor and Human Resources Subcommittee on Aging.

HANS MORAVEC is a principal research scientist in the Robotics Institute at Carnegie Mellon University in Pittsburgh, Pennsylvania, and the director of the university's Mobile Robot Laboratory. He received a Ph.D. from Stanford University in 1980 for his design of a TV-equipped, computer-controlled robot that could negotiate cluttered obstacle courses. His publications include *Mind Children: The Future of Robot and Human Intelligence* (Harvard University Press, 1988).

DAVID NORSE is a research associate for the Overseas Development Institute in London and a research fellow of the Environmental Change Unit at the University of Oxford in Oxford, England.

ANDRZEJ E. OLSZYNA-MARZYS is associated with the Pan American Health Organization's Unified Laboratory of Food and Drug Control in Guatemala.

HOWARD K. SCHACHMAN is a research biochemist with the Virus Laboratory at the University of California, Berkeley. He is also the chair of the American Society of Biochemistry and Molecular Biology's Public Affairs Committee and a special adviser to the director of the National Institutes of Health. He received a B.S. in chemical engineering from the Massachusetts Institute of Technology in

1939 and a Ph.D. in physical chemistry from Princeton University in 1948.

MILTON F. SEARL, now retired, was an energy supply economist for the Electric Power Research Institute (EPRI) in Palo Alto, California, which was founded in 1972 to conduct a broad economically and environmentally acceptable program of research and development in technologies for producing and utilizing electric power. A pioneer of research in the relationship between the use of electricity and real gross national product, he has been a consultant to the president emeritus of the EPRI since 1989.

JOHN R. SEARLE is a professor of philosophy at the University of California, Berkeley.

DAVA SOBEL is a science and medicine writer for several newspapers and magazines, including *Harvard Magazine, Omni, Good Housekeeping,* and the *New York Times Book Review.* A former science reporter for the *New York Times,* she is the author of *The Incredible Planets: New Views of the Solar Family* (Reader's Digest Association, 1992).

CHAUNCEY STARR is a professor emeritus and the former founding president and vice chairman of the Electric Power Research Institute in Palo Alto, California, which was founded in 1972 to conduct a broad economically and environmentally acceptable program of research and development in technologies for producing and utilizing electric power. He was a pioneer in the development of nuclear propulsion for rockets; in the miniaturizion of nuclear reactors for space; and in the development of atomic power electricity plants. In November 1990, he was awarded the National Medal of Technology from President Bush for his contribution to engineering and the electrical industry.

THOMAS S. TENFORDE is the chief scientist for the Life Science Center at Battelle Pacific Northwest Laboratories.

RICHARD G. TESKE is a professor of astronomy at the University of Michigan in Ann Arbor, Michigan, who specializes in the study of supernova remnants. He is also a former director of the Michigan–Dartmouth–MIT Observatory in Arizona.

STEVEN ZAK is an attorney in Los Angeles, California. He received a B.A. in psychology from Michigan State University in 1971, an M.S. from the Wayne State University School of Medicine in 1975, and a J.D. from the University of Southern California Law School in 1984. He has written about animals with regard to ethics and the law for numerous publications, including the *Los Angeles Times,* the *New York Times,* and the *Chicago Tribune.*

INDEX